Clann na Poblachta

Clann na Poblachta

Eithne Mac Dermott

CORK UNIVERSITY PRESS

First published in 1998 by
Cork University Press
University College
Cork
Ireland

© Eithne Mac Dermott 1998

British Library Cataloguing in Publication Data
A CIP catalogue record for this book is available from
the British Library

ISBN   1 85918 186 4   hardcover
       1 85918 187 2   paperback

Typeset by Tower Books, Ballincollig, Co. Cork
Printed by Redwood Books, Wiltshire

Contents

Illustrations

All photographs supplied by G.A. Duncan, Dublin unless otherwise stated.

Preface

It is very easy, and redolent of the sort of soporific academic study masquerading as 'scientific and objective analysis' to start a preface such as this with a blindingly obvious statement stressing that Clann na Poblachta has not received anything like the sort of attention, academic or otherwise, that such a subject probably merits. But, of course, it hasn't. Clann na Poblachta was a small, theoretically radical and republican party which emerged from a myriad, and rather confused, IRA ancestry to challenge Fianna Fáil for office, power and the right to ownership of the symbols of national identity in 1947 and in 1948. Their emergence as a political force was probably the single biggest factor leading to Fianna Fáil's defeat in 1948, and certainly, while they themselves did not succeed in gaining anything like the sort of numerical parliamentary representation – in other words, an overall majority – they had set themselves going into the election, they were to become the linchpin of the coalition government, which in itself was a novel political experiment. They were to supply bright, capable and idealistic ministers to serve in that government, and, ultimately, they were to cause its collapse, because when they fell, the fall of the government itself could not be far behind.

This book, then, is the story of Clann na Poblachta. To my way of thinking, the first function of a historian is to tell what happened, and, if possible, to supply reasons why one way rather than another. This means I am still something of a slave to historical narrative, despite the unfashionableness of this approach in some 'modern' quarters. As Eric Hobsbawm has so rightly observed, without the distinction between what is and what is not, without the distinction between what has happened, and what has not, there can be no history. How we choose to interpret the facts, and present the relevant evidence, sources, arguments and conclusions is, of course, another matter entirely, and here, the perspectives of the writer and how these influence the treatment of the story to be told are of central importance.

My own interest in the subject dates from the time I was in school. I used to take time off from school in Galway in the 1970s to travel to Dublin to attend major Dáil debates. While most of my class-mates looked up to stars such as John Travolta or Marc Bolan, the god, or hero of my life was Noël Browne. It was thanks to Noël Browne, then an independent Socialist TD, that I was able to attend every political event of importance in the Dáil between 1977 and January 1982 when he retired from active politics. He also encouraged my interest in such matters, earnestly discussing them with me over coffee, suggesting reading material, and sometimes sending me copies of articles he had written, or speeches he had made. I devoured everything that he suggested I read – he introduced me to the writings of Marcuse, Illich, Kafka, and Marx – and I watched, enthralled, as he fought Health Minister Charles Haughey's atrocious 1979 Family Planning Bill, by putting down forty-one amendments, all of which were defeated. In fact, the initial suggestion to 'write something' on this topic came from him, and, while originally, my intention was to heroically 'bat for Browne', the passage of time has shown that he was quite clearly perfectly capable of batting for himself.

In any case, the focus of interest inevitably shifted, becoming broader in the process, and ultimately settling on the Clann na Poblachta party. Clann na Poblachta was fascinating because it was a party run in the main by young radical – or supposedly radical – people. It was born in high drama, lived 'on the edge', so to speak, for much of its early political existence and came to grief in unbelievably theatrical circumstances. Is the fact that Clann na Poblachta was exciting a good enough reason to want to study it, and write about it? I think it is. Too much is written by people who have no sympathy, or, to put it another way, no empathy with the topics from which they make their living.

Equally, while political theory has produced a rich and challenging harvest, intellectual fashions which offer highly schematic versions of events, and which seek to systemise politics (and history) within a structured framework, can often run the risk of completely overlooking the human aspect, the human story. At a seminar a few years ago, I was asked if I had considered measuring the reasons for Clann na Poblachta's collapse 'scientifically'. Apart from harbouring grave doubts about the idea that all human relationships have a 'rational' basis, how on earth does one attempt to measure human relationships 'scientifically'? How does one measure dislike, or antipathy? By April 1951, Seán MacBride and Noël Browne could hardly stand the sight of one another, as a situation had arisen where policy disagreements and personal antagonisms reinforced each other in an accelerating chain reaction, to use a scientific metaphor. Now, this may not have been rational, or logical, and it was certainly not 'scientific', but it was a factor in the collapse of Clann na Poblachta, and is a salient fact in the story of the Clann. Of course history is about much more than loves and hates, but to ignore the impact of the human story on the grounds that it is not quantifiable, and therefore does not fit into the theoretical construct, is sometimes to miss the point entirely.

Therefore, one of the unshakeable convictions of this book is that history and politics are about people; this is a story of human endeavour. For what is politics but the human striving – both worthy and unworthy – after power? People matter, above all in history and politics, and the drama of human endeavour is present in the story of Clann na Poblachta in great measure. This is a story worth telling, for who they were, what they attempted to achieve, their occasionally muddled motives, intense relationships, their highs and lows, successes and failures and is a story rich in the stuff of high drama. Whatever else is made of this book, it is my earnest hope that the reader will at least take from it some of the heartfelt sense of passion, idealism, commitment, some sense of that high drama which attended the story of Clann na Poblachta.

A brief note about sources is usually appended at this stage. In researching Clann na Poblachta, I was exceptionally fortunate in that a good many of its active participants were quite young at the time the party was in its prime. Seán MacBride was only forty-four years of age when he challenged de Valera in 1948, and Noël Browne had just turned thirty-two when he was elevated to cabinet rank. I was able to interview a surprising number of the leading participants in the leadership of the Clann. Almost everybody I approached for interviews or information proved to be exceedingly courteous, and helpful. Very few, in fact, turned me down, Fine Gael's former leader, James Dillon, being a rare exception. MacBride and Browne both courteously agreed to give interviews, as did Jack McQuillan whose wonderfully warm hospitality and witty company I always greatly enjoyed. Others who agreed to meet with me included Con Lehane, Patrick Lindsay, Hector Legge, Labhrás Ó Nualláin, Liam Ó Laoghaire, Colm Ó Laoghaire, Fursa Breathnach, Ben Hooper, Oliver J. Flanagan, Liam Cosgrave, Peadar Cowan (son of Captain Peadar Cowan), George Lawlor, Colm O'Quigley, Roger McHugh, Johnny Prendergast, Florence O'Riordan, John McMenamy, and Seamus Pattison. A number of those who agreed to be interviewed requested anonymity as a condition of granting me an interview.

The Cabinet papers for that era are now available and offer a rich source of useful and interesting material. In addition to this, many of the 'leading lights' of some of the other political parties, such as Fianna Fáil's Seán MacEntee, and Richard Mulcahy, one time leader of Fine Gael, as well as Patrick McGilligan, have left fascinating private collections which are open to public perusal, and provide a rich vein of material on the era for anybody willing to engage in a spot of assiduous mining. Retracing the paths of past conflicts also meant that I managed to visit fascinating places such as Baltinglass and Kilbeggan, in the course of my research.

It is said that the past is a different country, and certainly, the Ireland of the 1940s and 1950s seems to have been a very different place, in the sense of both time and space, when compared with what we experience today. Although exceptionally distant in some ways, it is still sufficiently close for the trap of hindsight history to exist; by hindsight history, I mean the superimposing of current attitudes and outlooks on former contexts. Costello's attitudes in 1951 to the publication by *The Irish Times* of the details of the ecclesiastical interventions (an action which appalled him) is as inexplicable to us as our current attitudes on the topic would have seemed to him. However, his attitudes would have been shared by a good number of his peers at that time. Trying to understand something such as Costello's attitude (even if still witholding active sympathy for his position), trying to place yourself in the shoes of the past while refraining from passing the judgements of the present, is only a part of the – let us use a positive, uplifting, word – challenges, of the writing, study and researching of history today. Far more pressing is the lack of historical continuity, the disconnection with an engaged sense of the past. For, if it used to be said that the problem with Ireland and history was that Irish people never forgot their history (while the Ancient Saxon Enemy never remembered), this can no longer be said to be the case. Recently, I attended a function held to commemorate and celebrate, the life of Noël Browne. It took place in May 1998, exactly a year after his death, and opened with a showing of the Clann na Poblachta election film *Our Country*. Noël Browne, then a young medical doctor, appeared in the film discussing medical shortages; his party leader, Seán MacBride also addressed the camera, and called for political change. Several in the audience sniggered at the old world air of the film, at the affected acting in some of the scenes, and at the mannered diction of the man who did the voiceover, Noel Hartnett. At no time was the revolutionary impact of this film on Irish society and culture explained to the audience, for that film frightened the life out of Fianna Fáil in 1948, to such an extent that they went to heroic lengths to have it banned. It also set a benchmark for party political broadcasts which went unsurpassed for over thirty years. Hartnett, who was described to me by MacBride as being 'the Gay Byrne of his day', was not the only person who went unrecognised. As MacBride spoke, people sitting behind me (and they were not young) asked each other who he was. 'I wonder who that man is with that accent, he's certainly not Irish', one person remarked to her neighbour. There are a great many things one can say about MacBride, and his political career was an extraordinary testament to a life crammed with contradictions, but to deny MacBride his Irish nationality left me speechless. With the erosion of historical continuity, and a sense of engagement with historical memory (few who lived in Ireland at any stage from the twenties until the seventies could have not known who MacBride was), the need for historians to remember what others forget becomes even more essential.

Thus, in writing this book, I have attempted to bring the drama of the party that was called Clann na Poblachta to a wider audience. I actually enjoyed trying to put this together, and I leave it to the reader to sort the wheat from the chaff.

Eithne Mac Dermott
August 1998

Acknowledgements

At the end of the sort of long journey which researching and writing a book involves many debts of gratitude have accumulated, and need to be bestowed upon those worthy few, who have assisted this endeavour from its earliest stage, that of a twinkle in the eye and a split infinitive on the page. Redemption only seems possible with an apparently endless expression of appreciation in the acknowledgements section of the book. Indeed when reading history books as a youngster, I used to be struck by all of those thank-yous found in such introductions and yet now I find myself bowing to those exact same conventions.

The research for this book took place on and off for a good many years, much of it in Dublin. With that in mind, I would like to express my gratitude and appreciation for the endless courtesy, enthusiasm, and helpfulness of the staff of the various libraries I visited. Seamus Helferty and his staff, in the rich treasure trove of the Archives section of University College Dublin's library were always helpfully on hand with assistance, and to them I extend my warm thanks. Equally helpful were the wonderful staff at the National Archives, now located in Bishop Street, but working out of Dublin Castle for most of the time I availed of their facilities and services. Actually, I must confess that I loved the almost Dickensian atmosphere when I was studying the state papers in Dublin Castle, even though space was cramped, facilities limited, and all of the researchers were compelled to share one large table as they beavered away at their work. Again my warm thanks to them. Some of my early research was carried out in the National Library and in common with countless other scholars who have availed of their facilities down through the decades, I found the staff to be extremely understanding, helpful and supportive.

Illustrations for the book were only considered at quite a late stage, and thus I passed a fascinating day with Mrs Grace Duncan, examining her wonderful archive of photographic material which is probably the best private pictorial record or chronicle of events in Ireland in the twentieth century. A wonderful day was also spent with Frank and Bairbre Kelly perusing back issues of *Dublin Opinion*, and I thank them for their terrific company, warm hospitality and boundless generosity. Keith Ridgeway and Sunniva O'Flynn of the Irish Film Archive were helpfulness itself in procuring the Clann na Poblachta film *Our Country*; my thanks to them.

Friends and relatives supplied endless (or so it must have seemed) accommodation in the form of support, meals, beds and sofas on my interminable trips to Dublin. To those that supplied accommodation, house-keys, drink, coffee, food, futons and varying degrees of emotional support, my warm thanks. Therefore, heartfelt thanks to Dana Ward, Oran and Brenda Ryan, Aidan Crowley (and 'Higgy'), Gabrielle McAuley, and my ever supportive godmother, Ita Kelly. Sinead Conneely and Brendan Flynn were both incredibly supportive when this book was at a much earlier evolutionary stage, that prehistoric phase known as a thesis; warmest thanks to them. An even earlier enthusiast for the whole enterprise was Colman Keane, formerly of the Galway History Club, whose unswerving early support, encouragement and enthusiasm helped supply a much needed focus for my fascination with history, and with whom I spent many an enjoyable evening over the years, thrashing out some of the more deviant aspects of the Clann's profile, attitudes and outlook.

My former supervisor Professor Gearóid Ó Tuathaigh has been a superb and inspired teacher whose effervescent enthusiasm, eloquent wit, original insights and general all-round decency make knowing him a pleasure, and studying under him an enriching experience. He has been mentor, friend and a firm supporter of this work from an early stage; to him my gratitude and friendship. Another beacon of light in the history department of University College Galway, was Professor Gearóid MacNiocaill, whose warm humanity during his tenure was as treasured as his scholarship was respected by those of us who worked under him. Professor Michael Laver, who spent many years in Galway prior to his appointment to the Chair of Politics in Trinity College Dublin was also wonderfully supportive, and to him I extend my warm thanks.

Neil, my brother, has been an uncomplaining chauffeur, and great friend throughout this process. More recently he has approached the (shared) task of proofreading with diligence determination and enthusiasm; again I convey not just heartfelt thanks, but a sisterly love. My parents Phil and Charles, have been a wonderful support; my love and thanks to them.

1

Genesis of the Clann

'I hated politics in the normal sense. I hated the electioneering system, and the double think and double talk of politics . . . .'
Seán MacBride in an interview with John Gibbons,
in 'Spirit of Ireland', Autumn 1987

At a meeting held in Barry's Hotel, Dublin, on 6 July 1946[1] with the stated intention of founding yet another new republican political party – this time preferably bereft of the lingering whiff of cordite – a political party which was given the name 'Clann na Poblachta' (literally 'Children' or 'Family of the Republic') was formed. Presiding over this meeting were a number of stalwarts of the republican movement, who between them composed a distinguished roll-call of names possessing peculiar political pedigrees which spanned the thankless thirties and, in several cases, went harking back to the glory days of the original anti-Treaty struggle of the early 1920s. There were even some who could claim to have been 'out' during the Easter Rising of 1916, the ulti-mate legitimising symbol in the republican gallery of iconography.

The meeting was also attended by journalists assigned by *The Irish Times* and the *Irish Independent* – two of the Dublin daily newspapers – whose reports subsequently graced the pages of their papers,[2] as well as by members of Ireland's secret police, who furnished their ministerial paymas-ters with a detailed account of proceedings.[3] A document setting out the party's aims and aspirations was prepared and circulated to the media, the secret police report observing sarcastically that 'the signatories estimated themselves a Provisional Executive'.[4] It is a credit to the powers of observa-tion of the secret police that their account of events differs so little from that of the published versions available in the daily newspapers. Both accounts were in total agreement as to the composition of the provisional executive of the new party[5], itself a term more in keeping with the ghosts of revolutions past, rather than with the promise of a radical constitutional future.

At first glance, Clann na Poblachta itself seemed to be just another one, the latest one, of those ghosts of revolutions past, a long line of ghosts whose chief political task had become reduced to devising methods of engaging 'lawfully' with the apparatus of a hated, oppressive state, while at the same time offering an alternative (in other words, a republican) political vision. Such a task was quite difficult, as those ghosts which sprang from the intertwined branches of the anti-Treaty movement owed some of their ideological roots to the continued observance of traditionally republican policies such as abstention from the contamination of parliamentary activity, a policy which usually entailed the studied non-recognition of the underlying institutional structures as well. These were the ghosts whose thunder was to be largely stolen by the foundation of Fianna Fáil in 1926. Fianna Fáil's subsequent subtle evolution from being a 'slightly constitutional' party to one that would hold office after 1932 – and this while boasting an attractive programme of (some) social radicalism married to a robust nationalist rhetoric – ensured that most of the existing irreconcilables were reconciled not just with political mobilisation, but with the parliamentary form it actually took.

Those who remained outside constitutional politics were to feel doubly betrayed by this. Firstly, as Fianna Fáil inched their way towards government, inevitable adjustments were made, not only in their interpretation, but also in their application of republican ideology and policies; Eamon de Valera's 1937 constitution offers the best possible example of this in practice. The second betrayal occurred in the form of Fianna Fáil's response to the increasingly militant nature of fringe republicanism. Common republican roots counted for little when the Fianna Fáil government felt itself under threat from its erstwhile republican comrades, and sentimental attachments were jettisoned with unseemly haste as the full armoury of the state's police apparatus was brought to bear against the IRA, and the parties it had launched. This process took the best part of a decade to develop, but, by the time of the IRA's successful raid on the government's arsenal in the Phoenix Park in December 1939, few could have doubted the comprehensive and complete nature of the break between the IRA and their radical supporters, on the one hand, and the Fianna Fáil government, on the other.

For the battered remnants of the old Sinn Féin, crying 'foul', 'sell-out', or, most insulting of all, 'compromise', clinging to the cherished certainties of abstention, alienated from the constitutional politics of the pro-Treaty institutions, and, adding insult to injury, now to be outmanoeuvred by the majority of the original anti-Treatyites (who sought – and found – refuge in the new, horribly successful Fianna Fáil), the only solution seemed to lie in establishing successive political *movements* of increasing irrelevance – the very word 'party' being itself somehow tainted – and adopting ever more militant positions on the fringes of political activity. Ironically, in a jerky replication of the path already successfully trodden by Fianna Fáil, this increasingly militant approach was to co-exist with a barely perceptible progression towards engagement with the hated political process. In truth, these political and militant developments occurred more or less simultaneously, and in tracing Clann na Poblachta's immediate political ancestry, this is where one starts to search.

This means placing Clann na Poblachta in their proper context, both in respect of the Irish political party system and in terms of the continual tendency within the republican movement towards eternal fragmentation and regrouping. Looking at this enduring tendency within the republican movement towards fragmentation, or, to put it another way, examining the apparently effortless and endless capacity of the republican movement to endure split after split (for, as Brendan Behan once famously cracked, the first item on the agenda of any republican meeting was always 'the Split') as well as the subsequent regrouping, or re-forming, means having to take a brief detour into the somewhat muddled philosophical, or ideological, background of Irish republicanism, for where it actually came from and where it thought it came from were not always quite the same place.

As Garvin has rightly remarked, 'Democracy in the twentieth century has commonly, but not automatically, walked hand in hand with nationalism',[6] and, of course, historically, Ireland has been very much part of this path of political evolution. In this context, it is important to note that modern Irish democracy is republican in form, and that this is an aspect 'that immediately marks the main Irish political tradition off from its putative English forebear and equally immediately points to American and French inspiration'.[7] However, acknowledging American and French revolutionary ancestry begs questions along the lines of what sort of nationalism and what sort of republicanism are actually being discussed? In Ireland, while both of these concepts traditionally have been seen as virtually identical – or, to put it another way, mutually interchangeable, at least in everyday conversation – the subtle distinctions between them have led to some internal tensions within what can loosely be termed the Irish 'republican' movement. Historically, although the development of nationalism, republicanism, and democracy occurred simultaneously, and while what they were supposed to mean would overlap considerably, they were not always quite the same thing. To take an interesting Irish example, Garvin has commented on how there has been a tendency to 'equate republicanism rather negatively' with the absence of formal ties to Britain. This has meant seeing one's republican identity in terms of the absence of a monarchy, in addition to the attainment of full freedom and the achievement of an unequivocal sovereignty. He has argued, in this context, that the positive, civic connotations of republicanism have tended to be neglected, stressing that 'the values of free speech and the values of open government' have not always been exactly cherished in republican circles, especially the sort of circles inhabited by republicans such as Frank Ryan, who appeared blind to the paradox implicit in his infamous remark that 'there should be no free speech for traitors as long as Republicans had boots and fists'.[8]

In other words, the understanding of what was meant by the terms 'nationalism' and 'republicanism' developed two distinct meanings, within the general sense of the word.[9] Very broadly, these could be seen, respectively, as the right-wing and the left-wing versions of the idea of republicanism. A number of commentators have drawn attention to this distinction between leftist and rightist republicanism; Garvin has written

that the left-wing variant of republicanism 'would argue for the essential
equality of all people and advocate the political right of all citizens to the
suffrage, regardless of economic condition',[10] whereas the rightist version of
republicanism, 'with its preference for the virtuous middle-class or skilled
artisan citizen',[11] has argued that full membership, or full citizenship, of a
true republic ought to be confined to that proportion of the adult population (usually male) that was economically independent, 'or sufficiently
well-off to be able to express an independent political opinion'.[12] Thus, the
elitist view of republican political participation does not include everyone as
being worthy of the right of participation, and indeed, historically, has
served to exclude all those elements, or people, who were not viewed as
being 'morally fitted' for full citizenship and who could not therefore participate, such as the poor, women, the exceptionally rich, and so on. In fact, by
their possession of these elevated ideals, the 'rightist' republicans awarded
themselves occupancy of the moral high ground, for in their mind they
alone possessed the right to define what needed to be done, because the
citizenry could not always be trusted to come to the correct conclusion (this
clinging to erroneous states of mind would be loftily described by orthodox
Marxists as 'false consciousness'). De Valera's succinct remark that 'the
people have no right to do wrong' expresses this attitude even more graphically. This distinction had been made by Rousseau as far back as the
eighteenth century, when he differentiated between the 'general will' and
the 'will of all', the general will being the collective will of the virtuous elite
– what everyone would think if they knew what they should think – while
the will of all was merely adding up the individual wishes of the total population, the assumption being that these wishes were informed by neither
knowledge nor 'virtue'.

Moreover, Garvin goes on to argue that, at one stage, even the very names
of the two great American political parties, Democrats and Republicans,
actually referred to two different political philosophies, arising from this
distinction. Exploring this same theme, Eric Hobsbawm has observed how
'two quite different concepts of the nation meet: the revolutionary-democratic and the nationalist. The equation state = nation = people applied to both,
but for nationalists the creation of the political entities which would contain
it derived from the prior existence of some community distinguishing itself
from foreigners, while from the revolutionary-democratic point of view the
central concept was the sovereign citizen-people = state which, in relation to
the remainder of the human race, constituted a "nation".'[13] The upshot of all
this, to quote Garvin's delicate distinction, is that 'exclusivist and inclusivist
versions of ideological republicanism have therefore competed'.[14] Indeed, not
only have they competed over the future direction of the state, but sometimes these contesting visions have even contended with each other as
different strands within the one political movement, or party.

The history of the development of Irish political parties, especially Irish
republican political parties, is littered with the stiffened corpses of parties
attempting to contain, or reconcile, this fundamental distinction. Not only
did this distinction, or difference, create tensions, but it gave rise to a whole

plethora of parties in Ireland – Sinn Féin in its multiple reincarnations was the obvious example, but others, such as Clann na Poblachta, were also true to this tradition – who would try to straddle this divide and walk this tightrope. Perhaps, not surprisingly, some of them fell off and either disappeared or reconverted into one or other of the elements which had gone into making them. Parties attempting to marry nationalist republicanism with egalitarian-social republicanism were to constitute a particularly marked thread or strand of political party development in Ireland, and this is despite the fact that, traditionally, since independence, the Irish political system has been characterised as a two and a half party system, containing Fianna Fáil, Fine Gael, and a small, unthreatening Labour Party, once contemptuously dismissed by Seán Lemass as being 'a harmless shade of pink'.

The story of Irish republicanism, then, can be told in terms of an ongoing twentieth-century tendency towards the fragmentation and subsequent re-forming of the 'body' of the republican movement, which took the form of the hiving-off of key groups into constitutional politics. Similarly, and significantly, it also represents another manifestation of the age-old blending of the 'social question' with the 'national question'. This combination of the national question with the social question represented the site of a powerful set of instincts, or reflexes, concerning social justice, which, while they may not have been theoretically logical – sometimes, indeed, they capsized under the very weight of their manifold inconsistencies – were, nevertheless, still deeply felt. From the time of Sinn Féin onwards, this gradual initiation into democratic politics occurred in turn for each republican generation, one following after another. By taking the form of a drift towards constitutional politics, despite an innate hostility to parliamentarianism, the very political process itself would become further legitimised. Therefore, in each generational split, it is possible to detect a new version of the old vision of social egalitarianism within Irish republicanism, for this represented the site of one of the deepest reflexes of the movement, even if the impulses behind this desire for social egalitarianism owed more, perhaps, to Jacobin instincts than to socialist inclinations.

In any case, Clann na Poblachta epitomised one aspect of that recurring motif; essentially they represented the first major attempt since the election of Fianna Fáil to office in 1932 to reproduce something more republican in its constitutional integrity and more impatiently concerned with addressing social affairs than anything offered by Fianna Fáil. In effect, by attempting a burglary on the ill-guarded ideology bank of Fianna Fáil, with the objection that Fianna Fáil was delinquent on republican issues and manifestly not at all serious in tackling questions of social justice, Clann na Poblachta was to challenge Fianna Fáil on its own grounds. Returning to the tracing of Clann na Poblachta's immediate political ancestry brings us back to the late 1920s, with mainstream republicanism reeling in the wake of the latest split in Sinn Féin in 1926, which had led to de Valera quitting the party and founding Fianna Fáil, with the intention of contesting elections, taking oaths and taking seats, and, eventually, forming long and lasting governments.

Therefore, by the late 1920s, as Fianna Fáil tacked increasingly to the right in anticipation of ministerial office, it was perhaps inevitable that the initial republican response to this should take the form of a clarion call to the left. The first such response, Saor Éire, came into existence in September 1931 and represented an attempt to merge radical nationalism with supercharged socialism, the latter legitimised by reference more to Connolly than to Lenin. Fear and loathing best describe government reactions to the appearance of this *arriviste*. Episcopal condemnation – and an episcopal ban on membership – followed hot on the heels of official government abhorrence. Official Department of Justice files, dripping with delicate distaste, described Saor Éire as a 'quasi-political' organisation, while, at the same time, Saor Éire was denounced by the Catholic hierarchy as being 'frankly Communistic in its aims'.[15] Although founded jointly by Seán MacBride, Michael Fitzpatrick and Michael Price of the IRA's headquarters staff,[16] and Peadar O'Donnell, who at the time was actively promoting the anti-land annuities campaign, Saor Éire, in fact described itself as an 'Organisation of Workers and Working Farmers'.

Of the three delegates representing the IRA's headquarters staff at the inaugural meeting of Saor Éire, two, Seán MacBride and Michael Fitzpatrick, were to be present at the inaugural meeting of Clann na Poblachta and were to play an active role in the party. The third, Michael Price, was ultimately to quit the IRA and to end up supporting the Labour Party. Although the idea for the anti-land annuities campaign seems to have originated with Peadar O'Donnell, it effectively had its copyright stolen on being borrowed by de Valera and Fianna Fáil after 1932. (Indeed, O'Donnell had earlier offered the land annuities issue to the Labour Party, which had regretfully turned it down, fearing the inevitable 'Red' smear.) While much later in his long life the sobriquet 'veteran socialist' would be attached to O'Donnell, earlier police files baulked at such descriptive analysis, confining themselves to the oft-repeated use of the adjective 'dangerous'. In fact, O'Donnell was a multi-faceted character, whose many activities included editing and writing for the iconoclastic magazine, *The Bell*, renowned equally for its alternative political viewpoints and its prodigious – and widely respected – literary output.

As part of its platform, Saor Éire sought 'to achieve an independent revolutionary leadership for the working class and working farmers towards the overthrow in Ireland of British Imperialism and its ally, Irish Capitalism'.[17] While that much can easily be dismissed as typical of the hyperbole of the revolutionary rhetoric prevalent at the time, Saor Éire's other objectives were more interesting, for they also sought 'to organise and consolidate the Republic of Ireland on the basis of the possession and administration by the workers and working farmers, of the land, instruments of production, distribution and exchange'.[18] Nor did they omit to cultivate the obligatory furrows of the traditional nationalist discourse when they sought 'to restore and foster the Irish language, culture, and games'.[19]

Sniffing out rank communism, the police file enumerates Saor Éire's policies as being 'To abolish without compensation, landlordism in lands, fisheries and minerals; To establish a State monopoly in banking and credits;

To create a State monopoly in export and import services and to promote co-operative distribution; To make the national wealth and credit available for the creation and fullest development of essential industries and mineral resources through Industrial Workers Co-operatives, under State direction and management, workers to regulate internal working conditions'.[20] Other policies included the nationalisation of public transport, the provision of housing by the state, and the establishment of a social insurance scheme for old age, widows, orphans, and the mentally and physically incapacitated. These three policies are of considerable relevance, for each of them would make some sort of reappearance as policies promoted not just by Clann na Poblachta, but also espoused by the inter-party government.

Although Saor Éire had folded or disappeared within a year – Cronin has, perhaps, rather too kindly suggested that in the wake of the ecclesiastical denunciation the IRA convention of April 1932 simply 'decided not to revive it'[21] – it is of relevance for a number of reasons. Firstly, there was the very existence of a left-wing–IRA nexus, and an attempt to merge their respective ideologies, suitably tailored to an Irish context. Several decades later, after the collapse of Clann na Poblachta, some of the soi-disant socialists in the party argued that this collapse had come about largely because of the fundamental incompatibility of left-wing ideals with ardent nationalism, and that the former had only been grafted onto the latter as a belated exercise in electoral desirability.[22] Ideologically incompatible they may have been, but this argument misses the point that some sort of left-wing social vision apparently attended all of the fringe IRA forays into politics between the late 1920s and the late 1940s, when Clann na Poblachta was in its prime. Of even greater interest are the actual policies espoused by Saor Éire. Several of these, trimmed of their dottier tassels, would make a reappearance, not just as Clann na Poblachta party policy, but as actual government policy, during the inter-party government's term of office. By the early 1950s, many of these ideas would be regarded as perfectly legitimate goals in mainstream political thought almost everywhere in western Europe. A final point worth noting is that many of the founders and active members of Saor Éire would re-emerge in Clann na Poblachta, and that Saor Éire represented, for them, the first step on a long tedious path towards eventual political – and parliamentary – engagement.

Although, unlike its predecessor, the freshly minted Republican Congress was not explicitly condemned by the hierarchy, on emerging from the ashes of Saor Éire on 29 and 30 September 1934 in Rathmines Town Hall, it nonetheless offered an instructive example of the tensions implicit in containing conflicting ideologies. It split. This split occurred between, on the one hand, those who, like Michael Price,[23] wished to concentrate on the construction of a political organisation which would contest municipal and Dáil elections, and, on the other, those who preferred the revolutionary habits of secrecy, feeling that the time 'was not opportune'[24] for such a programme, and argued instead that the best way of political engagement was to operate in little burrowing cells which might, with luck, find their way into the trade union movement, for example. Peadar O'Donnell was the leading, though by no

means the only, exponent of the latter view.[25] There was a further complica-
tion which overlapped the earlier difference. Some of the comrades focused
on a post-Saor-Éire-style egalitarian rhetoric, and here Price and O'Donnell
were in complete agreement on the need for a socialist republic on the lines
suggested by Connolly. Others preferred to draw their inspiration from St
Thomas Aquinas, arguing that the proposed programme regarding land
ownership – and the denunciation of 'landlordism' – was not just 'Communist', but was also 'inconsistent with Christian ethics'.[26] With the episcopal
condemnations of Saor Eire still reverberating in their ear-drums the IRA
were rather wary of further involvement with similar organisations bearing
'left' agendas, such as the Republican Congress. They broke 'decisively' with
the Congress in March 1934 in a hotly-contested meeting.[27] This 'decisive'
break could be seen as yet another manifestation of the stresses found in the
vicinity of that eternal republican fault-line; in other words, does the nationalist vision of republicanism win out, or should the organisation place greater
emphasis on the attainment of the socialist aspect of the republican dream?
Significantly, those IRA members who chose to side with the Republican
Congress were subsequently expelled from the 'True Army'. The Republican
Congress itself further split in September 1934. Originally envisaged as a
means to forge some sort of unity between all existing 'anti-imperialist' forces
the Republican Congress, perhaps unsurprisingly, did not achieve its goal.
However, it continued to offer some sort of shelter as an umbrella for 'leftist'
Republicans; one of its last acts was to send abut 150 volunteers to fight with
the International Brigades in Spain in 1936.

The IRA were to spend most of the next decade lurching from one catastrophe to another. First of all, in this catalogue of self-inflicted disaster, they
were implicated in a series of grisly murders; in fact, the murders of Roderick
More O'Farrell, the elderly Vice-Admiral Somerville (whose only 'crime' was
to give letters of reference to local unemployed youths who wished to find
jobs in the British armed forces) and nineteen-year-old John Egan gave rise
to both substantial public unease and considerable government outrage, and
ultimately led to the banning of the IRA. This was followed by the planning of
an abortive – and fatuous – bombing campaign in Britain. However, the
culmination of a disastrous decade occurred with their inane attempt to plug
what they had supposed was a well-placed leak, with the kidnapping and
placing on trial of their own former chief of staff, Stephen Hayes, as a
presumed police spy. The grotesque comedy of what Ó hEithir has called 'the
sordid Hayes Affair'[28] now ensued, as Hayes was moved from one safe house
to another,[29] while being encouraged to write a lengthy and inculpatory
confession, prompted all the time by beatings and the steady application of
lighted cigarettes. He escaped his captors, and arrived – at a hobbled gallop,
covered in chains – at Rathmines Garda Station seeking sanctuary from his
former comrades. As a graphic symbol of how far the once proud IRA had
fallen, it could hardly be bettered.

Meanwhile, a succession of political 'movements' emanating from republican sources now followed. There was little to distinguish them from each
other, most of them bearing similar names, boasting of much the same

policies, and, broadly speaking, containing more or less the same faces. Sometimes, even the very venues where these parties first appeared remained the same. A very early variant from the late 1920s was an entity which was called Comhairle na Poblachta, which, despite the name, could hardly be classed as a political party at all, meriting instead the sharp observation from the secret police that 'This organisation is composed of the most virulent and active extremists in the country, and its sole object is the overthrow of the State by force of arms.'[30] From the jaded, and predictably jaundiced, point of view of the authorities, much the usual suspects were involved and a list of names was supplied with the file. They included Maud Gonne MacBride, Seán MacBride, George Plunkett, Count Plunkett, George Gilmore, Mary McSwiney, Frank Ryan, Michael Fitzpatrick, Tom Barry, and Michael Price, among others.

Having broken with the Republican Congress in 1934, it was not until December of the following year that preparations were made and constitutions were drafted for another new republican association. Although initially, and tellingly, referred to as an 'auxiliary organisation', the association was actually provisionally named the Confederation of the Republic.[31] Two detailed constitutions were prepared, one by Seán MacBride and the other by a colleague, identified only by his or her initials – 'M.D.' Mindful of where power actually lay within the new 'auxiliary organisation', 'M.D.' had urged in a section labelled 'Control' that 'Special attention should be given to the proposals on control.'[32] Among other matters, linguistic concerns troubled them, with 'M.D.' confessing in a covering page: '[regarding] Terms: I had in mind to use "Council of the Republic" instead of "National Executive" but decided against [it] . . . [this could] be interpreted as making that body superior to the Army Council . . . I don't much care for "National Executive."'[33] The need to strike the right revolutionary note was also evident in the draft constitution, for, in a wonderful salute to a venerable ancestor, the language of the French Revolution was respectfully invoked when 'M.D.' suggested 'Consider use of term "National Directorate" I have used, and also used by MacBride. (Directory would probably be better than Directorate.)'[34] MacBride's draft constitution clearly concurred: 'The Directorate shall be the supreme controlling authority of the Organisation when the assembly is not in session.'[35] Actually, most of MacBride's detailed constitution was more concerned with structural affairs – 'it shall be the function of each branch to . . . assist other organisations as directed by the National Directorate . . . hold public lectures and debates . . . encourage the learning of Irish'[36] – than with policy matters. Economic and social considerations did not feature at all, and the only political topic to be broached was the vexed question of parliamentary recognition: 'Under no circumstances shall such candidates, if elected, take part in the proceedings of either the Free State or the Northern Ireland Parliaments, or of any assembly which recognises itself bound by the Treaty of 1921, or by either the Free State or Northern Ireland constitutions . . .'[37] By the following March – probably bearing in mind the wishes of 'M.D.' who, clearly exercised by linguistic considerations, had earlier expressed a preference for Irish language forms: 'I would like if gaelic forms were adopted and popularised, both for the names of the Organisation and for terms'[38] – the Confederation of the Republic had metamorphosed into an organisation which called itself Cumann Poblachta na hÉireann.

A sense of *déjà vu* must, therefore, have attended the inaugural meeting of Cumann Poblachta na hÉireann, which was founded at the familiar republican watering hole of Barry's Hotel, Dublin (where Clann na Poblachta itself would come into being), on 7 March 1936.[39] The attendance at this meeting included Maurice Twomey and Seán MacBride representing the IRA; Fiona Plunkett and Florence McCarthy, officers of Cumann na mBan; Dr James P. Brennan, the Dublin county coroner; Madge Daly of Limerick; and Patrick McLogan, an MP for South Armagh. Diarmuid O'Riordan was appointed vice-chairman, and The O'Rahilly became treasurer. In addition, the IRA's own publication, *An Phoblacht*, was revived under the editorial eye of Donal O'Donoghue, in order to lend support to the new organisation. (Of those attending this meeting, The O'Rahilly, Brennan, O'Riordan, O'Donoghue and MacBride would all feature in Clann na Poblachta.) Cumann Poblachta na hÉireann attempted to reconcile the twin props of traditional republican political policy, namely non-recognition and abstention, by suggesting that while elections should be contested – thereby implying a degree of recognition of the detested institutions – any seats won should not be taken. The sole political importance of Cumann Poblachta na hÉireann lies in the fact that the IRA – whose creature the party, in fact, was – were actually prepared to contemplate the contesting of elections. Advocating an abstentionist platform, they contested the local elections in June 1936. Their impact was negligible,[40] despite the fact that at least one of their candidates – the redoubtable Madame Maud Gonne MacBride – enjoyed a considerable profile. Abstentionist policies had run their course, but it would take the organisations sponsored by the IRA a little longer to realise this. Breandán Ó hEithir put it rather nicely when he wrote: 'A quick glance at Irish history in the nineteenth century [had] been enough to tell [de Valera] that the Irish people had struggled far too hard to achieve the right to vote to negate it by electing Republican angels who would dance on the heads of ideological pins in Limbo.'[41] Indeed, de Valera himself had quit Sinn Féin just a decade earlier on that very same issue, in order to found Fianna Fáil, contest elections, and take such seats as he was elected to.

The same decision, ultimately, was reached by the successor party to Cumann Poblachta na hÉireann, an organisation bearing the startlingly similar name of Córas na Poblachta, which was founded in the Mansion House, Dublin, on 2 March 1940.[42] Yet again, the roll-call of those attending the inaugural meeting contained more than a few familiar faces, for the first meeting of Córas na Poblachta attracted an unusual cross-section of people, most of whom were to become actively involved in Clann na Poblachta: Seán Fitzpatrick, Seán Dowling, and Simon Donnelly from the National Association of the Old IRA – both Fitzpatrick and Donnelly would become founding members of Clann na Poblachta; Dublin county coroner, Dr James P. Brennan, who earlier was active in Cumann Poblachta na hÉireann – and earlier still active in 'the Christian Front' – and would make a reappearance in Clann na Poblachta; Peadar O'Donnell; and, strangely, General Eoin O'Duffy, formerly of the Blueshirts, who attended without committing himself further. Others who became involved with Córas na Poblachta and who would subsequently play some role in Clann na Poblachta were Seán Mac Giobuin, Con Lehane, Malachi Quinn, Roger McHugh – who was appointed editor of *Aicéin,* the organ of Córas na Poblachta's youth movement; Helena Moloney, and B. Berthon Waters, an economist. A striking absentee from the Córas na Poblachta inaugural meeting was Seán MacBride himself, who spent the 1943 general election in Donegal, canvassing support for a republican colleague, Seán MacCool, who at that time held the position of chief of staff of the IRA and, presumably, could not therefore canvass for himself.[43]

Having reluctantly decided to enter the political fray, Córas na Poblachta glumly concluded not only that elections should be contested, but that 'if necessary for the execution of the Plan, Córas na Poblachta will not shirk the responsibility of government', and continued, evincing a visible note of evident regret, 'that Córas na Poblachta must provide for the necessity of creating a government and that this will render, in present circumstances, the development of a political party unavoidable'.[44] In other words, if elected, they would take their seats in whatever institution – be it local or national – they had been elected to, and, in order to contest such elections with any sort of serious intent, they really needed to form a political party, regrettable necessity though that was. As events transpired, they polled dismally in both the local elections of August 1942 and the general election of 1943,[45] leading to the gratified conclusion drawn by the secret police: 'The complete defeat of the Party's candidates led to its speedy disintegration.'[46]

However, this ranked as more of a dissolution than a disintegration, for, within a year, a determined regrouping occurred with the intention of creating yet another new republican political party. With this aim in mind, several meetings were held between September 1944 and February 1945. The meeting which took place on 1 October 1944 earnestly discussed 'the feasibility of launching an organisation similar to SE [Saor Éire] and if it is feasible to draft heads of policy. It was agreed that the word "feasibility" should be read to mean "advisability".'[47] Present were a number of republican stalwarts, all of whom would become actively involved with Clann na Poblachta: Seán MacBride (presiding in the absence of Jim Killeen who was actually appointed chairman), Diarmuid O'Riordan, Michael O'Kelly, Con Lehane, Fionán Breathnach, and Donal O'Donoghue, who took the minutes. The minutes are clear and concise. Matters which should have been cleared up decades earlier surfaced yet again when the meeting found it necessary to note that 'After a discussion it was agreed that it would be futile to form an organisation unless it was prepared to contest parliamentary elections. It was further agreed that it would be futile to contest elections unless the candidates were prepared to take their seats in Leinster House.'[48]

A subsequent meeting held on 8 October took this particular discussion further still. Voicing concerns on behalf of an absent Northern comrade, Michael O'Kelly asked his colleagues 'to consider the point of not entering the 26 county parliament except as a majority party', adding that 'he feared the danger of a complete break with the past, and pointed out that many people have been sustained in their opinions by sentiment'. This appeal to the past received short shrift from those present. As the minutes tersely phrased it, the committee 'agreed that the question of entering the 26 County Parliament only as a majority party was impractical and inadvisable', adding, with a blunt recognition of unpleasant political realities, that 'The Twenty-six County Governmental institutions had come to stay, and had come to be recognised as a national central authority.'[49] 'Sentiment' as a valid consideration for preserving the time-honoured outlook of the past received equally short shrift when the committee felt impelled to respond to the Northern comrade by replying dryly: 'With reference to the danger of a complete break with the past; and to the fact that many people have been sustained in their opinions by sentiment, it was held that altered conditions have necessitated a change in outlook.'[50]

Despite giving every appearance of diligently preparing the ground for further republican political action, nothing much seemed to happen for the best part of two years, until exactly the same people gathered under the auspices of yet another new political party. This was Clann na Poblachta, which, as has already been noted, came into existence in Barry's Hotel on 6 July 1946.

2

The Children of the Republic

At first glance Clann na Poblachta seemed to be simply the latest offering in a long line of undistinguished republican attempts to scale the walls of the inaccessible Jericho. While Clann na Poblachta's linear descent on the distaff side of republican theory and practice, theology, and indeed ideology can easily be traced, less immediately clear are the reasons for the party's wide-ranging appeal and considerable electoral success. For, there was little at the time, in either the party's immediate ancestry, its stated policies, or even its current personnel, to indicate that within eighteen months of its creation it would play a crucial role in causing the biggest political upset witnessed in Ireland since Fianna Fáil took office in 1932. This was not merely a question of simply existing, fighting elections, and taking seats, although these pursuits in themselves generated considerable astonishment. Nor was Clann na Poblachta simply to be the means by which the politicisation of yet another generation of IRA men occurred, those irreconcilables who had hith-erto happily opted for the gun in preference to parliamentary contamination. Not only that, the Clann was also to be the chief conduit (though, as events would show, hardly the ultimate beneficiary) through which an entire politi-cal generation – those who had been too young to partake of the independence struggle and who, as a result, found themselves excluded from any meaningful participation in the nation's public life – found their political sealegs, as it were. However, if these people had not already been partially roused by contemporary events – such as the Irish National Teachers' Organ-isation (INTO) strike in 1946, dire economic conditions, the impact of the revelations of the inquest into the death of Seán McCaughey, and an arro-gant government apparently awash in scandals (all of which will be dealt with in the next chapter) – and simultaneously alienated by existing political parties, it is unlikely that Clann na Poblachta's revivalist form of republican-ism allied to social reform would have proved to be quite so alluring to them. Yet, the fact that the party succeeded in mobilising almost all of the remain-ing extraconstitutional republicans, as well as being the means by which much of a new generation was politically mobilised, points to the consider-able success achieved, which was in itself quite amazing, given the limited appeal enjoyed by the plethora of previous parties launched by much the same people as would lead Clann na Poblachta.

And here lies one of the paradoxes of the Clann. Most commentators stress the party's 'newness', 'originality', or, dare one say it, 'radicalism' in seeking explanations for the party's appeal and success. In fact, initially there was very little that was completely new in Clann na Poblachta – its leadership, a good many of its policies, even its very name were heavily redolent with echoes from the past. It looked new, and radical, and challenging, and different, without really being many of these things. Nor was this novel and attractive appearance necessarily solely a tribute to the persuasive power of advertising – although Clann na Poblachta were to run two superb campaigns in 1947 and 1948, greatly assisted by appropriate advertising and the deft management of Noel Hartnett. Neither the party's solid republican lineage, its current leadership, its striking mastery of public relations, nor its attractive social policies are sufficient in themselves as explanations for the appeal it exerted and the success it enjoyed.

Historically, what was to be of far greater importance was the fact that Clann na Poblachta actually went into government. This had three immediate results, the first two obvious and the other more long term. Firstly, by going into government, Clann na Poblachta effected a change of government, itself a good thing as Fianna Fáil had been in office far too long, with all of the problems attendant on that, a point conceded privately even by some of its own members.[1] Secondly, by supplying ministers of the undoubted calibre of Seán MacBride and, more especially, Noël Browne, Clann na Poblachta proved that platform rhetoric could actually be translated into administrative action. Thirdly, and most important of all, was Clann na Poblachta's role in helping to create a new form of government: the 1948 election was to mark the beginning of the end of the old civil war nexus, of the old system whereby Fianna Fáil and Fine Gael faced up to each other and fought elections head-to-head, the winner hopefully able to form a government on its own; after 1948, non-Fianna Fáil governments were to be formed on the basis of coalitions,[2] and voting patterns would, in time, reflect this altered political landscape. All of these points are relevant in highlighting the historical importance of Clann na Poblachta (and are all the more striking when contrasted with the negligible impact of its related republican predecessors), but they do not fully explain the reasons for the party's success and appeal. All of these reasons, while worthy in themselves, would not have been efficacious, and would not have worked, had the time not been opportune, to paraphrase Peadar O'Donnell. It is possible, therefore, to argue that 1946 was opportune in a way that earlier times were not, and that MacBride, who was to prove an inept leader in other respects, could at least see this, and seize the opportunity when it presented itself. But before addressing, in the next chapter, some of the reasons why 1946, as opposed to, say, 1943, or earlier, was to prove such a demonstration of the idea of *zeitgeist*, a brief introduction to some of the personalities and leading lights of Clann na Poblachta, and a discussion of the party's internal structures, are in order.

Among those who signed the document circulated by the party to the media (referred to in Chapter 1 above), and therefore found themselves sitting on Clann na Poblachta's provisional executive, was Seán MacBride, the man who was to become the leader of the party, but who in 1946 was rather better known as a barrister specialising in the defence of republicans who had fallen foul of the law. MacBride's background was extraordinary, and his republican antecedents impeccable. He was born in Paris in January 1904,[3] the son of a brief marriage between his mother, the redoubtable Maud Gonne, and Major John MacBride, who had distinguished himself in the Boer War, fighting with the Boers against the British, and who was later, in 1916, to take up arms against the British again, this time at the cost of his life. Maud Gonne, in Paris, not only inspired and tormented the poet W. B. Yeats, but also kept open house for republicans on the run who just happened to be passing through Paris. MacBride, as his biographer, Tony Jordan, remarks, 'was brought up in situations where he only met the important people in the Independence movement [and] behaved from boyhood as if he was one of them'.[4] By 1920 he had joined the IRA and, supporting the anti-Treaty side in 1922, rose up through the ranks, becoming chief of staff in 1936 and quitting the organisation in 1938.[5] Subsequently, he turned to the law, qualifying as a barrister in 1937, taking silk in 1943, and devoting much of his energy and most of his legal practice towards the amelioration of the lot of his former comrades in arms.[6] However, while MacBride really only came to public attention and political prominence in 1946, and that more for the McCaughey inquest than for the founding of yet another republican party, his political apprenticeship had been a long one, predating Saor Éire and taking in membership of almost all of the fringe movements launched by the IRA, or factions within it. As leader of the new party, MacBride initially seemed to have a lot going for him. His bizarre aristocratic background, French accent, and arresting appearance, combined with his undoubted administrative abilities and forensic legal skills, suggested that here lay the party leader of the future. However, the skills acquired during his long political apprenticeship were not necessarily the ones required to lead a political party (as opposed to, say, a paramilitary organisation), engage de Valera successfully in battle, or, for that matter, juggle issues to one's advantage at the Cabinet table, particularly an inter-party Cabinet table. Other skills were needed as well, skills which MacBride lacked, and here, in fairness to MacBride, he had the wit to recruit people who had them, in this instance principally Noel Hartnett and Peadar Cowan.

Unlike almost everybody else who was involved with Clann na Poblachta from the outset, neither Hartnett nor Cowan had the almost mandatory IRA background. What they did have, however, was political experience in spades, combined with a shrewd appreciation of how elections should be fought and election campaigns funded and organised. This expertise was evident even to the uninitiated, such as Noël Browne, who later wrote with a note of reluctant wonder that 'Hartnett was well skilled in the intrigues and intricacies of fighting and winning elections, learned over the years at the highest level in Fianna Fáil'.[7] This knowledge of the procedures of *realpolitik* meant that Hartnett's political judgement in particular, and, to a lesser extent, that of Cowan, were very much depended on by the rest of the party, and, more importantly, by the leadership of the party, in the early days. With time, they would find themselves in a situation analogous to that of all experts, or, to use the parlance of a later time, all handlers: namely, those who are acquired by political parties, and are admired, envied, depended upon – and indeed resented – for their expertise, but who, at the same time, are completely devoid of a support base within the existing network, or structure, of the party. They were to enjoy influence without power, a position which normally should not pose too many problems unless one happens to fall out with the party leader or become otherwise expendable. Of course, this was what actually happened in turn to both Cowan and Hartnett. Apart from everything else, their expertise was sorely missed by the time of the 1951 election, and certainly contributed to Clann na Poblachta's crushing defeat,[8] even though the reasons for their absence, as well as the reasons for the largely self-inflicted debacle faced by the Clann, were, to a considerable extent, MacBride's own fault.

Despite lacking the sort of mandatory republican background most of his new colleagues wore on their sleeves, Hartnett nevertheless found himself on the dais in Barry's Hotel, where he signed the statement circulated by Clann na Poblachta to the media. Noel Hartnett was a barrister whose legal activities as MacBride's junior counsel in a number of controversial cases – principally the McCaughey inquest – had led to the termination of his position as compère on Radio Éireann's popular *Question Time* programme at the behest of the Fianna Fáil government. Announcing Hartnett's dismissal, a piece in the *Irish Press*, on 30 May 1946, reported, 'The Minister for Posts and Telegraphs has notified the ITA that Mr Noel Hartnett is to be precluded from acting as Radio Compère for the ITA *Question Time* in future'.[9] Government requirements were masked by the generous application of large doses of self-righteous rhetoric, when the Minister for Posts and Telegraphs, P. J. Little, justified his action with the following remarks: 'Mr Hartnett has, since his engagement as a compère taken part in very vehement and dangerous political controversy; and the general practice of the broadcasting organisation must necessarily be insisted on that persons taking an active part (one might say with violent language) in such a controversy cannot be permitted to act as an announcer or compère, especially before a large gathering of the public. Mr Hartnett's speeches and Press Correspondence were entirely outside his professional work in the Courts of Law.'[10] Along with his family, Hartnett was a life-long admirer of de Valera, and was profoundly shocked at being sacked by the Fianna Fáil government – in what was accurately described by Noël Browne as an act of 'vindictive reprisal'[11] – for participating at an inquest in a professional capacity. Furthermore, Hartnett was something of a refugee from the higher echelons of Fianna Fáil, for he had once held a seat on the party's national executive. Stung on account of the sacking, Hartnett claimed that he had also fled the party in dismay at what he perceived as both its increasing corruption and its diminishing republicanism. Hartnett's hands-on experience was to lead to his appointment as Clann na Poblachta's director of elections, and his political nous was to prove invaluable to the Clann – amply compensating for MacBride's deficiencies in these areas – both in the by-elections of 1947 and in the general election of 1948.

Another political refugee (this time from Labour) was Captain Peadar Cowan, a solicitor, who also signed the Clann's founding statement. Cowan's own political background bordered on the perverse, for he had held a commission in the Free State army and had dabbled – briefly – with the Blueshirts before turning his attentions to Labour. Cowan could be viewed as emblematic – though as events were to show he was by no means representative – of the 'left' element in Clann na Poblachta. Long before his acrimonious fall-out with MacBride, Cowan had displayed a capacity for mercurial political relationships, having been in and out of the Labour Party with disconcerting dizziness throughout the 1940s. As chairman of the Fairview branch of the party, and holding a seat on the party's administrative council, Cowan had stood for election as a Labour candidate in the 1944 general election, in, of all places, the Westmeath constituency. Not surprisingly, he failed to take a seat, despite putting what even the secret police account grudgingly conceded was 'a tremendous amount of work and energy'[12] into his campaign. Shortly after the 1944 election he resigned from the Labour Party and set up 'The Vanguard' – veritable evidence of the communist cloven hoof indeed, as it actually styled itself a 'New Socialist Republican Movement'.[13] Notwithstanding the salacious response its appearance generated amongst the political authorities, 'The Vanguard' didn't actually last very long. Within a year Cowan had returned to the Labour Party, rejoining the Fairview branch and becoming honorary director of organisation for the party in the process, a position he resigned from in July 1946 when he joined Clann na Poblachta. His attendance at the inaugural meeting of the Clann meant that he obtained a place on the provisional executive and was subsequently appointed director of finance for the fledgling party.

Also on the platform was Con Lehane, another solicitor who, like Cowan, enjoyed a close professional relationship with MacBride and was to throw many briefs in his direction. As with so many of the other leading members of the Clann, Lehane had served his republican apprenticeship, in his case putting in time with the IRA's Dublin Brigade. After his arrest in 1936, he agreed to abjure violence and in a letter – subsequently described with evident satisfaction by the police as being 'very abject' – stated that he had severed his connection with the movement and wished to devote himself to his private practice.[14] In fact, Lehane's occasional political impulsiveness did not quite end when he left the IRA and began to make a career out of defending imprisoned republicans. Not only was he involved with some of Clann na Poblachta's dottier ancestors such as Córas na Poblachta, but he also dabbled in more esoteric pursuits. Nor was the meeting in Barry's Hotel the first time he had shared a platform with Peadar Cowan. A gloriously lunatic earlier example concerns a meeting in Jury's Hotel on 7 November 1943 (the secret police were there, too), when Lehane was spotted, along with Cowan, Robert N. Tweedy, Hilda Tweedy, and sundry others attending a lecture held to celebrate the twenty-sixth anniversary of the Russian Revolution, a meeting which opened with a rousing rendition of *The Internationale*.[15]

Some of the other signatories of the Clann manifesto had equally picaresque political backgrounds, managing to mingle some sort of socialist thought with their republican activities. As a traveller to the Soviet Union in both 1927 and 1932 – to attend meetings of the 'International Congress of the Friends of Soviet Russia' – Michael Fitzpatrick was bound to attract the wrathful attention of the secret police, especially when he returned and acquired a ballroom, which, with insouciant impudence, or maybe quixotic nostalgia, he imprudently named the 'Balalaika'.[16] On a more prosaic level, though equally subversive in the eyes of the authorities, files on Michael Fitzpatrick[17] also noted that while he had been 'constitutional since 1940',[18] he had over twenty years of solid republican activity behind him when he left the IRA, in the late 1930s, for he had been actively involved in every organisation created by the IRA, from Saor Éire onwards, taking in membership of Cumann Poblachta na hÉireann and Córas na Poblachta as well, before landing in Clann na Poblachta. Then there was Donal O'Donoghue – by the 1940s an accountant by profession – who was regarded by some as being 'an unlikely member of a guerilla army'.[19] The police files entertained no such doubts, remarking on his twenty years' service during which time he rose to be quarter-master general of the IRA and edited the IRA's magazine, *An Phoblacht*. Earlier editorial activity had included a stint with *The Workers' Voice*, the publication of the Workers' Revolutionary Party in Ireland,[20] and O'Donoghue had also involved himself with the 'League Against Imperialism' by attending several of their conferences. His family connections were also thought to be somewhat suspicious – for O'Donoghue had married Sheila Humphries, who herself was a signatory of Saor Éire's manifesto, and had also been actively involved with the 'Republican Congress'.[21]

Most of the remainder of the provisional executive came to constitutional politics with robust republican backgrounds, or, as Noël Browne put it when writing about Michael A. O'Kelly, 'a lurid record of violent underground military activities in the IRA'.[22] O'Kelly, whom Browne described as 'a tough and ruthless party apparatchik',[23] became Clann na Poblachta's first general secretary, until he was succeeded by Tom Roycroft, a teacher, who can best be regarded as one of the gifts bestowed on the Clann by the INTO link. Another was Fionán Breathnach, and here the police files could not agree on whether the 'Finian Walsh, a recently dismissed national teacher', of 1930, who was appointed business manager of *The Workers' Voice*, was the same as Fionán Breathnach, national teacher, who held a seat on Clann na Poblachta's provisional executive and whose brother, Cormac, was a Fianna Fáil TD, but they concluded that 'it is likely'.[24] National teachers were not the only ones drawn from the educational establishment – Clann na Poblachta reached into the universities too, and not just among the student body.[25] One of their founder members, Roger McHugh, at that time held a lecturing post in the English department at University College Dublin and would, years later, be appointed to the Chair of English there. His republican antecedents did not simply cover the dainty drawing-room pursuits of editing *Aicéin*, the youth magazine of Córas na Poblachta, but had also included placing his house at the disposal of those who held former IRA chief of staff Stephen Hayes captive and were trying to wring a confession out of him.[26]

What is of interest in this context, apart from the idiosyncratic life stories of some of the Clann's leading lights, is their actual social background. Apart from the sturdy republican lineage and relative youth of some of these people, their occupational profile is extremely interesting. In strict class terms, many of them could equally easily pass the port in the dining room and pass muster in the billiard room with the best that Fine Gael or any of the other parties could throw up. For all of its radical republican ancestry, Clann na Poblachta's provisional executive contained a surprising number of lawyers, company directors, and, inevitably, teachers, giving it – to say the least – a rather unusual class profile for a party with such a platform.[27] Admittedly, in no competitive political system are the parliamentarians, or the people who make up the executive bodies of political parties, anything like a microcosm of those who vote for them, and this tendency has been even more pronounced in parties which purported to be catch-all, as opposed to niche, or sectional interest, parties. However, as Clann na Poblachta were to set out their stall to attract the votes of disenchanted Fianna Fáil 'little men', as well as seeing Labour, and Labour's supporters, as being their natural ally, fishing pond, and constituency, it is of interest to note that in the case of the Clann, class divergences between the party leadership and many of those whom they planned to attract as supporters were more than usually wide for a political party at that time. This interesting class profile would become even more pronounced with the election (not, note, self-appointed selection) of the new – democratically renamed and diplomatically retitled – national executive after the party's first ard-fheis.[28] In fact, that ard-fheis did not occur until the very end of November 1947, that is, after the three by-elections which were to thrust Clann na Poblachta centre stage in the public consciousness. But before returning to the events of 1946 to 1948 which were to prove so propitious for the Clann, the internal structures of the party, the influence of its IRA ancestry on its attitudes and structures, and the style of leadership adopted by Seán MacBride need to be addressed.

As Clann na Poblachta's first ard-fheis was not held until well over a year after the foundation of the party, the provisional executive was, strictly speaking, neither elected by nor accountable to anybody, a point not missed by the secret police. Nor indeed, for that matter, was it missed by 'The National Advisory Council, Old Comrades Irish Republican Army' – an organisation which regarded itself as a gauntleted guardian of the clear wellsprings of republican thought[29] – who railed against this perceived lack of democratic accountability in a strongly worded statement issued from the familiar haunt of Barry's Hotel in the summer of 1947.[30] In it, disavowing any previous support for Clann na Poblachta, they 'regretted' the failure of the provisional executive of Clann na Poblachta to hold an ard-fheis, and deplored the fact that the party's decision to contest three by-elections 'was adopted by a self-constituted Provisional Executive, thereby, in effect asking the people of Dublin, Waterford, and Tipperary, to accept a policy which has not been put before a democratically constituted convention of their own party for consideration and ratification, and which cannot, therefore, be regarded as being seriously concerned with bringing about a democratically constituted national movement'.[31] As a parting shot, members of the association were asked to refrain from giving any support 'to a group of hand-picked opportunists whose background constitutes a grave menace to the National and Christian principles of the Irish people'.[32]

Strong stuff indeed, but no stronger than what Fianna Fáil would hurl at the new party once they became alert to the possible dangers its existence posed to them. Nor, for all Clann na Poblachta's subsequent prickly sensitivity to criticism, was such a disavowal anything to lose too much sleep over, for squabbles over the nature and ownership of elusive republican holy grails were hardly anything new – indeed this internecine faction-fighting had been a feature of the republican movement since the early 1920s and, as such, constituted an accurate strand of republican ancestry in itself. Of greater importance, in the context of republican ancestries, especially in the context of parties attempting to put a bit of democratic distance between themselves and their immediate republican ancestry, was Clann na Poblachta's regrettable tendency to lapse into old habits and cling to the *modus operandi*, if not the aims, of the hallowed ancestors. Poised to enter constitutional politics, was the party's initial failure to hold an ard-fheis an unfortunate oversight, caused by the accelerating pressure of events? Or rather, was it the characteristic continuation of the non-democratic attitudes which had prevailed before the conversion to constitutional politics? In fairness, by the time the party got around to holding its first ard-fheis in November 1947 it had been impelled to the centre of the national political stage, and would now be obliged to fight for its very life, for it had done much more than simply tweak the Fianna Fáil government's Roman nose. By taking two seats out of three, in three fiercely contested by-elections, Clann na Poblachta had, in effect, left the government with an unfortunate intimation of political mortality. Nursing their wounded pride, and dabbing their bloodied nose, Fianna Fáil viewed these losses as grand larceny akin to feloniously making off with the family silver, a fact which led to de Valera's immediate dissolution of the Dáil and consequent declaration of a general election for February 1948. For Clann na Poblachta, then, November 1947 was surely more a time to try to surf the tides of history, rather than to settle down to the boring business of the nuts and bolts of constitutional politics. The upshot of all of this was that Clann essentially tossed a constitutional chassis over the existing 'provisional' framework, leading ultimately to an expression of ambiguity in the very structures of the party.

This ambiguity was certainly illustrated by the role that would be played by the national executive of the Clann, and was to be reflected even more graphically in the powers accorded to the Clann's own standing committee, which was in charge of the day-to-day running of the party. For example, each of these bodies enjoyed considerable powers with regard to candidate selection, which, in the forties, was more usually considered to be the prerogative of the constituency convention of a party. According to the Clann's own constitution, constituency conventions were to be chaired by a member of either the national executive or the standing committee, or by somebody else appointed *in loco parentis*. Nothing much untoward thus far, it would seem, as all of the other parties employed a similar practice at constituency conventions. However, the Clann's constitution allowed the national executive, and/or standing committee, not only to determine how many candidates a constituency convention could nominate, but, much more importantly, enabled them to impose any additional candidates they wished upon a constituency convention, and this over the heads of the constituency convention. In addition, the standing committee had the power to refuse to ratify the nomination of any candidate.[33] Basically, the executive bodies could decide how many candidates were to stand in a constituency, they could impose whosoever they wished, and they could refuse to accept anybody chosen by the constituency convention. Admittedly, no political party could operate effectively if it consistently flew in the teeth of the wishes of its membership, but the point is that Clann na Poblachta's executive bodies had the potential power to do so if the need arose.

Certainly, the Clann's constitution awarded its executive bodies a degree of administrative power unusual in political parties at that time in Ireland, and, to that extent, it certainly reflected the vertical hierarchies of the military structures – such as the IRA – from which it had emerged. Vertical (and one-way) lines of authority and communication are valued in military organisations because the primary objective is to ensure that the commands given are obeyed and implemented. Political parties tend to aim for rather different goals, such as changing society, and, as a result, their structures are more usually used to stress some sort of democratic accountability. Theories of representative, or indirect, democracy generally imply both increased delegation and increased distance as one advances up the layers of the organisation. In political parties, this usually means that party branches elect delegates to attend the annual conference, or ard-fheis, and that, while there, they elect an executive body, which in turn elects its steering committee, with the party leader presiding benignly over the lot. Direct democracy was more the norm for revolutionary parties and their clones (including those spawned by the IRA), involving long, agonised debates on matters of principle and vigorous open voting on the part of the collective. In these situations, the executive bodies were merely supposed to carry out the clearly stated wishes of the assembled membership – and there was nothing to say that they couldn't attempt to persuade or sway the assembled membership! – while their very assembly in one place was often a boon to hostile police forces. What all of this meant for Clann na Poblachta was that the party's administrative bodies ultimately attempted some sort of fusion between the traditions with which they were familiar – direct democracy from the floor and an authoritarian leadership used to obedience, on the one hand, and the norms of representative democracy involving delegation of authority to theoretically accountable, and pretty powerful, executive bodies, on the other. Curiously, Clann na Poblachta's constitution was anything but confused on the seeming contradiction of where to place power. Its executive bodies, the national executive and the standing committee, enjoyed extensive powers, including the right to 'make, from time to time, such additional rules as they may decide', squaring this constitutional circle with the rider 'provided, always, that such rules are not inconsistent with this constitution'.[34]

Actually, while Clann na Poblachta's administrative structures were – with time – to help make some of their non-republican members (such as Noël Browne and Jack McQuillan[35]) very, very uneasy indeed, ironically, with the further passage of time, many of these ideas regarding candidate selection would be faithfully copied by the other major political parties.[36] Whatever about candidate selection, and there are strong arguments to justify occasional additional names on a ballot paper, one feature of the Clann's constitution which ultimately appeared in a peculiarly sinister light was the clause which empowered the national executive to elect a ten-member standing committee and, strangely, allowed or awarded the standing committee itself the power to co-opt an additional five members to its ranks.[37] MacBride's detractors (and their numbers grew with the years) saw in this his typically authoritarian desire to create in-built cushioned majorities, lest he be unexpectedly defeated by the democratically expressed distaste of the majority.

Of course, while the distaste of the majority would never pose any kind of problems for the leadership of the Clann, because a feature of their national executive meetings (and, indeed, ard-fheiseanna) for years to come would be 'the votes of unanimous confidence and unswerving loyalty in the leader proposed by some half-witted national teacher from down the country',[38] this administrative ambiguity was further reinforced by the position which was to be cultivated by MacBride himself as leader. This is an area which requires some attention, for MacBride's tenure as leader was to be quite controversial. Claiming to be simultaneously above politics while in politics, MacBride contrived to play a mediating role between his executive bodies and the general membership. This was an attitude which had its origins in IRA habits of mind, for the chiefs of staff – especially the politically inept ones such as MacBride, Tom Barry and Michael Fitzpatrick – had always had a characteristic disdain for the sordid realities of getting their fingernails dirty while digging for votes. Pure, in other words direct, democracy would instead prevail. Now, it is perfectly possible to cultivate the mystique of an unsullied leader in an authoritarian organisation – and the idea of the leader as a disinterested representative of the masses, interceding on their behalf with a bureaucratic, or corrupt, executive establishment, is as old as the hills, and older indeed in places such as Tsarist, or Soviet, Russia. What is disturbing about MacBride is that in constructing a political party, he seems to have thought that this was what leadership was all about. It wasn't, of course. Leadership at that level was all about having a 'handle on the vision thing'[39] (which wasn't really MacBride's particular problem), having your finger on every pulse, and having your hands (or the hands of trusted minions) on all of the necessary levers. MacBride seems to have understood the last of these quite well, but he was woefully ignorant about the second, and this certainly contributed to the long-term structural problems of Clann na Poblachta.

The irony of all of this was that MacBride, as leader, seemed to be regarded as one of the Clann's greatest assets, whereas in fact, his combined deficiencies would eventually make him something of a liability. These deficiencies included the aforementioned authoritarian tendencies, which, whether they were inherent in MacBride's personality or acquired as a result of his political apprenticeship (or both), made his – and his party's – effective functioning in a democratic system just that bit more difficult. Concomitant with that was the fact that MacBride, over time, would also manage to fall out with almost every senior member of the party *apparat*, above all those whose immediate political ancestry did not lie with the IRA. Granted, personality clashes existed, and while few can doubt that Noël Browne was 'highly-strung',[40] or that Cowan was 'pugnacious and truculent',[41] Hartnett was neither – and was a superb political operator to boot. Any party leader who could face the departure of such senior – and able – party members with equanimity could not expect to thrive politically, and especially not in a party which defined itself by stressing a broad-based radicalism, in addition to its nationalist background. Could anyone even contemplate the idea of de Valera jettisoning the 'radical' element which undoubtedly existed within Fianna Fáil, despite the fact that their message was hardly music to ears attuned to Arcadian bliss? Stifle them, yes, with the judicious use of the combined tactics of exhaustion and inertia (used to great effect at endless Cabinet meetings): but jettison them, never.

There were other deficiencies, too, for instance a failure to grasp the finer points of *realpolitik*, and these MacBride did initially attempt to address by recruiting people like Noel Hartnett to attend to these sordid matters of *realpolitik*, as well as by turning this supposed deficiency to his advantage with the argument that his presence in politics was fuelled by a need to rid the country of such foul politicking, thereby stressing that Clann na Poblachta stood for better things, such as a sublime sense of mission in public life. The other complaints which were to be made about MacBride as leader, for instance his cold, logical, platform manner (as mentioned by Inglis),[42] or his profound lack of knowledge of – and worse, manifest lack of interest in – matters close to the hearts of 'middle Ireland', such as Gaelic football and hurling,[43] were not the major drawbacks some thought them to be. Granted, in a pre-television age, a good rabble-rousing oratorical style was bound to entertain and impress, and for that reason, good platform skills were an important requirement for a party leader to possess, and this had been the case ever since public meetings had been used to influence political outcomes. In any event, opinions are divided on the merits of MacBride's platform rhetoric: Inglis, for example, regarded MacBride as 'a wretchedly

poor speaker, with an unattractive accent he had retained from his upbringing in France',[44] while, by way of contrast, his biographer Tony Jordan
quoted C. S. 'Todd' Andrews approvingly when the latter wrote that MacBride
'spoke in a peculiarly soothing manner'.[45] Another view comes from John A.
Murphy, who felt that MacBride was a 'colourful leader' and that a certain
'exotic element in his personality was an additional attraction in an Irish
political chief',[46] a point endorsed by Tim Pat Coogan, who wrote that
MacBride 'had an attractive French accent . . . and carried a romantic aura
akin to that of de Valera in his heyday'.[47] Notwithstanding differences on how
his platform persona was perceived, MacBride himself could point to the fact
that inflaming passions was the very antithesis of what he had sought to
achieve by entering politics.

Equally, a knowledge of sporting matters – and in the forties this essentially meant GAA sport – while a considerable help in Irish politics, does not
guarantee automatic success, nor does its absence imply comprehensive
failure. Moreover, MacBride was well able to convey his contempt for this sort
of 'populism', for, as he saw it, his platform persona declined to patronise his
audience with the sort of vulgar displays of populism which were implicit
with a declared interest in sport; and yet, he proved equally capable of simultaneously guarding his flank, for Clann na Poblachta were to attract an
unusually high number of successful GAA sportsmen to run as candidates.[48]
This process was already well in train as early as the 1947 by-elections, for
the Clann's candidate in Waterford, Seán Feeney, appeared to have been
recruited by the party first and foremost on account of his prowess on the
hurling pitch for his native county. A number of them would be elected to
various bodies, such as Jack McQuillan, who gained a Dáil seat in Roscommon in 1948 for Clann na Poblachta, having already won several All-Ireland
football medals with the county, and Andy Murphy, who was elected to
Carlow County Council for the party, having played football for Carlow and
Leinster.[49] In any case, charges of being out of touch with the icons of Irish
culture were rather inappropriate if applied to MacBride, for his very
upbringing had conspired to ensure his intimacy with almost all of the more
elevated icons of that same culture. One need only refer to his family's
extended relationship with the poet W. B. Yeats to reinforce this point.

Really, these are trifling complaints notwithstanding the coverage they
have received in some accounts,[50] for the real charge, and arguably the
greatest question over MacBride as leader, lay in the fact that he led a
supposedly radical party, and enjoyed a radical reputation, which does not
seem to be fully merited. Apart from his heady experience with the manic
messianism of Saor Éire (and MacBride's biographer, Tony Jordan, admits
that around that time MacBride 'was doubtful about becoming embroiled in
social issues'[51]), had anything else in MacBride's background or career justified this belief in his radicalism? What had he ever done to engender, let
alone encourage, the idea that he could be an agent for revolutionary or
radical change? Leading a party with a radical reputation, MacBride himself
had come to enjoy a reputation as a radical, or, at least, as a liberal. His
reputation for liberalism probably derived from his concerns with human,

or civil, rights, and, in turn, these evolved from the nature of his legal practice, for MacBride had come to constitutional politics as a vigorous defender of those who vigorously opposed the state. The type of liberalism which springs from human rights concerns is often based on a fairly narrow legal premise. In fairness to MacBride, his legal and his political careers both demonstrated a consistent thread of interest in human rights matters throughout his life. For example, during his stint in Iveagh House as Minister for External Affairs, he signed the European Convention of Human Rights on behalf of Ireland, and the long list of ground-breaking (and law-making) cases he was involved in amply illustrates his sustained legal interest in that area over a long period.

However, a nose for liberal niceties in law does not always translate into a comprehensive political and social vision, let alone a liberal one, and the argument that MacBride was a social radical is difficult to sustain in the light of his actions as a party leader, and especially his later behaviour as a party leader *and* minister during the Mother and Child Scheme debacle. In terms of retaining radical support, safeguarding one's radical ideological territory, preening one's radical image, and having a radical impact on government policy, Clann na Poblachta's key moment of choice was not the decision to go into government (although some of its more purist supporters saw this as the moment of choice), but was, rather, the choice made at the time of the Mother and Child Scheme crisis to back the cause of the vested interests opposing the scheme, and here, the blame for that choice must lie squarely with MacBride.[52] There were, of course, a dozen other factors involved, including Noël Browne's fraught relations with the Irish Medical Association (IMA), the Catholic hierarchy, and MacBride himself, but this merely serves to underline MacBride's lack of a strategic vision in terms of recognising the bases of his party's support and acting accordingly. From a radical perspective, the consequences were catastrophic, for, as Lee has put it in a devastating verdict, 'MacBride's ineptness as party leader ruined whatever chance existed of an opening to the left in postwar Ireland', adding pointedly that 'MacBride failed to provide his movement with the responsible leadership required to translate it from a party of protest into a credible party of government', and concluding, correctly, with the searing critique that MacBride's support of the conservative consensus during the Mother and Child Scheme served to 'split his party's support base instead of splitting the government'.[53] This is to anticipate what happens, for these choices were to lie in the future; but it is important to note that MacBride's leadership contained some of the root causes for the eventual failure of the Clann, and that these reasons for eventual failure had little enough to do with the decision to go into government and far more to do with MacBride's inherited IRA legacy of aloof authoritarianism, his failure to nurture and water the roots and branches of his party and help to build it up into a permanent feature of the political landscape rather than remain simply a vehicle for political protest, his failure to keep the various strands of the party united and heading in the same direction, and, above all, his failure to recognise where the sources, or bases, of his radical support actually lay and to realise that his continued existence as party leader of a serious radical party lay with retaining and sustaining, rather than splitting, such bases of support.

MacBride's detached status as leader, initially derived from his days with the denizens of the deep in the IRA underground, was subsequently justified by his heavy workload as Minister for External Affairs. The contrast with de Valera could hardly have been greater, despite some superficial similarities. De Valera may have contrived to give the impression that his attention was solely occupied by elevated constitutional matters, but few finer tacticians ever fought an Irish election, and his almost pedantic attention to detail was a successful part of his electoral strategy. All of this means that while Clann na Poblachta may have had the extensive IRA network to call upon, on the minus side they were to be hampered by dodgy notions of what constituted leadership and by administrative structures which owed more to the needs of running a subterranean organisation than to those of an evolving democratically accountable political party. Given time, the Clann probably would have evolved into a workable – and indeed, democratic – party machine, much in the manner of the parties (chiefly Fianna Fáil) upon which it was modelled. However, the strains of an early election, meteoric growth, and attitudes carrying over from the halcyon days of their doubtful ancestry combined to ensure that this did not happen.

3

The Summer of '46

As events transpired, the summer of 1946 was a good time to found a political party. It seemed equally propitious at the time. The significance of 1946 lies in the fact that a number of circumstances in the economy and in society at large were conducive to political change, in that they combined to bring about a fragmentation, or, in other words, a reduction in traditional patterns of support for the major political parties. Furthermore, since all of the postwar movements which challenged the status quo came from outside of politics as previously organised, any organisation which could act as a sort of junction, connection, and conduit for these movements, as well as for the beliefs which gave rise to them – as Clann na Poblachta was to do – possessed enormous potential for mounting a challenge in favour of change, and being the chief means through which such a challenge could be mounted. And here, of course, the key point is that Clann na Poblachta had come to be seen as just such a means, and was viewed by many as the main vehicle for change in Irish society by late 1947.

By 1946, de Valera had been in power for fourteen years, and had not been defeated in six consecutive general elections. At the most recent of these, held in May 1944, de Valera had gained an extremely comfortable Dáil majority of fourteen over all of the other parties put together. His tally of seventy-six seats seemed a vindication of his leadership during the war years, and a further vindication of his finely honed judgement in calling snap elections. Fought on the clever slogan 'Don't Change Horses in Mid-Stream', the 1944 election effectively saw off the twin challenge of the new small farmers' party, Clann na Talmhan, which had burst out of the mists of western obscurity to take ten seats in the earlier election of June 1943, and that of the newly revitalised Labour Party, which, capitalising on the widespread discontent and hardship occasioned by wartime conditions, had – even more alarmingly – taken seventeen seats in 1943. Not only did Labour's electoral success threaten to displace Fine Gael as the second largest party, but it also left de Valera in the position he hated most, dependent on the whims of others to retain office, for the 1943 election had left Fianna Fáil with a mere sixty-seven seats out of 138, and they were thus holding office as a minority government.

Poised to effect a major breakthrough, and crack, or at least disturb, some civil war political moulds, the Labour Party heroically split instead, over the re-emergence, past, and future role of 'Big' Jim Larkin in Labour politics.[1] The Irish Transport and General Workers' Union (ITGWU) appears to have played a rather murky role in helping to engineer this split, as it encouraged the setting up of National Labour and successfully prised away several of its members who happened to be Labour TDs from the Labour Party itself, while bleating about 'the Communist threat' posed by Larkin and his followers. To a certain extent, this was a short-hand for a rerun of the old 1920s row between Jim Larkin and William O'Brien, and which of their respective unions was to enjoy pre-eminence.[2] However, there was more to it than that. Of course, personal and trade union animosities played a part in the development of this sorry saga, which was mined assiduously for all it was worth by Seán Lemass and Fianna Fáil. Echoing the division between the two Labour parties, two trade union congresses emerged from this split, and while the two Labour parties reunited in 1950, the two congresses did not kiss and make up until 1959. Two parties crawled out of the ensuing wreckage, and de Valera recognised a golden opportunity when presented with such on a platter. He dissolved the Dáil, called an election, and romped home with a considerably increased majority, rid of his distasteful dependence on others. If one of the main arguments being put forward to explain the successful emergence of Clann na Poblachta as a party of change – or apparent change – is that the time was right for such a party (and this is one of the arguments being made), then it is necessary to pause for a moment and examine why this support was not directed at, or channelled through, the Labour party instead, as it already existed as some sort of vehicle for change.

For a moment, then, the question becomes, why not Labour? before we can return to, why Clann na Poblachta? The first obvious reason is the one which has just been addressed. The Labour Party had split in two, weakening the party as a result and presenting a sorry spectacle as trade union jealousies (on O'Brien's part) dating from immediately after the First World War were perceived to be of paramount importance in defining the party's image. Historically, the Irish left had suffered from having come from the most underdeveloped proletariat in western Europe, and it long remained the weakest, its support never exceeding 20 per cent of the national vote. Moreover, it had been marginalised in the great divide which followed the franchise extensions in 1917–18; in other words, because Irish politics split over definitions of national sovereignty, and stayed split over these fairly limited definitions, parties which remained aloof from that struggle were bound to become marginalised, especially parties which, privately, on account of their own ideological ancestry, were obliged to question the very nature and efficacy of nationalism, as parties coming from the left were supposed to do. Although parties coming from the left were supposed to query the efficacy of nationalism, and not just as *a* defining icon of the nation's identity, but also, as happened in the Irish case, as *the* defining cleavage, or division, in the political system, nevertheless, Labour's biggest problem lay in the effective marginalisation of its concerns by the other parties – the attitude best expressed by the comment 'Labour must wait' – as the other parties defined the political contours of the new state, in a manner which best reflected their own immediate political and ideological concerns.

Worse still, before Labour could successfully lay permanent claim to the mantle of 'the opposition' in the Free State's parliament,[3] de Valera led Fianna Fáil into the Dáil to snatch it from them. In addition, the ambiguity of Labour's relations with the trade union movement (most of whose members seemed to have voted for Fianna Fáil), successive – and some successful – 'Red' smears, the intensely Catholic nature of most of the electorate of that time, social snobbery, and, possibly most importantly of all, the fact that the twin issues upon which ideological fault lines could break down in Ireland (republicanism or, in other words, definitions of national sovereignty on the one hand, and, of course, land ownership on the other) were not issues which could be handled with any confidence by Labour – all this militated against the party ever putting down the sort of comprehensive roots required for a major party of government. Clann na Poblachta attracted a generation at least as much as a class (and within this generation exerted considerable cross-class appeal), and set out several stalls hoping to attract disillusioned republicans, Fianna Fáil 'little men', and what they could of the left/progressive (in other words, Labour) vote. They could do it, too, because of their republican heritage which meant that they could fight the traditional battles over national sovereignty, and symbols of identity, with aplomb, while still fishing for anything else which might bite. The bottom line was that despite everything it stood for, there were self-styled radicals, or people of a 'progressive' complexion, who would vote for Clann na Poblachta, but who would not vote for Labour. In a telling article, Winifred Trench, a prominent member of the Labour Party, wrote about attending a meeting called to form a new branch of Clann na Poblachta, early in the summer of 1947. She asked the chairman whether the difference between Labour and Clann na Poblachta was 'so fundamental as to justify the formation of Clann na Poblachta as a separate party'.[4] Continuing, she wrote, 'I knew him to have been instrumental in the formation of several branches but he was obviously unused to being asked questions. What his answer amounted to was "We have nothing against the Labour Party, it is more or less the same as our own. But people will join Clann na Poblachta who would not join the Labour Party, our leaders are men of energy who can be trusted to get things done. We are in a hurry and the Labour party is too slow."'[5]

By 1946, it seemed that both the formal and the informal opposition had been scattered in considerable disarray, with the twofold challenge of Labour and Clann na Talmhan effectively stymied, the IRA a shaken shadow of its former self, and the main opposition party, Fine Gael, content to settle even further into moribund somnolence as long as the slumberers were 'chaps', 'chaps' that is who had attended the correct schools and who wore clean white collars, 'chaps' whose idea of political activity was to commute between the Four Courts and Leinster House, taking in the smoking-rooms of places such as the Kildare Street Club *en route*. Fine Gael's vote had declined

at every election since 1932, and by the mid-1940s they frequently found
fielding candidates in elections something of a difficulty, a difficulty they
contrived to disguise by pleading the 'national interest'.[6] Put simply, the
party failed to attract any new blood. Throughout the entire 1940s they only
managed to acquire three new TDs, two of whom were the offspring of former
TDs, and one of these two, Liam Cosgrave, just happened to be the son of a
former Taoiseach. Although actually founded only in the wake of the Treaty
split, representing the pro-Treaty side, Fine Gael continued to behave as
though its ancestry hearkened back to the impenetrable mists of the nineteenth century and that therefore it needed to pay no heed to this brash new
century and the problems it posed. This 'gentleman's club' approach to politics combined archaic attitudes to the notion of mass membership – Fine
Gael charged by far the highest membership fee of any political party in
Ireland, presumably to ensure that membership remained confined to
'gentlemen' – with a magnificently lethargic indifference to the requirements
of fighting elections. In addition, the party's organisation was ludicrously
inept, and, until 1959, the positions of party president, Dáil leader, and,
when occasion warranted it, Taoiseach and indeed, Leader of the Opposition,
were all to be held by different individuals. Augmenting this particular
process even further was the unfortunate tendency of the Fine Gael leadership to become unhorsed in battle. A striking example of this occurred, when
General Richard Mulcahy, who had succeeded W. T. Cosgrave as party president in 1943, promptly proceeded to lose his Dublin Dáil seat in the general
election of that year. While awaiting the parliamentary return of the general
– Mulcahy captured a seat in Tipperary the following year, an election which
saw W. T. Cosgrave himself defeated in Cork – Fine Gael was led in the Dáil
by Dr T. F. O'Higgins, scion of one of their most formidable families and a
brother of the murdered Kevin O'Higgins. When contrasted with the towering
dominance enjoyed by de Valera – could anyone even contemplate the idea
of de Valera losing his seat? – the duality of Fine Gael's leadership seemed
especially feeble. The upshot of all of this meant that serious opposition to
the Fianna Fáil government was not likely to come from within the familiar
confines of Leinster House.

However, for those equipped to interpret such things, the astounding
performance of the Independent republican candidate, Dr Patrick McCartan,[7] in the 1945 presidential election[8] was an interesting harbinger of
things to come. McCartan polled extraordinarily well, obtaining over
200,000 votes, itself an interesting indicator of political alienation and a
useful signpost to those intending to enter politics that 'here be votes' for
anybody interested in trawling the murky waters where those who voted for
neither Fianna Fáil nor Fine Gael lived. From Fianna Fáil's point of view, the
transfer patterns made grim reading. In every single constituency far more
votes transferred from the republican McCartan to the 'Blacksmith of Ballinalee', namely the Fine Gael candidate, General Seán MacEoin – despite
their apparent political incompatibility – than transferred to the ultimate
victor, Fianna Fáil's then Tánaiste, Seán T. O'Kelly. At their minimum, these
votes transferred at a rate of three to MacEoin to one to O'Kelly, but that

was nowhere near the average, which was closer to six, or seven, to one.[9] Dublin city made especially disturbing reading, for McCartan – on a shoestring budget – actually outpolled MacEoin, and their combined vote threatened to nibble at the heels of Seán T. O'Kelly, who was on his first electoral outing as a presidential candidate.

Away from the precincts of Leinster House, matters seemed somewhat different. De Valera's policy of neutrality may have steered Ireland successfully through the hazards of the war years, but the effects of this had been to isolate and insulate Ireland from the dynamic of change found elsewhere in postwar Europe, changes which had been largely impelled forward by the needs and consequences of war, and changes in which the idea of state intervention played a large role.[10] In a broad sense, such total isolation gave rise to an attitude of detachment, the effects of which were beautifully captured by F. S. L. Lyons who used the marvellous image of 'Plato's cave' to convey a sense of the impact of neutrality – and the resultant detachment – on Irish society.[11] However, while the requirements of war had compelled the Fianna Fáil government to throw the sort of *cordon sanitaire* around Ireland that nationalists could only have dreamed about earlier in the century, this bizarre fulfilment of the conditions to meet such nationalist desires proved to be rather too revealing of some pressing problems. For the truth of the matter was that the war, rather than acting as the sort of catalyst for social, economic, and political changes which were to occur subsequently in Europe, served in Ireland to highlight even further the economic and social problems that had existed before it started.[12] These included a stagnant economy, deplorably poor housing conditions, widespread poverty – and, concomitant with that, an extraordinarily high rate of some of the illnesses associated with poverty, such as TB – a depressed agricultural sector, high prices, low incomes (wages had actually been frozen during the war following the implementation of the standstill order on wages which was introduced by Seán MacEntee as Minister for Industry and Commerce in May 1940[13]), and a staggering – and steadily increasing – rate of emigration.

Hardships which many associated with wartime privations returned with a vengeance. Bread rationing was reintroduced in January 1947, as was soap rationing, and beer, stout, and porter supplies were drastically reduced, being cut by 30 per cent. Private motoring had virtually ceased since 1943, and now public rail transport was itself curtailed, with trains sometimes reduced to running three days a week. The anodyne expression 'industrial unrest' masks the full impact of the dockers' strikes, bus drivers' strikes, teachers' strikes, and the threatened flour mill workers' strike on the party – Fianna Fáil – which claimed the greatest fluency in articulating workers' grievances, for it read their minds, looked into their hearts, and reclined on the Dáil seats bestowed by their votes. In fact, the threatened flour mills strike of May 1947 concentrated Cabinet minds wonderfully, to the extent that the party which enjoyed most working-class support contemplated the outright prohibition of the right to strike.[14] Even the weather conspired against Fianna Fáil, when the wet summer of 1946 was succeeded by a winter which was widely regarded as the coldest winter in living memory, a winter when snowdrifts and rationing impeded transport, a winter when in one notorious instance a coffined corpse was shoved into a snow bank to be retrieved and buried a week later when the weather proved less inclement,[15] a winter when Britain – encountering similar difficulties – suspended exports of coke and coal to Ireland indefinitely. By September 1947, coal rationing, last experienced in 1941, had been reintroduced.

Moreover, agriculture, the most important economic activity in the country, and the one sector which had profited enormously from Ireland's advantageous position regarding agricultural exports – chiefly cattle – to Britain during the First World War, derived no benefit from proximity to Britain during the subsequent conflict. In truth, not only did Irish agriculture not benefit from proximity to the UK during the Second World War, but total Irish agricultural exports to Britain actually decreased by 35 per cent from 1939 to 1946, a fact which the Irish side attempted to explain away by reference to inadequate UK prices.[16] The twin blows of the Economic War of the thirties, when Ireland's exports to Britain were curtailed as a retaliation for de Valera's earlier actions in withholding the land annuities, and the 1941 outbreak of foot-and-mouth disease, which decimated cattle herds, completely destroyed the export market on which much of Irish agriculture was based. Moreover, agricultural technology in Ireland was backward, and the actual land holdings – and their yields – were quite small. Taken together, all of this ensured that the flight from the land – a phenomenon witnessed across Europe for most of the century – continued apace. However, in Ireland there was an added bitter dimension to this traditional flight from the land to the cities, because the industrially underdeveloped urban centres could not provide the necessary employment either, and this meant that the only remaining option was wholesale emigration from the country itself. Apart from a short period during the war when all travel to Britain was banned by the British government (and Irish people seeking to circumvent that travel ban usually travelled first to that corner of Ireland which remained part of His Britannic Majesty's realm), emigration to Britain continued and increased. During these years, the number of people leaving Ireland to seek employment opportunities elsewhere (usually in the UK) numbered around 25,000 each year and net emigration in the ten years from 1936 to 1946 totalled 187,111.[17] With the outbreak of war – and the attendant wartime boom in the UK economy – employment opportunities beckoned, and thousands flocked to avail of them, serving as a safety valve by reducing the strain of unemployment in Ireland and augmenting the meagre incomes of those left behind by sending remittances.

However, it was not only the British authorities which sought to curtail travel, for, with the introduction of compulsory tillage orders, the Irish government expressly prohibited certain categories of worker from leaving the country during 'the Emergency'. Although originally and expressly intended to target the badly paid farm labourers, 'those with a minimum experience of agricultural or turf-cutting operations'[18] as the government innocuously phrased it – those, in fact, who had already displayed a disturbing tendency to flee Ireland and flock to the fleshpots in Britain in vast numbers, much to the dismay of their erstwhile employers, the farmers, some of whom had attempted to lobby the government to curtail this peripatetic trend – the measure prohibiting travel was gradually extended over the course of the war years, until, in addition to prohibiting travel to the UK for men on a special register of agricultural and turf workers, it also managed to include every man in any sort of job, young men under the age of nineteen, anyone who had been fired for misconduct or who had refused the offer of work in Ireland, as well as each and every man who was ordinarily resident outside a town of less than 5,000 inhabitants.[19] Nevertheless, female emigration was not restricted during the war, and indeed, continued to rise so sharply that Ireland would come to boast 'the highest rate of female emigration of any European country between 1945 and 1960'.[20]

Actually, while agricultural grievances did indeed give rise to the creation of a political party which represented agricultural interests, namely Clann na Talmhan (and they failed to mount a comprehensive challenge to the existing social and political order as their policies were largely confined to 'improving agriculture' without any clear strategy of how to undertake such a task), when faced with falling yields, falling numbers of small farms, and falling numbers of people working and living on these farms, Fianna Fáil were unable to confront the contradictions of their own rhetoric which extolled the virtues of good husbandry on smallholdings, preferably devoid of any kind of state intervention. In a society which cherished the concept of private property to the extent that Ireland has done, no political party could hope to 'reform' agriculture to the extent required and remain politically viable, and certainly no Irish political party, not even Labour, has ever publicly thought to do so.[21] Agriculture is of relevance because of its central importance to the Irish economy, for the fact that its multiple woes, while creating a political party, did not really hurt de Valera, and for the fact that Clann na Poblachta, after it came into existence, had absolutely nothing to say on the matter.

Clann na Poblachta's silence on the topic of agricultural reforms, in an otherwise extremely loquacious series of policy statements, aspirations, and letters to the newspapers, which offered opinions on everything else from currency reform to afforestation, and not forgetting the running sore of partition, was extremely revealing. It was revealing because Clann na Poblachta was a party which purported to be offering a radical, alternative, political and social vision, one which was designed to crack not just tiresome civil war moulds, but also those rigidly conservative – and dreadfully deferential – social moulds. Property ownership, land ownership, and the attendant land hunger were among the very few areas where traditional ideological fault lines broke down. Traditional voting patterns, too, could dissolve with astonishing speed whenever property rights or aspirations were challenged.[22] For example, within the previous decade, general elections had actually been won on the land annuities issue. Any party boasting the sort of ancestry Clann na Poblachta had – with the ghosts of Saor Éire thundering through their heads like hordes of Mongol horsemen, condemning 'landlordism' and tacitly condoning agricultural 'outrages', – and seeking to mount the sort of challenge to Irish society that the Clann seemed to have in mind, could hardly ignore the topic of property. Yet by ignoring the potential for change implicit in the property issue (apart from calling for the provision of state-built houses for married young people), Clann na Poblachta underlined their own essentially conservative social vision and demonstrated just how far political respectability had taken them on the road from Saor Éire. Of course, this also served to illustrate the fact that their Dublin-based strategists, while sharp-witted politically, did not view these matters as the sort of policy radical parties poaching votes in the west should interest themselves in.

Agriculture by itself would not put Clann na Poblachta – or, more relevantly, Clann na Talmhan – into office, but neither would it deprive de Valera of power. However, there were several other matters outstanding in 1946 around which organised grievances could – and did – gather. These included two of the great movements around which organised opposition to the government in the immediate postwar era occurred, namely the INTO strike and the campaign for the control of food prices, each of which would have a considerable impact on Clann na Poblachta.

Prices had more than doubled during the war, and residual rage at such high prices, scarce goods, and black-marketeering led to demands for government-sponsored price controls. The first of these, the Lower Prices Council – dismissed by the secret police as an organisation 'which has been so active throughout '47 in fomenting discontent in Dublin City'[23] – is significant for the fact that it succeeded in mobilising astonishingly large numbers of people outside of the framework of formal political activity as recognised by the political parties. Over 100,000 people turned up for some of their public meetings, including large numbers of women. The Lower Prices Council was formed by the Dublin Trades Union Council in 1947 and included representatives from the Irish Housewives' Association, the Dublin Trades Union Council, the Women's Social and Progressive League, the INTO, the Irish Conference of Professional and Services Association, and, from the world of politics, representatives from both the Labour Party and Clann na Poblachta. In a letter to the *Evening Mail*, dated 10 October 1947, the secretary of the Lower Prices Council, Maureen O'Carroll, pointed out that 'Clann na Poblachta did not, in fact, ask for representation on the Council for several weeks after it was formed' and went on to deny the 'inspiration' of the Clann on the Lower Prices Council.[24] (This was before the by-elections took place.)

As well as mobilising public opinion to 'agitate' against the increases in the cost of living, the Lower Prices Council recognised above all the need to highlight women's 'right to participate in the national housekeeping'.[25] Thus, the Lower Prices Council, along with the Irish Housewives' Association, went on to convene what became known as the 'Women's Parliament'.[26] Although any organisation questioning government policy came to be seen as a threat by the local government minister Seán MacEntee, calling for a spot of police monitoring, MacEntee's advanced state of paranoia is well illustrated by the fact that there is even a secret police file on the Irish Housewives' Association, which noted that the organisation was 'active in agitation in 46/47 against rising cost-of-living', adding that it wrote 'frequent letters to the press over the names of the joint Honorary Secretaries'.[27]

Originally envisaged as an association of women's organisations set up to deal with the cost of living, the Women's Parliament turned out to be an extraordinary example of political mobilisation, where 300 delegates represented a larger body of over 300,000 members. As Hilda Tweedy – herself a founder member of the Irish Housewives' Association, the Lower Prices Council, and the Women's Parliament – later recalled: 'An enthusiastic first sitting, attended by delegates from most women's societies, was held at the Catholic Commercial Club on 7 October 1947 at which nine resolutions were passed'.[28] Their eclectic programme called for 'better economic and social conditions for the community as a whole' by seeking the prohibition of luxury imports and giving priority instead to imports of fertiliser and agricultural machinery. In addition, they demanded the provision of hot dinners for every school child as well as the introduction of food subsidies. They also advocated a Prices Tribunal to regulate 'price controls based on cost and a fixed margin of profit', and called for government action to restrict the 'influx of tourists'.

This admixture of sound social policy and blinkered xenophobia struck an answering chord with some in Clann na Poblachta, and echoes of some of these policies were to be found in some of the Clann's own, later, policy offerings, for certainly, links existed (or were developed) between these organisations and the Clann. One of the Clann's founders, May Laverty, was involved with both organisations, as was B. Berthon Waters, who was later to become something of an economics guru for the Clann. (Years earlier, she had attempted to lecture the assembled membership of Córas na Poblachta on economic delights.)[29] There were other well-known subversives in attendance, such as Hilda Tweedy herself (who was trailed, faithfully, by the secret police) and Louie Bennett, who chaired the Women's Parliament, and whose links were with Labour rather than with Clann na Poblachta. It is worth recording that, unlike the teachers, the Lower Prices Council actually achieved a degree of success in their aims, for they persuaded the rather apprehensive local authorities in Dublin to establish a consumer–producer market, with fixed prices for both consumers and producers.[30]

Of the two movements, the Irish National Teachers Organisation strike is by far the better known. It had its origins in the dismissal by the government of a wage claim submitted by the national teachers' organisation as far back as 1939 and revived once the wartime wage freeze was lifted. The peremptory manner of the dismissal – 'boorish' is the usual adjective applied to Minister for Education Tom Derrig's treatment of the teachers – as much as the fact that it was actually dismissed by a government utterly disinterested in availing of the services of the recently established Labour Court,[31] contributed to the INTO's decision to take strike action. In fact, about the kindest thing that has been said of Tom Derrig was that he was 'a rather weak person at the best of times.'[32] Other accounts were considerably harsher – 'boorish, stubborn and dogmatic' was the dismissive opinion succinctly expressed by a respected member of his own party.[33] Worse still, in the eyes of the teachers, was the fact that Derrig had actually sprung from their ranks, for, having been a teacher himself, he was therefore expected to understand their grievances even if he could not exactly identify with them.[34] Consequently, his 'boorishness' really infuriated the teachers. Most independent observers, including two of the three Dublin newspapers, sided with the teachers, *The Irish Times* offering support in a series of trenchantly worded leaders which condemned the government for 'the boorishness of their conduct' and acidly pointed out that 'In this case where the Government itself is one of the parties to the dispute it has no right to act at the same time as defendant and judge.'[35] Some commentators feel that considerations of status were a factor in the INTO dispute.[36] Civil servants enjoyed a postwar wage increase which was denied to teachers who saw themselves as 'professionals'. An offer from John Charles McQuaid, the archbishop of Dublin – who was known to be tacitly sympathetic to the teachers' cause – to mediate in the dispute was brusquely rejected by the government.[37] Archbishop McQuaid's intervention on the teachers' behalf has been explained away by his known sympathy for those who toiled in the professions, and he certainly supported the 'ideal of a salary in keeping with the dignity and responsibility of your profession as teachers', as he put it in a letter to T. J. O'Connell, general secretary of the INTO.

The strike, when it came, proved to be a long and bitter one which lasted from 20 March to 28 October 1946, when the teachers, defeated but unbowed, returned to work. As strikes went, it took an unusual form in that the strike action itself was confined to the Dublin teachers, while their colleagues in the rest of the country, who carried on working, supported them financially. Striking teachers – brandishing banners – invaded the pitch at the All-Ireland football final in late September 1946, and were hastily escorted off it by the guardians of law and order, who, brandishing their truncheons, displayed a touch of overexuberance in the exercise of their duties.[38] The sight of respectable teachers being beaten up by the police certainly shocked a considerable number of the spectators present, including some members of the Cabinet, such as Seán Moylan, the recently appointed Minister for Lands (whose brother was a striking teacher), and led to further behind-the-scenes efforts to terminate the strike, but only on terms of unconditional surrender from the teachers. Those terms were met, following a further plea from Archbishop McQuaid for a return to work which was sympathetically and courteously phrased – but an enduring legacy of bitterness remained.[39]

This legacy was to have a number of interesting effects, some of which would redound to Clann na Poblachta's advantage. A great many teachers abandoned Fianna Fáil, which had been their traditional political hearth, and opted for the new party instead. Motivated and mobilised by the strike, they were to transfer these characteristics to the new party, which badly needed such organisational finesse. Apart from giving Clann na Poblachta a large degree of organisational gravitas, and some indispensable lateral clout where policies were concerned, the teachers actually supplied a considerable number of people to staff the Clann, a process which was to tone down – ever so slightly – the republican complexion of the party. Four members of the INTO's strike administrative committee, which totalled eleven, were actively involved with the Clann. Of the INTO's strike executive committee, which was the most radical and active of the lot (and bitterly regretted the termination of the strike), out of twenty-one members, a further four were actively associated with the Clann.[40] Moreover, the Teachers' Club in Parnell Square, hub and headquarters of the INTO during the strike, seemed to have become a virtual base camp, social centre, and meeting place for Clann na Poblachta itself in those early days. Perhaps that might help to explain Fianna Fáil's gruff hostility to the INTO. Unquestionably, the INTO and Clann na Poblachta initially influenced each other, but in truth, despite the best that Fianna Fáil could come up with by way of paranoid conspiracies, the teachers' influence over the Clann was always far greater than the Clann's influence over the teachers, even though Clann na Poblachta became one of the main vehicles through which the teachers channelled their dispute. Clann na Poblachta only formally came into existence in the middle of the teachers' strike, and while members of the INTO's strike committees did indeed become very active in the party, their strike activity was not directed by Clann machinations, but by their requirements as teachers.

Undoubtedly, both of these movements – the campaign for the control of food prices and the teachers' strike – assisted Clann na Poblachta, for they led to the mobilisation of large, previously unmobilised groups, groups which were mobilised outside of existing political frameworks, and this could only benefit a party which itself had come in from outside of previously existing political frameworks.

Although from 1946 Clann na Poblachta kept stressing 'its confidence in democratic institutions', as part of a sustained attempt to put a bit of democratic distance between itself and its pronounced republican ancestry (especially in the face of MacEntee's barbed gibes on the matter of such ancestries) one final strand of what went to constitute the party took the form of seriously rattling the government's cage. This was the Republican Prisoners Release Association (RPRA), which campaigned, as its name suggested, for the release of the many republican prisoners interned and imprisoned during the war.[41] A little disingenuously, perhaps, the RPRA initially denied any 'connection with the reported formation of a new Republican party', further saying 'that if there was any intention to form such a party the Association had no knowledge of it, nor connection with it'.[42] Actually the RPRA, which was supported by some of the republican lawyers – such as MacBride[43] and Lehane – who had legally represented those imprisoned, in truth contained a considerable number of those around whom the nucleus of the Clann would develop within a matter of months. MacBride, in fact, had acted as defence counsel in virtually every capital case involving republicans since the outbreak of the war,[44] but it was only with the lifting of wartime censorship and the attendant reporting restrictions that these cases became better known and began to have a wider political impact. Such an impact was greatest of all in the McCaughey case, which seemed to serve more as a detonator than as a catalyst when news of it broke. Coming when it did, it met several needs at once. Firstly, the timing was right in terms of putting the government on the defensive (and indeed, perhaps, assisting at the birth of a new party, although, at that particular time, such thoughts were dismissed as unworthy ones). Secondly, there were the circumstances of the inquest itself and the drama of the abbreviated exchanges between MacBride and the prison author- ities, doctor, and governor. Finally, and most importantly, with the lifting of the wartime censorship, such matters could now be openly reported.

Seán McCaughey died early in the morning of 11 May 1946, after a hunger and thirst strike which had lasted twenty-five days. He had commenced the hunger strike with a view to obtaining his release, but had died instead, as the government would not countenance giving in to his demands.[45] A few hours after his death, 'in the middle of the night', the prison governor was contacted by Con Lehane who 'spoke from Dublin over the telephone enquir- ing as to when it was intended to hold the inquest and informing the Governor that he, Mr Lehane, desired to be present as representing the next of kin'.[46] Thus, Lehane 'duly appeared' at Portlaoise Prison, 'bringing with him' Hartnett and MacBride, who turned up 'complete with wigs and gowns'.[47] MacBride even acted as one of the pall-bearers when the coffin was leaving the prison, prior to the funeral of McCaughey.[48] The sneering tone of the secret police report could not quite mask official unease when details of the inquest, and indeed, details of the conditions of McCaughey's imprison- ment, were finally published. In a celebrated exchange, MacBride asked four questions of the prison doctor.

> MR MACBRIDE: Are you aware that during the four and a half years he was here he was never out in the fresh air or sunlight?
> DR DUANE: As far as I am aware he was not.
> MR MACBRIDE: Would I be right in saying that up to twelve or thirteen months ago he was kept in solitary confinement and not allowed to speak or associate with any other person?
> DR DUANE: That is right.
> MR MACBRIDE: Would you treat a dog in that fashion?
> MR MCLOUGHLIN (*for the authorities*): That is not a proper question.
> MR MACBRIDE: If you had a dog would you treat it in that fashion?
> DR DUANE (*after a pause*): No.[49]

No further questions were permitted, and MacBride, Hartnett, and Lehane gathered up their materials and swept dramatically out of the room where the inquest was held.[50] When published, the exchange made sensa- tional headlines which left the government squirming with discomfort. Twelve Dáil questions were put down by Clann na Talmhan's Michael Donnellan, and the aggrieved response of the usually vitriolic Local Govern- ment Minister, Seán MacEntee, who attempted to argue that the 'questions improperly asked by Mr MacBride' were nothing more than an 'attempt to turn the proceedings into an occasion for IRA propaganda',[51] no more than de Valera's grumble that these were 'trick questions', indicated the defen- sive stance taken by the government.

Counterattacking, MacEntee took his case to the letters pages of the national papers, where he queried MacBride's patriotic values, among other matters stressing his lack of service in the wartime defence forces.[52] MacBride ably responded by drawing attention to the fact that his wartime correspondence to the papers had been suppressed outright by government order, rather than being merely subjected to censorship, and that in a suppressed letter, while he didn't exactly call for a wholesale flocking to the Local Defence Force, he did urge what was left of the republican rump to acknowledge Dáil Éireann.[53] This was the beginning of a comprehensive – and lengthy – duel, or joust, between the two men which was to be fought in the letters columns of the daily newspapers over a period spanning the following twenty-one months. In the absence of access to the radio waves (radio was perceived as an arm of the government, akin to the civil service, and not something which implied or even permitted political access), and long before the advent of television, letters to the newspapers were the principal means by which political arguments could take place, and political viewpoints could be articulated and simultaneously disseminated to a wider audience. Outside of the stilted confines of the Dáil chamber, the letters pages were quite literally the only venue for ongoing political debate at that time. As a consequence, they enjoyed the sort of prominence reserved today for the more popular radio or television interviews or debates. The speed of debate was quite rapid too, for replies usually appeared within a day or two of the publication of the original missive, and the more prolific performers and adept letter-writers (such as MacEntee) were not above stirring up a controversy from time to time. MacBride's own letters in the wake of the McCaughey inquest, while unblushingly disclaiming any political agenda – 'I have been asked repeatedly to form a political party; I have been asked repeatedly to stand as a candidate; I have so far refrained from doing so for various reasons'[54] – took pains to include a wider programme than simply the civil rights concerns implicit in the death of a man in such deplorable conditions, and, indeed, the wartime censorship of MacBride's own letters to the papers. Actually, MacBride's letters give the impression of a man who is preparing the ground for political action, and, despite the disclaimer quoted above, the time lapse is interesting, for the McCaughey inquest was held at the end of May 1946 and Clann na Poblachta materialised in early July.

Clearly, preparations for the formation of the party had been under way well before the meeting of 6 July in Barry's Hotel, and equally clearly, despite the deafening disclaimers from a number of the relevant organisations, Clann na Poblachta was in a position to benefit from their existence. Between July 1946 and late October 1947, when the three by-elections occurred, the Clann attempted to consolidate, by strengthening its roots, attending to its organisation and polishing its policies. During that period, apart from aligning itself with all of the available worthy causes, such as the INTO strike and the Lower Prices Council, and taking several sideswipes – along with every other political party – at a government increasingly engulfed in some stunning scandals, it gave little sign of the force it was to become. Most observers could have been excused for concluding that it was simply another fringe republican party, capable of making plenty of noise, but, as such, posing no real threat to existing political parties. In fact, in all of Fine Gael leader General Richard Mulcahy's voluminous correspondence and comments during the period of the three by-elections, the name of Clann na Poblachta is strikingly absent.[55] This is all the more interesting in view of the fact that one of the contested seats, that of Tipperary, lay within Mulcahy's own constituency, and a party leader presumably can be expected to sniff the direction of the wind accurately, especially as in this case the Clann happened to run a very strong candidate, Patrick Kinnane, in Tipperary.[56] Actually, Mulcahy worried much more about the potential threat posed to Fine Gael by the Clann na Talmhan candidate in Tipperary, and nowhere mentions Kinnane. While this might be explained away on the grounds that Clann na Talmhan were always likely to present a greater worry to Fine Gael than a new, supposedly radical, republican party, it still displays an astonishing lack of knowledge of how one should sniff the wind. (Of course, Fianna Fáil laboured under no such misapprehensions, and indeed, were sniffing so hard that a constituency revision was on the cards.)

To a large extent, at around this time, Clann na Poblachta also disappeared from official sources, for, after the ponderous police account of its formation, the Clann makes only one further appearance in the annals of the secret police, and this occurred at a meeting of the party which was held in the Royal Hotel, Bray, on 21 October 1946. During the meeting, as the Clann later complained in a letter to the Taoiseach, 'members of the association [!] had been subjected to police surveillance and that police enquiries had been made as to the proceedings of the meeting'.[57] The government's attempts at a straightfaced answer were anything but convincing: 'On investigation it was found that the police were on duty at the Royal Hotel in connection with the presence of a man suspected of petty larceny and that their presence there had no connection with the Clann na Poblachta meeting.'[58]

Some of this considerable police effort could probably have been better expended closer to home, for, in addition to all of their other woes, Fianna Fáil now appeared to have located the self-destruct button a later generation would label 'sleaze' as they stumbled from one scandal to another, the sort of scandals that usually attach themselves to a party which has been too long in power and has become far too practised in the slippery ways of patronage. Such scandals were to prove an especial boon to the party – Clann na Poblachta – which had been stressing the need for a 'new standard of political morality in public life'[59] ever since their inaugural meeting, and had repeated the message that they were the ones to provide this, with monotonous persistence, ever since. New parties invoking vocabularies of self-righteous zeal are nauseating enough in the jaundiced eyes of existing parties, but what must have made this especially galling for Fianna Fáil was that they themselves now presented a very inviting, and timely, target, as the emergence of these scandals and the emergence of the Clann as a party preaching political accountability more or less coincided, to the considerable electoral advantage of the latter. Occupancy of the moral high ground would not normally pose a pressing problem unless relinquishing the heights were to involve the loss of Dáil seats as a consequence. However, in this instance, that is exactly what happened, for not only was the timely emergence of the scandals efficacious for the Clann in that they enabled Clann na Poblachta to portray themselves as the guardians of political morality, in marked contrast to Fianna Fáil, who appeared to be steeped in sleaze, but, far worse from Fianna Fáil's viewpoint, was the fact that three by-elections loomed, and that they would now be obliged to fight on ground not of their own choosing electorally. Small wonder that de Valera threatened an immediate general election if the by-elections went against the government.

The first of these scandals was quite minor, and involved the unfortunate Dr Conor Ward, who in 1946 held the post of Parliamentary Secretary (i.e. junior minister) to the Minister for Local Government and Public Health. Health became a separate ministry the following year, but not before Ward was obliged to resign his position on account of charges of corruption concerning his links with the bacon factory owned by his family in Monaghan.[60]

It was the second scandal, the notorious affair concerning the bungled sale of Locke's Distillery in Kilbeggan, Co. Westmeath, which really did for Fianna Fáil, and introduced the very notion of serious sleaze to a puritanical political culture. A combination of the 'luridity of the foreigners'[61] involved, the illegality of the sale, and the connections, accidental or not, between elements of the Fianna Fáil party and this 'parcel of international crooks'[62] all combined to embarrass the government profoundly, and led to demands for a public enquiry. Questions in the Dáil concerning the sale of the distillery were first asked by Oliver J. Flanagan[63] on 18 October 1947, and matters speedily came to a head, with further questions from a number of deputies, – including Flanagan, several from Clann na Talmhan, and some from James Dillon – on 23, 25, and 27 October. Most sources are in agreement that many of the colourful innuendoes and extravagant allegations made by Flanagan amounted to a spectacular abuse of Dáil privilege, and certainly, the tribunal of enquiry, when it reported, seemed to endorse this view, for it soundly castigated Flanagan, dismissing one of his allegations as 'entirely without foundation [and] made with a degree of recklessness amounting to complete irresponsibility'.[64] However, it is worth noting that the terms of reference of the tribunal were designed to narrow its scope somewhat, by confining it to an investigation into allegations against ministers and members of the Oireachtas arising out of the negotiations for the sale of Locke's Distillery. Lemass later added an amendment to the effect that the tribunal should enquire into 'any other facts or circumstances connected with the disposal of the distillery, which, in as far as members of the Oireachtas are concerned, would be of public importance'.[65] An opposition amendment which was moved jointly by General Richard Mulcahy, the Fine Gael leader, and their exiled black sheep, James Dillon, and which sought to widen the scope of the enquiry to include all the facts and circumstances relating to the distillery, was swiftly dismissed by the government when it was defeated by sixty-seven votes to forty in the Dáil. Batting for the beleaguered government, de Valera's smug, yet sure-footed, response – 'but we cannot prevent wrong things from taking place in business. We cannot even prevent murder taking place in our community'[66] – allowed him to justify a tribunal with limited terms of reference as being 'what the public was interested in' while arguing that they were manifestly not interested in 'whatever manoeuvring there may have been between different parties interested in the sale of Locke's distillery, except in so far as it affected members of the Oireachtas'.[67] The tribunal sat from 1 to 18 December, when it reported its findings. Alas, for Fianna Fáil, its exoneration came far too late, for by then the by-elections had already taken place and had recorded verdicts against the party.

The initial background to the sale was fairly straightforward. Locke's Distillery – one of those ancient Irish-owned distilleries – had genteely gone out of business in early 1947, and later that year an international consortium, Trans-World Trust, Lausanne, offered to purchase it, lock, stock, and barrel.[68] Promises were given which suggested that the distillery might yet resume the production of whiskey, with particular attention being paid to overseas markets (especially South America), but not, of course, omitting the domestic market, and the members of the consortium drank to that with President Seán T. O'Kelly in his official residence, Áras an Uachtaráin, on 25 September. Also 'taking tea with the president'[69] that particular day were William Quirke, a 'prominent Fianna Fáil Senator',[70] who was a partner in the firm of auctioneers who were handling the sale, and the President's niece and her husband, a Dublin barrister. In fact, the attraction for the consortium lay not so much in the handsome stone buildings in Kilbeggan, nor in the resumption of whiskey production (which they had no intention of undertaking), but in the stock of 60,000 gallons of mature, immature, and maturing whiskey which the bankrupt company had in its vaults. Postwar Europe suffered from a serious dearth of quality alcohol, and anybody able to get their hands on a decent supply was assured of an excellent income, particularly on the black market.[71]

Doubts only arose when the consortium failed to come up with the deposit in time for the sale to be realised. Subsequent police investigations made the startling discovery that Trans-World Trust of Lausanne was an unsavoury collection of black-marketeers, for the consortium itself was made up of some of the most extravagantly exotic and fraudulent fauna – not to mention their assorted accompanying *femmes fatales* – ever to materialise in wholly pure Ireland. There was Hubert Saschell, an Austrian national, whose stated interest in Ireland lay in the twin pursuits of becoming managing director of a factory to be established in County Limerick for the 'assembling of Czechoslovak motor-cars', and exporting suspiciously vast quantities of Irish tweed, for which purpose he had bought a large farm near Gort, County Galway.[72] As if this did not suffice to sound the tocsins, there were also Georges Eindiguer, a Swiss industrialist, who even in the 1940s had a private plane, and Horace Henry Smith, 'Eindiguer's interpreter and dogsbody'[73] who travelled on a British passport, fraudulently obtained. Horace Henry Smith turned out to be a man named Alexander Maximoe, ostensibly Swiss but really Russian, who was wanted by the British police. Actually, Maximoe was generally regarded as having been Swiss, but this was denied by the Swiss authorities in a characteristically stuffy statement: 'The Swiss Legation in Dublin stated yesterday that Alexander Maximoe, otherwise Horace Henry Smith, who was deported from Eire on an order made by the Minister for Justice, and who jumped from the mail-boat in mid-channel, never possessed Swiss nationality. It had been stated at the time that Maximoe was Swiss.'[74] Maximoe was arrested by the police in Saschell's Dublin apartment and served with a deportation order, the fulfilment of which entailed the Irish police accompanying him on the mail-boat to Holyhead, where their British counterparts waited to take him into custody. *En route* to Holyhead, Maximoe gave his police minders the slip and escaped, his red-faced escorts saying that they had heard a splash as he dived (some said to his death) into the Irish Sea. Saschell – who, according to the tribunal's report, was 'mixed up in a couple of very unsavoury transactions'[75] – was also invited to leave the country, and he 'took a plane from Dublin Airport to Paris'[76] the very same day. Eindiguer had been located in his Dún Laoghaire hotel, and, as his papers were found to be in order, he left the country of his own accord and promptly disappeared.

Fianna Fáil's problem was twofold. Not only had the Department of Industry and Commerce blatantly supported Trans-World Trust's bid over that of all other tenders, but one of the partners in the firm of auctioneers handling the sale was Fianna Fáil senator William Quirke, who enjoyed strong social ties with President Seán T. O'Kelly and his family, among others. And then all this unpleasant business had to go and happen right in the middle of a rather testing series of by-elections, tainting Fianna Fáil by association, no matter what the tribunal said.

Noël Browne, Minister for Health

Seán MacBride, Minister for External Affairs

Election scene (1947), with Noël Browne (smoking) in bottom left-hand corner

Election scene (1947), with Seán MacBride on right of picture

MARCH 1948

Dublin Opinion

VOLUME XXVII

The National Humorous Journal of Ireland for over a Quarter of a Century

Humour is the Safety Valve of a Nation

FROM the Opposition benches on a clear day it is possible to see the mistakes you made when you were in power.

* * *

JOHN COSTELLO has grasped the tiller. James Dillon has grasped the tillers.

* * *

THE new Tanaiste —Just William!

* * *

WITH so many new brooms we're just sitting back comfortably waiting for the Sweep results.

* * *

"A bus stopped six inches from a falling wall at Bath." —*Sunday Express.* They won't stop anywhere here!

* * *

IT'S nice for a Government to have the Opposition in one nice handy compact block.

* * *

WELL the Taoiseach's first speech in his new capacity certainly showed that he wasn't a Jack in office!

* * *

THE Captain of Portmarnock Golf Club will not be likely to get the country into a hole.

* * *

AT the box office when the recent cinema tax comes off: "Two Paddy McGilligans, please!"

* * *

MOUNT Everett!

* * *

SHAKESPEARE on the Inter-Party Government: "*Richard is himself again.*"

* * *

THE man that said: "I am ill-fitted for this high office," has at least one quality that fits him for it.

* * *

THE hospitals will now be a Browne study.

THERE must be a feeling of relief amongst about 147 Deputies that things are settling down. People who have had the rain down the backs of their necks for a couple of months don't exactly want another tour of the constituencies.

SURPRISE OF CITIZEN ON WAKING UP TO FIND THAT, ALTHOUGH ONE PARTY DID NOT ACHIEVE AN OVER-ALL MAJORITY, THE COUNTRY WAS NOT DOOMED.

WE don't know what James Dillon is like as a golfer but we imagine that as Minister for Agriculture he is likely to replace some of the divots.

* * *

SEAN MAC BRIDE is Minister for External Affairs. That's not fair, to give one of the youngest of the Ministers all the rest of the world to deal with.

* * *

AND even John Costello, S.C., will consider £60,000,000 a big Bill of Costs.

AS Minister for Justice, Sean Mac Eoin shuld be able to make the sparks fly.

* * *

THEY should have made Oliver Flanagan Minister for Vocal Government.

* * *

SUGGESTED slogan for Mr. William Norton, Minister for Social Welfare—"Where there's a Will there's a way."

* * *

AS Minister for Lands, Mr. Blowick will be a notable addition to the long division.

* * *

WITH his success in the National Health Insurance dispute after a few days in office, Mr. Norton may be described as one of our earliest settlers.

* * *

THEY may have a narrow majority but they may have a broad outlook.

* * *

GEORGE WASHINGTON, says an American professional, would have made a good golfer. Nonsense, he couldn't tell a lie.

* * *

PEOPLE who move in artistic circles are inclined to get dizzy.

* * *

SOME of what looks like jay-walking is caused by people trying to dodge their creditors.

* * *

"*ALEA JACK-TA EST.*" as the National Labour Party might have exclaimed when they crossed the Rubicon.

* * *

A REASON suggested for the fact that some of the new houses are not papered is that the builders are afraid that papering them would make the rooms even smaller.

Eamon de Valera, Seán MacBride, Minister for External Affairs, Mrs Costello, Col. and Mrs McCormack (Chicago Tribune) and John A. Costello, Taoiseach

Dr John Charles McQuaid, Seán MacBride, Minister for External Affairs, Cardinal Dr John d'Alton, Monsignor Langan

4

'Two lovely black eyes could only mean a general election'

By late 1947, the first electoral contest since the presidential election of 1945 (and the local elections of the same year) approached, with by-elections due to be held in Dublin County, Tipperary, and Waterford. Scenting not just battle, but possible victory, Clann na Poblachta fielded candidates in all three constituencies. MacBride himself was selected in Dublin, and they achieved a notable success when they persuaded Patrick Kinnane – a veteran of the independence struggle who had been, as *The Irish Times* dryly phrased it, 'a vigorous opponent of the Treaty',[1] and whose considerable GAA and Gaelic League contacts had made him both well known and widely respected – to stand for the Clann in Tipperary. Their candidate in Waterford, a secondary teacher named Seán Feeney, was less well known despite having been an All-Ireland hurler with Waterford. Initially, Feeney enjoyed neither MacBride's growing fame and political presence nor Kinnane's extensive networks and reputation for stolid integrity, but ultimately, his greatest problem was that his campaign did not have the time to build up a decent momentum, for on paper he was a reasonably strong candidate.

From the very beginning of the by-election campaign Clann na Poblachta seized the initiative and went on the offensive, actively baiting the government and employing a wide variety of strategems designed to grab public attention and win public support. MacBride took to the letters pages of *The Irish Times* (who were broadly supportive of his campaign, or, at the very least, were strongly antagonistic to the Fianna Fáil government) and the *Irish Press* (who were nothing of the sort), and displayed a hitherto undetected aptitude for hand-to-hand combat as he locked horns with Fianna Fáil's vitriolic virtuoso and specialist in character assassination, the Minister for Local Government, Seán MacEntee.[2] Their correspondence was extraordinary, running simultaneously in two parallel and utterly different universes, where sweetness and light mingled with altruism and economic arguments in *The Irish Times* while the cumbersome baggage of MacBride's lurid past made an appearance in the *Irish Press*,[3] as MacEntee summoned up his heavy artillery in the form of extremely unsubtle references to the police files he had in his possession. Indeed, MacBride himself alluded to the difference in the tones employed by MacEntee in the respective papers when he referred to 'the honied words' used to convey 'an atmosphere of sweet reasonableness' in MacEntee's letters to *The Irish Times*, and contrasted this with the 'bitterness and invective' which distinguished his letters to the *Irish Press*.[4]

Adopting the measured modulation of an enlightened mandarin, MacBride refused to rise to MacEntee's taunts by loftily dismissing them in the sort of tones invoked by one of the Clann's more succinct advertising offerings, which advised the electorate to vote for the Clann because 'Instead of flag-waving, "national records", and personalities, what is needed is a policy based upon realities. Instead of recriminations and self-glorification based upon past events, the need is vision and planning for the future. If you want ability and honesty in public life vote No. 1 for MacBride, Seán in County Dublin, Kinnane, Patrick in Co. Tipperary, and Feeney, Seán in Co. Waterford.'[5] Rejecting MacEntee's charges of harbouring sympathies for authoritarian regimes, MacBride broadened the scope of the debate by introducing economic themes[6] in a comprehensive broadside which included his letters, his speeches, and some very effective, and attractive, advertising. The Clann's director of elections, Noel Hartnett, more than earned his keep, for the Clann kept up a steady barrage of inventive, pungent, and succinct advertising throughout the by-election campaign.

A particularly stunning example was the large advertisement the party placed in *The Irish Times* on 3 October, which took the form of a large chart and graph, and purported to be a contrasting analysis charting the rise in the cost-of-living in a number of countries from 1939 to 1947. Operating from a 1939 base of 100, the chart demonstrated how Ireland '(26 counties)' topped the cost of living league with a figure of 176. The others cited were the UK (131), Canada (127), and New Zealand (114). After discussing the significance of these figures, the Clann advertisement went on to argue for their policies with the stirring statement: 'The Real Solution: A policy of Full Employment and Production based on the development of our natural resources backed by our national credits. In the meantime the cost of living can and MUST be reduced IMMEDIATELY by temporary remedies; Food subsidies; Price Control; Tribunals representative of Producers and Consumers and free supplies of fertilisers.'[7] Further advertisements appeared, including one taking the clever – and masked – form of a letter signed by many worried worthies urging support for the Clann. This 'letter', a very subtle and upmarket approach to advertising, appeared in *The Irish Times* on Monday, 27 October, and ran as follows: 'We appeal to all the electors of Dublin county to give their utmost support to Seán MacBride, SC. We know him to be a man of integrity, courage and ability, whose views and criticism[s] in the Dáil will be an asset to the nation. Irrespective of party politics and past political affiliations, we appeal for you to give him your utmost support by voting for him and working for him from now until next Wednesday (29th). [Signed] Dr Patrick MacCartan, Frank Hugh O'Donnell, Dr Daniel Deasy, Michael Chadwick, Dr Niall O'Rahilly, John J. Donoghue, Mrs Kathleen Clarke, Dr Joseph P. Brennan, Jerome Hurley, Gerrard L. McGowan, William Toomey, and

Patrick Gallagher.' Two points are worth noting. The first is that a number of those who signed the letter had been involved with the Clann from the outset, so that their bona fides – or, more to the point, their actual distance from the party – may not have been as great as the letter may have implied. Secondly, this was clearly a pitch for the 'progressive bourgeois vote', assuming such a contradictory beast existed, for most of these signatories came from the fairly well-heeled segment of society. Clann na Poblachta was attempting to demonstrate its potential in attracting cross-class support, while simultaneously trumpeting a progressive, or 'radical', but not, Heaven forbid, a 'communist', manifesto. Nor was that all, for, despite some earlier misgivings, MacBride proved as able on the hustings as he was effective in print, and his lieutenants, such as Lehane and Hartnett, proved themselves the equal of anything that Fianna Fáil could throw at them.

And throw they did, for Fianna Fáil took the by-elections very seriously, so seriously, in fact, that the threat of an incipient general election was made half a dozen times at least during the campaigns. To take just two examples – Lemass announced that 'clearly, therefore, a defeat for the government in the by-elections must mean a general election',[8] and de Valera with his characteristic blend of bullying cajolery stated that 'This is a vote of confidence in the government. If that vote is not given, if there is any weakening of the government, then we will have no choice whatever except to go to the people and have the matter treated at a general election.'[9] Technically, de Valera did not need to call a general election before the summer of 1949, and his Dáil majority was so secure that even in the unprecedented event of his losing all three seats, his Dáil majority over all others combined remained untouchable. However, trifles such as having more seats than were required had never before dulled Fianna Fáil's appetite for the fray, and October 1947 was to be no exception. Tactically, they pulled out all of the stops, even though they were already embroiled in both the aforementioned scandals and a series of strikes which involved workers in the banks, buses, and insurance sector. Admonishing the striking workers with patronising paternalism, de Valera had let it be known that 'We are particularly anxious, therefore, that we shall not have strikes.'[10] The strikes also upset Minister for Industry and Commerce, Seán Lemass, whose fingers clearly itched as he grumbled that 'the problem of strikes is probably the most difficult which democracy has to face'.[11] Most of his colleagues were in no doubt as to where the danger to democracy – as understood by Fianna Fáil – actually lay, and they concentrated their fire accordingly. This involved a spot of selective disinterring of the embarrassingly extensive police files on MacBride, and, for good measure, some vigorous stirring of blushing crimson paint pots, in a sustained attempt to make the 'Red' smear stick. It also involved dispatching all available ministerial manpower to the front lines in the constituencies, with mixed results. In their very different ways, Lemass and MacEntee showed their mettle, but could not prevent the sort of occasional disasters as were bound to attend the utterances of Minister for Education, Tom Derrig. Derrig, whose crass insensitivity had already aggravated matters during the teachers' strike, now told an election meeting in Nenagh 'that if workmen were not prepared to stay at home, the Fianna Fáil Government was not going to stop them going away', adding, in a spectacular *non sequitur*, that the government 'deplored emigration'.[12]

Fielding candidates strong enough to take on the threat presented by the Clann proved to be something of a problem and obliged Fianna Fáil to reach deeply into their reserve basket of candidates. They nominated their general secretary, Tommy Mullins, himself a veteran of the War of Independence and founding member of Fianna Fáil, to contest Dublin County against MacBride.[13] Neither of their two remaining candidates, Seán Hayes in Tipperary and J. Ormonde in Waterford, enjoyed a national profile, but both had extensive links in their respective constituencies. In Tipperary, Seán Hayes had a War of Independence background to square up to Kinnane's, and Ormonde had been a Waterford hurler, in common with his Clann opponent, but, unlike the *parvenu* from the Clann, Ormonde had also been interned during the War of Independence and had latterly served prominently in the Local Defence Force.

With hindsight, it is fairly easy to pick out the signposts leading to the Clann's success. At the time, it was harder, and here one must acknowledge the prescience of some sources, principally in Fianna Fáil, who never underestimated the challenge they were facing, and also, the reporting of *The Irish Times*, which, despite the absurd amount of attention they still devoted to the icons of empire ('The Hon. Clarissa Bletherington-Smythe "came out" in London yesterday' style of reporting), ran a very perceptive by-election diary, written by Brian Inglis as 'Quidnunc'. By the end of October, *The Irish Times* was predicting strong support for MacBride in Dublin.[14]

However, nobody at any time thought that Tipperary would turn on Fianna Fáil, least of all Fine Gael, whose leader Richard Mulcahy nowhere, but nowhere, mentioned the Clann's campaign, or the Clann's candidate, or even the Clann itself, in any of his vast quantity of correspondence concerning the by-elections. Nevertheless, he did devote considerable attention to his party's relationships with all other parties,[15] and especially Fine Gael's relationship with the farmers' party, Clann na Talmhan.[16] An illuminating insight into Fine Gael's – and Mulcahy's – mindset at this time can be found in a letter he wrote to J. J. O'Dwyer, the recently appointed Fine Gael 'national organiser', concerning 'Special Groups [to be contacted] For Finance'.[17] The 'special groups' Mulcahy had in mind appeared on a neatly typewritten list he dispatched to O'Dwyer and included 'Publicans, Solicitors, Barristers, Doctors, Auctioneers, Drapers, Retail Grocers', while the belated handwritten addition of sources such as 'builders' and 'investments' indicated second thoughts as to what constituted the appropriate money-generating classes in the country. It hardly needs pointing out that Mulcahy's *weltanschauung* did not include the vast majority of the population in the constituencies where he, and his party, would be touting for votes. Fine Gael's candidates in the by-elections comprised a nice, young, anonymous, insurance broker from north Dublin named Eamon Rooney, a former Free State luminary in Tipperary, Colonel Jerry Ryan, and Nick Sheehan, a large farmer from Waterford. Among Labour's candidates were two, Seán

Dunne in Dublin and Tom Kyne from Waterford, who would both gain election to the Dáil in the far and distant future, but in October 1947 the
spotlight shone elsewhere.

Polling took place on 29 October, and by the evening of the 30th, it was
clear that MacBride had achieved a historic victory, securing the Dublin
County seat with ease. He had polled extraordinarily well, and at the end of
the first count was lying just under 200 votes behind Fianna Fáil's Tommy
Mullins. Two counts later, aided in no small way by an astonishing surge of
transfers, courtesy of Labour and Fine Gael, in that order, MacBride found
himself more than 9,000 votes ahead of Mullins, and was declared elected.[18]
Striking a suitably bashful pose at the conclusion of the count, MacBride
stated that he 'did not know that he felt very happy "now that I have a great
responsibility as the first spokesman of a new movement in Ireland"'.[19]

While the loss of Dublin was regarded as 'grave'[20] by Fianna Fáil, the
subsequent loss in Tipperary could only be seen as catastrophic. Initially,
reports from the constituency implied that all was well, and, when the
incomplete count was adjourned for the night, *The Irish Times* opined 'that
as Mr Hayes (FF) is leading from P. Kinnane (CnP) and Col. J. Ryan (FG), the
Fianna Fáil candidate, Mr Hayes would take the seat'.[21] As events transpired,
'Mr Hayes' did not take the seat, and was eventually overhauled by 'Mr
Kinnane' who was the recipient of an ever-increasing number of transfers as
count succeeded count.[22] Waterford did at least provide Fianna Fáil with
some sort of solace, for their candidate actually held the contested seat; but
even there, the omens were ominous enough, for Fianna Fáil's own vote had
fallen drastically, and their candidate only retained the seat because of the
spectacular ineptitude of the opposition parties, where their failure to transfer votes to each other cost them the seat, in marked contrast to the other
two constituencies.[23]

Comment on the by-election results focused on the precipitate decline in
Fianna Fáil's first preference vote in all three constituencies, and on the
novel transfer patterns which had recently appeared, *The Irish Times* 'admitting' that Fianna Fáil's loss of two seats 'had come as a big surprise'. Such
surprise was all the greater when the fact that Fianna Fáil had led on the first
count in both Dublin and Tipperary was taken into consideration. Greatest
surprise of all was reserved for the outcome, which had come about because
'in both cases the bulk of Fine Gael's second preferences went to Clann na
Poblachta'. Rather nonplussed, *The Irish Times* concluded, 'This totally illog-
ical development is a sign of the times.'[24] If the print media were nonplussed,
or otherwise 'surprised', Fianna Fáil were incandescent with rage. Of all who
could survey such, they alone could read the tea-leaves, and discern thousands of missing votes. Moreover, they realised that the three hapless
constituencies were, rather unfortunately, a representative national sample.
Action would have to be taken, especially if manners were to be put on the
brash new kid on the block, who gave every sign of turning into an upstart.
Action along these lines entailed de Valera making good his threat of an
almost immediate dissolution of the Dáil, at least before the two Clann TDs
had a chance to make themselves comfortable in their new surroundings.

Correctly divining the government's intent, 'Quidnunc' in *The Irish Times* wrote with almost satanic glee of how 'The Government might have ignored one lost seat if they had gained the other; two lovely black eyes could only mean a general election.'[25]

However, before an election could be called, de Valera had several matters to attend to, such as the ongoing trade talks with the UK (MacBride sent him a cheeky telegram offering the 'chief' his full support for the duration of these talks[26]), the tardy passage of the supplementary budget, and, what must have been most pressing of all, the planned constituency revision, which had been crawling through the Dáil during the earlier part of October, but unfortunately had been sidelined due to the regrettable appearance of the Locke's Distillery scandal. The Electoral (Amendment) Bill provided for an increase in the number of TDs, from 138 to 147, and this, as Lee acerbically points out, was to materialise despite a massive drop in population due to sustained emigration.[27] Tucked away in the small print was the strategem devised for dealing with constituencies prone to the blandishments of attractive suitors like Clann na Poblachta. Under proportional systems, large constituencies tend to favour smaller parties, and so it was proposed to radically alter the number of large constituencies. The largest constituency size of all, the old seven-seaters (and there were three of them), were to be abolished outright – it would never have done to allow the Clann a precarious toe-hold in such fertile territory. Both the four-seaters and five-seaters had their numbers increased, the number of four-member constituencies increasing from eight to nine, and the number of five-seater constituencies increasing by a similar amount, from eight to nine; but this was merely to mask the largest change of all, which was the enormous increase in the number of the smallest constituency size, the three-seaters, which were set to increase from fifteen to twenty-two. Defending this rather suspicious preference, the government attempted to plead geographical homogeneity when they unblushingly offered the argument 'In the re-arrangement of constituencies it has been the object to constitute as many three member constituencies as possible, and thus form as uniform a unit as possible throughout the country.'[28]

Meanwhile, the two newly elected Clann na Poblachta deputies took their seats on 5 November, to the barely concealed discomfiture of Fianna Fáil. Quidnunc, writing a marvellously descriptive account for *The Irish Times*, wondered if the assembled Fianna Fáil deputies could feel 'the cold east wind gathering in the background', and asked whether they had 'sensed anything explosive in the atmosphere' of the 'unusually crowded' Dáil chamber. MacBride's entrance was memorably sketched by Quidnunc: 'The new deputies were then brought in and introduced to the Speaker. First Mr Donnellan (Farmers) brought in Mr MacBride who at times bears a vague resemblance to Boris Karloff – off the films I hasten to add: Karloff is not sinister in the flesh . . . Mr MacBride bowed, shook hands, bowed again, and made good his retreat into the back-benches, shaking hands with Mr Dillon on the way . . . Mr Kinnane was introduced by Mr Commons, also of Clann na Talmhan . . . Mr Oliver Flanagan led a round of applause, which was taken up in the public galleries, despite shhhhhhhing from the Government benches. The Speaker rose to rebuke those members who gave out tickets to visitors without first warning them of the impropriety of applause.'[29] MacBride the parliamentarian got off to a flying start, inundating the government with questions and private member's motions.[30] However, before he could make any sort of name for himself as a specialist in the nuances of Dáil debate, de Valera tried to pull the rug from under him by dissolving the Dáil on 15 December and calling a general election for 4 February 1948. During that time the initial indifference of Fianna Fáil to MacBride's presence (Quidnunc had compared the masked shock of the Fianna Fáil deputies to 'the stoic calm of French aristocrats awaiting the tumbril') gave way to a more familiar exchange of unwatered venom on both sides.

In fact, for Clann na Poblachta, the whole period from early October 1947 until after the formation of the government in February 1948 must have seemed akin to a long spin in a centrifugal machine, for life appeared to have turned into one long election campaign. De Valera's choice of an immediate election deprived the Clann of a much needed breathing space, let alone the time they certainly required to build up and strengthen their organisation, and, of equal importance, to adjust, fine-tune, and tinker about with some of their policies, especially those which might cause voters to take fright. Mindful of his own ascent of the path to power, de Valera well recalled that Fianna Fáil had been allowed six vital years' consolidation and growth between the time of their formation and their eventual assumption of power. Such luxuries were not to be accorded to others, and here de Valera's instinctive, and lethal, sense of timing comes into play, for he was perfectly capable of weighing up competing claims and plumping for a short-term loss to himself, if, on the balance of probabilities, this could overstrain, and eventually obliterate, the Clann. This is not as fanciful as it appears, for informed opinion immediately after the by-elections argued that victory for Fianna Fáil would be unlikely if de Valera made good his 'preposterous'[31] threat and actually dissolved the Dáil. As *The Irish Times* put it, in a strangely prescient article penned just after the by-elections, 'So far as can be gathered, the general opinion seems to be that Mr de Valera will again have the largest party, but shrewd observers are convinced that it will no longer have the overall majority that it has enjoyed in the past. What then? A coalition? And if a coalition, with what group?'[32]

While the campaigns for the by-elections and the general election essentially dove-tailed into one another, and must have seemed like one long blurred rush of adrenaline to Clann na Poblachta, in effect they were two separate campaigns, with different requirements. By-elections offer an opportunity to slap the government on the wrist, highlight local issues, and (in 1947) model the attractions of the new party. General elections offer the opportunity of government removal, and government formation. Clann na Poblachta's stunning successes in the by-elections shocked the entire political establishment (even Mulcahy had acknowledged the existence of the Clann by January 1948 in his private papers), and allowed the Clann to take itself seriously as a potential party of government riding the crest of a wave. Certainly, the similarities with pre-1932 Fianna Fáil – or, for the more starry-eyed, pre-1918 Sinn Féin – were very pronounced. All were young parties, bursting wild-eyed onto the centre of the political arena and energetically preaching a messianic message of social radicalism married to robust republicanism.

Faced with the challenge of a general election, the Clann went into overdrive. They kicked off their campaign with an effective – and stunning – slogan, which, notwithstanding MacBride's cerebral complexity in other areas, had the merit of direct simplicity. 'Put Them Out' was all it said. If their grasp of public relations had been arresting, clever, and stimulating during the by-elections, it reached new heights during the consequent general election. Once again, Hartnett excelled as the Clann's director of elections, awake as always to the power of nuance and symbolism, and equally prepared to seize bold new initiatives. Yet again, the letters pages of the newspapers were used to conduct political debate, and MacBride and MacEntee resumed their earlier combat inhabiting two parallel universes as they used the letters pages of both the *Irish Press* and *The Irish Times*, to fight two completely separate battles. The campaign also involved endless speeches, and here MacBride's relative youth (at forty-four, he was on average almost twenty years younger than the other party leaders) showed to his advantage, not merely in terms of presenting himself and his team as energetic young brooms promising the proverbial clean sweep, but also in purely physical terms, for he was physically able to do more than de Valera, and it showed. MacBride's punishing schedule of four to five meetings a day contrasted with the three to four a day addressed by de Valera, to the disadvantage of the latter.

MacBride was careful, too, and aware of the impact of status symbols. He drove himself to meetings in his small Ford, which inevitably was contrasted with the massive ministerial Dodges used (and indeed abused) by government ministers. (Noël Browne described how Paddy Smith, the Fianna Fáil Minister for Agriculture, 'was said to have brought his calves to the fair for sale in his Ministerial car'.)[33] Sometimes MacBride even left his small car parked discreetly outside villages, which he would then enter, on foot, conveying an image of the Man of the People.[34] The general election campaign of 1948 was one of the most exciting for years, and certainly brought to mind the thrill of the knuckle-duster days of campaigns past (especially the memorable election of 1932), with torch-lit processions and enormous public meetings, all heavily redolent with the scent of change in the very air.

With Hartnett to guide them, MacBride and his staff did not have to rely solely on speeches, letters, and the clever advertisements of the by-election campaign to drive their electoral message home. Calling upon his considerable experience of the national airwaves, from his days as a radio compère, Hartnett was able to come up with stunningly effective additional alternatives. To Hartnett's immense regret, the Clann were not to enjoy access to the national radio, because radio was perceived as an arm of the government, and was thus not available to any political party,[35] but they were to go one better when they commissioned a short film.

Called *Our Country*, this film was the first political documentary ever shot in Ireland, and, as such, regardless of its electoral role, it enjoys a justly celebrated status.[36] Cinematically, it was superbly constructed, combining sharp social commentary with arresting, and bleak, imagery. Nine minutes long, it opened with Noel Hartnett, seated with his back to the cameras, slowly swivelling around and, as he came to face the cameras, proceeding to give a graphic account of the problems facing Ireland.[37] Rural depopulation and poverty were depicted, complete with scenes of empty fields and ruined houses. Urban deprivation and decay also featured, the camera trailing slowly over slums and picking out a woebegone child, standing barefoot in a puddle of muddy water. Emigration was shown, as were shortages, poverty, and unemployment. Shops were shown stocked with goods which only the well-off could afford to purchase. A young TB specialist named Noël Browne, at that time the assistant medical superintendent at Newcastle Sanatorium in County Wicklow, was interviewed about the dreadful shortage of facilities for patients suffering from this terrible illness. Seán MacBride himself was also interviewed, and informed the camera, – and, by extension, the viewers – that 'it's your country', and that only they themselves could change their own society, but change it they could. Nowhere was the name of Clann na Poblachta mentioned, but the inference to vote for change was obvious. For its time (and it has aged well), this was a superb film, a devastating documentary, and a stunning example of the potential of film as political propaganda.[38] It was filmed on location in December 1947, and mixed, and completed, in the Elstree Studios in Hertfordshire in England, because Ireland had no film-making facilities at the time. In effect, this film was Clann na Poblachta's manifesto.

Fianna Fáil recognised a thrown gauntlet when they saw one, and steps were immediately taken to minimise the impact of this piece of cinematic effrontery. MacEntee once again took to the letters pages of the *Irish Press*, where his condemnations of the film were couched in very virulent terms. Dismissing the film as 'a bogus film', 'a typical carrion-crow production',[39] MacEntee proceeded to condemn the appearance of 'a certain Liam Ó Laoghaire' in the film. 'In this film', fulminated MacEntee, 'he was acting as a bogus grocer's assistant, pleading a bogus scarcity to a bogus customer.'[40] In a conclusion heavily laden with menace,[41] MacEntee went on to express the hope that 'the managers of reputable houses would refuse to show it because it was one brazen lie from beginning to end. If they did show it, the public would know that they were showing it not as the proprietors of picture-houses, but as political propagandists.'[42] This strong hint was taken, for, despite the astonishing fact that *Our Country* – to everyone's amazement – actually passed the Irish censor, the J. Arthur Rank Organisation declined to show it on their 'Eire circuit'.[43] Maura Laverty, one of the film's scriptwriters, hastily travelled to London, to try to persuade Mr Rank of the injustice of this 'allegedly political censorship'. A number of other circuits followed the lead of Rank, Abe Elliman of Odeon (Ireland) Ltd informing the sponsors of the film that 'the circuit would not take sides in the forthcoming general election'.[44]

Liam Ó Laoghaire never denied playing the part of the grocer's assistant, but he argued that the shortages and scarcities portrayed in the film were authentic, and went on to accuse the minister of using 'jack-boot methods' in seeking to suppress the distribution of the film, acidly pointing out that MacEntee 'would deny the Irish public the right to see our slums or to hear the statistics on TB. He would like to pretend that there is no emigration or no unemployment.'[45] The requirements of film-making, especially film-making to a tight deadline and limited budget, necessitated another little bit of sleight of hand, which fortunately remained undetected by MacEntee. This involved the stunning – and cinematically extremely effective – shot of the forlorn child standing barefoot beside a puddle of dirty water. As Liam Ó Laoghaire later explained, because the film was shot in December hardly anybody was barefoot in Dublin. If necessary, people would borrow money to buy shoes or even steal footwear to keep their children in shoes over the winter, if they could not otherwise afford them. 'So we said to this young fella, here's sixpence, go and take off your shoes and socks and stand in that puddle of water.' Looking suitably miserable, the 'young fella' did as he was asked.[46] The fact that Fianna Fáil did not see fit to condemn the shot of a barefoot child indicates that they did not find barefoot children a sufficiently unusual sight to take issue with the film on.

Deprived of the distribution networks of the large cinemas (although several of the smaller, independent cinemas did show the film, where it was 'well-received'), the Clann resorted to taking the film with them on the hustings, showing it against gable walls, for example, thereby adding, if that were possible, yet another touch of exotica to Irish elections. Around about this time, they also made an LP (long-playing record) of MacBride describing Clann policies.[47] A growing number of people had phonographs, or the newer record players, designed for the shellac discs of the time. It could be said that this was simply a pitch for the vote of young 'wannabees', the sort who would possess phonographs, and would be intrigued by the idea of a party leader cutting a disc. A more likely reading is the influence of Hartnett, and the openness of MacBride himself to experimentation with new, and novel, means of communication.

Whichever was the case, the fact remains that in terms of what a later generation would term mastery of 'public relations' skills, Fianna Fáil were comprehensively outclassed. In fact, about the best that they had been able to dredge up by way of creative endeavour during the 1948 campaign was an advertisement which announced 'Your bottle is better and cheaper than anywhere else in the world today – thanks to good old Dev.'[48] Their only hope lay in the chance that the new party would overreach itself, and they watched avidly as the election campaign took its toll on the new party's fledgling organisation. Entering the election campaign with thoughts of emerging from it as a government, Clann na Poblachta selected ninety-three candidates nationwide, second only to the number put forward by Fianna Fáil themselves. This was easily enough to form a government if they were all to gain election, but, of course, that was an unlikely scenario, for the Clann's very structures creaked ominously with the strain imposed upon them by the election. At one level, this was simply a problem of too much growth too quickly, for membership increased enormously in the wake of the by-elections and the Clann lacked the immediate means of coping with this. Moreover, they were now obliged to construct a national organisation with alacrity, for they now presented themselves as a national party, seeking to form a national government, and thus required a national base. Naturally, they had no experience in anything like this, and worse, they had to do their building at a gallop, or, on the run, to coin an unfortunate phrase, for they were fighting a particularly enervating general election, which was itself a fight to the death. Furthermore, there was the problem of candidate selection, and here the ancestral ghosts returned for a short visit and infused some in the party with their particular perspective, leading to some rather strange choices in terms of candidate selection.

The by-elections had alerted the Clann to the need for strong candidates who could boast extensive networks in their respective constituencies, or were otherwise well known, and, in addition, could preferably come to the party with some sort of republican past. Of course, it was not always possible in the gadarene rush to acquire candidates possessing all of these characteristics, and the Clann generally made do with one or the other, usually fielding two candidates per constituency who between them were well known, and possessed a republican past. As with so much else to do with the Clann, on closer examination this duality concerning candidates emerged in a curiously disturbing light. Those who had come to the party from routes other than the IRA ultimately saw in this a republican conspiracy to enable the IRA candidates with whom they were linked on the ballot paper to soar easily into the Dáil on the backs of transfers supplied by the merely 'well known', whose job it was to put them there.

In Roscommon, former Army lieutenant[49] and Roscommon All-Ireland football winner Jack McQuillan stood for the Clann, alongside Michael A. Kelly, formerly of the IRA but who at that time was the Clann's general secretary. Kelly's unpleasant attitude to his running mate was summed up when he rather unwisely informed a friend, 'With McQuillan's boots, and my brains, I'll be elected in Roscommon.'[50] This process appeared to be at work in some other constituencies as well. In Dublin South-East, for example, Noël Browne's running mate, Donal O'Donoghue, was an infinitely more agreeable character than the boorish Kelly, but Browne eventually came to feel that his 'function' was to 'be used as political mounting blocks for others, the ex-IRA' to 'ease' their passage into the Dáil.[51] Meanwhile, across the river in Dublin North-East, Clann candidate Captain Peadar Cowan noted, fuming, that his role in life was to elect 'senile Mrs Tom Clarke' as part of the same strategy.[52]

Undoubtedly, the 'old guard' probably preferred the idea of those who had put in the time-honoured apprenticeship in the 'real army' as potential parliamentary colleagues to these more recent recruits, but does that make this preference a republican-inspired plot? In fact, we are back to that old IRA conundrum, scarcely removed from first principles, where one has to ask, 'cock-up or conspiracy'? If this was an IRA-style conspiracy (and almost everything in the collective political unconscious of the Clann's republicans points to their preference to doing business in this manner when put under pressure), then it bore the usual IRA fingerprints of ineptitude, for it back-fired gloriously. Neither Kelly, O'Donoghue, nor 'senile Mrs Tom Clarke' actually gained election, whereas McQuillan, Browne, and Cowan did.

In finding for 'IRA cock-up' (as opposed to any other kind), and the perva-sive influence of, and difficulty in dispensing with, the mental habits of a lifetime, it is of relevance to note that other types of 'cock-up' occurred too, and owed even less to conspiratorial casts of mind and more to the exigen-cies of running an election on a tight budget, and finding candidates – fast. This, too, led to a few farcical situations, situations where individuals who could come up with the deposit of £100 out of their own pocket could be considered as candidates.[53] (£100 was a lot of money at that time. By way of contrast, one need simply note that TDs' annual salaries stood at £624.) Most of the parties managed to nominate a few spectacularly awful candidates, but the problem for the Clann was partly one of image ('we have the people to lead you to the promised land', when in fact, they hadn't, or, at least, not a full complement) and partly one of overstretching, which had been part of Fianna Fáil's plan for the new party all along. When one adds the constituency revision to that, one sees the grounds for the quietly reason-able optimism indulged in by de Valera as polling day approached.

Apart from organisation (and here the experienced world-weariness of Fianna Fáil proved to be a more durable beast than the Clann's heady ideal-ism), and stunning use of public relations (a contest the Clann won hands down), this was an election where personality differences were augmented by policy differences. Initially, this was MacBride's doing. Partly because he personally preferred a more cerebral approach to politics, and partly because the Clann's very *raison d'être* was to dispense with the political and social cleavages as defined by civil war politics and define a new type of politics, of which they were to be the leading examplar – hence their attempt to inject new themes and topics into the national political discourse – policy differ-ences came to play a large role in the 1947 and 1948 elections. Earlier, MacEntee had failed to lure MacBride into an old-style 'personality' debate, and instead, as early as the by-elections, had himself been obliged to respond to MacBride's successful attempts to broaden the scope of the debate by introducing considerations of policy. Policy was not MacEntee's particular forte, and his frustration at this unwanted direction taken by the letters tourney expressed itself in ever more splenetic outbursts. Lemass, whose strength *was* policy, played a relatively minor, and muted, role in the 1948 election, and while he dutifully denounced most of the economic policies proposed by the Clann, his endless battles with MacEntee at Cabinet over the future direction of economic policy indicated a private sympathy for a more interventionist, and expansionist, set of economic policies.[54]

These policy differences, and their importance to the Clann's self-image, had come about largely because MacBride and his immediate lieutenants had come to the realisation that a party based simply and solely on revanchist republicanism was hardly likely to meet with much electoral success by the mid-1940s.[55] Policies addressing social issues would have to be included, as well. Of course, this particular debate had raged on and off ever since the halcyon days of Saor Éire, a debate which had included questions on the sort of emphasis to be given to social and economic policies (as opposed to purely republican ones), and also raising the little matter of which particular social policies were to be emphasised. Insofar as Clann na Poblachta rediscovered the importance of radical social policy, one can argue (and MacEntee did, vehemently) that they derived their social radicalism from ideas sprouted by Saor Éire. While Tony Jordan, MacBride's biographer, states that most of Saor Éire's objectives 'remained part of MacBride's political philosophy',[56] and while it is incontestable that ideas that were first mooted during the Saor Éire era did indeed play a role in the Clann's vision of how the country could be governed, it was the differences between the earlier Saor Éire policies and the subsequent policies eventually espoused by the Clann which were to provide a clear indication of how far they had travelled on the road away from their radical ancestry.

This difference was most clearly expressed by the emphasis given to policies boasting other ancestries to the economic and social policies put forward by Saor Éire, policies which could best be described as a cocktail made up of elements from the Dignan Plan, Minority Report No. 3 on the Banking Commission, and some toned-down derivations dating from the days of Saor Éire. The Dignan Plan came, as its name suggested, from the pen of Dr John Dignan, the bishop of Clonfert, who had been appointed chairman of the National Health Insurance Society, ironically enough as events turned out, by Seán MacEntee. In October 1944, Dignan had issued a pamphlet entitled *Social Security: Outlines of a Scheme of National Health Insurance*, which, while attempting to bridge traditional Catholic social teaching with contemporary health insurance requirements, proposed a radical overhaul of all Irish social services.[57] Dignan's recommendations were dismissed out of hand by MacEntee in 1945, and the bishop himself was dismissed a year later, when MacEntee declined to re-appoint him to the chair of the National Health Insurance Society, appointing a more malleable civil servant instead.[58]

The outright (and virulent) rejection of Dignan's scheme by the government meant, in effect, handing aimed weaponry over to the government's critics. Clann na Poblachta were delighted (not that they could openly say so), but, in essence, this was to legitimise their call for radical social action. By publicly siding with the injured party – the martyred bishop – Clann na Poblachta could appear to be both socially radical and progressively Catholic, and, while they were at it, consign some of the more glaring references of their Saor Éire ancestry to the dustbin of history, or, at the very least, to short-term memory loss. From the date of their inception, the Clann called for the implementation of the Dignan Plan, and it materialised, approvingly quoted, in their election literature in both 1947 and 1948. Most tellingly, MacBride himself emphatically supported the Dignan Plan in the Clann's film *Our Country*. In fact, the film contained several shots depicting quotes from the Dignan Plan – including one shot of a newspaper headline announcing the fact that Minister MacEntee had sacked Bishop Dignan.

Fianna Fáil could not readily oppose Clann na Poblachta on those grounds, (especially as they had never made clear their reasons for opposing the Dignan Plan[59]), and it fell to the 'dismal science', economics, to provide Fianna Fáil with some sort of policy cudgel with which to hit the Clann. As matters transpired, Fianna Fáil failed to fully seize their opportunity, for fighting elections on economic theory – as opposed to definitions of sovereignty, dressed up as economic theory – was new to them, too. In addition to ideas which owed their genesis to Saor Éire (not that this copyright was always acknowledged), the other chief source of MacBride's own economic thought, from which he culled both ideas and inspiration, was the *Report of the Commission of Inquiry into Banking, Currency and Credit,* Minority Report No. 3 by Mr P. J. O'Loghlen (1938). This was a very able, iconoclastic, and challenging document, which attacked the whole premise of Irish economic policy as pursued by native governments since the 1920s. Citing papal encyclicals[60] among other sources in support of its stance, it questioned the validity of the link with sterling, stating that 'when a country attaches its currency to sterling, it subordinates its domestic policy to the views of the authorities who manage sterling . . . England goes her way, and if we attach ourselves to her, like a row boat to a battleship we can only expect to be dragged in her wake.'[61] Nor was that all. O'Loghlen questioned the justifications for the idea of a central bank, doubted the capacity of the private sector to remedy unemployment or to provide any meaningful economic growth, and called for comprehensive government intervention in the provision of capital, capital development, and the provision of full employment itself, because 'Our first duty is to consider what measures are practicable which may lead to a state of full employment, both of natural resources, and of labour requiring employment.'[62] He suggested a state afforestation policy as one way of meeting each of these needs – namely government intervention and visionary leadership, *and* employment creation – at the one time.[63]

It is not clear when exactly MacBride came across O'Loghlen's report, but he seems to have been instantly smitten by its contents.[64] Large tracts of O'Loghlen's thinking featured in the Clann's economic policies (the ideas on repatriation of sterling assets, an intensive programme of capital development, afforestation, land reclamation, public authority housing, and the link with sterling itself were all borrowed more or less intact from O'Loghlen), and, moreover, one of the people who most influenced the final direction of the Minority Report No. 3 would herself enjoy a considerable and continuing influence on MacBride. This was B. Berthon Waters, who was one of the most hostile witnesses examined by the Banking Commission and who, along with Fr Edward Cahill, SJ, and Bulmer Hobson, influenced O'Loghlen in the writing of his report.[65] Ten years later, MacBride himself was taking copious advice from this group, and Berthon Waters was, moreover, writing economic memoranda for MacBride, at his request, and continued to do so long after he had been appointed to Iveagh House.[66] His own later economic offerings come with strong genetic fingerprints concerning both the link with sterling and afforestation,[67] the latter issue later a particular source of tension between MacBride and the starched collars in the Department of Finance. Clann na Poblachta's economic policies did not meet with unqualified approval. Fianna Fáil condemned them in whinging – but strangely unconvincing – tones, and certainly failed to mount any kind of serious rebuttal. Silent disbelief was the inarticulate response from the other parties, while *The Irish Times* (usually sympathetic) sneered condescendingly that the Clann 'represents something new, although its declared policy is as old as Sinn Féin, and its economic programme scarcely deserves to be taken seriously'.[68] Less enamoured still seemed to be the population at large, a considerable number of whom took fright at both the tone and the content of this debate.

For one Clann stalwart, the major memory of that election campaign was the sight of MacBride, elegantly attired as always, earnestly lecturing some down-at-heel slum youngsters on 'the incompatibility of sterling'.[69] 'I know in my case that our Director of Elections used to wince each time I made a reference, during the course of the General Election campaign, to the need for economic and financial reform', MacBride recalled ruefully over a year later.[70] He had good reason to be rueful, for, in the hands of some of the Clann's less polished speakers, the notion of the repatriation of sterling assets acquired bizarre permutations, which in turn gave rise to genuine fear on the part of many voters, voters, for instance, who had savings in British banking institutions, or received British military or civil service pensions, and who feared to lose them if the Clann were elected. Somewhat grimly, MacBride further recalled, 'I know, too, that the other political parties [and here, he can only have really meant Fianna Fáil] seized upon any statement I did make concerning our economic position for the purpose of suggesting to the electorate that if the Clann were returned to power the savings of the people in the Banks would no longer be safe and chaos would result.'[71]

Be that as it may, it should be noted that, no matter how inexpert some of their platform speakers, Clann na Poblachta were probably the first political party in Ireland to fight an election on some sort of coherent social and economic policy. Despite the electoral cost, MacBride remained unrepentant, as a speech made a few years later made abundantly clear: 'I have devoted a considerable amount of time, and often probably bored audiences throughout the country dealing with economic matters, as I believe it essential to focus the attention of our people on the exact nature of these problems.'[72] They were the first political party to stress the importance of policies on matters such as afforestation, and campaigned hard not just for public housing and land reclamation, but also for the increased provision of beds for TB patients, the provision for which was to come from the public purse. These latter policies were what won the enthusiastic support of some of their younger candidates such as Jack McQuillan (who also claimed responsibility for some of the development of their policies on land reclamation and, more especially, afforestation)[73] and, of course, Noël Browne, who had made the eradication of TB the prime business of his life and who was standing for election to the Dáil as a TB specialist for the party.

It was this mix of boundless enthusiasm, interesting policies, brilliant public relations, and an overstretched organisation which faced polling day. Clann na Poblachta appeared to have been riding the crest of a wave, always a tricky balancing act and one that proved difficult to sustain. Indeed, in the last few days before polling day, MacBride himself 'sensed that the tide had turned'[74] and that habits of caution would prevail, as electors declined to desert their traditional political allegiances in the droves required to give MacBride his landslide. Reflecting years later on the results of the election, MacBride himself was to make this very point to RTÉ's John Bowman, when he remarked 'Strangely enough, if the elections had been held roughly a fortnight previously before the date they were held, we would have got about 30 to 40 seats. We lost in the last ten days of the election campaign . . . Our economic policies frightened the people . . . I could feel the people being scared that last ten days.'[75]

5

'Mr de Valera's abhorrence of coalitions is proverbial'

Polling day fell on 4 February 1948, and, from very early in the various counts countrywide, it became evident that the projected landslide to the Clann was not going to take place. Later on, it became equally evident that the electoral system, so beneficial the previous October, was doing the party no favours this time out. By the end of the nail-biting count, Clann na Poblachta had gained ten seats, with 13.2 per cent of the national vote (almost 20 per cent in Dublin), from their ninety-three candidates.[1] They were bitterly disappointed with this result. The mirage of Sinn Féin's 1918 sweeping victory had proved to be just that – an illusion. In terms of votes cast, the Clann, with their 13 per cent of first preferences, came third in the country. Fianna Fáil, of course, led, with 41.9 per cent of the first preference vote (down considerably from their 1944 total of just under 50 per cent); this won them sixty-eight seats, a drop of eight seats, despite an increase (from 138 to 147) in the number of deputies returned to the Dáil chamber. Fine Gael's vote had also declined, dropping from 20.5 per cent in 1944 to 19 per cent in 1948. During the war, Fine Gael had found themselves unable, even, to run a sufficient number of candidates to form a government – in the 1944 election just fifty-five candidates contested seats for Fine Gael. However, matters had improved slightly by 1948, for, with the appointment of a national organiser, eighty-two candidates were selected to contest seats for the party. Fine Gael obtained thirty-one seats, an increase of one. Between them, the two Labours achieved 11.3 per cent of the national vote, less than Clann na Poblachta, but for that they pulled in 19 seats (14 for Labour and five for the God-fearing comrades in the splinter party, National Labour). The farmers' party, Clann na Talmhan, received 5.6 per cent of the national vote (and were strongest, naturally enough, in their western fastness), and seven seats.[2] A total of twelve Independent deputies were also returned, their support coming from a very wide variety of constituencies, and, in some cases, reflecting much more than simply local concerns.

In fact, the Clann were desperately unlucky not to have won more than ten seats, which was, itself, a very creditable result for a party fighting its first election. Strict proportionality would have given them nineteen seats,[3] a bit of luck, up to twenty-five. Some of their candidates were beaten by only a few votes for the final seat in a number of constituencies (for example, this happened with Noel Hartnett, fighting for the final seat in Dún Laoghaire–Rathdown).[4] The Clann themselves regarded this as a bitterly disappointing result, a view which confirmed it as a failure in the eyes of the voting public, and a view the other parties were only too willing to endorse. Having entered the election campaign with such high hopes, even the merest brush with reality would have rendered the results a disappointment in the eyes of the Clann. The fact that the Clann saw the election result almost in terms of a defeat had the unfortunate result of reinforcing conservative voting tendencies in Ireland, and it would take another few decades before sustained fresh attempts would be made to drill into the ancient moulds. Moreover, it is worth pointing out that as no coalition government had actually held office up to that time, coalition voting patterns had not yet emerged as a salient feature in Irish elections. (In fact, they would begin to do so from 1951.) In addition, the Clann were seeking to replicate the successes of the catch-all parties, and posited themselves as such. This meant that transfers from other parties did not come to them in anything like the numbers required, and, in one or two bizarre cases, Clann candidates did not even transfer to each other.[5]

There was more to it than that, of course. De Valera's multiple gambles had paid off. The constituency revision worked, and so did the idea of an early election, for it achieved just what that astute reader of Machiavelli had planned – it meant that the Clann overreached, overstretched, and overstrained themselves, and that the party's resources, and ultimately their support, were spread too thinly.[6] MacBride himself later made this very point in an interview with RTÉ's John Bowman, when he remarked, 'To a certain extent, de Valera was quite correct in his strategy to call a general election before we had time to organise',[7] adding that it was his definite opinion that 'if we had another year or so to organise I think we probably would have won an overall majority'.[8] It meant that de Valera had seen off the first serious challenge to his particular cabbage patch since the foundation of Fianna Fáil itself. In the words of Coogan, 'de Valera had correctly targeted the enemy who would unhorse him'.[9] But had he? In putting together this exceedingly elaborate equation, de Valera seemed to have omitted one factor, and this factor, while irrelevant in the context of destroying Clann na Poblachta, came into play immediately after the counts were completed.

Actually, there were two aspects to this factor. The first was that the election results had left de Valera and Fianna Fáil in a minority position, *vis à vis* all the other parties put together, and the second was that all of these other parties might just feel impelled to make common cause against de Valera, in the sort of movement MacBride's succinct slogan 'Put Them Out' had already possibly presaged.

Originally, this was not even envisaged as a problem, as de Valera had unaccountably found himself in a minority situation several times before in his career (for instance, in 1932 and 1943), and, as these matters quite often resolved themselves in terms of who blinked first, de Valera had managed to retain office. The closest he had come to parliamentary defeat had occurred in 1943, when Clann na Talmhan, fresh to parliamentary existence, had given him support as Taoiseach on the grounds that he led the Dáil's largest party. After a year's rumination on the topic, they arrived at the conclusion that they had committed an error of monumental proportions, and thus, by the following year, when they voted against de Valera for Taoiseach (not that he cared; he had an overall majority by then), they had changed their minds so completely that they were the first party to advocate coalition government as an alternative to Fianna Fáil. Given de Valera's propensity for Houdini-style escapes, and given the fissiparous nature of the five parties making up the opposition, not to mention the fact that twelve Independent deputies had also been returned, de Valera could take comfortable solace from the fact that firstly, those parties were unlikely to agree amongst themselves, and secondly, even if they did, some of the Independents would have to row in with them, just to make up the required numbers.

However, there was another consideration, another dimension, to all of this. As his biographer succinctly phrased it, 'after sixteen years in power [de Valera] could not bring himself to face the fact that he was widely disliked'.[10] Many a great friendship has begun on little more than an acknowledgement of the cementing bonds engendered by a common enemy. Acknowledgement of these cementing bonds does not necessarily mean instant, or enduring, friendship, but can express itself in mere political arrangements, an infinitely more accommodating beast, especially when the common enemy was so gratifyingly visible.

While the general election had occurred on 4 February, because of a curious postscript – concerning the Carlow–Kilkenny constituency – the final results did not become clear until 10 February.[11] When the Dáil assembled on 18 February, de Valera found himself voted out of office by a combination of Fine Gael, Clann na Poblachta, Clann na Talmhan, Labour, National Labour, and eleven of the twelve Independents,[12] who went on to form a government, carving up the ministries amongst themselves in accordance with their respective parliamentary strengths. Disgusted, de Valera embarked upon what he grandly termed an Anti-Partition World Tour, leaving his party in the capable hands of Seán Lemass, his predicament the subject of some smothered giggles. De Valera's lengthy journey was to take him to America, India, Pakistan, New Zealand, and Australia, and would fulfil the various functions of removing him from the depressing reality of loss of power while generating plenty of publicity for him, and simultaneously keeping the new government under pressure in the stakes of anti-partition rhetoric. This didn't impress *Dublin Opinion* in the slightest, who reported with a straight face that during the American leg of the world trip, 'At Tulsa, Oklahoma, Shuna Tona, Chief of the Otoe Indian tribe installed Dev as a brother Chief giving him the name of Drahri Turahi meaning "good friend from across the sea"', adding, wickedly, 'If Dev had been made an Indian Chief before these Emergency Duties were put on, he'd have been able to read the smoke signals better.'[13] Meanwhile, in faraway Melbourne, another unexpected repercussion of the change of government occurred when it was noted that 'Archbishop Mannix didn't speak at all for two days after the result'.[14]

This was the first coalition government, better known to history as the first inter-party government. While there was some public amazement at this rather unexpected outcome, behind the scenes there had been considerable activity ever since the outcome of the general election had made Fianna Fáil's minority position clear. De Valera was well aware of the vulnerability of his situation, but chose to sit tight and confine himself to acerbic attacks on the very idea of coalitions, in the hope that the other parties would not be able to make common cause against him when the time came for the Dáil vote to select the Taoiseach. However, de Valera can hardly have been unaware of the fact that coalition government had become the norm all of a sudden in western Europe. It was not that coalitions had somehow become contagious, but the idea had become very familiar from its extensive operation in postwar 'Popular Front' governments found all across Europe. Closer to home, Britain had also experienced a National Government during the war (and, indeed, during the earlier Great Depression as well, although that unhappy administration remained far from everyone's active recall), and, as no political experiment could be contemplated without already having been undertaken by the Ancient Saxon Enemy, this, presumably, put a further seal of approval upon a hazardous endeavour. In fact, by 1948 most of the parties operating in Ireland were broadly in favour of the idea of coalition.

As long ago as the immediate aftermath of the by-elections *The Irish Times* had remarked, 'the general opinion seems to be that Mr de Valera will again have the largest party, but shrewd observers are convinced that it will no longer have the overall majority that it has enjoyed in the past,' asking presciently, 'What then? A coalition? And if a coalition, with what group? Mr de Valera's abhorrence of coalitions is proverbial.'[15] By the time the general election took place, murmurings concerning coalition could be heard from every party. The earliest advocate – and, for a long time, the only advocate – of coalition was Clann na Talmhan, and they were presently to be joined by Labour's Roddy Connolly, who pushed hard for links to be forged between Labour, Clann na Poblachta, and Clann na Talmhan in a sort of 'Republican–Labour–Farmer' grand alliance towards the end of 1947.[16] Presenting his case, Connolly argued that Clann na Poblachta 'is looked upon by the people as a battering ram to break the power and privilege of the present government and that combined with Labour and Clann na Talmhan would contribute largely to the overthrow of Fianna Fáil'.[17] Moreover, he felt that Labour should take the initiative in promoting such a scheme. Replying to Connolly on 15 November in the Labour Party's own publication, the *Irish People*, Joe Deasy gave a guarded welcome to Connolly's idea but felt the inclusion of Clann na Talmhan in any sort of grand alliance to be 'inadvisable'.[18]

However, the most important convert to the idea of coalition was the leader of Fine Gael, General Richard Mulcahy, who would turn out to be the key player – as MacBride's was the key party – in the creation of the coalition. Even before polling day, in his characteristically tortured syntax, he was referring to the swing against Fianna Fáil as possibly having the effect of 'putting any Government or a group of them as a group Government into power', adding that 'the ordinary Irish people can be trusted; their Leaders can be relied upon to come together and express the desire of unity of their people'.[19] Mulcahy sincerely believed not only that was it 'inconceivable' that Fianna Fáil would obtain an overall majority, but that it would be 'almost inconceivable' for de Valera to be elected Taoiseach in a new Dáil.[20] Determined to do what he could to assist the 'inconceivability' of de Valera's becoming Taoiseach, Mulcahy dropped further hints about the direction his thoughts were taking when he spoke in Kilkenny on 8 February: 'Fine Gael will resolutely oppose his re-election as Taoiseach . . . Fine Gael is prepared to co-operate with other parties in forming a Government.'[21] Carrots of co-operation were dangled tantalisingly in front of the other parties with a mixture of praise – 'There is a unity of interest in these matters . . . and there is a fundamental unity of outlook on them on the part of the Leaders of all the Opposition parties' – and ringing rhetoric: 'The present opportunity demands their co-operation. It is one of those great national opportunities calling for recognition . . . The country doesn't need another General Election in the near future . . . it wants Party leaders to stand up to their responsibilities. There is a national duty on the various opposition Parties in the Dáil . . . to take power out of the hands of a man and of a Party incurably dictatorial and arrogant in their spirit.'[22] He concluded with an astonishing request to his supporters in Kilkenny, when he suggested that they support Fine Gael at polling the following day on the novel grounds that this would serve 'to strengthen the hands of Fine Gael to work for co-operation among the party leaders'[23] – surely an unusual motivation when seeking votes from one's own supporters.

The best account by far which discusses the formation of the inter-party government comes from Mulcahy himself. Nearly twenty years later, John A. Costello was preparing for an extensive series of interviews with the political correspondent of *The Irish Times*, Michael McInerney, and he wrote to Mulcahy for help.[24] Above all, he wanted his memory prodded on the details concerning the formation of the inter-party government. 'My recollection is that the suggestion originally came from Seán MacBride but I am not sure whether the suggestion of an Inter-Party government came from him or from you or from Bill Norton.'[25] Mulcahy was more than happy to put him right, and he replied to 'My dear Jack' in an extraordinarily detailed letter,[26] having earlier commiserated with Costello on the choice of interviewer: 'I might have wished you a more attractive detonator than McInerney.'[27]

According to Mulcahy, after the results had become clear on 10 February, he 'consulted' with Dan Morrissey who was recovering from an illness.[28] He put it to Morrissey, whose judgement he trusted, that he 'had it strongly in mind to write to the leaders of the various parties and invite them to come together and form a government to oppose the setting up of a Fianna Fáil government'.[29] Morrissey seemed to be quite taken with the idea and replied 'in a cheerful Morrissey way that the Government so formed would probably last six months, and that our last state would be worse than our first, but that

I would have to do it (the inviting)'.[30] Thus fortified, Mulcahy wrote to all of the other leaders on 11 February, inviting them to meet him two days later at Leinster House. On Friday, 13 February, they all turned up at Leinster House (with the exception of James Everett's National Labour, who were otherwise detained), and Mulcahy was pleased to find that the three other parties (Labour, Clann na Poblachta, and Clann na Talmhan) 'had apparently considered the proposal favourably'.[31] Provisional agreement was even reached on Mulcahy's proposals concerning ministry allocation and the numbers of portfolios each party was to receive.

However, there was a snag, and this was that there were those who did not wish to serve under Mulcahy himself as Taoiseach. Describing this years later to Costello (who, of course, did not attend this meeting), Mulcahy was delicate and discreet: 'Norton intimated that he did not think that his party would agree to serve in a government under the leadership of one who had been the leader of another party.'[32] Disappointed, Mulcahy still managed a surprising answer: 'My reply to that was that if there was an agreement to form a government on the lines I suggested, while the Fine Gael party might feel that I should be the leader of the government, they could have my assurance that, if the other parties were prepared to form a government on the lines I suggested, that I would not stand between them and the setting up of such a government.'[33] This must have astonished the other party leaders, and they readily fell in with Mulcahy's proposal 'that there should be no delay in meeting me again and that they should meet again the following day'.[34] Furthermore, Mulcahy recommended that 'the persons' attending the meeting the next day 'should be those who were going to be designated as Ministers by the party concerned, and Norton asked if I could bring you particularly for the purpose of your advice and help. There was a general feeling that you should be so asked and I had no difficulty in assuring them that you would be there.'[35] Mulcahy saw Costello on the Friday evening and 'reported the position' to him. Together, they both visited Patrick McGilligan at his house the following day and 'discussed the situation'. Saturday evening saw them all assemble in the Mansion House, as arranged. 'The attendance comprised [James] Dillon, the prospective ministers for the Fine Gael, Labour, Clann na Talmhan and Clann na Poblachta [parties] (except that in this case MacBride was accompanied by the O'Rahile[36] who was not intended for the ministry by MacBride until he ascertained at that night's meeting what second ministry would be held by his party). The ministry having been outlined and agreed to, you were then invited to become Taoiseach. It was arranged that we would meet again on Sunday night to hear your decision.'[37] Actually they met before that, as Mulcahy reminded Costello, for, when Sunday arrived, 'You met the Fine Gael group in the forenoon at Lissonfield House [Mulcahy's home] and all met again at the Mansion House at nine o'clock that evening to hear your decision.'[38]

This detailed account omitted to discuss the role played by National Labour, on which de Valera was undoubtedly pinning whatever hopes remained for his retention of office. In fact, with this in mind, de Valera had earlier despatched the Minister for Justice, Gerry Boland, to have a chat with the National Labour deputies in the hope that something might yet be salvaged from the approaching disaster of loss of office. Recalling all this with wry amusement many years later, Gerry Boland remarked to *The Irish Times'* Michael McInerney: 'At this stage the Government Ministers all loved power, even Dev although you might not believe it. I was sent off to see what I could do with James Everett of the National Labour Party, in the way of securing their votes for Dev, as Taoiseach. But I didn't make much of an effort, and just asked him if we were to pack our bags or not. There was some equivocation, so I reported that they would vote against us. We had a Fianna Fáil meeting before the Dáil met, and I spoke at it to the effect that we were all getting too high and mighty, and were thinking that we owned the country. "I even think it myself", I said, "It will do us no harm to be in Opposition for a while."'[39]

National Labour had not attended any of the earlier meetings, and were perceived by the giant transport union, the ITGWU (which had promised financial support to the party in 1947), as an obedient mouthpiece for the union's concerns. After the 1948 election, the central council of the Congress of Irish Unions (the breakaway congress sponsored by the ITGWU in open opposition to the Irish Congress of Trade Unions) recommended that the five National Labour TDs support the re-election of de Valera as Taoiseach when the Dáil resumed. In fact, the five TDs turned up over an hour late for this meeting with their union 'minders', and when they did materialise, they rejected the union's advice 'unceremoniously'.[40] Not only did they announce their intention to vote for the inter-party government, rather than for de Valera (a decision the union grumbled 'was not cricket' and denounced as 'a betrayal of the trade unions'), but they justified their decision by pointing out that they were answerable to their constituents, and not the ITGWU.[41]

In fact, Fine Gael accounts show a great deal of sympathy for National Labour in those trying times, and a surprising understanding of the pressure that was then being exerted on National Labour by the transport union (and, presumably, by extension, by Fianna Fáil). As Mulcahy expressed it in another letter he wrote to Costello two years later, in April 1969, 'You may remember feeling or knowing that the National Labour party had a great spirit and faced many difficulties and temptations at that time.'[42] Costello did indeed remember, for, as he had earlier told Michael McInerney, 'Talking about heroes, James Everett was the hero of the Inter-Party Alliance. No man was under heavier pressure to support the then Government both from his union and from Fianna Fáil.'[43]

National Labour's role was described in greater detail by Mulcahy in this later (1969) correspondence with Costello. Because of the pressure being exerted on them by the ITGWU, James Everett, the party leader, was only able to meet Mulcahy on the Tuesday (17 February), the day before the Dáil met, 'and when he and his men had a talk with me and agreed to the formation of an Inter-party Government on the basis of representation already suggested by me to the other parties at their first meeting with me, I called in Dan Morrissey who was in the neighbourhood to meet them'.[44] Mulcahy himself was impressed by National Labour: 'As Dan and I moved from my room to yours after they had gone my remark to Dan in admiration of the attitude of Everett and his men was "Well, Dan, it would be hard to say who the hero of this episode was."'[45] Concluding, Mulcahy heaped further praise on Costello: 'I am sure you don't forget that their experience under you caused them to become a united Labour Party.'[46]

Each of these letters (those of April 1969 and July 1967) was a typical Mulcahy offering. They were both neatly typed, contained several additional handwritten amendments, and were extremely detailed. However, Mulcahy's original account does raise some interesting questions, for it features some rather interesting omissions. These concern the roles played by Clann na Poblachta and National Labour (neither of which are really mentioned in his earlier, more detailed account), and the part played by some within his own party, such as Dr T. F. O'Higgins, which is overlooked in a classic instance of averted eyes. Mulcahy's own role and bona fides have never been doubted – 'selfless' is the adjective most usually applied to him[47] – and his decision not to persist in seeking the position of Taoiseach when doubts about his suitability were raised by some of the other parties is fascinating. Party leaders are considered egocentric by nature – it comes with the package – and if nature has not endowed them with the necessary insatiable appetite for privilege, power, and prestige, circumstances usually contrive to make good nature's lack. Mulcahy's immediate response must have left the other leaders dumbfounded, and, for that matter, it must also have contributed to the air of baffled wonder (mingled with the faintest contempt) with which he continued to be regarded. More importantly, it certainly put Fine Gael in a very strong subsequent negotiating position; Mulcahy had, in a way, surrendered the biggest prize without a murmur (even though it was to remain with Costello), and this meant that the other parties could not be any less magnanimous when it came to sharing out the spoils. This is what probably lay behind the fact that Fine Gael enjoyed a disproportionately large number of ministerial posts and received a dispro-portionate number of the more powerful portfolios. Fine Gael's subsequently powerful political presence at the Cabinet table cannot be explained away by Mulcahy's guile, for Mulcahy was no predator, certainly, and neither was Costello – not initially at any rate.

Moreover, he had been handed a Cabinet on a plate, rather than actually choosing one for himself. This brings us to the other matters of interest in Mulcahy's chronicle. As mentioned, in his original account there is little reference to National Labour (although he remedied that in his subsequent account) and, yet again, there is hardly any reference to Clann na Poblachta, either in terms of an ideas input into these negotiations or even in the context of vetoing Mulcahy himself as Taoiseach, which is what they are supposed to have done. Most sources are agreed that Clann na Poblachta was the prime agent in ensuring that Mulcahy did not become Taoiseach.[48] Yet, rather surprisingly, Mulcahy himself completely overlooks this little detail, for he fails in any respect whatsoever to even refer to the part played by the Clann.[49] In fact, about the only Fine Gael based source which does refer to the role played by the Clann is that penned by Patrick Lynch. Lynch, who went on to serve as Costello's economic adviser (and occasional secretary), wrote that 'On Saturday, 14 February, when he returned from a game of golf at Milltown, Senator James Douglas called with the news that Seán MacBride wished Costello to become Taoiseach of an 'Inter-Party' government. That afternoon MacBride personally informed Costello that all the parties opposed to Fianna Fáil would form a government on condition that he agreed to be Taoiseach; no one else would be acceptable.'[50]

From Clann na Poblachta's perspective, and, to a lesser extent, that of Labour, it is ironic to consider that if they had left the General in place, they probably would have enjoyed even more leeway, and been able to assert themselves far more in Cabinet than they actually did. Mulcahy was so anxious to form a government, and to ensure that such a government lasted, that he was prepared to go to considerable lengths to make certain that matters ran smoothly.

In fact, while Mulcahy was vetoed, not because he 'was the leader of another party' (as Norton tactfully phrased it), but because of his role in the Civil War, there were some who suggested that elements in Fine Gael wished to see him ousted as leader (or Taoiseach), and contrived to use the Clann and Labour to achieve this end.[51] Presumably this is a reference to the relationship Mulcahy enjoyed, or, more to the point, didn't enjoy with certain elements within Fine Gael, such as Dr T. F. O'Higgins. O'Higgins had led Fine Gael during the brief period Mulcahy had lacked a Dáil seat in 1943 and had relinquished it upon the General's return to the Dáil in 1944. It is possible that some sort of tension existed between the two of them, for Mulcahy's relationship with the brother of T. F. O'Higgins, the murdered Kevin O'Higgins, had been anything but smooth.[52] This is not to suggest that such feuds are automatically passed on from one family member to the next, but it is worth noting that Mulcahy's detailed account features at least one further omission, for it neglects to mention that O'Higgins was also involved in the negotiations leading up to the formation of the inter-party government. It would have been extremely surprising if he were not, given the positions he held (and had held) in Fine Gael. However, it is equally clear that O'Higgins (unlike, say, Morrissey) did not enjoy the trust, or confidence, of Mulcahy, and neither was his advice sought by Mulcahy.

Costello's own memories were slightly different, and originally, when he first wrote to Mulcahy, he recalled, almost tersely, that 'Senator Douglas came to me on Saturday afternoon. On Saturday night I met you and Dr Tom O'Higgins, Dan Morrissey and others in your house, and we discussed the matter. I saw Arthur Cox on Sunday evening, made up my mind and told you of my decision. That night I think I met Seán MacBride and the others in the Mansion House. I subsequently met Jim Everett in Leinster House. I am glad to hear that you are playing golf and keeping well.'[53]

This note to Mulcahy gave no indication of the shock Costello received, when, having been asked to attend the Saturday meeting as an adviser, he was invited – apparently abruptly – to become Taoiseach. Nor does it give any indication of the role played by either Senator James Douglas, MacBride's emissary, or indeed MacBride himself. However, Mulcahy's lengthy letter must have jogged his memory somewhat, for, by the time he actually gave the long-planned interviews to *The Irish Times'* Michael McInerney, he had remembered Mulcahy visiting him on the Friday night with this suggestion. 'I was appalled at the idea. I never wanted to be Taoiseach but the pressure began.'[54] This pressure continued when 'we met Mr Patrick McGilligan on Saturday with the late Dr Tom O'Higgins, and that night the party representatives at the Mansion House all asked me to be Taoiseach. I think my resolve was shaken mainly by the appeals made to me by Tom O'Higgins at Mulcahy's house.'[55] On the Sunday, Costello took his dilemma with him onto the golf course, and, later, called on his old friend Arthur Cox for advice.[56] 'I valued his advice, and secretly hoped that he would advise me against. But he was logical. "You have been in politics for 30 years and you cannot refuse the top post. If you play with fire you must expect to get burned some time."'[57] Costello did get burned, but it was a financial burning, not a political one. The prospective loss of earnings was his real reason for hedging when the post of Taoiseach was first offered to him, not that he could say so publicly at that time.[58] Both Mulcahy and Costello are agreed that William Norton, the Labour leader, was the first person to put forward Costello's name as adviser and putative Taoiseach, while Patrick Lynch remained convinced that it had been MacBride who had come forward with the suggestion.[59] Neither Costello nor Mulcahy mentioned Clann na Poblachta in this context, and so it is not quite clear whether they wished to deprive Clann na Poblachta of the credit for a bout of successful muscle-flexing (unlikely – Mulcahy was not that subtle, and he detested those who were), or whether this was a joint Clann na Poblachta–Labour endeavour, with MacBride content to let Norton do the running (possible, but not really in keeping with MacBride's conduct as an 'energetic prowler' both in the Dáil and in the Cabinet).[60]

When Costello was appointed Taoiseach, he was handed a ready-made Cabinet. Unlike most prime ministers, he had absolutely no input whatsoever into the composition of the Cabinet, because this had already been thrashed out at the various meetings held in the Mansion House and in Leinster House. At these meetings the first problem had been to determine how many portfolios were to be given to each party, and that seemed to have been decided fairly quickly.[61] More time was taken on the thornier question of just which portfolios were to go to each party. If, as MacBride has said, 'There was an understanding that each party leader would select and be responsible for his own ministers',[62] Mulcahy's lack of authority becomes even more pronounced. Not only was he not going to become Taoiseach, but it is inconceivable that he chose the portfolios staffed by people such as O'Higgins and General Seán MacEoin. It is far more likely that they chose them themselves, while Mulcahy's opinions, of course, were sought on such matters. Credence is given to this by the sequence of scribbled-out names in McGilligan's rough notes on these discussions.[63]

Having settled the position of Taoiseach to their satisfaction, the chief problem remaining to the party leaders seemed to lie in finding a suitable portfolio for the leader of Fine Gael, Mulcahy himself. This process meant that Mulcahy's name originally appeared alongside the words, 'External Affairs', where it was crossed out and replaced by MacBride's name. Next, Mulcahy found himself pencilled in beside 'Finance' (and in McGilligan's account Finance lay beneath External Affairs). That must have been an extremely interesting discussion, for Mulcahy's name is crossed out not just once, but twice, before being replaced by McGilligan's own name. This was intriguing for two reasons. Not only was the unfortunate Mulcahy scratched out twice – indicating considerable thought on the topic – but, before these negotiations took place, MacBride would have been considered the more likely choice for Finance, given his predilection for economic debates and his reputation as an expert on economic matters. After all, it was the Clann which had campaigned on exotic economic policies, not Fine Gael. Furthermore, McGilligan's own prior reputation was as a tough constitutional lawyer, holding ferociously right-wing views on financial orthodoxy; it was he who, speaking as Minister for Industry and Commerce back in 1924, had made the extraordinary statement that 'There are certain limited funds at our disposal. People may have to die in this country and may have to die through starvation.'[64] Presumably this is why he, rather than MacBride, ended up as Minister for Finance, for it appeared that the unsettling effects of MacBride's heterodox economic heresies had extended far beyond the unease already registered by the hapless electorate, and even now lapped at the polished toe-caps of the mandarins in the Department of Finance. However, in a curious postscript regarding the discussion concerning the distribution of this particular portfolio, Patrick Lynch has written: 'But such was the influence of MacBride in the shaping of the new Government that he was able to have McGilligan appointed Minister for Finance rather than General Mulcahy who had been McGilligan's own choice for the post.'[65] The starched collars in Finance must have heaved a huge sigh of relief not to have been lumbered with MacBride and his strange notions, but they were to be in for a shock with the effects of the appointment of McGilligan. This was the beginning of Fine Gael's increasingly marked tendency to concentrate most of the available ministerial economic fire-power in their hands in coalition governments, a practice which would become even more pronounced in subsequent coalition governments.

A suitable post was eventually found for Mulcahy, who was slotted into Education, an area of interest to him given that he had devoted a lot of attention to educational matters, especially the position of the Irish language.[66] Justice was given to General Seán MacEoin, the defeated Fine Gael candidate in the 1945 presidential election. The Defence berth was assigned to Dr T. F. O'Higgins, ensuring that traditional law and order concerns remained in safe Fine Gael hands. Fine Gael also received Industry and Commerce, Mulcahy's confidant and friend, the 'hapless, blundering and inept'[67] Dan Morrissey, finding himself appointed minister. McGilligan's list left a blank space beside the Minister for Posts and Telegraphs (which had been provisionally earmarked for National Labour), while Local Government and Social Welfare were both first noted as being 'Labour'. This was amended when the Labour leader, William Norton, suggested himself for Social Welfare and nominated his colleague Tim Murphy for Local Government;[68] National Labour duly took Posts and Telegraphs in the form of party leader, James Everett. Agriculture seems to have been initially intended for Clann na Talmhan (for the name of party leader, Joseph Blowick, was crossed out), but it went instead to the chairman of the Independent TDs group, James Dillon.[69] Blowick was allocated a more congenial ministry, that of Lands and Forestry, where his tenure was less than distinguished.[70] This left Clann na Poblachta, whose numbers entitled them to two ministries. As already noted, External Affairs (rather than Finance) went to MacBride, and he in turn nominated the thirty-two-year-old Dr Noël Browne to the Health portfolio. Commenting on this years later, MacBride pointed out: 'I had no say in the choice of the Ministers other than in the Ministers of my own party.'[71] Given that MacBride enjoyed a considerable stature among the other party leaders at this time, on account of both his party's respectable performance and his own extraordinary reputation, and, in addition, given that the prevailing atmosphere at these talks was exceedingly flexible while yet underscored by a great determination to reach agreement, thus entailing close attention to and rapid recognition of any particular little problems that might exercise the minds of the party leaders (such as their unease with the idea of Mulcahy as Taoiseach) – given all these factors, MacBride's statement that he 'had no say' in the choice of ministers is not really credible.

However, MacBride does seem to have lost out on the distribution of junior ministries (or parliamentary secretaryships, as they were known then). McGilligan's scrawled notes indicate that none of the three posts on offer were originally destined for Fine Gael.[72] No portfolios are mentioned, but three names came up. These were Brendan Corish of the Labour Party, Oliver J. Flanagan, who served as secretary for the group of Independents, and Con Lehane from Clann na Poblachta. Between that hectic weekend and the time the new government were sworn in, changes must have been made which were broadly to the detriment of the smaller parties' – or, to be more explicit, Clann na Poblachta's – representation. By the time the appointments of the parliamentary secretaries were formally ratified in the Dáil, on 24 and 27 February, both Lehane and Flanagan had disappeared from the potential line-up, to be replaced by Liam Cosgrave of Fine Gael and Michael Donnellan from Clann na Talmhan. Corish alone remained of the original nominees for junior office.

A number of points need to be made about the whole saga. The first concerns the role of the Fine Gael party and their leader(s). Costello, the prospective Taoiseach, was not to enjoy the sort of political 'clout' conferred by party political strength, for he did not lead Fine Gael and his authority, such as it was, derived solely from his occupancy of the Taoiseach's chair. On the face of things, he appeared a strange enough choice, having been chosen primarily because he was acceptable to all of the other party leaders in a way that nobody else was. Moreover, there were questions which could be raised regarding his suitability for the post. Certainly, all of the other party leaders were united in recognising that Costello was to make an excellent 'chairman', to invoke the parlance first used by Farrell.

Temperamentally, though, 'the qualities as caused him to be selected as Taoiseach in 1948', according to Michael McInerney who interviewed him, were his 'rough charm, straight direct manner, without any of the charisma of a Pearse, a Griffith or a de Valera',[73] qualities which would not find themselves in great demand in the field of high diplomacy – or in the more subtle confines of the Dáil chamber and domestic politics, for that matter. A sympathetic observer who has also commented on Costello's character is Patrick Lynch, who wrote, 'As a man, the Taoiseach was kind and generous, qualities often masked by a manner, blunt and gruff',[74] adding that Costello's 'experience as a lawyer was not always an advantage' in government.[75] This was an opinion which would come to be fervently held by the British, as well. Writing to his government towards the end of 1950, the British ambassador, Sir Gilbert Laithwaite, caustically observed that Costello's 'leadership lacks distinction',[76] adding, pointedly, that 'his manner frequently suggests that as head of the Government, he is carrying with reluctance and without enthusiasm a burden for which he is not well qualified by temperament or experience'.[77]

However, it also appeared that the man who did lead them, Mulcahy, did not enjoy the authority conferred by leadership, either. He does not seem to have had much choice in deciding who served with him as part of the Fine Gael team, apart from probably insisting on Morrissey's inclusion, and, certainly, there was little indication of his 'leadership' status, as such, during the tenure of the inter-party government. Theoretically, this twin leadership – with Costello unsure of his authority as Taoiseach (especially as he was attempting to follow in the footsteps of the redoubtable de Valera) and Mulcahy unable to fully exercise his authority as party leader – should have left Fine Gael quite incapacitated politically, above all in the field of ideological theft, in which they were to prove themselves astonishingly adept. In theory, this vacuum of authority at the heart of the government should also have left them exposed. This sort of vacuum was a situation ready-made for someone capable of cleverly exploiting it, as MacBride appeared to be. But it is a testament to Fine Gael's stubborn resilience that they emerged from the inter-party government considerably stronger than when they had entered it. In fact, Fine Gael's highly refined, and much commented upon, appetite for political cannibalism only developed much later, during the course of the inter-party government, and then only in response to opportunities presented to them by the Clann's increasing vulnerability. Of course, the Fine Gael leadership 'never fully trusted MacBride'[78] and 'were simply waiting to crush him',[79] but this they could never have begun to even contemplate, let alone actually attempt, if he had kept a judicious eye on both his party machine and his ideological territory. This was to be his downfall, and their success, but that in no way suggests that Fine Gael entered government with the intention of devouring small parties. Entering government with an entire leadership cadre suffering from shock, and a disoriented pair of leaders unsure of their respective authorities, the very notion of a successful career in political cannibalism would have struck them as being wildly improbable.

The other points which need to be made concern the Clann. The first of these, the major one, concerns the decision to actually go into government, and support, prop up, and otherwise take part in the inter-party government, and the other concerns the selection of Noël Browne as their second ministerial nominee, in preference to anybody else. Ideological arguments about small parties and coalition governments date from this time and come in the familiar twin format. There is the argument put forward by the purists, such as Noël Browne, who has written: 'A succession of minority party leaders in the last forty years has failed to reconcile their membership of a coalition with their responsibilities to their own electorate.'[80] In other words, involvement in a coalition frequently swamps small parties, for it often involves decisions which come to be seen as unpalatable compromises, or 'insoluble contradictions' in Noël Browne's words,[81] above all with regard to their own policies, and this, in turn, means betrayal of their electorate and of the interests of that electorate. This is especially true in the case of small parties with a clearly defined ideological profile. Their policies are subject to adjustment, or amendment, if not outright compromise in a coalition arrangement. This argument contends that the sole purpose of the small parties is to keep the larger parties in power, and that, at Cabinet, voting will often degenerate into straightforward divisions along party lines, where the will of the majority (i.e. the larger parties) will prevail.[82] In fact, consistent – and mutual – compromise is a perennial feature of coalition government, and it is a basic requirement for political survival. Large parties do not usually survive long in such governments if they insist on pushing their own perspectives, policies, or viewpoints through at all times, irrespective of the cost to the government, or the cost to the prestige or self-image of the smaller parties. It is simply not clever politics to insist upon having your own way all of the time. The argument presented by the purists seems to rest on the idea that the very concept of compromise is obnoxious, and a betrayal of one's own interests. They also have a stronger argument, which is the fact that such compromises as do occur are not always evenly spread. Both large and small parties compromise in coalition governments – they have to – but the ratio of compromise is quite often different for the various parties. Smaller parties are required to compromise that bit more. Therefore, the resultant *modus operandi* for small parties often hinges not simply on just compromise, for coalitions by their nature are compromises, but on which issues are appropriate for compromise and which are to be prioritised.

The main argument justifying small parties entering coalitions is based on pragmatism. Parties which receive small electoral mandates cannot expect to be in a position to implement all of their proposals, and, therefore, seeking to implement some of their proposals is often the best that they can hope for. Other options, such as supporting minority governments from outside the 'council chamber' (i.e. Cabinet meeting room), tend to lead to a double drawback in that parties declining to participate in government suffer the negative consequences of government participation – in terms of lost votes from an irate electorate – without any of the compensating advantages of the fruits of office, which can range from ministerial motor cars to the successful implementation of long-sought-after policy objectives. While Ó hEithir has argued that 'if Seán MacBride had played his cards differently after the election, by using his party outside the coalition, Clann na Poblachta could have survived and the course of Irish politics changed dramatically',[83] a diametrically opposed view was taken by the Clann leader himself.

Justifying his decision to enter government, MacBride explained: 'We had campaigned throughout 1948 on a slogan which consisted of three words 'Put Them Out'. That's what we campaigned on. We certainly couldn't Put Them In.'[84] He pointed out that 'the mandate we got was not a mandate for government' and that this left the Clann with a difficult choice. 'Who were we going to vote for? Vote for the government we had campaigned to put out? Or vote for a Fine Gael government which we didn't agree with either? The only realistic alternative was to try and work with a government which would at least go part of our way.'[85] Wasn't that a compromise? 'Yes, to a certain extent. We would have been compromising much more if we had voted for Mr de Valera. I think in politics you have to compromise all of the time, and particularly in that situation. Undoubtedly, if we had gotten a mandate and come back to office with eighty seats, then we probably shouldn't have compromised. We got ten seats. This was the least of the compromises.'[86]

'The least of the compromises' was ratified by Clann na Poblachta's national executive. Some of the members objected to going into government with that 'bloody murderer',[87] General Mulcahy, but MacBride impressed upon them the need to steer away from civil war politics, break old moulds, and set off in new directions – and, in the process, implement a fair number of the Clann's policies. This latter context was the one he used to justify the nomination of Dr Noël Browne as Minister for Health. Browne's background was no less singular than MacBride's own, and considerably more traumatic and poverty-stricken. While still a young child, the dreadful disease tuberculosis had killed both his parents, and, later on, led to the death of his brother and one of his sisters. Another sister succeeded in securing an education for him at an English prep school, where she worked, and then managed to facilitate his transfer to Beaumont College, a Jesuit public school. After her death (also from TB), the benevolence of a wealthy Dublin family had enabled him to attend Trinity College Dublin (where he himself contracted TB) and qualify as a doctor. Upon qualification, he specialised in TB, and made the eradication of the disease the prime business and motivation of his life.[88] By 1947, Browne held the post of assistant medical superintendent in Newcastle Sanatorium in County Wicklow,[89] and it was there that he met Noel Hartnett, who used to visit a friend of his, a patient at the sanatorium named Harry Kennedy, who was employed as a journalist with *The Irish Times*. Hartnett was at that time helping MacBride in the framing of various policies for the new party, and he was impressed by the passion and enthusiasm of the young TB specialist. Already quite well known in the sort of circles where TB was an issue – Browne had co-founded the Irish Tuberculosis Society,[90] and many of his more fervent supporters were former TB patients – Noël Browne was recruited by Clann na Poblachta and given a free hand to draw up the party's policies on TB and related matters. In fact, the mortality rate from TB was horrifyingly high, while the resources devoted to combating the disease were embarrassingly, and disgracefully, low. Browne was an able and attractive candidate (for example, Brian Inglis, who wrote the 1948 election diary for *The Irish Times*, regarded Noël Browne as 'the most impressive' of the Clann's candidates),[91] representative of the 'new' generation who had no background in any aspect of the 'national' struggle(s), and his speeches focused attention on the sort of social matters parties looking to the future rather than dwelling in the past preferred to discuss. Actually, Browne had been explicitly instructed to confine himself in his speeches to his medical brief after he had burst out at one meeting 'The country is sick of 1916!' in response to a particularly irritating Fianna Fáil heckle of 'Where were you in 1916?'[92]

After the election, Browne found himself returned as one of the ten Clann na Poblachta TDs, and, two weeks later, he was appointed Minister for Health, on MacBride's recommendation. Considerable surprise was expressed that this position did not go to one of MacBride's close associates (such as Con Lehane), but, in fact, MacBride had a number of reasons for appointing Browne, whose proposed elevation initially did not go down at all that well with the republican comrades in the Clann's national executive. 'I had tremendous difficulties in getting Noël Browne accepted [as minister] in the party, because of his background and because he had never been involved in anything before, and he wasn't trusted by everybody in the party.'[93]

Having fought an election on the need to forget the Civil War and all it entailed, MacBride preferred to opt for someone without an IRA background as his Cabinet colleague. Therefore, to appoint as Minister for Health a representative of a generation which had nothing whatsoever to do with civil war politics, on a platform – progressive social change – which was equally innocent of reference to civil war matters, would amply demonstrate his commitment to such change. 'I had campaigned very strongly on the basis that people should be appointed in government irrespective of their past political affiliations, and that had a progressive political viewpoint, and were capable of trying to change conditions in the country.'[94] For the same reason, he declined to appoint any of his old republican comrades as his ministerial colleague, pointing out that 'people would say that the Clann was just another "IRA party"', rather than a party espousing social change.[95] Moreover, as he further explained, quite a number of the Clann's new deputies were dark horses, so to speak, and, apart from one or two such as Lehane, MacBride didn't really know them that well. In a rather telling remark, he commented: 'There was nobody that I knew, or trusted, that had any experience of government. Therefore, I had no idea of how they would behave in government, particularly people who've never been in government before.'[96] In any case, the Clann had to be seen to implement some of their policies, so why not TB? MacBride no doubt considered himself more than capable in looking after the more traditional concerns of the Clann's republican supporters, and, with the appointment of Browne, the 'social' side would now be taken care of.

The decision to go into government was not without cost for the Clann. From the very beginning, they were shedding members on such matters of principle. Among those who left the party on this issue was Seán South, who would reappear, several years later, in a rather different guise when he took part in the 'Border campaign' of the mid-1950s.

A much greater loss to the Clann was Captain Peadar Cowan, for whom a parting of the ways was also in order. Cowan had been elected to the Dáil as one of the Clann's TDs, and, almost immediately, seems to have fallen out with MacBride. Their disagreements centred on the decision to enter government, which Cowan contested, the appointment of Noël Browne to Health – ironically, in the light of his own, later, fervent support for Browne, Cowan thought that he was too young and inexperienced to be appointed a minister – and finally the decision to seek Marshall Aid as part of the European Recovery Programme, which Cowan believed would turn the country into 'a nation of beggars and mendicants'.[97] According to Cowan's account, he and MacBride met for lunch at Bailey's to discuss the formation of the government. A curiously recurring motif of MacBride's tenure in office would take the form of these meals, invariably consumed in salubrious surroundings, with political crisis providing an unusual counterpoint to the proceedings. MacBride's decision to accept the 'moribund' Department of External Affairs astonished Cowan. Justifying his choice, MacBride explained that such a department would leave him with more time to build up the Clann, while Cowan wrote that he later learned that MacBride had employed a rather different technique in obtaining the department: '[He] was running around saying how unfit he was for anything big . . . saying that if they gave him External Affairs he would be content with that.'[98] As Cowan recalled, MacBride was tired and tense, and he 'appeared to have been burning the candle at both ends' for 'his submissions smelled of the midnight oil'.[99] Clann na Poblachta's national executive were due to meet a few days later to ratify the decision to go into government, and MacBride wished to secure Cowan's agreement in advance. Cowan disagreed with MacBride's position, and voted against entry into the coalition the following Saturday at the national executive meeting. A true iconoclast, Cowan idiosyncratically objected to membership of the government on the grounds that membership would serve to muzzle Clann members from criticising or questioning the government.[100] However, it was not until July 1948, when Cowan had actually voted in the Dáil against accepting Marshall Aid[101] – which was one of MacBride's cherished projects – that he was, perhaps inevitably, expelled from Clann na Poblachta. In his defence, Cowan pointed out that the Dáil vote on Marshall Aid had been a free vote, and he therefore queried the moral justification for his expulsion from Clann na Poblachta.[102] With that, what had commenced as a policy disagreement turned into a form of mutual personal detestation, as he and MacBride were to spend a considerable amount of time over the next few years exchanging a substantial volume of personal abuse in the Dáil.

Ministerial office had granted MacBride access to the secret police files which had been kept on himself and his colleagues, and, if he ever had occasion to peruse any of the files on Cowan, doubtless they would have drawn a nod of rueful recognition. The police file regarded Cowan as having 'plenty of initiative and drive' and noted that he 'is personally an able fellow', adding presciently, 'However, he is rather pugnacious and truculent in his manner, and this may prove a set-back in his political career.'[103]

In fact, Cowan had earlier been targeted by MacEntee during the by-election campaigns in October 1947 and the general election campaign of 1948 as meriting special attention. This attention had taken the form of letters to the papers alluding to Cowan's curious political past (especially his dalliances with fringe activities such as The Vanguard) and a determined trawl through Cowan's Army record in the hope of a fruitful yield.[104] Actually, there was a serious political agenda to all of this muck-raking, for MacEntee had shrewdly divined where one of the Clann's ideological fault lines lay, and he was resolved to exert pressure at that point. For, as he wrote to Tommy Mullins, 'if the material [on Cowan] were used properly it would probably do one of two things, either split Clann na Poblachta by driving Cowan and his followers out of it or else kill Clann na Poblachta in the rural areas'.[105] What MacEntee couldn't possibly have foreseen, though, was that Clann na Poblachta would prove to be more than perfectly capable of splitting itself, without any outside assistance whatsoever. At the time, however, Cowan's prodigal response to MacEntee's taunts and accusations took the form of a hostage to fortune. Writing in the *Irish Press* on 17 January 1948, Cowan's expressions of affection for MacBride were couched in extravagant terms: 'I am sure that Mr MacBride will be as surprised as I was to read Mr MacEntee's statement that Mr MacBride and I had quarrelled, and that Mr MacBride was trying to force me out of Clann na Poblachta. The statement is, to my knowledge, false, malicious, unscrupulous, and reckless. Seán MacBride and I are personal friends and loyal colleagues and as joint founders and executive members of Clann na Poblachta we are working loyally together to attain the aims and objects of Clann na Poblachta.'[106]

MacBride's reasons for seeking to sever his links with Cowan were more complex. At the national executive meeting when he was expelled, the official charge seems to have been a variation on the good old 'Red' smear theme,[107] which appears to have been a convenient excuse. True, Cowan's personality was 'truculent' and his political career was bizarre and characterised by wanderlust. However, he was an able administrator, and had proven himself capable during his tenure as the Clann's director of finance. Moreover, he had the sort of political experience that most of MacBride's colleagues lacked, the sort of experience that MacBride possibly felt was no longer necessary as the Clann were now in government. For, if Cowan was unable to remain for any length of time in any political organisation (as his previous and subsequent careers amply demonstrated), then MacBride, too, experienced difficulty in relating politically to his colleagues, for he appeared to be congenitally incapable of coping with anybody who disagreed with him except by resort to expulsion or exclusion. The fight with Cowan could easily be explained away as a personality clash, for both men were strong-willed, but MacBride would also fall out with his director of elections,

Noel Hartnett, his only ministerial colleague, Noël Browne, and his own departmental secretary in External Affairs, Frederick Boland,[108] before his term of office would be complete. This is a fairly comprehensive list of personality clashes, and begs questions about the way in which MacBride coped (or, as the case may have been, didn't cope) with conflict or disagreement. As Browne correctly points out, the result of MacBride's inability to keep those with whom he disagreed on board meant that he was, in effect, driven back into the arms of the old republican comrades for support, and this, in turn, was to leave him fatally vulnerable when it came to future elections.[109] Moreover, MacBride's further inability to keep (or even to wish to keep) the various strands of the party together and heading in the same direction ensured that Clann na Poblachta never transcended its early image as a party of protest, and that it never grew past the 'Put Them Out' way of thinking to develop into a credible party of government.

6

'Ireland still remains the
sacra insula[1]

The inter-party government took office on 18 February 1948, and from its very inception demonstrated a capacity to contest ownership of the symbols of national identity with Fianna Fáil, who now languished in opposition. Significantly, almost the very first act undertaken by the inter-party government was their decision to send a telegram to the Vatican desiring 'to repose at the feet of Your Holiness the assurance of our filial loyalty and of our devotion to your August Person, as well as our firm resolve to be guided in all our work by the teaching of Christ, and to strive for the attainment of a social order in Ireland based on Christian principles'.[2] As Keogh points out, 'No Irish Government can afford to be suspected of anti-clericalism or anything less than ardent Catholicism. Accordingly, when de Valera was replaced by a coalition somewhat more liberal in complexion, it had been necessary, for political reasons, to demonstrate its devotion to the Holy See.'[3] In an interview with John Bowman, conducted a good many years later, MacBride saw nothing wrong with having sent this telegram, and a spirited argument ensued.[4] MacBride, in fact, attempted to draw a parallel between the papal visit to Ireland in September 1979 and Costello's telegram on behalf of the Irish government in 1948. 'Do you see anything wrong with the Pope coming to Ireland?', he angrily asked John Bowman in a reversal of the more usual roles of interviewer and interviewee. Bowman responded by pointing out that the Irish hierarchy had invited the Pope to Ireland, not the Irish government, a difference MacBride (tellingly) professed not to see.[5] Although the Cabinet may have felt an overwhelming need to demonstrate their collective filial loyalty to the Holy See, a dissenting note was sounded by the Cabinet secretary, Maurice Moynihan, who resolutely disagreed with the idea of the Irish Government reposing at the feet of any other authority, for he felt strongly that 'no civil power should declare that it reposed at the feet of the pope', but his objections were overruled.[6]

Almost the next action undertaken by the Cabinet was the decision to exclude Moynihan from Cabinet meetings. Each of these actions illustrated an important facet of inter-party Cabinet behaviour, the first indicating how eager they were for a slice of the action in vigorously contesting for the ownership of the symbols of national identity, the other illuminating their blundering approach to Cabinet administration and, in addition, throwing a useful light on MacBride's mingled paranoia and influence. Patrick Lynch profoundly regretted the exclusion of Moynihan, describing him as 'a very wise man with a keen sense of political niceties.'[7]

The exclusion of Moynihan will be treated in greater detail in the next chapter, as it had profound implications for the manner in which the inter-party government actually functioned, or, more to the point in certain situations, failed to function. However, before turning to the internal workings of the inter-party government, and the dramatic life and spectacular death of Clann na Poblachta, it is first necessary to take a look at the pervasive influence of the Catholic Church on Irish culture and society, for without an understanding of the position of the Catholic Church in Irish society, and the role it sought to play within that society, what happened in 1951 seems inexplicable.

That the Catholic Church was powerful was already quite well known. That it was also an exceedingly enthusiastic political actor with a preference for an actively engaged approach where possible was widely suspected in some liberal quarters. Such unworthy suspicions lurking in liberal breasts notwithstanding, until the debacle of the Mother and Child Scheme exploded into the public arena in April 1951, the verdict on the degree and extent of ecclesiastical prompting of government policy could only have been 'not proven'. For, of course, the inter-party government is best remembered for what became known as the 'Noël Browne Mother and Child Scheme', where the excessive enthusiasm of ecclesiastical interventions resulted in such interventions becoming public knowledge for the first time. The actual details of the Mother and Child Scheme debacle will be dealt with in greater detail in chapter 8; for the moment, what is of significance is the context, or, to put it another way, the political and social culture, within which both Church and state operated in those years. This means having to take a look at how and why this context, or political culture, had developed in this way, and it is to that which we now turn.

With that, we can return to the implications of Costello's telegram of filial loyalty to the Holy See. That Costello should deem it necessary to demonstrate his Irishness, in addition to his Catholicism, with such an extravagant display of 'filial loyalty' illustrates all too clearly the importance of Catholicism as a defining icon, or symbol, of Irish national identity at that time. For, of course, by the 1940s, Ireland had become one of the most self-consciously Catholic countries in the world, and had articulated a comprehensive Catholic vision of itself which was expressed in the everyday culture, the everyday life, and the everyday law of the country. These enduring links between Catholicism and the emerging Irish national identity had been forged and tempered in the trying conditions of the nineteenth century. In practice, this meant that it was not only Irish political and social culture, but the essential nature of Irish politics itself, which was to be hugely influenced by the convergence of Catholicism, democracy, nationalism, and liberalism, a heady mix Garvin aptly dubs 'O'Connellism'.[8] Indeed, for the newly emerging Irish elites it could be said that 'Their most unin-hibited political loyalty was to a Catholic democratic idea, one that was theoretically pluralist and invented by Daniel O'Connell rather than Theobald Wolfe Tone or Patrick Pearse.'[9]

Democratic values had not always co-existed easily with Catholicism. For that matter, not only had Catholicism, historically, been adverse to democ-ratic values, but it is worth noting in this context that Ireland was one of the few functioning Catholic democracies in the *world* by the late 1930s. Indeed, internationally, democracy and Catholicism were almost mutually exclusive until after the Second World War, for, as Garvin remarks, 'Certainly, the international Catholic Church was deeply ambiguous about the coming of democracy elsewhere in Europe and was commonly to flirt with various fascist and other right-wing authoritarianisms in the inter-war years.'[10] This is an important point, for Catholicism and democracy – especially the sort of democracy which arrived on the coat-tails of a successful revolution – were not always the happiest of bed-fellows, and indeed it is instructive to contrast the situation in Ireland with the position which had existed in Italy, where, with the victory of Garibaldi's forces, the Vatican had 'effectively outlawed' democracy, which meant that the emergent Italian democracy was, essen-tially, run by anti-Catholics, a state of affairs nicely described by Garvin as 'one of the greatest ecclesiastical own-goals of all time'.[11] Actually, histori-cally, the political preference of the Catholic Church 'had commonly gravitated to the support of authoritarian and fascist regimes. International Catholicism did not abandon its liking for authoritarian political systems until after the Second World War.'[12] This tacit, and sometimes blatant, support for authoritarian and fascist regimes had deep ideological roots, roots predicated upon the notion of a hierarchical and structured society. In other words, in an organisation which saw bishops as superior to priests, and priests as infinitely superior to the easily led-astray laity, with the Pope presiding over the lot and invoking Scripture to do so, doctrines preaching the essential democratic equality of the masses were going to fall on barren ground. Garvin made this very point when he wrote: 'A common self-image of the priest was that of the Good Shepherd; naturally, this imputed some-thing of the character of sheep to lesser human beings. A religion that structured human society in such a way was bound to be less reverential towards doctrines of popular sovereignty.'[13] This point needs to be stressed, for while the ardently Catholic complexion of Irish politics and society has been much commented upon – as it will be also in this chapter – the fact that Ireland combined ostentatious public piety and a functioning democracy was to be an almost unique achievement in the political life of Catholic states up to the Second World War. Of critical importance, therefore, in influencing the direction and form of Irish democracy was 'the fact that the Catholic Church, despite some deep intellectual reservations, came down on the side of Irish electoral democracy', and this was to be 'crucial to the development of a voter-driven and open polity in Ireland'.[14]

However, while this tells us that the Irish Catholic Church facilitated, or, at the very least, certainly did nothing to obstruct the development of democratic forms and institutions in Ireland in the 1920s, possibly because, unlike both the IRA and their erstwhile fellow Catholic hierarchies abroad, they felt that the people could be trusted to 'do the right thing', it does not fully explain the peculiarly Catholic evolutionary path taken by the political and social culture in the new Irish state. Therefore, addressing this means first having to take a look at why Ireland became so Catholic, before attempting to describe the way, or manner, in which this Catholicism was expressed in the everyday life and law of the state. Most commentators are agreed that a key feature in explaining why Ireland became so Catholic, and managed to maintain this incredible degree of devotion to the institutional Church, was the church's control of education, for, as Whyte put it, in Ireland the Catholic Church came to enjoy 'a grip on education of unique strength',[15] leading, in Ó hEithir's view, to an educational system which 'seemed to train people to be physically fearless and morally cowardly'.[16] The importance of this lies in the fact that almost from the inception, or the introduction of the national school system, the state funded the national schools, while the Catholic Church ran and largely staffed them. This, in turn, has created a situation where, as Tom Inglis has written, 'Religious tradition is not simply a set of beliefs and values which are held within the mind and passed on from generation to generation. It involves a physical and moral control which has been mainly exercised over the Irish people by priests, nuns and brothers.'[17] Secondary education was also to be not just denominational, but run by the clergy, and, uniquely, independent Ireland was also to boast denominational third-level education, when an ecclesiastical ban on Trinity College, strictly enforced by the archbishop of Dublin, ensured that young Irish Catholics were obliged to seek their higher education in the – presumably Catholic – colleges of the National University of Ireland.[18]

Apart from coming to control education, another reason adduced for the increasingly influential position enjoyed by the Catholic Church was that this increased influence and the growth in institutional adherence in Ireland (in other words, practising one's religion by attending Church services regularly) were part of a 'modern civilising process that had been spreading throughout Europe since the sixteenth century'.[19]

An even stronger argument is that the growth in religious practice, sometimes referred to as the 'Devotional Revolution', had its roots in a reaction to becoming Anglicised, or, put another way, that this increased religiosity was a response to the loss of language and cultural identity which had attended all of the social upheavals – such as the decimation of the population wrought by the catastrophe of the Great Famine of the 1840s – that had taken place in the nineteenth century. Indeed, it is difficult to overemphasise the catastrophic effects of the Famine, effects which were still being felt decades later and which had led to a complete transformation in attitudes to both agriculture and religion in Irish society. Agriculture was utterly altered with the abrupt discontinuation of old patterns of inheritance, such as subdivision of farms, in favour of handing the entire farm over to one designated son. In turn, this led to a radical transformation of the patterns of family organisation, with 'stem-family' practices prevailing, and, with that, all of those other extraordinary traits which came to be associated with Irish family life in social science literature in the twentieth century, such as an obsession with property, repressed sexuality, late marriage, high fertility, enormous rates of emigration (especially female) for those who could not marry, and high rates of permanent celibacy for up to 30 per cent of the population, a great many of whom joined religious institutions and orders.[20]

In fact, the Catholic Church was the single institution which enjoyed the greatest growth, and the most rapid expansion in the country in the century after the famine. As Lee points out 'the number of priests sextupled, and the number of nuns rose even faster'.[21] The rural cliché that the three most useful things an Irish farmer could possess were 'a bull in the field, a pump in the yard, and a priest in the house' contained more than a germ of truth. The growth in vocations was not confined to the domestic Irish Church, but also included an enormous increase in the numbers flocking to join missionary orders as well, in the process attracting 'some of the finest performer talent in the country'.[22] For over a century, the Irish Catholic Church attracted some of the best minds in the country to its ranks, and these people would, in turn, supply leadership, administrative skills, and organisational abilities in their roles as priests, nuns, sisters, brothers, nurses and teachers both in Ireland and abroad. However, one of the striking features of Irish Catholicism was its complete inability to come up with creative, innovatory, or original ideas, in other words, its utter lack of intellectual dynamism. Instead, it played a great defensive game, and was at its best in defence of itself, its ideas and its institutions. Whether or not this can be laid at the door of an authoritarian, anti-intellectual society (faithfully fostered, and indeed, mirrored by the very institutions of the church itself) is still very much a matter for debate, but, in this context, it is of interest to note that in over a century of drawing some of the best minds in the country to itself, the Irish Catholic Church has still to produce a theologian of international stature.

One of the major new roles of the Catholic Church in this altered society was to supply a theological justification, or moral framework, for these changed circumstances; in Whyte's words, 'the role of religion has been to reconcile the Irish peasantry to this fate'.[23] This theme has been developed extensively by Tom Inglis, when he commented, correctly, 'Because the Catholic Church was the means behind this new system of moral discipline and social control, Irish Catholics became socialised into an ideology of spirituality, frugality and celibacy',[24] a state of mind which was perhaps best illustrated by de Valera's notorious frugal comfort speech. On St Patrick's Day, 1943, de Valera took to the airwaves of the national radio station, Radio Éireann, and proceeded to articulate his vision of an ideal Ireland with the sort of bravura performance that could only be classed as a deathless definition of Arcadian bliss '. . . let us turn aside for a moment to that ideal Ireland that we would have. That Ireland which we dreamed of would be the home of a people who valued material wealth only as the basis for right living, of a people who were satisfied with frugal comfort and devoted their leisure to things of the spirit – a land whose countryside would be bright with cosy homesteads, whose fields and villages would be joyous with the sounds of industry, with the romping of sturdy children, the contests of athletic youths and the laughter of comely maidens, whose forums would be forums for the wisdom of serene old age. It would, in a word be the home of a people living the life that God desires that man should live.'[25]

Pressing his case, Inglis has further argued that this Catholic ideology was maintained 'through practices which centred on individuals surrendering to the interests of Church, family and community, and through an uncritical commitment to traditional rules and regulations'.[26] Indeed, Inglis goes on to argue, fairly convincingly, that a conservative religious outlook, conservative religious practices, and conservative agricultural practices went together, hand in glove, when he wrote that 'It was partially for these reasons that Ireland did not develop a mature system of capitalist agricultural production and modernise fully until the second half of the nineteenth century',[27] also making the important observation that 'the growth of piety was paralleled by a growing consumer consciousness, rising material expectations, and a ruthless commitment to land possession, almost irrespective of the human costs involved'.[28] Indeed, this ruthless commitment to land possession, this obsession with property ownership – the staunchly defended sanctity of property – was to have extraordinary long-term repercussions in Ireland. In fact, in independent Ireland, property was to receive greater protection in law than did people, while crimes against property evoked greater outrage (and greater sentences) than did crimes against the person. The cliché of the farmer stuffing his money into the straw mattress for safe-keeping rather than investing it in financial institutions found an answering echo in the unimaginative investment policies pursued by the financial institutions themselves. Capital, for example, tended to be sunk in housing or property, and not in creative or productive enterprise. This led to a situation where the health of the economy was measured not in terms of exports, but in terms of the state of health of the construction industry – in other words, in how many new houses were built in a given year – while the very tax system was constructed around the idea of property acquisition, leading to a situation where, by 1995, Ireland boasted the highest rate of private home ownership in the *world*.[29]

For, of course, there were extensive links between post-Famine agricultural society and the newly prominent clergy. These links were shared backgrounds, attitudes and outlooks which gave rise to a shared authority or hegemony. The social classes which might have contested this position were mostly dead or had emigrated, for the Famine had virtually wiped out the poorest social classes. The sort of values cherished by the clergy found a resounding echo in the materialistic perspectives tenaciously held by the new inheritors of the earth, those horny-handed sons (rarely daughters) of the Soil, who made up the new small-farmer and shop-keeper class. Very often, the social composition of both the clergy and the new property owners came from the same sources, leading to a well-based suspicion in some quarters that the clergy were basically 'strong farmers in cassocks'.[30] In other words, those recruited by the religious orders came largely from the social classes which had benefited most from the massive social changes sweeping through late nineteenth-century Irish society, and the materialistic values they preached were the values instinctively shared by the class from which they had come.

In an interesting and complex analysis, Inglis has argued that this linkage between agricultural society and the Church took the form of an alliance of power. 'For just as the Church was reconstituted as a power bloc in and through the new tenant farmers, these farmers were constituted as the dominant economic class in modern Irish society in and through the Church. The Church offered these farmers the means of becoming civil and moral.'[31] The advantages of the acquisition of such moral authority were twofold – it awarded these farmers the same social status and the same economic power as the displaced Protestant gentry: 'Through an adherence to the Church's new moral discipline, these farmers could not only attain the same social prestige as the Protestant gentry who had dominated their lives but also, hopefully, the same economic class. Through the Church they were to become more Puritan than the Protestants themselves.'[32] However, the creation of a new class of resolute and tenacious landowners does not usually lead to economic or social dynamism: 'it was because these farmers became a power bloc in and through the Church, that once they had consolidated their holdings and the struggle for ownership of the land had ended, they became a highly conservative force. They were limited by the rules and regulations which had made them civil and moral. It was this limitation which inhibited the economic individualism central to the development of a fully mature capitalist agricultural mode of production.'[33] However, these rules for making a people 'civil and moral', this rhetoric of morality, tended to emphasise some forms of morality, to the almost total exclusion of all the others. In Ireland, this would find vivid expression in an official obsession with sexual morality, with less emphasis being placed on 'the observance of less relevant commandments than the sixth'.[34] This obsession with control of sexual morality, especially female sexual morality, has been viewed in terms of the creation of another power alliance: 'It was primarily through the dependence of mothers on the Church for moral power within the home . . . that the Church maintained control of women and sex and was able to develop a rigid adherence to its rules and regulations.'[35]

Simultaneous with these all-encompassing social changes was the fact that the Catholic Church itself underwent a determined restructuring in the latter part of the nineteenth century, becoming more organised, more centralised, more 'Roman', and more 'muscular' in its mission as it attempted to address, and if possible counterattack, the sort of challenges – such as the evil twin blandishments of liberalism and socialism – a changing world brought in its wake. As part of this process, the Irish Church was modernised and thoroughly overhauled in a sweeping series of changes spearheaded by Cardinal Paul Cullen, making it more subject to central control – in other words, the control of the Roman Curia – in terms of both doctrine and administration, and, as a result, more able to take positive and proper advantage of any opportunities which might arise to exert itself in the lush fields of moral policing or the promising pastures of political activity. However, possibly the most important aspect of all was how Catholicism came to be seen as an integral part of the Irish national identity. Catholicism and the concept of being Irish fused towards the end of the century, as various concepts of Irishness were being explored as part of the 'national revival' movement. Taken together, the Church's control of education, its strategic links with certain dominant social classes, its ability to set – and implement – the righteous and reverent rhetoric of the new state (in other words, the moral agenda), as well as its genetic identification with the sense of national identity of the new state – all of these combined to ensure that by the 1920s the Catholic Church enjoyed both moral authority and political power in the newly independent Ireland. This authority and power, it must be remembered, were not contested with any vigorous degree of dissent in the new state – indeed, they met mostly with approbation and approval – and the one province which most certainly would have entered a vigorous note of protest had itself been partitioned off to partake of a stagnant and sterile independence when it was constituted as the state of Northern Ireland.

Initially, the growing influence of the Church found physical expression in a construction boom,[36] culminating in the building of vast numbers of churches, which, significantly and symbolically, usually occupied prominent positions wherever they were built. However, while the number of churches built continued to rise in the early years of the Free State, the Catholic complexion of the new state was increasingly expressed in terms of the laws passed which conformed to Church teaching. In fairness, the institutional façade presented by the Irish Free State to the watching world owed far more to British ancestry than to any other paternity, with some significant exceptions. These exceptions were to be found in the areas of health, education, social matters, the primacy of private property, and anything to do with the exalted notion of the 'family', and from the early years of the Free State legislation setting forth Catholic principles in these areas found its way onto the statute books, as the Catholic contours of the state were sculpted onto the sort of tablets of stone which carry the force of law. Divorce, which, since the time of Henry VIII, had been possible with the passage of a private member's bill, was prohibited by statute in 1925, a prohibition which was robustly reinforced when de Valera's 1937 constitution was enacted, for it contained a constitutional ban which could only be removed by referendum. Laws were passed which outlawed the advertising, sale, importation, and use of contraception. Further laws were passed – with the active support not just of Catholic ideologues, but of large sections of the trade union movement as well – which obliged women to resign their positions of employment upon marriage. In 1944, the topic which exercised the collective minds of the Irish hierarchy at their Easter meeting was the availability and use of the new sanitary tampons, Tampax, a product which, it was felt, 'could harmfully stimulate young girls at an impressionable age'[37] and about which the hierarchy harboured grave misgivings. Thus, they respectfully requested the relevant minister, Dr Conor Ward, who was parliamentary secretary to the Minister for Local Government and Public Health, to consider taking steps to prohibit their sale. Ward readily complied, for he shared the grave misgivings of the hierarchy, and tampons were duly outlawed.

De Valera's constitution of 1937, designed as a more authentic representation of Irish national needs (he saw the earlier 1922 constitution as representing an imposed order), contained republican rhetoric in spades. It also contained a number of articles which owed their inspiration to Catholic social teaching, namely Articles 41 to 44, which dealt with the position of women, the prohibition of divorce, and the 'special position' accorded to the Catholic Church. The 'special position' accorded to the Catholic Church was hammered out in consultation with a number of Church notables, such as the future archbishop of Dublin, John Charles McQuaid, who at that time was president of Blackrock College and sometime adviser and friend to de Valera and his family.[38] Later, Rome was also consulted in order to outmanoeuvre the more enthusiastic of the native clergy, who were pushing hard for the Catholic Church to be acknowledged as the One, True, and, preferably, Established Church. De Valera was having none of that, and packed Joseph Walshe, ex-seminarian and secretary of the Department of External Affairs, off to Rome with a version of the controversial Article 44 for the Vatican to peruse.[39]

For the outside world, though, the notorious, and ultimately farcical, laws on censorship were what most defined the Catholic cultural contours of the Irish state.[40] Almost every writer worth his or her salt was banned. The roll-call of banned writers is astonishingly long, the international list taking in Steinbeck, Freud, Salinger, Proust, Orwell, Greene, Capote, Durrell, Hemingway, and Sartre among countless others; banned Irish writers – and this is by no means an exhaustive list – included Frank O'Connor, Brendan Behan, Seán O'Faolain, Austin Clarke, George Bernard Shaw, Kate O'Brien, John McGahern, James Joyce, Samuel Beckett, and Edna O'Brien. By the early 1950s, it was calculated that the Censorship Board was ardently banning an average of two books a day.[41] Probably the most ludicrous manifestation of the literary *cordon sanitaire* girdled about the country occurred in the Upper House, the Senate, in 1943, when one intrepid senator, Sir John Keane, attempted to question the banning of *The Tailor and Ansty* by reading some of the offending passages from the book into the record of the Senate. Appalled that this record would be available to the general public 'for a few pence', the Senate voted to censor its own record, instead.[42] In an interesting explanation, Lee has argued that the psychological function of this extensive censorship was to provide moral reassurance by presenting the illusion that Ireland was 'a haven of virtue surrounded by a sea of vice', adding that censorship 'helped rivet the remunerative impression that immorality stopped with sex'.[43] It can be argued that states that feel the need to practise censorship have a delicate sense of self which needs sturdy protection from the chill winds of anything – such as the truth – which might threaten this fragile self-image. It might also be argued, as it is by Lee, that in such states a classic means of reconciling image with reality is to reduce the range, or sphere, of 'real morality' to those teachings which 'happen to conveniently coincide with the objective material requirements of the dominant groups in society'.[44] In any case, the dynamic of state censorship is the same wherever it is practised, while the precise form it takes may differ from country to country. Other countries have also experienced censorship, and the contrast with the form of censorship later practised in the 'socialist republics' of Eastern Europe is instructive; there, the censors more usually focused on political subversion, whereas in Ireland, official attention was more usually reserved for matters sexual.

It is a moot point as to whether the main impulse behind these laws (and attitudes) came from the Church or from some of its more enthusiastic lay followers, for while Lee has commented that 'the Church did not invent these values. But it did baptise them',[45] Ó hEithir has drawn attention to how some bishops 'bleated loudly'[46] when the Censorship Act was slightly modified. In any case, censorship could prove to be a double-edged sword, as some bishops found out during the 'Emergency' when their Lenten pastoral letters were censored by government order. Not only that, but a statement from the Vatican newspaper, *Osservatore Romano*, refuting rumours that the Pope favoured Mussolini and Hitler was also censored, on the grounds the rumours to which it referred had not been published in Ireland.[47] When the security needs of the government came into conflict with the pastoral needs of the hierarchy, only one outcome would exist, even in Ireland, and that is why it is important to note that while the influence enjoyed by the Church was extensive, it also had its limits. An interesting illustration of this occurred during the Spanish Civil War, when some sections of the Irish hierarchy, along with most of Fine Gael, attempted to put pressure on de Valera to withdraw recognition from the legitimate, elected, republican government of Spain, and recognise General Franco instead. Using the guarded diplomatic policy of the Vatican (who themselves were in no hurry to recognise Franco, despite the enthusiasm of the Spanish Catholic Church for the Generalissimo) as a useful benchmark, de Valera declined to recognise Franco until February 1939, when the forces of the republic were all but defeated.[48]

Of course, Cosgrave, de Valera, and, indeed, Costello were all devoutly practising Catholics, leading a nation of devoutly practising Catholics. Opposition to the confessional ethos of the state was far more likely to come from the eager, mobilised laity, who saw the state as being delinquent in its duties by not promoting an even more robust form of Catholic identity in its laws, than from the fragmented fearful left, the polite self-effacing Protestant minority, or even, with some notable exceptions amongst the hierarchy, the official Catholic Church itself. For this was also the era of the Catholic social movement, whose adherents drew their theological justification and their intellectual fortification from the doctrines of 'vocationalism', doctrines they preached to successive governments with a crusading zeal. Vocationalism had fallen out of intellectual fashion in Catholic circles on the continent in the period just after the Second World War, but, having arrived late in Ireland in the first place, it achieved its full, influential flowering precisely in the period when it had fallen into disfavour in mainland Europe. Above all, the 1940s was the time of the passionately engaged lay organisation, epitomised by bodies such as, perish the thought, the Knights of Colombanus and Maria Duce, meriting the following wry observation from Whyte: 'Perhaps it was only a lunatic fringe, but it was still of interest as a symptom. One can learn something of the tendencies in a society by observing on which particular fringe of it the lunatics break out.'[49]

In any case, W. T. Cosgrave's devotion coincided almost completely with the ethos and values of the state he led. De Valera had to be a little more circumspect at first, for, when he came to power, a sizeable portion of the hierarchy regarded him with grave mistrust – after all, the republican side in the Civil War had been denounced from many an altar, and some of them had even been excommunicated. This gave rise to an exquisite ability to split theological hairs which could be found in the more sophisticated circles of the republican movement, such as recognising the right of the Church to pronounce on matters of 'faith and morals', while doubting their competence in the sort of sensitive area covered by the 'national question'. As Noël Browne, relishing the irony of the situation, put it, looking around the table at a meeting of the Fianna Fáil national executive during his brief sojourn in that party in the 1950s, 'Well, I am the only one of you who has not been excommunicated.'[50] In fact, squaring this theological circle was not an especially taxing ideological – or even intellectual – exercise (as Frank Aiken later said, with disarming simplicity, 'we knew they were wrong'), and de Valera was well able to reassure the doubtful with the sort of displays of public piety as surrounded his attendance at the Eucharistic Congress in 1932. Any lingering doubts about his devotion to Catholic ideals were laid to rest when he unveiled his new constitution, complete with sturdy Catholic buttresses.

Costello, although personally at least as equally devout as the man he replaced,[51] was nowhere nearly as adroit, and his time in government would be interspersed with unusual ecclesiastical encounters, of which the infamous Mother and Child Scheme was only the last and most dramatic. Demonstrating adherence to Catholic values and institutions by sending telegrams of 'filial loyalty' to Rome was one thing. However, within weeks of taking office, Costello's government had an opportunity to demonstrate their 'filial loyalty' in more concrete terms, for they found themselves playing a surreptitious role in 'defence of Christian Democrat Italy' by helping to channel funds to the electoral war-chest of the Italian Christian Democrats. Diplomatic reports had indicated that the combined left were poised to take power in the 1948 Italian elections, leading to the unthinkable outcome of a possible communist take-over, and had argued that the most pressing need of the right was for funds with which to counter the communist menace. In Ireland, a flurry of fund-raising followed, ably spearheaded by the hierarchy, especially the archbishop of Dublin, John Charles McQuaid, and assisted, behind the scenes, by the Irish government. This succeeded in collecting more than £60,000 from Irish Catholics, which was then sent to Italy via the good offices of the Irish Department of Finance, the Irish Department of External Affairs, and the indefatigable efforts of the Irish ambassador in Rome, Joseph Walshe.[52] It is only fair to point out that these fund-raising activities came about due to the combined enthusiasms of Walshe and the Minister for External Affairs, Seán MacBride, for the Christian Democrat cause, rather than in response to specific Vatican requests for money or action.

In fact, the inter-party government were to devote considerable attention to their relationship with the Holy See, a relationship perceived as being of paramount importance by all Irish governments at the time. However, despite a common accord on many matters, a difference of opinion emerged with the appointment, by the Vatican, of Ettore Felici as the new papal nuncio to Ireland, to succeed the popular and tactful Pascal Robinson, who had been the first nuncio appointed to Ireland and who had died in August 1948.[53] The attempts of the Irish government to block the appointment of Felici – citing arguments that he was too old, and, much more importantly, that, being Italian, he would not possess the 'background of knowledge', a posting to Ireland should entail – proved unsuccessful. Despite fighting a lengthy rearguard action, lasting several months, the government was eventually obliged to accept the appointment of Felici.[54] It is of interest to note that the nuncio 'crisis' and the blundering repeal of the External Relations Act (which will be discussed in the next chapter) occurred more or less simultaneously, leaving MacBride, for one, with very full hands, as he attempted to juggle competing claims on the government's attention. In fact, MacBride attempted to buy time on the question of the appointment of the new nuncio, with the explanation (among others) that, pending the repeal of the External Relations Act, he did not think that the 'Holy Father should be placed in the position of accrediting his representative to one of the most Catholic countries in the world through the head of the Anglican Church'.[55]

Notwithstanding the temporary little difference of opinion caused by the appointment of Ettore Felici, relations quickly resumed their former cordial warmth. The Holy Year of 1950 presented the inter-party government with the sort of opportunity to demonstrate their devotion by publicly proclaiming their Catholicism that the Eucharistic Congress of 1932 had earlier afforded de Valera. Such an opportunity was far too good to miss, and thus a large number of ministers, starting with MacBride himself – whose visit 'was an unqualified personal success'[56] – and including the Taoiseach, John A. Costello, as well as the President, Seán T. O'Kelly, proceeded to beat a path to Rome to attend the Holy Year celebrations. These celebrations commenced with the dramatic opening of the Holy Door; 'as part of his duties as Foreign Minister Seán MacBride was photographed at the formal opening ceremony of the Holy Door',[57] Noël Browne later recalled, adding, with an exquisite and meticulous note of malice, 'they let him hold the key'.[58]

As an indication of the importance of the link with Rome, and the relationship with Rome, in the official Irish mind in the 1930s and 1940s, it is worth noting that, at the time, the position of Ireland's diplomatic representative to the Holy See was regarded as one of the most prestigious, and desirable, that could be held within the Irish diplomatic service, and only some time later was a more realistic sense of proportion attached to the posting. On a related point, it is equally interesting to note that the Irish travel industry can trace its roots to the organisation of pilgrimages to places such as Lourdes and Rome. However, in deference to changing times, by the 1960s such excursions often offered a week in the sun at the conclusion of the more reverential aspects of the trip, and by the 1970s the reverential aspects had frequently been dropped entirely from the itinerary.

However, while relations with the Holy See remained exceedingly cordial, the inter-party government was to experience a somewhat less equable relationship with the domestic Catholic Church in Ireland, and this despite heroic efforts on the part of the government to ensure that proposed legislation remained compatible with Church teaching when objections were raised. And vigorous objections were raised, for example, when attempts were made by rural publicans, supported by the government, which was initially sympathetic to the case made by the licensed trade, to regularise pub opening hours on a Sunday. This endeavour was firmly quashed – twice – by the hierarchy (in fact, their statement was described by an awed Whyte as being of 'so formidable a nature' that he quoted it at length) during the term of office of the inter-party government.[59] William Norton, the Tánaiste, ran into difficulties with his Social Welfare Bill, even though he had taken extensive precautions to safeguard his ecclesiastical flank in the preparation of the Bill.[60] Also quashed were Minister for Justice Seán MacEoin's attempts to introduce formal adoption procedures. Years later, Noël Browne recalled 'Seán MacEoin . . . as kind-hearted a man as you could meet, came in late to the [Cabinet] meeting. Clearly disappointed, he threw his brief on the Cabinet table and, as he sat down muttered "He won't allow it."'[61] 'He' was the archbishop of Dublin, John Charles McQuaid, and 'it' was the 'compassionate attempt', in Browne's words, of the government to allow for the legal adoption of children. Although the formal, eventual, objections stated by the government (prompted in a stage whisper by Archbishop McQuaid, on behalf of the Church) were expressed in terms of an apprehension that the rights of 'natural parents' would be 'irrevocably' undermined, it is thought that the real reason for the formidable opposition faced by the well-intentioned legislation was a fear that it would facilitate proselytism.[62] In other words, the possibility that Catholic children would be adopted by people not of their faith aroused fear and loathing in ecclesiastical circles, and in some of the more enthusiastically interventionist lay circles as well. As Tom Inglis has accurately noted, 'It is obvious from this . . . that any direct input from the Bishops in terms of law creation has been confined to moral conduct in general, and family, education, and health, in particular.'[63]

It is appropriate to close this chapter with a Tale of Two Funerals; both men had held the office of President of Ireland at different times, and each had filled it with distinction; each was Protestant, and the funerals of both would take place in St Patrick's Cathedral, Dublin. There the similarities ended, for, of all the expressions of Catholic fidelity uttered by the inter-party government, undoubtedly the most bathetically ludicrous note of punctilious piety was struck with the attendance of the Cabinet at, or, more to the point, outside, St Patrick's Cathedral, where the funeral of Dr Douglas Hyde was taking place in 1949. First President of Ireland, founder of the Gaelic League, distinguished scholar, and son of a rector from County Roscommon, attendance at the funeral of Douglas Hyde, a Protestant, ranked with poitín-making, perjury, and membership of an illegal organisation as a reserved sin, a sin so grave that it required absolution from a bishop to cleanse it from the soul. And so, in the immortal words of the poet, Austin Clarke,

> 'Tricoloured and beflowered,
> Coffin of our President,
> Where fifty mourners bowed,
> Was trestled in the gloom . . .
> At the last bench
> Two Catholics, the French
> Ambassador and I, knelt down.
> . . . Outside . . .
> Costello, his Cabinet,
> In Government cars, hiding
> Around the corner . . .[64]

Fortunately, matters had changed somewhat for the better by the time Erskine Childers died suddenly in 1974. On this occasion – attendance at a Protestant service no longer considered a reserved sin, or indeed any kind of a sin – Church and state combined, this time inside St Patrick's Cathedral, to bid a heart-felt farewell to a distinguished servant of the state.

The importance of Catholicism as a defining icon of Irish nationality, and the influence of the Catholic Church in prompting – or swaying – government policy, would re-emerge during the Mother and Child Scheme debacle three years later, but, before that, a major test of the inter-party government's ability to redefine the symbols of national identity would appear, with their handling of the repeal of the External Relations Act. In this instance, the conflict over the ownership of the symbols of national identity was to take the form of a concealed conflict between Fine Gael and Clann na Poblachta. This, as much as the intended wrongfooting of Fianna Fáil, is where the true significance of the repeal of the External Relations Act lies, for this illustrates, almost better than anything else, not only how the government functioned, but also the first faltering steps towards that eventual political ascendancy which was to be enjoyed by Fine Gael, and, concomitant with that, MacBride's inability to safeguard his ideological territory, a tendency which would become ever more pronounced the longer the government lasted. It is to this that we now turn.

George Garrett, US Ambassador, Seán MacBride, Minister for External Affairs and Patrick McGilligan, Minister for Finance signing the Marshall Plan

Senior Clann na Poblachta party members. Back row: Pádraig Ó Nualláin, Dick Battersby, unidentified, Joe Barron, Mac O'Rahilly, Jim Killeen; Front row: Maire Dennehy, Mick Kelly, Seán MacBride, Donal O'Donoghue, Tom Roycroft, Margaret Skinnider.

Noel Hartnett, founding member of Clann na Poblachta

Con Lehane, founding member of Clann na Poblachta

Captain P. Cowan, founding member of Clann na Poblachta

Jack McQuillan in front of Leinster House shortly after his election in 1948

THE GOVERNMENT, FEELING THAT THINGS ARE GOING WITH AN ALMOST
ALARMING SMOOTHNESS, TOUCHES WOOD

Dublin Opinion (July 1948)

7

'The Fine Gael Party had a sudden brainwave that they would steal the "Long Man's" clothes'

Like Banquo's ghost, the confusion and controversy surrounding the repeal of the External Relations Act simply refuse to go away. As an example of the inter-party government's early *modus operandi,* it is quite illuminating, revealing, as it does, a number of features such as the lack of communication between ministers, the initial lack of authority – and probably confidence – of the Taoiseach, the haphazard manner in which some decisions were taken or arrived at, and their inability (due to MacBride's paranoia) to avail of the benefits bestowed by the Cabinet secretariat. Inevitably, this resulted in the failure to note or record some of the decisions which were taken – assuming, that is, that such decisions were actually taken in the first place. As each of these points merits further examination, they will be returned to later.

As an example of Clann na Poblachta's influence in government, the repeal of the External Relations Act serves at least as much to illustrate the activities of various external players/actors – ranging from the machinations of Captain Peadar Cowan, plotting mischief and 'vingince' from the back-benches, to the dubious, nay, diabolically suspicious inspiration vouchsafed to Hector Legge, editor of the *Sunday Independent,* as he announced that the External Relations Act was 'to go' in his edition of 5 September 1948 – as it does to highlight MacBride's early predominance in government, where he sought to implement his party's stated policy objectives.

Unlike the Mother and Child Scheme debacle where the sequence of events, or basic facts, are not really a bone of contention between the various parties to the dispute, the repeal of the External Relations Act has given rise to vastly conflicting versions, not only as to what did or did not happen, but why it happened, and, odder still, how it came to happen. None of this would be of major importance almost half a century later, were it not for a number of reasons, chief among them Costello's oft-repeated conviction that this was one of the major achievements of the inter-party government. Not alone did it regularise the formal and legal status of the state, a matter of no little importance given that a civil war had been fought barely a quarter of a century earlier over just such matters as the titles and status of the state, but also, bearing this very much in mind, Costello was to argue that the repeal of the Act enabled 'the gun to be taken out of Irish politics'.[1] Whether this was a spot of retrospective justification in an attempt to kick over the embarrassing traces of how exactly the External Relations Act actually came to be repealed, or was a passionately held conviction, or both, is still very much a matter for debate. While no one ever doubted the sincerity of Costello's convictions on that, or indeed any other topic, the stress he subsequently laid on 'enabling the gun to be taken out of Irish politics',[2] in accounts and interviews he gave then and later, indicated someone who appeared to protest a little much.

Such protestations also took the form of indignant denials that the repeal of the External Relations Act had anything to do with Costello himself having been 'influenced by or subjected to any pressure by Mr MacBride or any of his followers'.[3] This is a little disingenuous. While MacBride did not make the repeal of the External Relations Act a condition for the formation of the coalition,[4] Clann na Poblachta, in so far as it possessed any sort of public image, presented itself as a seriously 'republican' party, spiced up with a liberal dash of social and economic reform. That must have been reflected in the Cabinet, given the tendency of MacBride as 'an energetic prowler'[5] to pronounce on topics he was known to take an interest in, as well as on others which did not really lie within his immediate orbit or sphere of influence. Moreover, at Clann na Poblachta's 1948 ard-fheis, which was held early in the summer, the Clann's *Clár* contained a number of motions stressing the Republican and 'separatist' aspects of the party's policies, and demanding that steps be taken which would implement these policies. Several other motions called for the repeal of the External Relations Act.[6] As this was MacBride's own immediate electoral swimming water, so to speak, he could hardly have ignored it, even if his own background and reputation as an ardent republican had been disregarded.

For all that he was determined to minimise MacBride's role in governmental policy formation, Costello was quite keen to stress that the government had concluded that the External Relations Act should be repealed, and not merely because this was 'nationally desirable'.[7] A need also existed for the government to be seen to have acted on their own initiative rather than be prodded or 'forced to do so', by the introduction of a private member's bill moved by one of the Dáil's loose cannons, Captain Peadar Cowan.[8] Not only was Cowan perfectly capable of moving motions on the External Relations Act, or anything else which took his fancy, but, from the time he was expelled from Clann na Poblachta in July 1948, he took a special delight in provoking and embarrassing MacBride. However, Cowan was not the only source of external pressure on the inter-party government's apparently vulnerable republican flank.

De Valera was embarrassingly visible, too, especially during his well-publicised – in the *Irish Press*, at least – global travels, ostensibly (and ostentatiously) labelled an Anti-Partition World Tour, which took place almost immediately after his removal from office. Such ostentatious anti-partitionist rhetoric was bound to have an immediate and jittery impact upon a coalition government a little unsure of itself, and uncertain of its anti-partitionist credentials – and this despite the prominent presence of MacBride in Cabinet – a point not missed by some of the shrewder observers, such as John Hickerson who remarked that de Valera's tour was responsible for the inter-party government being 'required to demonstrate to the Irish electorate that it is equally zealous, and in consequence has been spurred to action which it otherwise might not have taken'.[9] Although one commentator has remarked on how 'the attendant publicity put Clann na Poblachta and the coalition government under pressure to prove their republicanism',[10] and the British representative in Dublin, Sir John Maffey, privately grumbled that 'there is the smell of a Fianna Fáil party stunt about this American trip. Mr de Valera is batting for his Club, not for all Ireland',[11] the government would have done well to take a leaf out of *Dublin Opinion*'s treatment of de Valera's anti-partition peregrinations. With a pun on de Valera's former occupation as a teacher of mathematics, *Dublin Opinion* offered the following 'problem' for the consideration of their readers: 'Mathematical Progression: 1) Mr de Valera goes to the Country; 2) Mr de Valera goes to the Countries',[12] and continued, chortling, in the same issue, with a reference to an *Irish Press* headline which had announced 'Mr de Valera's plane struck by lightning', to which *Dublin Opinion* added, bitingly, 'That's nothing, after the last General Election.'[13]

Equal indignation was evident in Costello's refutation of 'the most extraordinary, fantastic and completely unfounded statements' that he had 'without any consultation or authority [from his government colleagues] in a fit of pique . . . on my own responsibility declared the intention of my colleagues and myself to repeal the External Relations Act and declare a Republic in Canada'.[14] As these 'imaginative circumstances', in Costello's words, have gained considerable currency, both then and subsequently, and as the tone of Costello's own written account offers reasons why this might have been so, it is worth taking a look at the whole saga of the repeal of the External Relations Act again; what happened, and how and why it came to happen.

For these reasons, it is also worth taking a brief look at the provenance, purpose, and effects of the Act itself. The External Relations Act dated from 1936, and, in its initial *political* intent, represented yet another step devised by the labyrinthine mind of de Valera to further loosen the Treaty-based ties which still bound Ireland to the ancient Saxon Enemy, while simultaneously serving, without any apparent sense of contradiction, 'to provide a bridge between North and South'.[15] In taking full advantage of the opportunities presented by the problems posed not only to the British government, but also to the British 'constitutional' establishment, by the crisis concerning the abdication of Edward VIII in December 1936, de Valera displayed his undoubted virtuosity in the narrow, but demanding, field of Anglo-Irish relations. However, the *legal* impact of the External Relations Act was to lead to considerable confusion, as, within a year of the abdication, a brand new constitution was to be enacted in Ireland, one, moreover, which made provision for the creation of an (admittedly truncated) office of the head of state, in other words, an elected President, to whom it was obviously intended that many of the functions of the now redundant monarch would eventually devolve.

The following year, 1938, saw the selection of the founder of the Gaelic League, Dr Douglas Hyde, to the new office of President, meeting several of the symbolic needs of the new state at once. However, Lee has commented on the 'characteristic ambiguity' of this situation, 'which left Ireland effectively a republic in her internal affairs, while retaining the king as a symbolic sleeping partner in external relations'.[16] Even the very name of the state, so often a source of self-indulgent angst amongst the branches of the revolutionary movements charged with the disinterring of the native culture, was somewhat unclear. Names are important, and, as studies of colonialism and similar relationships of power tell us, those who rule, as a rule, tend to define and name the ruled simply because they have the power to do so, and usually in a foreign language at that.[17] That is why language revival movements play such a powerful and important role in independence movements, and are so often an accompanying feature of the organisations, parties, or groups which seek political independence in newly emerging nations. It is also why the name of the newly independent nation state is almost always the first word to be altered or changed after the departure of the colonial power.[18]

Thus in the Treaty of 1921, Ireland acquired dominion status and answered to the name of the 'Irish Free State', an appellation nowadays employed as a particular term of abuse by a bizarre combination of obdurate unionists and radical republicans. With the introduction of the 1937 constitution, the state's name became simply 'Ireland', or, *as Gaeilge*, 'Éire'. Nowhere in the constitution was the dread word 'Republic' even whispered, although that did not prevent James Dillon, ebullient as ever (rumoured to have been put up to it by the irascible American minister in Dublin, David Gray, who detested de Valera[19]), from seeking to elucidate further the exact nature of this nebulous republic. Thus, Dillon was at his needling best when he taunted de Valera in the Dáil on 11 July 1945 by asking, 'Are we a republic or not, for nobody seems to know?'[20] De Valera's snapped response was terse: 'We are, if that is all the deputy wants to know.' Subsequent events would amply demonstrate that it would be perfectly possible to be both a republic and, simultaneously, a member of the (British) Commonwealth of Nations. India was the first country to avail of this route, to be followed in time by many of the other former imperial possessions of Her Britannic Majesty's Empire. Regretful cluckings that this possibility was neither spotted nor seized upon by various Irish governments can be found in Lyons's account, as he gloomily concluded that 'equality, it seemed, was no substitute for nationality',[21] glumly noting, in addition, that Ireland's membership of the Commonwealth seemed to reinforce the lesson that 'not even the most imaginatively conceived association of states can fulfil the inner demands and compulsions of a passionate sense of nationality'.[22]

Ambiguity rather than a 'passionate sense of nationality' was what characterised Ireland's position with regard to the Commonwealth from the mid-thirties onwards. This ambiguity was reciprocal, for, by the time the war broke out in September 1939, some British politicians, as well as members of the Irish opposition, were querying whether Ireland was still even in the Commonwealth. Ireland, after all, had not attended any of the

Commonwealth conferences since 1932, the year de Valera had come to power. Within a week of the British declaration of war on Nazi Germany, the various dominions had all followed suit[23] – all, that is, except Ireland, which chose to pursue a policy of neutrality. As Fisk rightly points out, this 'was not just an exercise in sovereignty, [but] was also an experiment in independent foreign policy'.[24]

Whether such 'exercises in sovereignty' were compatible with membership of the Commonwealth engaged the agonised attention of the British Cabinet in late October 1939. In what appears to have been a fairly intense meeting, opinions ranged from an understanding of 'Eire's' position, and a recognition of its legality,[25] to the view that 'Eire' should be 'expelled' from the Commonwealth.[26] Characteristically, Winston Churchill – newly recalled as First Lord of the Admiralty – was the most vehement advocate of 'expulsion', even going so far as to request the Lord Chancellor to examine the 'legality of terminating Eire's Commonwealth membership'.[27] The Law Lords subsequently submitted a ten-page memorandum which argued that this could cause Britain more trouble than it was actually worth as 'such action might imperil the existence of the whole Commonwealth'.[28] If 'push came to shove', it is worth noting that long before Costello's display of awkward acrobatics caused Ireland to 'leap' out of the Commonwealth with anything but balletic grace, a sharp shove administered by Churchill's Britain could well have 'pushed' it out. That this didn't happen, even after Churchill became Prime Minister, can be attributed in equal measure to the totemic, rather mystical notion of 'the indivisibility of the Crown' and to the fact that the other dominions probably wouldn't have stood for it.

Nevertheless, while neutrality was extremely satisfying to the nation's *amour propre*, allowing, as it did, for the exercise of an independent foreign policy, visible expression of sovereignty, and a degree of success in the safeguarding of gains which had been made since independence,[29] certain features of existing constitutional arrangements did rather tend to cramp the Irish government's style. Despite having a President ensconced in the Governor-General's old residence in Dublin's Phoenix Park, diplomats, for example, were still accredited to their respective stations in Ireland or abroad by the British monarch, having, of course, been approved by the Irish government in advance. Even rubber stamps have their flaws, however, particularly those wearing crowns in times of war. In practice, this meant that while Ireland's diplomats remained *in situ* in Germany after war was declared, appointments to ambassadorial rank could not be replaced, as such replacements required the King's signature. Thus, in 1943 when Con Cremin proceeded to take up his post as Ireland's chargé d'affaires in Germany, he did so chiefly because the Irish government were unable to appoint him ambassador, the secretary of the Department of External Affairs, Joseph Walshe, prudently deciding 'not to risk British apoplexy by requesting the King's consent'.[30]

While satisfying the symbolic requirements of sovereignty, the wartime exercise in neutrality also revealed its limitations. Whether such constraints were serious limitations or whether they merely added to the 'characteristic ambiguity' of Ireland's actual status with regard to the Commonwealth remained unclear. Charged with this in the Dáil, de Valera offered the opaque observation that 'in all political systems there are relationships which it is wiser to leave undefined'.[31] For all that, on 17 July 1945, partly in response to earlier goading (from Dillon, among others), de Valera returned to this tiresome topic. In this instance, the master of nuance, specialist in pellucid confusion, and expert in the elasticity of political vocabularies found himself obliged to seek recourse to the written word in order to shed further light on that unfortunate expression 'republic'. In order – as he helpfully phrased it – to save the Dáil 'the trouble of looking up references',[32] de Valera, as subtly devious as ever, attempted to prove to the Dáil, with the assistance of an armful of dictionaries, that Ireland satisfied every possible requirement of the term 'republic', short of actually formally bearing the title. Furthermore, he pointed out that 'This External Relations Act is a simple statute repealable by the legislature and not a fundamental law.'[33] Would nobody rid him of this troublesome word?

The inter-party government would shortly do so, employing the novel device of appropriating the term for themselves, with the declaration of the Republic. As to whether de Valera himself would have done more than tinker with existing arrangements in pursuit of the elusive republic remains open to question. Some sources argue that he had been 'moving towards repealing the Act'[34] when the fickle finger of fate, taking the cloaked form of a general election, led to his removal from office. According to this version, de Valera explained to Sir John Maffey, Britain's envoy in Dublin, that the Act had failed to fulfil its intended functions. Not only had the Act failed 'to provide a bridge between North and South' – although it is difficult to see how de Valera took this argument seriously unless he intended to address the 'problems of partition' from under the umbrella supplied by the structure of the Commonwealth – it was also causing 'confusions' in Southern politics.[35]

A salt-mine to hand would be an agreeable commodity when contrasting that account with the version put forward by Keogh, who spoke with Frederick Boland.[36] Secretary of the Department of External Affairs from 1946 until 1950, Boland maintained that de Valera would not have repealed the External Relations Act, but, rather, would have chipped away at it, by removing all references to the Crown, 'although we would have been prepared to acknowledge the King as head of the Commonwealth if others did it. That was Dev's idea all along.'[37] Stressing that had de Valera 'remained in power, we would have remained in the Commonwealth', Boland went on to recall a meeting between Churchill and de Valera which occurred in 1953. By then both men had been returned to power in their respective countries, and Boland was Ireland's ambassador to the Court of St James. Churchill wanted to know whether Ireland would have left the Commonwealth had de Valera still held office. De Valera's response was a surprisingly straightforward 'No'. Clarifying his 'Chief's' position, Boland pointed out that his objection had never been to the Commonwealth *per se*, but to the oath of allegiance which was owed to the King as King of the Commonwealth. In addition, as de Valera himself explained to Churchill, he had formed the opinion that the Commonwealth was 'a very useful association for us',[38] principally because the other

Commonwealth countries 'had a strong interest in Ireland',[39] as they felt that they could find common cause with Ireland on several issues, chiefly the need to clip the wings of the former imperial power by ensuring that any attempt by Britain to 'enlarge their role' in the organisation would be met with immediate, and stiff, opposition. Of course, this raises the question of why, if de Valera found the Commonwealth so 'useful [an] association for us', he declined to attend any Commonwealth conferences from the time he had first attained office in 1932.

This is an appropriate place to return to the innovations, trials and (some would argue, largely self-inflicted) tribulations of the inter-party government. Commonwealth conferences when viewed as political catalysts have much to recommend them, but in this instance, the catalyst, if that is what it was, seems to have resulted simply from the invitation to attend the conference which was scheduled for October 1948, in London. The invitation arrived in the middle of August, and, in addition, sought the views of the Irish government, along with those of the other Commonwealth countries, as to the continued usage of the term 'High Commissioner', and their thoughts on the potential precedence of such a personage in matters of protocol. An informal agenda of sorts was appended, and the Irish government were invited to add topics of interest to them to this list. It was this invitation, and the need to respond to it, which appears to have given rise to the first recorded Cabinet minutes on the topic.[40] As usual, Captain Cowan was fast out of the starting-blocks, for, as far back as early June, he had asked the Taoiseach 'whether an invitation has been received by the Government to be represented at a Dominions Conference in London this year, and, if so, whether the invitation has been accepted'. Significantly, Costello took this question himself, his secretary noting in a handwritten aside to MacBride's secretary that the Taoiseach 'is not prepared to authorise the transfer of the question to the Minister for External Affairs'. In addition, MacBride's suggested reply, 'The Answer is NO' was altered by Costello to read 'No such invitation has been received.'[41] And, indeed it hadn't, not by the time Cowan received his answer in the Dáil on 8 June.

Too much can be read into this, but a number of points can be noted, some of which hearken back to the observations made about the government's *modus operandi* at the outset of this chapter. The first one is obvious, that of a Taoiseach attempting to assert his authority. Costello was no de Valera, neither in personality nor – as perceived at the time – in the possession of the exquisite political skills of the departed Chief, and the motley crew he presided over bore little resemblance, in public at least, to the disciplined monolithic façade presented by the Fianna Fáil party to the world at large. His authority, such as it was, derived solely from his occupancy of the Taoiseach's chair. He was not party leader of Fine Gael, and the party he did not lead not only lacked an overall majority in the Dáil, but also did not have a majority within the construct or structure of the inter-party government itself. Lacking the immediate source of 'clout' conferred by party leadership, Costello was obliged to resort to other tactics. In addition, the very fact of coalition government was, in itself, a startling political innovation, one which necessitated the reordering of priorities, and the rewriting of the political rule-book. In other words, as it had not been tried out before, it was necessary to feel one's way in the establishment of new structures and in the working out of a totally new *modus vivendi* between the various parties in the government. While it is clear, to invoke Farrell's useful distinction, that Costello was much more a 'chairman' than a 'chief ',[42] several commentators have drawn attention to the fact that, as time went on, he increasingly asserted himself,[43] to such an extent that by the time he came to be Taoiseach in the second inter-party government his control over his Cabinet – as opposed to his own party or theirs – was essentially complete.

From quite early on, this attempted assertiveness took the form of clipping MacBride's wings whenever opportunity arose, as MacBride – loquacious, opinionated, new on the scene, and the linchpin of the coalition – was the obvious 'alternative Taoiseach'.[44] Equally important in this context was MacBride's portfolio. The Minister for External Affairs was frequently out of the country (which, in fact, was something of a new departure), and this left him vulnerable in the domain of domestic politics. Needless to add, had Clann na Poblachta's discipline, experience, and organisation been anything like as rigorous as those of Fianna Fáil, or even, dare one say it, Fine Gael, it is possible that MacBride could have been better protected. As much of Clann's structural weaknesses were of his doing, ultimately he was to pay the price in the form of increasing vulnerability. Each of these aspects will be addressed subsequently, especially the theme of MacBride's declining influence and stature within the Cabinet, but on the question of Costello's 'asserting' himself *vis à vis* MacBride, it is worth noting that Taoisigh commandeering aspects of the External Affairs portfolio was nothing new. Indeed, de Valera had been his own Minister for External Affairs from the time he had been first elected Taoiseach in 1932 until 1948, and in later years still occasionally spoke *ex cathedra* on topics relating to foreign issues. Costello himself, for that matter, had been his party's foreign affairs spokesman for the previous fifteen years,[45] and had electoral results turned out differently (in other words, had Fine Gael obtained more seats) it was quite conceivable that he would have found himself Minister for External Affairs, rather than Taoiseach.[46] Electoral hiccups notwithstanding, Costello 'attempted to assert his position as the principal source of foreign policy in the government', according to Keatinge.[47] Thus, while Costello's appropriation of External Affairs questions (and rewritten answers for that matter) was, of course, very much intended as a salutary lesson to the upstart Minister for External Affairs (and any other party leaders who might be watching), it was also a continuation of an existing practice. Nor would this be the last time Costello acted in such a manner. A few months later, he chose to pilot the Bill taking Ireland out of the Commonwealth through the Dáil himself, an act Noël Browne viewed (probably correctly) as a snub of sorts – referring to it as being 'both ill-mannered and ungracious of Fine Gael and Mr Costello' to 'deprive' MacBride, as the relevant minister, of the right to steer the Bill through the Dáil.[48] However, as even Browne conceded, not all of Costello's interventions in the Dáil, in representing portfolios other than his own, can

be attributed to a desire to put manners on his Cabinet. With evident gratitude, Browne recalled an occasion when Costello 'took on' Seán Lemass on
behalf of his young Minister for Health, admitting that he himself 'was
certainly not up to that level of competition yet', and that Costello 'good
lawyer that he was' had 'no trouble with his brief', which was to deal with
Lemass's unwelcome attentions and questions.[49]

Viewed benignly, the inter-party government's interpretation of *Dáil*
procedure was certainly flexible, as it probably had to be given the coalition
nature of the beast. However, their interpretation of *Cabinet* procedure
brought flexibility to the very limits of its possible elasticity. Problems in this
instance were the need to display flexibility in the new, potentially
combustible coalition context, where strong ideological differences existed –
'even within the admittedly narrow spectrum of Irish doctrinal discourse'[50] –
and where the big egos of small parties, and the bruised egos of the larger
parties, required constant soothing.

Equally culpable, of course, was MacBride's obsessive paranoia about the
civil service in general, and the Cabinet secretariat in particular. This
distrust of institutional structures seems to have been shared by Clann na
Poblachta's pair of ministers, an attitude which probably had its roots in the
arcane ancestry of the party itself. Years later, Browne confessed his early
fears that his civil servants would 'set out to control' their minister, adding
that he 'resented and feared the possibility of being "managed"'.[51] As events
transpired, Browne was to develop an enormous respect for the enthusiasm
and integrity of his departmental staff, one which would be reciprocated by
many of them. No such change of heart occurred with MacBride. His
innately suspicious nature[52] had received further refinement in the precise
circumstances of his political apprenticeship, where he had toiled with the
denizens of the deep in the republican underground. Skills honed in such an
environment did not necessarily successfully translate to party political
management in a 'modern western democracy', and subsequent activities
defending republicans who had fallen foul of the law did little to ease his
defensiveness. Thus he first entered Iveagh House with 'a most suspicious
and untrusting attitude',[53] and on his arrival immediately demanded from
Boland, his departmental secretary, 'a list of all of the British agents'[54]
employed by the department.

This paranoia extended to the Cabinet secretariat, which, at MacBride's
behest, were not permitted to attend Cabinet meetings. Thus, for the first
time since the foundation of the state, there was no member of the Cabinet
secretariat present at government meetings. The Cabinet secretary, Maurice
Moynihan, did in fact attend the first two meetings of the inter-party
Government, those of 19 and 24 February 1948, and is noted in the minutes
as having done so.[55] Subsequently , he was excluded from attending Cabinet
meetings, MacBride entertaining lurid suspicions that, after sixteen years of
Fianna Fáil rule, Moynihan[56] must have become contaminated by association with the grubbier aspects of the *ancien régime*, – Patrick Lynch coyly
referred to the fact that Moynihan 'was suspect politically because of his
long and close association with Mr de Valera by, at least, one of the

Taoiseach's colleagues'[57] – that his loyalty to the new administration must have been questionable, and that, as a career civil servant, he was probably 'a tool of British interests'. Patrick Lynch, who served as Costello's economic adviser, deeply regretted the fact that Costello was unable to fully avail of Moynihan's expertise, and felt that it limited Costello's options, 'was a severe disadvantage', and hampered his government's effectiveness. Referring to this, years later, Lynch remarked that 'Maurice had immense ability, integrity and experience with an exquisite mastery of language, spoken and written in Irish and English. Moreover, he was a very wise man with a keen sense of political niceties,'[58] adding, with perceptive insight, that 'had Costello 'the benefit of more extensive advice from Maurice Moynihan, also a devoted Catholic with a very subtle mind, on delicate issues of the relations between the State and the churches, the history of the first inter-party government might have been different'.[59]

Unimaginative, the civil service may have been, but a tool of foreign interests, it most certainly was not. Apart from the 'sabotage' regularly indulged in by the higher echelons of the Department of Finance towards anything which smacked of expansionist economics, ministers who supplied clear guidelines as to desired goals, and offered serious leadership in attempting to achieve them, found a motivated civil service a pleasure to work with.[60]

Moynihan was despatched to another branch of the civil service, there to await the return to office of his former master, and the Cabinet called in Liam Cosgrave, the Government Chief Whip and Parliamentary Secretary to the Taoiseach, to take the minutes instead. This was all a very far cry from the procedures pursued by the administration led by Liam Cosgrave's father, W. T. Cosgrave, in the 1920s, when the Cabinet secretariat in the form of Diarmuid Ó hEigeartaigh sat in on all Cabinet meetings, those dealing with party political matters as well as the more usual government business.[61]

Cosgrave's minutes were, for the most part, precise and confined to the noting of decisions which were taken. He did not see it as part of his job to make notes on how discussions evolved or how decisions were arrived at,[62] and, needless to add, he did not have shorthand. Neither did MacBride, who 'was not a competent short-hand writer', as Noël Browne acidly pointed out.[63] Few professional males of that generation and time – outside of the occupation of journalism – had shorthand.[64] That this 'procedural laxity' gave rise to 'administrative uncertainty'[65] is beyond doubt. That it also hampered Cabinet communications and ultimately weakened the government is equally evident. By the time of his second administration, in 1954, Costello's steep learning curve had included the valuable lesson of not jettisoning such experienced personnel. Thus, Moynihan returned to the Cabinet table as secretary and minute-taker, being asked to withdraw only when party political matters were under discussion,[66] and procedures, on the whole, were notably tighter. It probably helped matters considerably that MacBride was no longer a member of the Cabinet, although, had he been, it is likely, given the rather different manner in which Costello approached the task of 'chairing' his second administration, that such paranoid delusions as were entertained by MacBride would have been given short shrift. Of course, this was not the case with the earlier administration, where the 'procedural laxity', compounded by poor communication and a haphazard approach to the formal taking of decisions, was best exemplified by the capricious approach taken over the repeal of the External Relations Act.[67]

The invitation to the Commonwealth conference was the first item on the agenda of the Cabinet when it met on 19 August 1948.[68] Inevitably, one of MacBride's multifarious memoranda accompanied the topic.[69] This, interestingly enough, recommended that the government 'should not be represented at the meeting of the Commonwealth', on a number of grounds, some of them spurious, and several of them self-evidently contradictory. MacBride grumbled at the lack of a formal agenda, and grudgingly conceded that the British government's only communication to Costello, concerning the diplomatic status of high commissioners – and one which was also conveyed to all of the other Commonwealth countries – might possibly have been prompted by positive impulses such as the desire to ascertain the views of the participating governments, and, in so doing, 'to remedy in advance the anomalous position concerning their diplomatic status'. He derived considerable satisfaction from noting that perhaps not all of the Commonwealth countries intended to attend the conference, and of those that did, it was possible that not all would send their prime ministers. In the absence of a formal pre-set agenda, he proceeded to speculate as to the topics which might arise, listing a number of likely subjects which included defence and military co-operation within the Commonwealth; the establishment of machinery for 'closer consultation between London and the Commonwealth countries'; the alteration of the King's title; the continuance of the term high commissioner; the European Recovery Programme (some of the Commonwealth countries had difficulty with the 'concept'); migration from Britain to the Commonwealth; and Britain's policy in the south-east Pacific.

Having speculated about a possible agenda, MacBride loftily proceeded to dismiss it as such, remarking that 'it will be readily appreciated that we will have very little interest in many of the matters under discussion', and continued, in a passage entirely lacking in any sense of contradiction or, for that matter, of irony, 'indeed, some of these matters might raise questions of considerable difficulty from our point of view'.[70] If such a display of logic failed to suffice, precedent remained, and MacBride readily invoked it, reminding his readers that since 1932 no Irish representatives had attended any Commonwealth conferences, 'though some have been held'. Then came the *coup de grâce*, containing interesting information doubtless new to the Cabinet, when he pointed out that, 'In view of the fact that we are not members of the Commonwealth',[71] Ireland should not really consider attendance at the conference. Pursuing this point, he added that if representation at this conference were to be contemplated, it should be contingent upon certain conditions being met 'by an agreed exchange of correspondence in advance' recognising that such attendance occurred, not in the capacity as 'members of the Commonwealth', but, doffing a hat of a different hue, rather 'because of our desire to co-operate in matters of mutual interest'. Topics that MacBride felt fell into these categories, and ought to be raised in the event of Irish participation, were – inevitably – partition ('the meeting would be the appropriate place at which to raise, formally and definitely, the question of Partition)',[72] the elimination of Ireland from the King's title, and the abolition of the title of high commissioner.

MacBride's recommendations were accepted by the Cabinet only insofar as they agreed that Ireland should not be represented 'as a member of the Commonwealth' at the proposed meeting. As the Cabinet minutes ponderously phrased it, in a piece displaying the input of many sticky fingers: 'Consideration of the question whether Ireland should be represented at the meeting, otherwise than as a member of the Commonwealth, for the purpose of discussing any particular subject, was deferred pending the receipt of further information which the Minister for External Affairs undertook to procure.'[73]

In fact, MacBride had been busily procuring plenty of relevant material ever since June. That 'the evolution of the Commonwealth' exercised at least some government minds over the summer is therefore evident from the available sources. At the time of Cowan's unwelcome Dáil question concerning attendance at the Commonwealth conference, in early June, MacBride seems to have compiled a fairly comprehensive dossier of clippings from the British and, interestingly – in the light of what was to happen there in September – the Canadian press on the 'evolution of the Commonwealth', which he laid before the Cabinet with the remark that he had 'evidence that these excerpts reflect accurately a current trend of thought in British official circles'.[74] The articles, which came mostly from 'quality' periodicals, offered intelligent and perceptive analyses of such questions as the possibility of the Commonwealth including both monarchies and republics, how the political choice involved was not confined to dominion status or secession, whether association in the Commonwealth had become compatible with 'real independence', and the value of the Crown as a symbol of unity, as well as a recognition that in the case of Ireland, South Africa, and India this function had not been fulfilled. Almost all laid stress on the positive direction the Commonwealth was taking, instancing symbolic changes such as the alteration of the title of the Secretary of State from that of 'Dominions Secretary' to 'Secretary for Commonwealth Relations' as evidence of the emergence of a new Commonwealth, 'equal in status' and tolerant of divergence.

Further cuttings were added to the file over the summer, including one from *The New Statesman and Nation*, dated 31 July, which treated the news that 'A Bill to repeal the External Relations Act will shortly be introduced into the Dáil' in a cheerfully optimistic manner, adding breezily, 'this fulfils the promise recently made by Mr Costello, the Irish Premier'.[75] The article went on to explain to its readers that this act would break 'the last formal link between Eire and the British Commonwealth', but argued that the result of this would be 'that the Irish irreconcilables will have lost their last grievance' and that this, in turn, would help 'to make Anglo-Irish relations even closer than they are today'.

That the articles were circulated to the Cabinet is certain, that they were actually read and discussed at Cabinet is likely, and that they helped to lead to discussion and perhaps to a decision to repeal the External Relations Act and leave the Commonwealth at some stage is very possible.[76] It defies belief that this matter was not (at least tentatively) explored at Cabinet in the wake of Peadar Cowan's bombshell – the timing of MacBride's compilation was hardly a coincidence – and in the light of MacBride's predilection for memoranda and obsession with Ireland's international position, apart from all other considerations.

Of course, it is possible that such a discussion did not take place at a full formal meeting of the Cabinet, but at a meeting of a Cabinet subcommittee, of which there were several. No records exist of these meetings, and while both Costello and MacBride served on virtually all of them, none had been specifically established to deal with matters unique to External Affairs. Some of these, such as the 'Economic Sub-Committee'[77] or the inter-departmental subcommittee established to co-ordinate the work of various departments involved with the administration of the Marshall Aid programme, had a very broad canvas, whereas others were set up to deal with a particular set of circumstances.[78] Given the 'administrative flexibility' known to have been the hallmark of that government, it would be very surprising if straying or trespassing into somebody else's ministerial territory was not a regular occurrence at meetings of these subcommittees.

Equally, it is possible that such a discussion did take place at Cabinet (perhaps in June rather than in August), but, owing to 'procedural laxity' and other administrative oversights, was not actually recorded as having occurred. No records exist to indicate that this topic was raised at Cabinet in early June, although, for the reasons referred to earlier, this is not, in itself, an absolute guarantee that it didn't come up. That Ireland's attendance at the Commonwealth conference, the evolving nature of the Commonwealth itself, and Ireland's relationship with the Commonwealth came up at Cabinet both at the time of Cowan's Dáil question in early June and when the invitation to attend the conference itself arrived in August, seems more than likely. Indeed, during the adjournment debate in the Dáil on 6 August, de Valera had raised the question of the continuing relationship with the Commonwealth, quite possibly in an attempt to expose fissiparous strains in the government. If that was his intent, it failed to reveal the desired cleavages, as the government responded equably by sending in William Norton, the Tánaiste, to reply on their behalf. Norton remarked that the External Relations Act 'was a fraud on the people' and that 'it would do our national self-respect good both at home and abroad if we were to proceed without delay to abolish the External Relations Act'.[79] De Valera, a connoisseur of such things, could readily appreciate the subtlety of a well-executed counterattack, one which, moreover, threatened possibly to outmanoeuvre him. His response was confined to a muted 'Go ahead . . . you will get no opposition from us.'[80] Therefore, that Ireland intended to formally leave the Commonwealth at some stage in the indeterminate future seemed to be well known and fairly widely commented on, in arenas as varied as Dáil Éireann and *The New Statesman and Nation*, to mention just two.

However, whether an agreed formal Cabinet decision had actually been taken to leave the Commonwealth is still unclear. While Costello claims – several times – in his memorandum that this decision had been taken,[81] no such decision was actually recorded anywhere in the Cabinet minutes prior to his departure for Canada. In fact, as his own memorandum almost guiltily admits, 'I cannot say positively whether or not this decision is recorded in the Cabinet Minutes as at that time neither the Secretary nor the Assistant Secretary of the Government attended Cabinet meetings.'[82] Even when speaking to the ultimate of insider sources, the Fine Gael youth magazine *The Citizen* in May 1967, Costello's tone echoes with culpable doubts – 'I can't say if this Cabinet decision was put into the ordinary form of a Government minute' – although he went on to stress: 'that it was taken I have no doubt whatever'.[83] This uneasy air of guilty knowledge surfaced yet again in an interview with Michael McInerney of *The Irish Times* in September 1967, when Costello 'said that he was not absolutely certain whether the decision was entered in the Cabinet minutes'.[84] Such guilty hints imply that Costello seems to have known perfectly well that this decision was never actually committed to writing, at least not before he travelled to Canada. Moreover, one should note the clue-strewn path which he laid out for Brian Farrell, F. S. L. Lyons, and Michael McInerney – one which they had no difficulty following and one, in fact, which they hardly attempted to subject to serious questioning.[85] Lyons even went so far as to offer some extremely gentle extenuating circumstances, for, when he commented on the 'uncertainty about the precise date' as to when the decision was taken, he allowed for 'some confusion of ministerial recollections about the occasion (not unnatural after a lapse of twenty years)'.[86] Even Hector Legge, a stalwart supporter of Costello's position for decades, recently amended his long-standing account of events when he wrote that 'Subsequently it became clear that no actual government decision had been taken but the ending of the External Relations Act had been discussed by individual ministers.'[87]

However, Hector Legge was not the only observer to feel obliged to amend aspects of his story with the passage of time. Other commentators would also profess themselves 'surprised' at the astonishing gaps in the Cabinet minutes, or, put another way, by the complete lack of written records on the matter,[88] when a clue-strewn path already existed offering tantalising pointers suggesting that this decision may not have been taken at all. Indeed, it might be argued that if Hector Legge could 'read between the lines' to anticipate government actions, then surely the same could have been done about Costello's oft-stated and frequently cited doubts as to whether this decision (if made) was actually recorded. For, of course, five[89] separate sources exist where Costello confessed his doubts as to whether this decision 'was put into the ordinary form of a Government minute', suggesting, pretty strongly, that he was perfectly aware that it was never minuted, and also giving a fairly clear indication that a firm decision to leave the Commonwealth (as opposed to an understanding that an intended departure was on the cards) had yet to be taken. Equally, whether a precise date had been decided on upon which to leave the Commonwealth seems very unlikely, and, of course, needless to add, Costello had not been authorised in advance to take the unilateral decision he did.

Noël Browne, for one, has always been adamant that no decision was ever taken by the Cabinet to leave the Commonwealth, and that they blundered into having to do so on account of 'Mr Costello's Canadian capers'.[90] Browne himself did not recall any such decision ever having been taken, and subscribes to the view that the repeal came about because of Costello having lost his temper as a result of the diplomatic insults or slights which occurred at the first – and famous – Ottawa dinner.[91] However, it is worth noting that for a number of reasons, among them recurring ill-health and the fact that he begrudged anything – including attendance at Cabinet meetings – which served to drag him away from the Department of Health,[92] Browne's attendance at Cabinet meetings was, to say the least, extremely erratic.[93] Available Cabinet records show that while he was present at every meeting of the Cabinet held in June 1948, and managed to attend seven out of the eight meetings which took place in July, he actually missed four out of the five meetings which were held in August, including, crucially, the all-important meeting of 19 August at which attendance at the Commonwealth conference was discussed.[94] Regardless of what was discussed at that meeting (as opposed to what was recorded), Browne would not be able to recall it for the very simple reason that he was not present when it came up. Likewise, it is worth noting that MacBride, rather than Browne, was the Clann na Poblachta nominee to serve on the plethora of Cabinet sub-committees which came into being during the life of the government. That being the case, matters which arose under the auspices of these subcommittees, or topics which were dealt with by them, are further subjects that Browne could not possibly recall, not having been present when they arose. The handful of sub-committees which Browne actually served on were usually confined to matters relevant to the Department of Health or connected in some way with his portfolio.[95]

It is against this background that Costello's Canadian visit should be viewed. In its original context, this took the form of an invitation issued by the president of the Canadian Bar Association to Costello, then recently appointed Taoiseach, to attend their proposed gathering in Montreal scheduled for 31 August, and for the first three days of September, as the guest of the Canadian Bar Association.[96] Learning of this, the Canadian government subsequently invited Costello to be their 'official guest' for the duration of his visit in Canada.[97] Although several official receptions were held in Costello's honour by the Canadian government – only the first one of which was to be the venue for some of the misunderstood or notorious 'incidents' – the trip was not, as such, a state or official visit. Therefore, in terms of protocol, the visit seems to have been something of a hybrid, being neither a state nor an official visit, for while Costello was regarded as an 'official guest' by the Canadian government, the Canadian Bar Association were Costello's hosts for the first part of his visit, rather than the Canadian government. This confusion over the context of the visit was to have interesting repercussions, as Costello was really in Canada in his capacity as a barrister who happened to be a Prime Minister, rather than as a Prime Minister who just happened to be a barrister. What this was to do to a Taoiseach newly appointed to the position, possibly insecure in his occupancy, unsure of his authority over a fractious Cabinet, and, probably most importantly, expected to shine as he followed in the distinctive footsteps of the redoubtable de Valera – all of this on his first trip abroad in an unclear capacity, representing, but yet not fully representing, his government and country – can only be guessed at. Thus, Costello travelled accompanied by his wife, his ADC, Commandant Byrne, and his economics adviser and secretary, Patrick Lynch. As this was not an official visit, he was accompanied neither by his Minister for External Affairs, Seán MacBride, nor by any other departmental 'minders', an omission which would have unfortunate consequences.

Before he left Ireland, Costello drafted his speech on a subject of his choice which, as the guest of the Canadian Bar Association, he considered it to be his 'duty and privilege' to give.[98] 'After considerable thought', as he phrased it, Costello opted for the tendentious topic of 'Ireland in International Affairs'.[99] The completed speech was submitted to the Cabinet for scrutiny, where it met with 'unanimous approval', MacBride commenting later that it was 'a good lawyer-like speech'.[100] According to Costello, when drafting the speech he had been informed by the knowledge that a government decision had already been 'unanimously taken' to repeal the External Relations Act.[101] This was supposed to happen when the Dáil resumed, normally sometime in October, but in the meantime, the approved speech was to be essentially backlit with knowledge its formal text could not divulge. Costello's party of four left Cobh on 22 August, and arrived in New York five days later, on 27 August. Their two-day stopover in New York appears to have been an extremely pleasant interlude, as they were 'received and entertained by Mayor O'Dwyer', treated royally by the brahmins of New York's Irish community, and had an enjoyable time meeting 'many notabilities', including a good many 'numbers of distinguished men of Irish origin' who had, as Costello was subsequently to describe it, 'given signal service during the struggle with the British'. This was a classic instance of usurping de Valera's territory or patch, literally, metaphorically, and rhetorically!

With these heady nationalist fumes swirling all around them, on the evening of 29 August, Costello and his compatriots departed from New York's Grand Central Station on the overnight sleeper to Montreal, arriving there the following morning, where they were met by the president of the Canadian Bar Association, Senator John Hackett, and John Hearne, the Irish representative in Canada.[102] Costello was to stay in Montreal as the guest of the Canadian Bar Association until the morning of 4 September, when he left for Ottawa and the 'official' part of the visit.[103]

At a press conference on the morning of his arrival in Montreal, he explained to the assembled media that as he regarded himself as being *then* (my italics) in Canada as the guest of the Canadian Bar Association, he did not 'think it was proper . . . [to] express any views on controversial political subjects'. This was interesting, coming from a man who intended to make a speech entitled 'Ireland in International Affairs', which, as he admitted himself, had been written after the government had made its 'mute inglorious' and unrecorded decision to leave the Commonwealth, and presumably was somewhat informed by that decision, even if it could not allude publicly to the fact.

For the duration of Costello's stay in Montreal, while he was the guest of the Canadian Bar Association, everything went smoothly, above all, the speeches. In fact, the speeches went so smoothly that some of the audience of over a thousand left early,[104] and others, such as Patrick Lynch, also found them rather trying. Costello's offering, the belaboured 'Ireland in International Affairs', took over an hour and a half to deliver when Costello spoke to the Canadian Bar Association on 1 September, and was later described by Patrick Lynch as 'tedious',[105] while the speech given by A. T. Vanderbilt, chief justice of the State of New Jersey, was felt by Lynch to have been 'an address of stupefying banality'.[106] In addition to the speeches, everything else also ran smoothly, the awards, and even the Bar Association's formal luncheon, at which the later little problems regarding the toasts were solved by giving one to 'the King' and another to 'the Heads of Other Sovereign States'. That seems to have been as much for the benefit of M. Rebet, *Bâtonnier* of the Paris Bar, and A. T. Vanderbilt, who represented the Bar Association of the United States at the dinner, as it was for Costello, who, ominously, found himself being asked by M. Louis St Laurent (Canada's Minister for External Affairs), when the toast for the King was given, 'doesn't that cover you?' Costello replied that it didn't, and attempted to 'explain the position', which was that the King was not the head of state in Ireland, while privately admitting in his written account that he 'personally was not convinced that this was at all clear'.[107]

Problems, however, did arise at the infamous dinner which was hosted by the Canadian Governor-General, Lord Alexander,[108] in Ottawa on Saturday, 4 September, in Costello's honour. This notorious repast has entered political folklore more because of what did not happen – the President of Ireland was not toasted, Costello did not make a scene, and Ireland did not leave the Commonwealth, not that night anyway – than because of what actually occurred. What actually occurred was odder still. One toast was offered at the dinner, and that was to 'the King' – which Costello, although he usually 'did not drink port', honoured – rather than the two that Costello had been led to believe were agreed to in advance. This breach of a prearranged undertaking, as much as the omission of the toast to the President of Ireland, 'seriously perturbed' Costello, who was inclined to point the finger at the Governor-General, Lord Alexander – one of those old warhorses put out to pasture in the further reaches of the British Empire – rather than towards the Canadian government.

In any case, the dinner was to prove something of an ordeal for Costello, since even before Costello was confronted with the decorative silver cannon, he had 'found the going hard', because, while he himself was a 'good talker', the Governor-General 'was a man of few words and limited conviviality'.[109] Adding insult to injury were the nature of the dinner table decorations. Little silver replicas of artillery festooned the table in front of the Governor-General, who brightly informed Costello that these had been presented to him on a visit to Derry, and that they represented the cannon used in the siege of Derry, one of them being a replica of 'Roaring Meg', the most infamous of these. Accompanying Costello to the fateful dinner, Patrick Lynch has written about how the Governor-General 'seemed either anti-social or slightly hostile in his few exchanges with Mr Costello', a personality trait the Irish high commissioner, John Hearne, attempted to account for with the tactful explanation that the Governor-General's 'manner tended to be dour and that too much should not be read into it'.[110] Equally, it is possible – but stretching credulity considerably – to suggest that Lord Alexander was one of those slightly obtuse colonial administrators who felt that anything originating in Ireland would delight his guest. Perhaps he even mixed up the two Irelands. If so, he would not be the only person or institution to do so, as, just before the inaugural meeting of the Council of Europe in 1949, Ireland's Minister for External Affairs, Seán MacBride, found himself seated behind an odd designation, which informed viewers that this representative hailed from 'Irlande du Nord'. Remedial action was hastily undertaken, which resulted in the bottom half of the offending plaque being sawed off, leading to the sadly truncated version which is visible in photographs of the event.[111]

Whatever the intent, crass ignorance or botched hospitality, Costello's account – where he admitted to being 'certainly annoyed' – leaves us in no doubt as to the strength of his feelings on these matters. Somewhat defensively, he accepted that while the display was 'not intended to be provocative', it was definitely 'tactless' and, given that this display decorated the table at a dinner at which he was the official guest, he 'considered the matter as being in very bad taste'.[112] Patrick Lynch, who was present, has dryly referred to Costello's 'silence' and to how 'subsequent conversation between the two men could not be described as animated, but the Taoiseach displayed an unusually subdued manner until the formalities ended'.[113] His annoyance appears to have been shared by William L. Mackenzie King, the Canadian Prime Minister, who asked what the artillery represented in the polite conversation which took place 'after the ladies withdrew'. His Irish guests, Costello and John Hearne, duly enlightened him, drawing from him the sharp observation 'Will these people never learn!'.

Apart from that exchange, Costello made no comment concerning the incident during or after the dinner, preferring to 'discuss the matter' subsequently with Hearne, as to 'what action', if any, should be taken in the wake of the incident. Of course, the very fact that Costello brooded over 'what action' ought to be taken indicates quite clearly his defensive state of mind. Representing his country abroad, he was more than ordinarily sensitive about the symbols of sovereignty and as to slights, real or imagined, which might be offered. De Valera had attended many such dinners and, by selective application of the Nelsonian principle – in other words, by turning a blind eye – had managed, sometimes quite literally, to overlook anything likely to give offence. In a long career punctuated by subtle finessing and extremely fine hair-splitting, de Valera, begetter of Document No. 2 and taker of empty formulaic oaths, had found that the Nelsonian approach sometimes paid handsome dividends.

Not so the unfortunate Costello, who, while nursing his bruised pride, had concluded that these oversights, namely the failure to honour the prearranged toast to the Irish President and, to a lesser extent, the offensive positioning of the controversial cannon, were 'deliberate actions'. From the outset he was 'completely convinced' that Mackenzie King, who in any case had always tended to be extremely sympathetic towards Ireland, knew nothing about the agreed prior arrangements with regard to the toasts, and 'did not appreciate [the importance of] the happenings'. However, for 'some considerable time', until at least 1961 it appears, Costello remained 'of the opinion' that Lord Alexander's actions (or omissions) were 'deliberate actions'.[114] In the course of an interview with *The Irish Times* in March 1961, Lord Alexander recalled the dinner and remembered 'that we put flowers on the table as a compliment to your Prime Minister', adding that his 'vivid recollection' was that the flowers came in fetching shades of green, white, and yellow. Replying to a question that it was as a result of some action of his 'that Mr Costello was goaded into declaring the Republic', Lord Alexander evinced distinct surprise and could only recall that 'there were no speeches'. Pondering over this interview, which took place more than a decade after the events it examined, Costello rather tetchily conceded that it would have been 'an extraordinary action' for the Governor-General to take 'on his own initiative', and continued, more it seemed in an attempt to convince himself of Lord Alexander's bona fides than anything else, that he 'would not have been guilty of such conduct', and that it would have been 'inconceivable' that Lord Alexander 'would deliberately take a step which would be an insult to this country', and frankly astonishing that, 'had he done so [that] he would have forgotten about it'.[115] Having obviously digested the interview, Costello, in an instructive use of language which is evident throughout his memorandum, proceeded to 'acquit' Lord Alexander of 'any complicity in omitting to propose the Toast of the President of Ireland'.

In the immediate aftermath of the Ottawa dinner, Costello was still brooding over 'what action' to take when his hand was effectively forced. Normally fairly cautious, he had instructed Hearne to try to find out 'the cause' behind the omission of the toast, and beyond that intended to confine himself to reporting back to his colleagues on his return to Ireland. It is possible that this is where matters would have rested were it not for the *Sunday Independent*. Costello had passed an agreeable Sunday as the guest of Charles Burchill, minister resident of Newfoundland, 'some fifty miles from Ottawa', and had attended a civic reception given in his honour by the mayor of Ottawa. Later, he 'did a broadcast over the Ottawa radio.'[116] Later still, Hearne received a telephone call from one of the journalists who had attended the previous night's dinner. Hearne's caller, a journalist from *The Ottawa Journal* named Grattan O'Leary, informed him that an article had appeared in that day's issue of the *Sunday Independent* stating specifically that the government intended to repeal the External Relations Act ('External Relations Act to go' announced the *Sunday Independent* of 5 September

1948), and, in time-honoured journalistic fashion, he wished to know whether Costello had any comment to make. An inevitable 'no comment' was issued by Costello, via Hearne. However, Costello was not nearly as nonchalant as he appeared. Privately, he confessed that the report caused him 'great worry' and presented him with a 'very formidable problem', not least because he was to face a prearranged press conference two days later in the press gallery of Canada's House of Commons, where, in addition to the usual platitudes, this question – one which he 'certainly did not anticipate' – was bound to arise. By now a thoroughly convinced conspiracy theorist, Costello felt that it was 'quite obvious' that the article, penned with such 'apparent authority', could not have been written on the basis of 'intelligent anticipation', and, in a passage squirming with evident distaste, concluded dourly that it 'was the result of a "leak", doubtless emanating from some 'person with inside knowledge'.[117]

Once again, a glum acquittal was wrung from Costello, as his account lugubriously tells of how he had 'since been informed by the writer of the article that there was in fact no leak'.[118] The writer of the article was Hector Legge, editor of the *Sunday Independent*,[119] and the second of the key outside/external players to influence the outcome of this particular saga. Legge was one of those old-style 'gentleman editors', who circulated in polite society and was a seasoned *habitué* of the gentlemen's clubs surrounding Dublin's fashionable squares. Such people had no need to dirty their fingernails engaging in anything so sordid as unearthing a story. Stories came to them, sometimes on silver salvers, along with the clipped cigars and the port. Here, the important thing to remember is that some members of Costello's Cabinet shared not just a political preference, but also a social class – and its attendant circle, attitudes, beliefs, and prejudices – with the editor of the *Sunday Independent*. Close personal links existed between the professional members of the Cabinet, especially the Fine Gael ones, and Hector Legge, a fact which did not escape Costello's jaundiced eye. Combining known circumstances with the dubious coincidence of the article's appearance just then, along with his burgeoning defensiveness, enabled Costello to deduce that the 'person with inside knowledge' was an actual member of the Cabinet. The 'usual suspects' in this instance were considered to be MacBride or James Dillon, both of whom graced the relevant social scene, and cultivated the necessary media contacts. Asked to disclose who vouchsafed him the information contained in the 'leak', Hector Legge has always denied that a leak occurred, stressing that an intelligent reading of the available evidence could have led anybody to draw the conclusion that he did. He argued that a close reading of the Dáil Debates on the adjournment debate, for example, supplied ample evidence as to which way the government was thinking, and that the repeal of the External Relations Act was only a matter of time.[120] Naturally, as a newspaper editor, he delighted in his intuitive scoop, and hugely enjoyed his subsequent notoriety, but was always to maintain that his aim was not to unsettle the government, much less push Costello over the edge.

Pressed to explain how, apart from the extraordinary – even suspiciously inspirational – sense of timing, the belief in a leak arose, Hector Legge pointed to his known close friendship with Dillon, even more than his involvement with certain social circles. This closeness can be gauged from the fact that Legge had introduced Dillon to the woman Dillon would later marry.[121] For all of that, Legge remained adamant that Dillon possessed a strong sense of the dignity of his office and the duties imposed by this position, and that he would not have contemplated, not even for friendship's sake, the violation of Cabinet confidentiality.

Ultimately, Costello, rather reluctantly abandoning his suspicions, accepted Hector Legge's statement that no leak had, in fact, occurred. What this omits to take into account is the apparently ambiguous role of MacBride. Doubtless released by MacBride's demise, which allows for the telling of some stories long kept under wraps, Louie O'Brien, MacBride's private secretary of many years, recently revealed that he was the source of the disputed leak.[122] According to one source,[123] it was only a good many years later, and then by chance and through a third party, that Louie O'Brien learned that the person responsible for the leak was none other than MacBride himself, a discovery which appalled her : 'It was the first glimpse I got of the feet of clay! So many dishonest and dishonourable acts followed with the years that I became totally disillusioned.'[124] It is worth noting that Louie O'Brien herself is a source who has commanded respect from all who have met her.[125] This version maintains that MacBride ensured that the newspapers received an advance copy of Costello's speech to the Canadian Bar Association – the speech which had been 'unanimously approved' by the Cabinet prior to his departure – and that the wilier ones were able to read, as it were, between the lines, and draw the relevant conclusions.[126] In fact, it is normal practice to circulate speeches considered to be important in advance to the media, to ensure adequate and detailed coverage. However, the implications of this story would seem to indicate rather more than an uncomplicated desire to inform the media of thoughts fluttering about in the nether regions of the government's collective head. In this context, Ian McCabe's suggestion is worth noting, for he has written that 'There is a suspicion that MacBride gave Costello's speech to the Canadian Bar Association his imprimatur because he mistakenly believed that it heralded the official announcement of the repeal of the Act, and then prompted the Irish newspapers with an advance release of the speech through the Department of External Affairs.'[127] If there is any truth in this version, then this is where classic conspiracy theory comes to life, as this meant that with the publication of the story, Costello was to be effectively pushed into a situation from where he would be forced or obliged to implement what was essentially Clann na Poblachta policy on the Commonwealth. In other words, Costello would have been manoeuvred into a position where he was to be allowed no option but to repeal the External Relations Act, given that he would be unable to deny the veracity of the reports. This perspective, which regards Costello as a prisoner or pawn of conniving conspirators, such as MacBride, fails to take into consideration a number of factors, the most important of which seems to be that most of the available accounts see matters as being very much the other way around, namely, that MacBride ended up as the pawn, with Costello playing an increasingly assured role as puppet-master.[128]

It is necessary for a number of other reasons to treat the belated 'revelation' that MacBride leaked this story with considerable caution. Hector Legge has always denied that a leak occurred. Over almost half a century, his version of *his own* participation in this saga has remained remarkably consistent,[129] and in his letter of January 1992 he was contemptuously dismissive of the conspiracy theory which views the repeal of the External Relations Act as a sort of time bomb expected to explode when Costello was in Canada, as advanced by Louie O'Brien.[130] It is, of course, possible, that in stressing the lack of external influences in the writing of his article, Hector Legge was seeking to further highlight his own role in the whole process.

However, all of this fails to take into account MacBride's actions at the time, for, immediately after the appearance of the notorious article, MacBride despatched a telegram to Costello, advising him to answer with the time-honoured 'no comment' when asked the inevitable questions at the dreaded press conference. Had MacBride been guilty of the 'leak', this would have been a curious response to make, prompting the observation that if this was conspiratorial politics, it was so subtle as to be almost invisible. However, MacBride appeared to have had some inkling in advance of how matters would turn out at the press conference – whether because he had planned or discussed it with Costello (which is possible but unlikely), or had been responsible for a 'leak' (unlikely but not impossible), or simply knew his man and could gauge how Costello would react – for, when he met with Sir John Maffey, the British representative, on the *morning* of 7 September, it seems that he informed Maffey that it was the government's intention to proceed with the repeal of the External Relations Act.[131] Conspiracy theorists could view this as an example of MacBride pushing a particular course of action by pre-empting Costello's press conference, but a more likely reading is to see it as an attempt to smooth the path of the government, in advance of a fairly bumpy ride.

The appearance of Hector Legge's explosive article had received widespread publicity in Canada through the news agencies and had generated 'great interest' there. Bracing himself for his inevitable ordeal, Costello turned up in the press gallery of Canada's House of Commons on the morning of Tuesday, 7 September, two days after the appearance of the article, to find 'a very large attendance of pressmen', which included, interestingly enough, 'the representatives of the Russian papers'. As with everything else to do with this tale, conflicting accounts exist as to what happened at the press conference. Some accounts seem to feel that Costello lost his temper, but the more interesting debate centres on whether he lost his head. For reasons best known to himself, but alluded to in his memorandum, Costello decided to ignore the proffered advice of his Minister for External Affairs. In his memorandum, he states that this advice, 'though well-intentioned', was one he 'would not be permitted to adopt'.[132] Perhaps the attraction of asserting his position 'as the principal source of foreign policy in the government'[133] was quite difficult to resist.

Confessing that it presented him with 'a very formidable problem', Costello stressed that, before the press conference, he had given 'the most anxious consideration' as to the approach he should take, and pondered over 'what it was proper for me to do'.[134] Perusing the options open to him, Costello concluded that there were just four. He could take MacBride's advice, which was to offer a firm 'no comment', and 'decline' to make 'any statement or suggestion', however great the 'needling' of the press might be'.[135] The second and third options were to deny the truth of the report, or, alternatively, to admit its accuracy. Finally, there was the bolt-hole offered by saying that the matter would be dealt with on the reassembly of the Dáil. Contemplating his available choices, Costello argued that to say 'no comment' or to state that the matter would be dealt with by the Dáil on its reassembly would be tantamount to 'at least a qualified admission' of the truth of the report, and that the assembled journalists would be 'sufficiently intelligent' to realise that. As to his other options, Costello, with touching probity, noted that 'It would of course be quite wrong for me to deny the report, and I certainly never contemplated any such course.'[136] This was to leave him with only one course of action, which was to confirm the essential accuracy of the report; or, as he put it himself, as the report was true, and as the government fully intended to repeal the External Relations Act on the resumption of the Dáil, 'there was nothing in honesty and decency open to me but to admit the truth'.

Justifying his actions to himself, Costello continued with the comment that 'telling the truth' was the 'wisest course' to adopt, adding 'and I still think so'.[137] More relevantly, he insisted that this action was entirely his own decision, and that he had taken it 'with a full sense of responsibility'. Further protestations that this deed had nothing whatsoever to do with 'anything that had occurred' after his arrival in Canada, but had been prompted solely by the questions which arose in the wake of the *Sunday Independent*'s article, can be found in his memorandum. There, he tells of how the 'very first important question' was put to him by 'Mr Mears of *The Montreal Gazette*', who asked whether it was his 'intention to promote legislation to repeal the External Relations Act'. Costello confirmed that it was, and proceeded to give 'suitable replies' by way of answer to several 'subsequent supplementary questions' as to the effect these proposals would have. A little disingenuously, he added that 'naturally the reply gave rise to widespread publicity'.[138]

Inevitably, an alternative version of even the press conference exists. This version contends that not alone was the announced repeal not prearranged government policy, but that Costello's apparently considered responses – after he had mulled over his various options – had not even been planned. According to Cedric W. Sowby, whose stated source was John Hearne, Costello, when answering the blunt question, 'Are you going to repeal the External Relations Act?', is supposed to have said 'I'd like to . . . but'. The pause between the 'to' and the 'but' was so long that a number of the correspondents present dashed away and telephoned the news to their papers that Costello was about to repeal the Act.[139] If there is any truth in this version, then there is little wonder that Costello, in his exhaustive memorandum, laid such stress on the autonomous nature of his action, as the alternative – namely that he blundered into the declaration by accident – is considerably less attractive than an account which purports to have the Taoiseach the author of his own destiny. In that situation, whether Costello announced his intention to repeal the Act because he lost his temper, or whether the appearance of Hector Legge's article forced his hand, becomes almost immaterial, as long as he is seen to have taken such action himself.

Whatever about the communications between Costello and his colleagues in Government before his press conference (Costello had merely made reference to MacBride's telegram advising 'no comment'; MacBride himself had mentioned 'phone-calls'; whereas Louie O'Brien, on the other hand, recalled that 'the wires between Canada and Ireland lit up that night as Costello sought advice from Dublin'),[140] the wires were certainly fairly sizzling after the press conference. The story made international headlines, and Costello commented that there were 'rumours' that the Canadian government had 'met to discuss the situation'. For the remainder of his visit, Costello was to be subjected to a succession of official dinners, replete with the relevant toasts (a fact which he noted with considerable satisfaction), as the Canadian government attempted to feel their way and find out exactly what had happened. Describing these, Costello seemed somewhat defensive when he observed that, 'notwithstanding the announcement that I had made that morning', the Canadian Prime Minister, Mackenzie King, 'was very friendly indeed with me'.[141] In fact, the entire Canadian government, 'all of whom were very friendly', attended one of these repasts. There they sat through what must have been a surreal experience, as Mackenzie King proceeded to make a lengthy speech (described by Costello as 'long and excellent') stressing the similarity of the spiritual values held in common by Ireland and Canada, and omitting entirely any reference to Costello's earlier action. Fortunately, although Costello does not phrase it like that, the Governor-General was unable to attend any further dinners. After the third of these meals, a lunch hosted by Mackenzie King at his country retreat at Kingsmere, two days after the press conference, the pair plus advisers[142] – Costello was accompanied by Hearne – finally got down to serious business and held discussions on what must have been uppermost in their minds. Now that il gatto had been let out of il sacco, Costello's chief remaining task was to engage in a serious spot of damage limitation, soothe Canadian sensibilities (although, in truth, they gave little sign of being too ruffled), and, if possible, bring the Canadians onside, in an attempt to persuade them to support the Irish position at the forthcoming Commonwealth conference, which the Irish would now be obliged to attend in some contrived capacity, if only to tie up various loose ends.

Coincidentally or not, one of the loose ends had earlier presented itself for the consideration of the Irish government. The British representative, Sir John Maffey, was 'being pressed' by his government to find out whether Ireland intended to be 'represented' at the conference, 'and, if so, by whom', and had phoned MacBride on 6 September seeking the relevant information.[143] They met to discuss the matter on the *morning* of 7 September (weekly lunch at the Russell Hotel being their usual preferred option), where MacBride 'explained that the matter had not been fully considered by the Government' and that the government 'would require some further information concerning the matters that are likely to be discussed'.[144] Thereupon Maffey fished out a detailed agenda from his file, which included a further invitation to add 'any items' of interest to the Irish government to this list, and expressed the hope that 'less formal gatherings' and 'informal discussions between individuals' would predominate at the conference.[145] MacBride 'promised' to try to have the matter 'considered immediately' by the Cabinet, and to let Maffey know their 'decision' as soon as possible. Of course, the very fact that the Cabinet, according to MacBride's memorandum, had not 'fully considered' whether or not they should attend the conference by early September strongly suggests that this was not the only 'decision' which had yet to be taken. The matter would be 'considered more immediately' than anyone had supposed, once news of Costello's incredible press conference had filtered through to Dublin. However, more must have been discussed than was alluded to in MacBride's memorandum, for Maffey dashed off a communication to London that afternoon stating that MacBride had informed him of the Cabinet's intention to repeal the External Relations Act.[146] While Costello's press conference had not yet taken place when MacBride and Maffey met – 'given the time differential Costello could only have preceded MacBride's communication to Maffey had he addressed the press in Ottawa at sunrise'[147] – obviously it cast a compelling shadow upon their proceedings. This does not necessarily mean that Maffey was warned in advance about Costello's forthcoming press conference: rather he merely seems to have been informed of an intended policy initiative. Within a matter of hours, this general policy initiative would assume incredibly concrete proportions, leaving Maffey, when he learned of the contents of Costello's press conference – while dining with MacBride in the Russell Hotel – as dumbfounded as some of Costello's own Cabinet. With retrospective disingenuousness, MacBride was to speak of this meeting years later, remarking: 'I didn't want him [Maffey] to be in an awkward position regarding the press conference. I don't know how he could have been so misinformed about the feeling of the Cabinet. Possibly he felt he should have known and didn't know.'[148]

Maffey was not the only person to be astounded, however, for it appears that Costello's announcement had come as a bolt out of the blue for some members of his own Cabinet, despite the fact that it had been (supposedly) decided in advance by them. Noël Browne later confessed to having been utterly astonished by the news,[149] although, as noted earlier, he had been absent from the one meeting – that of 19 August – where this matter had definitely arisen. Considerable shock was also in store for Frederick Boland, then still secretary of the Department of External Affairs, when he learned of Costello's action. Boland, who was not privy to the inner workings of MacBride's mind,[150] was reduced to special pleading when he informed his British counterparts that, 'speaking personally, he felt that 'Ministers had gone too far,'[151] adding feeble reassurances as he nursed his telephones to the effect that 'All we could say is our Prime Minister has simply made an awful gaffe'.[152] MacBride's reported reactions come in a mass of contradictory accounts, some of these versions claiming that MacBride himself, appraised of the announcement while dining at the Russell Hotel with Sir John Maffey, also exhibited signs of surprise. (MacBride's dinners – usually held at some elegantly soignée spot such as the Russell Hotel – form a curiously recurring motif of his time spent in Cabinet.)

Keogh,[153] states that it was Boland who 'informed' MacBride of Costello's announcement when the latter, inevitably, was 'dining at the Russell' with Maffey. Boland's own surprise is certainly genuine, and he thought that MacBride was 'amazed' by the news. Moreover, in an interesting footnote, Keogh[154] also cites Maffey referring to both his and MacBride's surprise. Another source, Lyons,[155] mentions that Maffey himself thought that MacBride 'had looked surprised' when he learned of Costello's announce-ment on the *evening* of 7 September, in, of course, the Russell. Given that the pair had met earlier in the day, and bearing in mind the nature of their discussions (as recalled by MacBride) such surprise – on MacBride's part – seems rather superfluous. As MacBride stressed to James Downey,[156] 'This was no surprise to me or to any other Minister.' In that same interview, MacBride also wondered how Maffey 'could have been so misinformed' about the intentions of the Cabinet with regard to the intended repeal of the Act. In remarks made some years earlier to Lyons,[157] MacBride was equally at pains to lay emphasis on his total lack of surprise. Another contemporary source, MacBride's Clann na Poblachta cabinet colleague, Noël Browne,[158] goes along with the idea of Boland as the amazed messenger *en route* to the Russell in his account.

While this does not preclude the possibility of MacBride possessing infor-mation which he chose not to share with his Departmental Secretary, it should be pointed out that virtually every source (apart, obviously, from MacBride himself) remarks on his 'surprise' on learning of Costello's action. Another source, Cedric Sowby,[159] who also referred to the dinner, stated that MacBride's fellow diner on this occasion was R. M. Smyllie, editor of *The Irish Times*, rather than Maffey, and that the news 'came as a shock' to MacBride. Again, while this could be treated with some slight caution as Sowby's stated source happened to be John Hearne, who was safely stuck in Canada, looking after Costello, it is of interest to note that even Hearne, appar-ently, was aware of MacBride's 'shock'.

The upshot of all this is that it is difficult to escape the conclusion that Costello's precipitate action left the Cabinet (including MacBride) absolutely flabbergasted. This means that it is also difficult to avoid drawing the inference that both Costello and MacBride proceeded to provide cover for each other's stories of actions and (reputed) reactions for the rest of their lives. Just as it was in Costello's interest to stress that the government had taken a decision to repeal the External Relations Act at some stage in the indeterminate future, so it was clearly in MacBride's interest to stress his total lack of surprise at Costello's precipitate action. Otherwise, of course, each of them would have looked extremely foolish, and for the rest of their lives, they both stuck to a version of the events which supported Costello's action and MacBride's version of his own reaction. Of course, MacBride would have looked extremely silly if he had confessed to any degree of surprise. Domestically, and politically, he had to be seen to make at least some of the running on an issue of this sort.

Meanwhile, back in Dublin, the Cabinet had gone into the sort of defensive huddle an Afrikaner *laager* calls to mind. They met on the afternoon of 9 September, lacking six of their number. Actually, for MacBride, matters must have suddenly become very trying, for the 'crisis' concerning the Vatican's intention to appoint Ettore Felici as the new papal nuncio to Ireland, which the government attempted to resist, had just broken at exactly the same time.[160] MacBride and Browne were both present, as was the Attorney-General, Cecil Lavery, who in any case attended most of the meetings of the Cabinet. However, the secretary, Liam Cosgrave, was not present – this was the first Cabinet meeting he had missed since he replaced Moynihan – and this prompts the inevitable question of just who took the minutes for this particular meeting, and, more relevantly, what exactly it was that they chose to record.[161] Predictably, the available minutes are anything but revealing about such matters. What they do reveal is a Cabinet galvanised into action, as matters which had been deferred for months were abruptly addressed. It seems to have been MacBride who rode to the rescue on this occasion, as he turned up with several memoranda, a draft Bill transferring the functions of the King to the President of Ireland, and a recommendation (reversing his previously held opinion) that Ireland should attend the Commonwealth conference, following 'further' discussions with the British representatives as to 'the question of Ireland's being represented at the conference' as long as their 'relation' to the Commonwealth 'was made clear'. Having persuaded the Cabinet to accept the invitation, even if the tortuous conditions they ringed it with were such as to render it the political equivalent of the lotus position, what MacBride then least expected – Maffey noted that 'he appeared somewhat disconcerted'[162] – was for the invitation to be suddenly withdrawn, as the British belatedly aroused themselves and decided to retaliate. According to Maffey, MacBride's disconcertion sprang from the fact that 'the question had apparently been handled by him in the Eire Cabinet on the basis that an invitation had been extended to them'. Further contortions were to develop when the British withdrew the invitation (after all, Ireland was supposedly no longer in the Commonwealth), and the Irish government, who initially were contemplating attendance in the capacity of a rather reluctant bride specialising in the crossed 't's' and dotted 'i's' of a complicated prenuptial agreement, not only were reduced to angling for an invitation, but also found it necessary to lobby their (former) fellow Commonwealth members to ensure that they received it.

To this end they now addressed themselves, lobbying the governments of Australia, Canada, New Zealand, and South Africa in advance of the Commonwealth conference. Thus MacBride headed off to Paris between 3 and 9 October, ostensibly for a meeting of the Council of Ministers of the

Organisation for European Economic Co-operation (OEEC). As is usual (for those times), the available Cabinet minutes are exceedingly detailed where expenditure is concerned – MacBride's trip to Paris is noted as costing the Exchequer £116, including 'gratuities to police escorts' and to an 'extra chauffeur' which came to thousands of francs[163] – yet are astonishingly opaque where the actual business of the government is concerned. While in Paris, MacBride seems to have engaged in an extensive round of networking with several of the Commonwealth ministerial representatives, such as Australia's Deputy Prime Minister, Herbert V. Evatt, who were in Paris on UN business, prior to attending the initial part of the Commonwealth conference in London.[164] Evatt turned out to be a particularly valuable ally for the Irish team during the subsequent Chequers meetings, for it seems that his insistence was crucial in ensuring that the Irish were finally invited to attend the conference, and he also appears to have been instrumental in rejecting the argument of the British hard-liners, such as Jowitt the Lord Chancellor, that, henceforth, Ireland should be treated as a 'foreign' nation, with a consequent loss of rights and privileges for both Irish trade and Irish nationals. Saner counsels soon prevailed, for, alerted – by Evatt among others – to the electoral implications (for the British Labour Party) of the disenfranchisement of the Irish Diaspora in Britain, the Prime Minister, Clement Attlee, and his advisers quickly dispensed with this proposal. Originally, the British view seemed to centre on the premise that to invite the Irish government (after their precipitate action) to attend the conference would, in effect, be a prelude to accepting the Irish position as a *fait accompli*, and that this, in turn, would serve to undermine the very fabric of the Commonwealth. Evatt countered with the argument that to exclude the Irish government from the conference, and to fail to forge the closest possible links with the Irish authorities, would most certainly undermine the Commonwealth. Mindful of the fact that Ireland had been Britain's oldest colonial possession, and, more importantly, that Ireland had been something of a testing ground for the theory and practice of both the making and the unmaking of the British Empire – and now, possibly, of the Commonwealth as well – the other Commonwealth countries paid very close attention to the developing saga. This close attention also took the form of strong support for the Irish position, even from countries such as New Zealand, which MacBride – and the rest of the Irish government – had initially regarded as 'a Union Jack country'.[165]

Chequers was the venue for the Commonwealth conference when it finally got under way on 17 October. Supported by the rest of the Commonwealth, the Irish attended as invited 'observers', a formula which satisfied everybody. They were represented by MacBride from External Affairs and the perspicacious Patrick McGilligan from Finance, but, significantly, not by Costello, who was after all the Taoiseach.[166] McGilligan's dual role lay in the (unspoken Fine Gael) need to keep an eye on MacBride, and by extension on the evolution of foreign policy, and, more importantly, in the fact that he was manifestly a safe pair of hands, something nobody could say at that juncture for Costello himself. Frederick Boland's dismissive opinion of the crude

Costello diplomatic style – 'Jack Costello had about as much notion of diplomacy as I have of astrology'[167] – seems to have been shared by the British. Telegraphing Secretary of State for Commonwealth Relations, Philip Noel-Baker on 15 October, two days before the start of the Commonwealth conference, Maffey's pointed observation that 'Mr Costello personally has conducted this business in a slap-dash and amateur fashion'[168] was obviously noted. In his politest, most unpressing tones, Sir Norman Brook, secretary to the British Cabinet, had asked Clement Attlee, the Prime Minister, 'Presumably Mr Costello should be pressed to come himself. But should he be asked to bring Mr MacBride as well?'[169]

The Irish negotiating position was, in effect, to ensure that having formerly been 'a republic in all but name', Ireland would now contrive to be in 'in the Commonwealth in all but name' – this was where the formula 'non-British, non-foreign' came from. Therefore, the challenge lay in attempting to preserve those advantages which had formerly accrued to Ireland, while severing the symbolic ties which bound the two countries.[170] Speculating as to what might happen in the event of these advantages being suddenly withdrawn, were Ireland now to be regarded as a 'foreign' country, as originally recommended by Lord Chancellor Jowitt, didn't really bear thinking about – a conclusion arrived at, after much thought, by both the British and Irish delegations. In the short term, Ireland emerged from the Commonwealth conference no longer a member of the Commonwealth, but with all of its Commonwealth 'advantages', privileges, and usages intact, something which could hardly have been achieved without the strong support of the other Commonwealth countries.[171]

In the meantime, Costello had returned to Ireland, landing at Cobh on 1 October.[172] Apparently, he then took his time about reporting back to the Cabinet, for he did not put in an appearance at a Cabinet meeting until 11 October. This is a rather strange hiatus, and it defies belief that Costello – especially in the light of his unilateral action(s) in Canada – did not hasten to brief his colleagues earlier than that. The minutes for the meeting of 11 October are quite clear about the fact that all of the Cabinet – including minute-taker Liam Cosgrave – were present, and offer the following enlightening account of Costello's activities as 'item one': 'The Taoiseach reported on his recent visit to Canada and the United States of America and gave an account of the discussions he had with the various people whom he had met and of the addresses and interviews he had given during the course of his journey through the two countries. The action taken by the Taoiseach during his visit to Canada and the United States of America was approved.'[173] Now this smacks very much of not merely padlocking the stable door after the departure of the proverbial bolting horse, but of constructing miles of unnecessary minefields, watch-towers and barbed wire in order to prevent yet further equine escapes.

For it seems that Noël Browne's extraordinary tale of what transpired upon Costello's return to Ireland could well have some basis in fact. Characteristically dissenting from the 'unanimous' version agreed by the rest of the Cabinet, Browne claimed that a 'caucus' meeting of the Cabinet did in fact occur 'one Sunday afternoon soon after the Taoiseach's return to Dublin'.[174] Representing Clann na Poblachta in MacBride's absence abroad, Browne has written about how Costello, 'visibly distressed and unhappy', attempted to explain himself and his actions, even going so far as to offer his resignation as Taoiseach. Needless to say, there are no records suggesting that such a meeting ever occurred, but, given the butterfingered carelessness with which that Cabinet treated this topic – both in what they chose to record and in what they omitted to record – this is not necessarily a drawback.

While Browne himself was not always a totally reliable source, there are a number of reasons for paying this story some attention. Boland – no fan of MacBride's then or later – tends to agree with Noël Browne.[175] And some of the facts seem to, also. As has already been noted, MacBride *was* abroad (in Paris, where he was networking furiously) between 3 and 9 October,[176] and, as Browne normally stood in for him at Cabinet and in the Dáil during his trips abroad, representing Clann na Poblachta at Costello's 'caucus' would have been nothing new. Moreover, the suspicious length of time it took Costello to formally report back to the Cabinet is simply not credible; for one thing the Cabinet was no longer on holiday, and, in addition, the British were bombarding Costello with memoranda,[177] for Costello himself had drastically altered the parameters of the diplomatic game by which Ireland had defined itself since the 1920s – namely the nature of the relationship with Britain. Furthermore, the *draft* of the first item (the final version of which is quoted in full earlier) on the agenda for the meeting of 11 October merits closer inspection, for it seeks clarification on two points, firstly asking, for 'Approval of terms of above minute', and secondly, wondering 'Is minute to be dated last Thursday or today?'[178] This is almost certainly the ghostly thumbprint of the 'caucus' described by Browne, for, if an earlier (mute, unrecorded) meeting had not actually taken place, it would surely have been unnecessary to ask whether the date of 'last Thursday'[179] (in fact, 7 October) or 'today' (11 October) should appear at the head of the minute.[180] Naturally, none of the rest of the Cabinet concurred with this story. Presenting a united front to the world, the Commonwealth conference, and most importantly, the Dáil, the government was to argue that repeal of the External Relations Act represented the culmination of a coherent plan long in the making.

Of course, it was nothing of the sort, and, to conclude, it is necessary to look at the effects of the repeal of the External Relations Act, and what significance this had for the inter-party government and governmental policy formation in general, and for Clann na Poblachta itself – and not only as a member of government – in particular. Most commentators are agreed that the immediate effects were two-fold.[181] Ireland succeeded in safeguarding her Commonwealth advantages, while, at the same time, the repeal unintentionally served to copper-fasten partition and its attendant unionist stranglehold on the institutions and structures of government in Northern Ireland, as the British government retaliated, within a year, with the passage of the Ireland Act, which in effect guaranteed the Union. Other effects involved a name change for the state, Ireland from now on answering to the long-sought-after appellation of the 'Republic of Ireland'. This, in fact, aroused considerable unionist displeasure and gave rise to unionist attempts to lobby the British government with alternative suggestions – such as 'Republic of Southern Ireland' and 'Irish Republic' – which they might care to use in lieu of the offending 'Republic of Ireland'.[182]

As a display of diplomatic acrobatics, the entire episode provokes strong commentaries, ranging from Lee, who regards it as a 'shambles from start to finish, perhaps the most inept diplomatic exhibition in the history of the state',[183] to Keogh's acerbic observation that these 'decision-making skills' were more reminiscent of 'the Marx brothers than with government in a Western democracy'.[184] Noël Browne, no mean connoisseur of acidic contributions himself, uses terms such as 'irresponsible, incredible and ludicrous'[185] to describe these events. Perhaps the most telling comment of all comes from Sir John Maffey, who accepted that this was all 'part of the game of internal politics, and that the hand has been very clumsily played by the Costello Government'.[186] This was a view which was also held by Maffey's successor to Dublin, Sir Gilbert Laithwaite, who grumbled a little over a year later that 'There is a strong feeling that [Costello] mishandled and unwisely forced the pace over the severance of Eire from the Commonwealth.'[187]

The coda to the repeal came the following year, when the Republic was formally inaugurated outside the GPO on Easter Monday, coinciding with the launch of the anti-partition campaign. Along with the President of Ireland, Seán T. O'Kelly, Costello even reviewed the celebratory parade. MacBride did not attend these celebratory march-pasts, not because he was making a 'pitiful protest' in Browne's words, but rather because he was in the United States for the best part of a month on government business.[188] This invocation and meshing of the symbols of historical legitimacy, as well as those of an ongoing national identity, must have been as satisfying for Costello (who had come to be viewed by Maffey as 'emotional on this question') and the rest of Fine Gael, as it was possibly bewildering for their supporters, accustomed as they were to the party's unfortunate addiction to cod liver oil politics by making grimly unpopular virtues out of necessity.

For the repeal adventure had, of course, been Costello's own almost from the very beginning: the snatching of Cowan's question from under MacBride's nose, the 'Canadian capers' to use Noël Browne's expression, even the fact that Costello, as already noted, chose to pilot the Bill repealing the External Relations Act through the Dáil himself rather than leave it to MacBride as the appropriate minister – all of this indicated a Taoiseach very much determined 'to assert his position as the principal source of foreign policy in the government'[189] and, in the process, not only cut his Minister for External Affairs, but also that minister's department, out of the picture. In this context, MacBride's activities chasing around Europe in search of Marshall Aid, attending OEEC meetings, involving himself in the construction of the Council of Europe, and so on do not seem to have counted as the 'real' matters of foreign affairs. What really seemed to have counted, where the action lay, was where the action had always been found, namely in the nature of the relationship with the former colonial power, and historically these were the parameters within which Irish attempts at self-definition had been expressed. These were also the areas on which MacBride – and his party – (as opposed to, say, Costello and *his* party) had originally come to prominence, and given MacBride's past record, and his current portfolio, it was reasonable to expect any offerings or outbursts on the nature of the relationship with Britain to have originated with him. That this did not originate with MacBride serves to highlight the audacity of Costello's clumsily executed act of grand larceny, and the inability of MacBride to prevent such ideological theft. This was a two-pronged robbery, aimed as much at de Valera as at MacBride, for in donning the natty nationalist rain-gear of de Valera, and in stealing the republican raiment of the bathing MacBride, Costello did not merely appropriate their garments, but also enabled Fine Gael to reclaim their nationalist ancestry and heritage, and to lay claim to a portion – their portion – of the national iconography and the symbols of national identity, thereby shedding their unfortunate *démodé* allegiance to the Commonwealth. Certainly, this was how Maffey viewed the matter. Writing to Sir Eric Machtig on 30 September, he noted how 'strangely enough' the demand for the repeal had been 'brought up . . . by Fine Gael who had such a grim time in the Cosgrave Government defending what they did not really believe in'. This didn't really impress Maffey, who thought it both hypocritical and dishonest of Fine Gael to abandon the Commonwealth position they had held since the 1920s. Lamenting that 'it is a great pity that action for the repeal of the External Relations Act did not come to be taken by the Fianna Fail Government, as Fine Gael would certainly have rallied very strong elements in the country to defend the existing links', Maffey went on to argue 'The fact is that the Fine Gael Party had a sudden brainwave that they would steal the "Long Man's" clothes'.[190]

Clann na Poblachta were outmanoeuvred, outgunned, out-thought, and outfought in an area where their greatest strengths should have been evident. The fact that they were unable to safeguard their ideological territory on this matter boded ill for their influence in other matters and for the future. Viewed in that light, Costello's stated subsequent justifications, offered with the twenty-twenty vision of hindsight, for the repeal of the External Relations Act – which included his wish to 'take the gun out of Irish politics', the need to pre-empt or stymie any unwelcome interventions from Captain Peadar Cowan, and, most important of all, the desire to clear up the constitutional confusions that lay in the wake of the Act[191] – certainly sound like those of a man who may have protested too much.

8

The gradually diminishing eminence
of the 'Grey Subsidence'

On his appointment to Iveagh House as Minister for External Affairs in the inter-party government in February 1948, Seán MacBride enjoyed an extraordinarily high reputation, and yet, by 1951, that reputation, as well as the political base which served to reinforce it, was effectively in tatters. In a little over three years, the 'rival Taoiseach'[1] had become transformed into a 'Grey Subsidence'[2] presiding over the precipitous decline of his authority within the Cabinet, and the complete collapse of his party both in the government and in the country at large. If the debut of Clann na Poblachta – and MacBride – on the political stage had been accomplished with a bow and a flourish, their disintegration would be no less dramatic, and considerably more destructive.

There are a number of obvious signposts charting that decline, such as the gradual increase in John A. Costello's confidence and authority – and, by extension, that of Fine Gael – even in areas of expertise not traditionally associated with the party such as an 'emotional' stance on partition, and, more subtly, in the economic sphere; the apparent and ominous collapse of Clann na Poblachta's vote by early 1950; a couple of scandals, one of which, the Baltinglass affair, didn't even involve Clann na Poblachta, but which redounded poorly on the party all the same; and, naturally, the infamous Mother and Child Scheme debacle, which placed intolerable strains on already exceptionally stressed relationships within the Clann, and split the Clann rather than splitting the government – an action which, in effect, brought down the government[3] and, of course, ultimately destroyed the Clann. Each of these will be treated in turn, for the purpose of this chapter is to chart the decline of Clann na Poblachta, as a party and as a force for radical change in Irish society.

Both Lee and Keogh refer to the extraordinarily high standing enjoyed by MacBride immediately after the formation of the inter-party government, Keogh even going so far as to describe MacBride's stature as being that of a 'rival Taoiseach'.[4] Such was his reputation that even the very term he had used to describe the government – 'I coined the phrase inter-party government' he later informed James Downey of *The Irish Times* – came to be readily utilised by the other members of the Cabinet.[5] His stature at the time certainly equalled that of the Taoiseach, for MacBride was privately rated by the CIA as being 'a brilliant and successful barrister, he is noted for his forceful advocacy and remarkable talent for cross-examination. He is probably the best debater in the Dail. He is definitely of Prime Ministerial caliber . . . charming, affable, and intelligent, and an excellent diplomat.'[6]

At Cabinet, too, his reputation had preceded him. His party and Cabinet colleague, Noël Browne, has written about how MacBride would 'scan the Cabinet agenda, and on those subjects on which he had a special interest, would submit a treatise to the Taoiseach. In the early days this memorandum was carefully unfolded and conscientiously read out by the Taoiseach to a politely attentive Cabinet. It was treated with some respect.'[7] Actually, the Cabinet minutes themselves tend to support this recollection, for memoranda from MacBride appeared regularly, and dealt with a comprehensive range of topics, which were not always confined to matters relating to his portfolio. Trespassing into the unguarded territories of other ministers' portfolios was to become a regular feature of MacBride's Cabinet interventions, one, in fact, which would not be curbed for quite some time. Many of these contributions were extremely worthy, able, and iconoclastic – and, naturally, some were not. Circumstances contrived to assist MacBride's tendency towards 'energetic prowling'.[8] Cabinet procedure and administration were initially lax, because the Cabinet secretariat, as discussed earlier, had been stymied. Moreover, inter-party Cabinet discipline was loose – as it had to be, given the range of personalities and views to be accommodated – and, of course, the very idea of an inter-party government was a startling political innovation, one which necessitated the rewriting of the political rule-book and the devising of new, and of necessity flexible, structures designed to cope with the new political situation. This gave ample scope in the early days to a trespasser, especially one entering Cabinet with the sort of intellectual reputation MacBride possessed.

MacBride's considerable impact on the general direction and form of government policy was reinforced by his high profile as Minister for External Affairs. Writing to his government in March 1950, on some of the effects of MacBride's tenure, the tone of the remarks of the British ambassador, Sir Gilbert Laithwaite,[9] was barbed: 'As Minister for External Affairs, he has missed no opportunity of figuring [as] prominently as possible whether at international gatherings or in this country. He has greatly expanded the External Affairs Department and has increased the diplomatic representation abroad of the Irish Republic on a scale which has been criticised as inappropriate for a country both poor and lacking in personnel.'[10] Actually, as Minister for External Affairs he gave the department the sort of prominent profile it had hithero lacked, supplying a sense of articulate direction and undertaking much needed administrative reforms.[11] A rather sympathetic observer, Patrick Keatinge, has commented that MacBride 'can be said to have grasped firmly the few opportunities open to Ireland in those years for pursuing an active foreign policy'.[12] These included joining both the Organisation for European Economic Co-operation and the Council of Europe, and also the establishment of the Irish News Agency, for MacBride fervently believed that world perceptions of Ireland as portrayed by the British media needed drastic remedial action, and argued that this could be best undertaken by the creation of a domestic news agency.[13]

Admittedly, the positive gains to be had by membership of such organisations was squandered to an extent by the constant repetition of the 'sore thumb' policy – namely, raising 'the problem' of Partition at every possible forum, and at every possible opportunity. While MacBride used the Council of Europe to sign the European Convention of Human Rights, stress the importance of civil liberties, and highlight the plight of political prisoners, he also used it to emphasise 'the evils' of partition, to a patently uninterested audience. At that time, with the war a recent memory, Britain was basking in the warm afterglow of that continental regard which was still accorded to her as 'The Liberator' of most of the western part of the continent from a grimmer tyranny than anything Ireland's historic Oppressor had considered possible.[14] By contrast, Ireland's concerns regarding partition were deemed an irrelevance in the wider European picture, and this obsession with the issue of partition continued when the Irish government declined to join NATO on the grounds that 'the continuance of partition precludes us from taking our rightful place in the affairs of Europe'.[15]

In fact, the problem with MacBride and partition was not just that he availed of every opportunity open to Ireland to broaden the country's perspectives and then proceeded to squander some of these net gains by harping on about partition, but rather that he failed to guard his flank, which meant raising partition in the one arena where it did count, namely the domestic Irish context. This was left to others, thereby ensuring, for a short spell, that some elements in Fine Gael, such as Costello – who had already successfully, if awkwardly, snatched the repeal of the External Relations Act from under MacBride's nose and who would go on to play a leading role in the All-Party Anti-Partition Mansion House Conference in 1949 – were to become strongly identified in the public mind with the anti-partition campaigns. And it wasn't only on the public mind that Costello's anti-partitionist features had became firmly fixed. Others noticed them too, and some, such as the British ambassador, found them rather trying, as the following dry note to his government made abundantly clear: 'Mr Costello continues to hold his Government together. Personally very friendly and approachable, he appears to feel bound from time to time to make speeches, particularly on the partition issue, which are uncalled for and unhelpful.'[16]

Uncalled for and unhelpful all of this may have been from a British point of view, but the truth of the matter was that this anti-partitionist perspective not only failed abjectly to undermine any kind of connection with Britain, but simply served instead to further cement whatever ties already existed. In campaigns of this type, the main function of rhetoric is reiterative bonding – sort of like the manly chest-thumping of the New Zealand rugby war-dance, the *haka* – rather than a serious attempt at persuasion of the other side of the merits of one's own point of view. For, of course, theirs was a view of partition which was primitive and very, very basic, a view which owed far more to geographical idealisation (islands are 'natural' units, and divisions of countries were wrong for they defied 'natural' geography) and an old-fashioned view of atomic physics (an atom is indivisible) than any sort of political reality.[17] Having stressed that point with some rather attractive imagery, the anti-partition campaign proceeded to emphasise the considerable grievances and privations endured by the nationalist community in Northern Ireland.[18]

In fact, none of the parties operating in the Republic of Ireland at that time displayed any sense of an understanding of the kind of cultural, social, and political problems which would have to be addressed in the event of anyone seriously contemplating grappling with 'the problem' of partition, which meant, in other words, acknowledging the existence of the unionist perspective.[19] Years later, it was put to MacBride that his description of the unionists as 'quisling Irish' in publications produced by the Mansion House Conference was hardly calculated to win support for an anti-partitionist position, at the very least in the context of unity with consent. Audibly wincing, he replied, 'I probably would not use the word quisling at the moment – but, I would regard the attitude of any Irishman that sides with Britain against the majority of the Irish people as being, certainly, not being a good Irishman.'[20] The key point to be made about MacBride's policies on partition, if one can justify the use of the word 'policies' in this context, is not just that they were traditional full-blown declarations of orthodoxy and as such characteristically deficient in any sort of critical analysis, nor that the Clann was expected to espouse such almost by definition, nor even that MacBride discussed this at every international forum open to him while neglecting the domestic one (which was the only arena that really counted in Irish political terms), but is simply that even in this particular area – supposedly his greatest strength and strongest suit – MacBride was virtually outmanoeuvred by Fine Gael, to the extent that Costello's voice came to be recognised as being at least as authentically 'emotional'[21] on the evils of partition as that of the leader of the more republican of the two parties. Certainly, Laithwaite, writing with gritted teeth, seemed to see it as such, commenting dryly on Costello's 'intemperate public references to the partition issue',[22] and drawing irked attention to 'his threat, as unwise as experience has shown it to be impracticable, to hurt Britain in "her pride, her prestige, and her pocket"'.[23]

Initially, in accepting the External Affairs portfolio, MacBride possibly sought, like de Valera before him, to ascend into an international sphere reserved for such elevated concerns, and to be identified in the public eye as 'Mr Ireland' plying his trade abroad. 'Mr Ireland' plied his trade with considerable panache abroad, and turned out to be an extremely talented, dedicated, energetic, and hard-working Minister for External Affairs. Representing his country abroad – and MacBride as minister travelled far more than any of his predecessors had ever done – MacBride introduced the notion of a peripatetic Minister for External Affairs to the Irish body politic for the first time. This did not meet with universal approval, even among the faithful in Clann na Poblachta. In the spirit of the times, such disapproval found ample expression in the composition of scurrilous ditties by the less reverent,[24] and a wide variety of wisecracks, of which Peadar Cowan's sardonic offering – 'he flew round like a spring butterfly only his boundaries far extended those of the Botanic Gardens'[25] – at least had the merit of lyricism. MacBride robustly defended the need for his extensive travels. When asked in Clann circles why he travelled so much and 'what good all this would do for Ireland', he loftily told the party not to be 'so parochial in outlook'.[26]

Of course, ultimately, this meant, in the context of MacBride's personal and political preferences, neglecting his party – and his party's interests – at home, an oversight not missed by Laithwaite, who so elegantly put it: 'He is thought by some to pay less attention to holding his little Clann na Poblachta party together than is wise.'[27] It is perfectly possible to be an excellent Minister for External Affairs – as MacBride was – and, simultaneously, to require tuition in party political leadership, in the niceties of maintaining and nurturing the party structure, and in how to safeguard one's ideological territory.

Despite not possessing the Finance portfolio, MacBride still found plenty to say on economic matters, particularly matters of economic development which suggested a role for some sort of state planning.[28] In time, he would encounter opposition not merely from cabinet colleagues, anxious to curb his influence, but also from some in the civil service, especially from the mandarins of the Department of Finance, who came to be MacBride's particular *bête noire*. Farrell mentions an interesting incident, from early in the life of the government, where officials from Finance attempted to cut across MacBride's personal negotiations with a foreign diplomat concerning funding of afforestation programmes with moneys from Marshall Aid.[29]

MacBride's tendency to pronounce on economic policy was due partly to his continuing interest in such matters and partly to the fact that circumstances conspired to present an almost unique opportunity to those who regarded themselves as proficient in the uncharted waters of economic planning. The European Recovery Programme (Marshall Aid) had just been launched, and MacBride's early pre-eminence in Cabinet had enabled him to ensure that everything to do with the European Recovery Programme, the OEEC, the applications for Marshall Aid, and the elaborate 'plans' for spending it – plans which were disguised as a Long-Term Programme for economic planning and development which itself was a prerequisite before the disbursement of Marshall Aid funds could even be considered – were handled by External Affairs, rather than Finance.[30] Interestingly enough, Finance never enjoyed any influence over attempts to secure Marshall Aid, for, even in 1947, the Fianna Fáil administration had dispatched Seán Lemass, at that time Minister for Industry and Commerce, rather than Frank Aiken, the

Minister for Finance, to Paris for the initial negotiations concerning Marshall Aid. Thus, by the time the inter-party government took office, a precedent for the exclusion of Finance from matters concerning Ireland and the OEEC had already been set, and MacBride was quite content to persist with this course, for he had plenty of long-term ideas on how Marshall Aid should be allocated (for example, land rehabilitation and afforestation), while Finance, in a classic demonstration of its intellectual poverty, could offer nothing better than a suggested rejection of the proposed funding, and, failing that, a recommendation that it be used to reduce the national debt.[31]

Finance were to fight a vigorous rearguard action, but, in truth, they would never have managed to circumvent MacBride's agility and ability without the deft touch supplied by their own minister, the perspicacious Patrick McGilligan.[32] Regarded by many as the best mind in the Cabinet – the British ambassador, Sir Gilbert Laithwaite, considered McGilligan to be 'shrewd and well-informed . . . he is eminently balanced and has a full appreciation of the factors in the economic field',[33] while Noël Browne has referred to McGilligan's 'panache, brilliance, and intellect'[34] – McGilligan's was indeed a deft touch, the application of which owed absolutely nothing to traditional Finance prejudices or attitudes. For, if McGilligan eventually succeeded in prevailing against MacBride, it was at the cost of moving onto MacBride's territory,[35] by embracing some form of expansionist economic thinking[36] – an outcome which must have horrified the mandarins and caused their starched collars to stand on end. Indeed, the mandarins of Finance were not the only august body to take umbrage at the new, and original, direction that the policies of the Minister for Finance seemed to be steering the country towards. Grumbles were also heard from the sort of groups considered likely to support traditional Fine Gael policies, the sort of upright pillars of society and stalwart members of the business community whose outraged – but polite – howls of protest started to land on McGilligan's desk as they made their displeasure known to sympathetic friends on the Fine Gael advisory committee, who, being stalwart businessmen themselves, viewed with equal dismay the new direction taken by their Minister for Finance, as a series of internal 'Confidential' minutes make clear.[37] 'The portion of his [McGilligan's] speech in the Senate relating to profits not only failed to correct the previous impression as to his attitude but it left the members of the committee who heard it with the feeling that there is a fundamental difference between his views and those held by the members of the committee', the chairman of the Fine Gael advisory committee noted with consternation and disbelief.[38] Appalled indignation at the subversive thoughts the minister appeared prone to express emerged later in the same confidential document: 'Mr McGilligan made an extraordinary statement in which he said that business people had assets to leave to their children and most other people had not. I consider it ridiculous and unfair to make a general statement of this kind.'[39]

Actually, the astonishing conversion of McGilligan, Costello, and Mulcahy to the delights of Keynesian economics – 'we introduced Keynes to Ireland', as Costello, replete with satisfaction, phrased it years later[40] – together with the conviction with which they were to express their complete conversion to economic planning and development on the part of the state, is one of the major mutations undergone by a political elite since the foundation of the state. Adopting the satisfied tone of the total convert, Costello was to tell Michael McInerney that Mulcahy 'is a man of idealistic principles and he is receptive of advanced economic or financial ideas. In fact, he and McGilligan today have very advanced opinions about the role of the Central Bank in the Irish economy.'[41] Continuing along this line, he proceeded to explain how 'in recent times, Mulcahy was a strong supporter of the ideas of my son Declan, and the Just Society and the social and economic programme which was debated in Fine Gael recently'.[42] Just so.

In fact, a major influence in securing the conversion of both McGilligan and Costello to such economic heresies was the role played by Patrick Lynch, who was seconded from the Department of Finance to the Department of the Taoiseach, to serve as Costello's personal economic adviser, and occasional secretary. Described by Lee as 'a gifted and idealistic economist',[43] Brian Inglis goes still further with his comment that Lynch 'shared many of my left-wing opinions, though as a civil servant he had to take care not to profess them publicly'.[44] Discussing his role, Lynch himself has written about how he 'prepared for the Taoiseach drafts of speeches influenced by what seemed relevant of Keynesian economics'.[45] Lynch was to push the notion of a 'double budget system' – making a clear distinction between capital and current expenditure as practised in countries such as Sweden – on his immediate boss, Costello, and on McGilligan as Minister for Finance. Both proved to be quite receptive to Lynch's earnest entreaties on the need for a 'capital' budget. Recalling this, Lynch later remarked: 'I was anxious that the principle of the two budgets should be formally adopted. My attempts to secure the introduction of explicit Keynesian thinking into economic policy required caution and discretion if my position were not to be misrepresented. I had to choose my words with care.'[46]

Ireland's first capital budget was presented to the Dáil on 3 May 1950 by Patrick McGilligan.[47] Apart from introducing the notion of deficit spending for capital expenditure, it is also worth noting for the fact that Seán MacBride, possibly the first Irish politician to utter the word 'Keynes' in an Irish political context, and certainly the first to introduce economic policy as an electoral weapon, seems to have had very little to do with the preparation of this budget. Certainly, he did not feature on the Cabinet committee which was established in February 1950 to address the question of the draft estimates for the public services for the year ending 31 March 1951 and 'to devise a programme of capital works to be undertaken by the State over a period of years'.[48] This interesting committee was a small one which contained Costello, the Tánaiste, William Norton, McGilligan himself, and the Minister for Agriculture, James Dillon. MacBride's omission, on a topic close to his heart, was probably deliberate, and offers an interesting pointer as to his declining clout – or Fine Gael's increasing confidence – in Cabinet at about this time.[49] Indeed, it is reasonable to assume that, but for McGilligan's indifferent health which meant that he missed quite a few Cabinet meetings and attended them by phone instead, which sometimes entailed him being on the line for hours at a stretch – MacBride put it down to hypochondria, 'That's how he stays alive. He takes to his bed at the first sign of a cold.'[50] – MacBride's own position in the Cabinet could have been even weaker by 1951. Laithwaite, for one, wrote with evident regret about how McGilligan's 'indifferent health results in his playing a less prominent part in public than his abilities would justify',[51] adding that if on account of his poor health, he had been obliged to change portfolios, accept a legal appointment, or leave the government, he would have been 'a very real loss'.[52]

Notwithstanding their common accord on the need for Keynesian-style economic planning, MacBride and McGilligan frequently expressed economic policies known to be at variance with each other, a divergence of opinion McGilligan was prepared to argue for in the Dáil when he asked rhetorically, 'Have we got to the stage when men, just because they join the government circle, must all, as one deputy said, when they go out of the council chamber, speak the same language?'[53] Not only were they not speaking the same language, but their discordant tunes even caught the attentive ear of the British ambassador, who wrote about this to his government in a barbed note, where he commented that MacBride's 'tendency to announce the decisions of his colleagues in the Government and to trespass in their fields has attracted unfavourable comment. It has been particularly marked in respect of finance and economics where his contributions, which suggest an imperfect grasp of the principles involved, have frequently been sharply at variance with the official view of the Finance Minister.'[54] In a later letter, Laithwaite dispensed entirely with such sardonic understatement when he drew pointed attention to the fact that MacBride's financial policy 'is wholly at variance with that of the Finance Minister'.[55] Whether McGilligan was wholly at variance with MacBride, or whether he prevailed against MacBride at the cost of becoming a fellow convert to Keynes – or both as seems more likely – while important in the context of the evolution of economic policy, is not as important in the context of Clann na Poblachta in government as is the fact that, ultimately, McGilligan and Fine Gael prevailed against MacBride in economic matters, supposedly his area of greatest expertise, much as they had prevailed earlier in republican rhetoric, which was supposedly where MacBride's greatest electoral, and rhetorical, strength lay.

Economic policy was one thing, and while parties attempting to define themselves as fluent in their command of this sort of exalted rhetoric would have done well to pay close heed to the fact that their leader was gradually losing ground in Cabinet, other more pressing problems loomed, which suggested that the Clann itself was losing ground in the country at large.

Ominously, it appeared that the Clann was losing a lot of its previous political support. At a by-election held in Donegal in early 1950, the Clann's candidate lost his deposit, and polled only half of the vote the party had amassed in the previous general election.[56] Worse was to come in the local elections in September of that same year. Results from these elections showed that the Clann's vote – instead of consolidating and increasing – had actually decreased enormously, for it had reduced by more than half, their general election first preference total of over 13 per cent falling precipitously to give them a reduced national total of around 6 per cent.[57] As one commentator has rightly remarked, 'This would seem to indicate the poor condition of the party's organisational structures. It appears that little effort had been made following the 1948 general election to plan for subsequent electoral contests.'[58]

In fact, for a party which harboured dreams of supplanting Fianna Fáil, and putting down roots as a nationally based catch-all sort of party, the 1950 local elections starkly illuminated the Clann's electoral limitations. Both in design and in execution, the Clann's catastrophic local authority campaign threw into sharp relief the undeniable fact that Clann na Poblachta was not going to supplant Fianna Fáil and eventually become a national movement of venerable age, enviable flexibility, and spectacular tenacity where the acquisition and retention of power were concerned. Instead, by offering the stark image of a party in decline, Clann na Poblachta served notice that their dream of becoming this type of national movement was pretty much moribund. In the local elections of 1950, the party only managed to run 159 candidates, and of these only 29 succeeded in capturing seats on any of the local authorities.[59] There were a number of reasons for this, of course, chief among them the conspicuous incapacity of the Clann as a party to attract new blood – in fact, astonishingly few new names ran for election to the various local assemblies under the Clann na Poblachta banner. Equally appalling from the party's point of view was their patent inability to retain some of their old blood (in other words, astonishingly few of their *unsuccessful* general election candidates from the 1948 election thought to consolidate their local base by seeking election to the local assemblies), and worst, much the worst of all was the startling fact that only one of their *successful* Dáil candidates of 1948 thought to fortify his electoral base at a local level – something which is surely considered one of the cardinal rules of Irish political behaviour, where it is generally accepted that without a comprehensive and well-nurtured network of local contacts, and a solidly secured local base, a candidate's chances of election to the Dáil are remarkably slim.

Jack McQuillan in Roscommon was the exception to this widespread myopia, a myopia that amounted almost to culpable political negligence, for it demonstrated all too clearly that Clann na Poblachta's Dublin-based leadership possessed remarkably untuned political antennae. McQuillan ran for the local council, topping the poll and bringing in a party colleague on his coat-tails. His recognition of the importance of a strong local base served as an illustration of his shrewd political judgement, and is possibly one of the reasons why he was able to retain his Dáil seat as an Independent long after he left Clann na Poblachta in 1951.[60] The best way of placing these horrendous results in context is probably to point out that while Clann na Poblachta won six Dáil seats in the greater Dublin area in the general

election of 1948, they could only manage to win two seats on Dublin Corpo-
ration in the 1950 local elections. This left them with a grand total of four
local representatives on Dublin local authorities, the new pair, Joseph Barron
and Michael ffrench-O'Carroll, adding to the two Clann councillors elected to
Dublin County Council two years earlier.[61] This was a horrifying collapse of
their vote, even allowing for the fact that party allegiances can often become
strangely flexible during local elections, as traditional political ties temporar-
ily succumb to local attractions. At the very least, such an electoral
hammering must have contributed further to the undermining of MacBride's
position at the Cabinet table.

Laithwaite, an astute and perceptive observer of the domestic Irish political scene, was well able to chart this decline, even if MacBride himself wasn't.
By late 1950, the fulsome adjectives in diplomatic communications which had
greeted MacBride's appointment to Iveagh House had been replaced by a tone
of baffled wonder. While noting that 'Mr MacBride remains enigmatic', Laithwaite also noted, with his customary keen acuity, that MacBride 'remains
most anxious to attract the limelight, but his incursions into the field of his
colleagues have been less marked during the period of this report'.[62]

Some months previously, when alluding to the Donegal by-election results,
Laithwaite had already shrewdly pinpointed one of MacBride's political weaknesses when, as was seen earlier, he informed his government that MacBride
'is thought by some to pay less attention to holding his little Clann na
Poblachta party together than is wise'.[63] Holding a party together, especially
one emitting signs of chronic decline, calls for certain skills, for internal
strains sometimes have an unfortunate tendency to manifest themselves as
visibly as possible. Of course, MacBride and Peadar Cowan had already
parted ways – a split foreseen by Seán MacEntee long before it actually
happened and assiduously mined for all it was worth.[64] However, while Clann
na Poblachta could cope with the unfortunate loss of Cowan, the loss of Noel
Hartnett – their director of elections – was a blow the party could ill afford,
and smacked of what Lady Bracknell would have termed carelessness. The
minutes of the standing committee of Clann na Poblachta noted with an ill-
concealed lack of grief on 9 February 1951 that 'A letter of resignation from
the party was read from Noel Hartnett. It was unanimously decided to accept
his resignation.'[65] Their national executive did a little better, when they
instructed the party general secretary at their meeting of 10–11 February to
write to Noel Hartnett 'informing him that his resignation has been noted
with regret'.[66] Hartnett had submitted his resignation to the Clann on 8
February, but it was only published in the national press in the aftermath of
the Mother and Child Scheme debacle, in April. In his letter of resignation he
argued that the Clann had 'compromised on those principles of political
honesty and clean administration which we induced our supporters to
believe were fundamental in our policy',[67] and continued with a denunciation
of the sort of policy which determined action on the basis of whether they 'a)
precipitate an election, or b) prove popular with the electorate. This may be
realpolitik, but it is nevertheless amoral.'[68] According to Hartnett, this amoral
cynicism had expressed itself most recently during the 'Baltinglass' affair.

The 'Battle of Baltinglass', as it came to be known, arose because of an improper political appointment made at the behest of the National Labour Minister for Posts and Telegraphs, James Everett, to a post office in Baltinglass, Co. Wicklow,[69] a small town which despite its existence just inside the borders of 'the Pale'[70] also happened to lie within the minister's own well-tended constituency. In fact, a surprising amount of time at Cabinet was already taken up with post office appointments, and dismissals, not all of them owing everything to political patronage.[71]

Everett's portfolio meant that he was also in charge of the national radio station, Radio Éireann, where he 'remarked more than once, that his yard-stick for programmes was the man lying on his settle-bed in Wicklow after his hard day's work'.[72] Such wide cultural interests notwithstanding, Everett appointed Michael Farrell,[73] a political supporter of his, to the position of sub-postmaster in Baltinglass over the head of the other candidate, Helen Cooke,[74] who already held the position which her family had held for the previous eighty years. The crassness and the blatant injustice of the appointment infuriated many in the town, and a successful and prolonged – though ultimately very ugly – boycott of the new post office run by Farrell was mounted.[75]

Throughout all of this, Everett continued to stick to his guns, and persisted with the appointment of Farrell despite mounting evidence of sustained – and increasing – opposition to it. Although they presented a united front to a contemptuous world, the Cabinet were not at one on this matter. While Noël Browne tended to give the impression of a complacent Cabinet supporting Everett, this was not strictly true. The requirements of inter-party politics at Cabinet meant that Everett, as the sole representative of his party, had to be given some leeway on such matters, but that did not mean he had the unanimous approval of his colleagues, as Noël Browne seems to suggest.[76] In fact, privately MacBride was as horrified as Browne over the Baltinglass debacle, on account of its doubtful political morality, the political ineptitude displayed in the way it was (mis)handled, and the inevitable – and expected – negative political fall-out, but the difference lay in the fact that he did not consider it an issue worth bringing the government down over,[77] whereas Hartnett, in his letter of resignation, obviously did. It is only fair to point out that Hartnett was not alone in holding this view. Several of the Baltinglass Boycott Committee felt this way also, including Ben Hooper,[78] who felt that 'jobbery in a rural post office was an ideal matter to fight an election over'.[79] Asked whether he considered this an appropriate issue on which to bring down a government, he replied, tartly, that it was a considerably better issue than the one upon which they eventually fell.[80] Within Clann na Poblachta, the Baltinglass scandal acted as a sort of prism, focusing attention (almost by proxy) on the respective positions – principled or otherwise – held by those on the different wings of the party. Pressed by Hartnett and Browne to make a public protest over the Baltinglass appointment, MacBride – according to Browne – 'pleaded weakly "that unsavoury matters are inseparable from politics"'.[81]

In Baltinglass, Farrell eventually resigned his position, and Helen Cooke was restored to her rightful place, presiding over her family's post office.

Theoretically, this should have redounded against Everett, but, electorally, it didn't. However, it did cause a crisis of confidence in the one party which had campaigned consistently against 'corruption and jobbery in public life', namely Clann na Poblachta. MacBride himself, while he readily conceded the point about jobbery, and argued that this was not an issue upon which to bring down a government, also felt quite strongly that this was not Hartnett's real motivation in quitting the Clann. According to MacBride, Hartnett had 'left the Clann because I didn't make him a Senator'.[82]

In addition to ministerial portfolios, the first inter-party government also undertook to share out the eleven positions in the Senate normally reserved for the pleasure of the Taoiseach. Costello's hands were tied in this context, too, for he simply carried out the prearranged distribution of seats, without himself having any say in the division of these spoils. Under this arrangement, Clann na Poblachta received two Senate seats. One of them was bestowed on Dr Patrick McCartan, the 1945 Independent presidential candidate, while the other went to Captain Denis Ireland, a truly peculiar choice. Actually, Denis Ireland came from unionist stock,[83] and MacBride ostensibly appointed him on the grounds of building bridges between the two traditions on the island.[84] There were some in the party, Noël Browne being one (and Hartnett, himself, would become another), who eventually were to view Denis Ireland's appointment to the Senate with the gravest of suspicion as being indicative of some sort of hidden agenda on MacBride's part.[85] MacBride staunchly defended the selection of both McCartan (a choice nobody took issue with) and Ireland. Moreover, as he plausibly pointed out, he had not entered public life to indulge in patronage for his political cronies,[86] and he certainly would have regarded the elevation of Hartnett to the Senate in that light. Despite that, Hartnett was 'deeply hurt'[87] by MacBride's refusal to appoint him to the Senate, especially in view of the prevailing belief that 'it is generally accepted that a campaign director, following a general election, has some right to recognition by the party leader'.[88] Moreover, Hartnett apparently also made representations to be put in charge of the newly created Irish News Agency – a position to which he would have been eminently suited – representations MacBride also turned down, ostensibly for the same reason that he had refused to appoint Hartnett to the Senate.

Despite the fact that Hartnett had resigned from Clann na Poblachta's national executive, had also resigned membership of its standing committee, and had actually quit the Clann na Poblachta party itself by February 1951, notwithstanding these multiple resignations, within a month, strangely enough, Hartnett had been asked to accompany MacBride on an official visit to the USA, as his factotum and speech-writer. His function appeared to lie in his ability to generate vast quantities of the sort of maudlin nostalgia which was the preferred diet of audiences consisting of Irish-American republicans, and for the first half of the visit all appeared to have worked out quite well. However, somewhere in the middle of that trip, Hartnett and MacBride had one last, 'blazing row',[89] and Hartnett returned home early to Dublin, by himself.

In the normal course of events, Hartnett's fall-out with MacBride would have had unfortunate organisational repercussions in Clann na Poblachta – as it, in fact, did – but what conferred an added dimension to this split were three additional factors, namely Hartnett's close relationship with Noël Browne, the latter's increasingly strained relationship with Seán MacBride, and the absolutely extraordinary position, or role, that the Catholic Church enjoyed in everyday life and everyday law in Ireland at that time, especially on matters relating to 'faith and morals', health, or education.

It was somewhat characteristic of Noël Browne to suggest, years later, that he disagreed with Hartnett's multiple resignations when he wrote, 'While I agreed with him about the principle involved . . . I felt that he tactically was mistaken in resigning . . . reluctantly, I must conclude that this was an essentially self-indulgent, petulant gesture on his part. It was ill-judged, and serious in its consequences for those of us who remained on in the party.'[90] At the time, however, a different interpretation can be inferred from Browne's actions, for he sided publicly enough with Hartnett, to the extent that he himself resigned from the Clann's standing committee on 15 February 1951, while still remaining a member of the national executive.[91] In fact, *The Irish Times* of 21 February was alert to the possibility of a serious split in Clann na Poblachta, for their political correspondent reported that there was a cleavage between those who, like 'Mr MacBride, who believed that the present government should be maintained, and those, who like Dr Browne and Mr Hartnett, argued that the party was in danger of losing its soul and must cleave to its principles at the expense of quarrelling with the other parties in the government'.[92]

The relationship between 'Dr Browne' and 'Mr Hartnett' went back to 1947, when Hartnett had recruited Browne into the Clann, after meeting him at Newcastle Sanatorium, where Browne had been treating a friend of Hartnett's. To a certain extent, Hartnett became Noël Browne's political mentor[93] – Whyte uses the expression 'intimate friend'[94] – and, perhaps, it was inevitable that when Hartnett and MacBride fell out, the ties which bound Browne to MacBride would diminish.

For the first three years of the government, these common ties gave every indication of being sufficiently sturdy to withstand the strains imposed upon them. At Cabinet, Browne was by far the youngest person present, and was seen very much as being MacBride's junior companion. To his relative youth – he was only thirty-two when he was elevated to ministerial rank – could be added the fact that Browne was, comparatively speaking, something of an unknown quantity in a political sense, for, despite the fact that he had been appointed Minister for Health on his very first day as a TD, he did not have the sort of prior reputation some of his Cabinet colleagues – even those who had not previously served in Cabinet – enjoyed. Moreover, Browne's Health portfolio was a new one too, having only come into existence in 1947, thereby ensuring that its position in the cabinet pecking order was a fairly low one.[95] In addition to that, Browne's own preference at Cabinet was to concentrate on Health matters,[96] whereas MacBride dealt with everything else – and this served to reinforce Browne's somewhat subordinate status.

Likewise, the fact that, in MacBride's absences abroad, Browne stood in for him as acting Minister for External Affairs, at Cabinet and in the Dáil, tended to reinforce this perception, as well as throwing an interesting light on the manner in which the inter-party government actually operated, where port-folios were seen as belonging to the party to which they had been allocated, rather than belonging to the government at large.

Before turning to Browne's deteriorating relationship with MacBride, a brief look at his own tenure in Health is required. When Browne abruptly resigned as Minister for Health in April 1951, the manner of his resignation (he was asked to resign by MacBride, who was backed by Costello), as much as the matter over which he resigned (a no-means-test health scheme which resulted in ecclesiastical pressure being brought to bear), created a political sensation. The fact that Browne had taken care to guard his flank by simul-taneously arranging for the publication – in the only newspaper likely to accept such a subversive offering, the liberal, Protestant-owned *Irish Times* – of all of the surreptitious correspondence which expressed these ecclesiasti-cal doubts contributed even further to the sensation, and meant that such matters now had to be openly discussed. However, striking though the manner of his departure from office was, the very fact that it was Browne who quit office, as opposed to almost any other minister,[97] was what conferred that blend of drama, farce, and tragedy for which the Mother and Child Scheme debacle is best remembered.

For Browne had enjoyed a richly merited reputation as an outstanding Minister for Health. He brought to his task a vision of what he wished to achieve, and he proved himself a gifted administrator and an idealistic, and deeply motivated, minister. This is the standard view found in almost every source,[98] including – perhaps surprisingly – the assessment expressed by his Cabinet colleague, and party leader, Seán MacBride, who later recalled, 'Noël Browne was a first-class Minister for Health. He did a first-class job of work on the eradication of TB.'[99] Even Costello, the Taoiseach – whose parsimonious lack of praise for the two Clann na Poblachta ministers in his Cabinet stands in stark contrast to his frequently expressed warm recollec-tions of the various Labour Party ministers – was reluctantly obliged to admit that 'Browne was a very hard-working Minister until the disaster of the Health Plan'.[100] In fact, Browne's passionate involvement with the concerns, goals, and problems of his Department of Health gave rise to a quite typical response from James Dillon, which took the form of coining a characteristically cruel nickname – 'My Bleeding Heart' – for him.[101] Harry Hitchcock has called Noël Browne 'an angry young man, to use today's parlance',[102] which he was, in the best, righteous sense of the word, but he was also very much a man with a mission, his mission being to mastermind, direct, and superintend, the eradication of the frightful disease of TB by whatever means lay at his disposal.

In tackling the problem of TB, Browne 'showed a restless, tearing energy',[103] the sort of energy his colleagues at Newcastle Sanatorium would readily recall, as one of the nursing sisters explained to Harry Hitchcock, who had just arrived to join the medical staff there: 'It is unbelievable how he straightaway lifted the morale . . . Just wait; his enthusiasm is infectious, he's a great motivator. All the younger staff are motivated by him.'[104] Driven, Browne employed a number of stratagems. His most pressing initial problem was in acquiring a sufficiency of beds to meet his immediate short-term needs, while on a long-term basis, the Department of Health was committed to an intensive programme of hospital construction. Browne was fortunate in enjoying untrammelled access to his own funds and being completely independent of the parsimonious fingers of the Department of Finance. This was the Hospitals Sweepstakes Fund, and Browne solved his financial problems 'brilliantly by a radical redeployment of his department's resources'.[105] He liquidated all of the assets of the Department of Health, and mortgaged the next £10 million which was expected to accrue from the Hospitals Sweepstakes Fund. With funding secure, he embarked on a recruitment drive to staff these new institutions, infecting most of his own departmental staff with enthusiasm in the process. Disused or underutilised buildings, such as a barracks in Dublin and a former mental hospital in Castlerea, were pressed into temporary service as hospitals. Furthermore, advances in medical research had led to the development of new drugs, such as streptomycin and BCG, which were designed to combat TB.

As minister, Browne encouraged the use of such new drugs, and saw to it that their availability was funded from the public purse. Generally, while relations between the Minister for Health and the main interest group representing the interests of the doctors, the Irish Medical Association, were fairly good in the early years of the inter-party government, some disagreements did occur. In fact, Browne's decision to ensure that the control and distribution of the scarce and expensive drug streptomycin remained with the Department of Health, rather than in the hands of the medical profession, provoked the first clash between Browne and the IMA,[106] with the latter resisting the idea of what they saw as 'state control', and the Minister for Health irritated with what he viewed as the 'uncompromising hostility of a section of the profession'[107] towards the introduction of much needed reforms in the health system. Another early bone of contention was the order from the Minister for Health directing local authorities to report to him personally within twenty-four hours any complaint made against medical officers in the performance of their duties,[108] an order which was greeted with barely concealed anger by the medical profession, who saw it as undermining their authority, and was defended robustly by Noël Browne, who regarded this as the sort of accountability the institutions of a state preaching democratic values should practise.

Also funded from the public purse was an enlightened programme of public education concerning health in general, and TB in particular, which was attractively presented and availed of the best that modern methods of communication could offer, for example publishing 'stylish'[109] pamphlets in both Irish and English. The Department of Health commissioned health education films, and Noël Browne himself frequently took to the airwaves of the national radio station, where he explained his department's goals and achievements to the country at large. As Ruth Barrington has noted, his high profile was successful 'because of his youth, obvious compassion, his own history of illness, and his commitment to eradicating the disease'.[110] Looking back, years later, Browne was to write that 'Those three years working in the Department of Health, among civil servants led by Mr Kennedy and Mr Murray, were the most educative, satisfying, and memorable years of my life.'[111] Browne's prescription for action – involving administrative expertise, political will, as well as securing and directing state funding – produced spectacular, and visible, results. The death rate from TB in Ireland – once one of the highest in western Europe – had halved by 1951, and was to be further halved again by 1954.[112] These were immensely impressive achievements, and contributed to Browne's growing reputation. By the summer of 1950, with the problem of TB well under control from an administrative perspective, Noël Browne was able to turn his energetic attention to other matters. Some of these other matters badly needed attending to, for a horrifying fact was that neutral, well-fed Ireland had one of the highest rates of infant mortality in Europe. However, there was a means to hand to address this and it was nothing less than the 1947 Health Act, lying virtually ignored since the departure from office of Dr Conor Ward. Prepared before Ward left office, the 1947 Health Act made provision for free medical treatment of expectant mothers, and of all children up to the age of sixteen years.

Unknown to the inter-party government, this Act had already been the subject of some covert ecclesiastical communications. These had been made privately, to de Valera, immediately before the general election of February 1948, and had been left unanswered by him while he fought an election to retain power.[113] Browne was not aware of these private approaches when he sought Cabinet approval for the redrafting of the 1947 Health Act on 25 June 1948.[114] The Cabinet gave the minister approval to proceed with the Bill, and to redraft the Act. There matters rested until the late summer of 1950, when, with TB already dealt with, Noël Browne returned to the redrafted Health Act with the intention of reviving and implementing it. Almost immediately the scheme ran into trouble on two fronts. The first of these were the objections put forward by the medical profession, who would be expected to staff and run the scheme. Their objections were couched in the familiar squawks of consternation concerning 'socialised medicine', for they feared that the implementation of the scheme would result in a salaried state system which would gradually supplant the notion of private practice.[115] Lee has commented rather acidly that 'had "socialised medicine" been considered likely to increase professional incomes, its ideological horrors might have been more stoically endured'.[116] The doctors – through their mouthpiece the IMA – stated their objections to a scheme without a means test, and, when the minister persisted with his preference for just such a scheme, the doctors summoned up their heavy artillery, which took the formidable, and powerful, form of the Irish hierarchy. Closer links existed between sections of each of these august bodies than were, perhaps, realised at the time. Ó hEithir, for one, has referred to the IMA 'as a posse of not so silent and not so holy Knights'.[117] Indeed, the Knights of Columbanus have been regarded as a repository of reactionary Catholic values, espousing an especially militant form of 'muscular Christianity', and it is of both interest and relevance to note that at least four of them could be found in the inter-party Cabinet. These were William Norton – the man Noël Browne subsequently labelled with caustic accuracy, 'a fake Labour leader'; Joseph Blowick – the 'hopeless' Minister for Lands, in MacBride's words; Richard Mulcahy – whose private papers show an absolutely astonishing amount of correspondence with religious orders and personnel; and Seán MacEoin – 'the Blacksmith of Ballinalee', Fine Gael's presidential candidate in 1945, who was a decent man, a devout Catholic, and held the position of Minister for Justice.[118]

While the Cabinet were uneasy about the idea of a brawl with the IMA – for some of the Cabinet actually enjoyed close relations with the doctors, Dr T. F. O'Higgins being one such – the potential of a public clash with the hierarchy filled them with undiluted horror. On 10 October 1950, Bishop James Staunton of Ferns, acting as secretary to the hierarchy, wrote a letter to the Taoiseach, setting out the hierarchy's objections to the Mother and Child Scheme. A committee of the hierarchy, consisting of Archbishop John Charles McQuaid, Bishop Michael Browne of Galway, and Dr Staunton, was set up for the purpose of 'seeing' the Minister for Health and 'informing him as a matter of courtesy' of the protests of the hierarchy before they transmitted their letter to the Taoiseach. The following day, 11 October, they saw the minister, who, in his own words, had been 'peremptorily ordered' to attend Archbishop's House. Although Browne had asked to bring along his departmental secretary, Patrick Kennedy, this was refused, leaving him facing the objections of the hierarchy without a witness at his side. They read their letter, and Browne attempted, verbally, to rebut their objections, a reaction later described by McQuaid – who was probably more used to deference – as 'incredible'.[119]

The hierarchy's objections centred, naturally enough, on such absurd aspirations as 'socialised medicine', but also on the health-care and education aspects of the programme, which included 'education in respect of motherhood' for pregnant women. These features were feared by the Church on the dubious grounds that the scheme might lead to pregnant Catholic women being treated by doctors not of their own religious denomination, and worse, that 'education in respect of motherhood' might perhaps come to include unthinkable areas such as contraception and abortion. Moreover, they intimated that the scheme would involve such taxation 'as to morally compel the population to avail of it'.[120] The most benevolent thing that can be said about the hierarchy's actions is, perhaps, that they were 'well-intentioned' but hopelessly out of touch. At the other end of the scale, it could be argued that the hierarchy, by allowing themselves to be used by the doctors, had allied themselves with a wealthy and powerful vested interest, rather than taking the broader picture of mass need, and mass deprivation, on board. Some commentators have suggested that it can be seen as a 'turf war', in that two competing versions of how health should be provided for, namely whether it should be controlled by Church organisations or answerable to state authority, were contested. [121]

Not only were the hierarchy's objections completely unrealistic, but they strongly smacked of being woefully detached and completely unaware of the realities of life in the poorer sections of Ireland, where poverty was widespread, infant mortality horrifically high, and unemployment endemic. Because of the war, neutrality, the association of Catholicism with Irish national identity, and the elevated position enjoyed by the Catholic Church in both everyday life and everyday law, the Church had enjoyed a sort of protected position, which, in effect, had insulated it from the mundane everyday concerns the rest of the population were obliged to pay heed to. However, the otherworldliness of their worries over the Mother and Child Scheme did not mean that the government could ignore them, quite the contrary, if anything. Noël Browne (acting on Cabinet instructions) hastened to reassure them. 'Education in respect of motherhood' meant correct diet during pregnancy and related matters, not the sort of stuff the bishops were coming up with by way of perfervid objections. In fact, Browne not only attempted to meet their objections in an elaborate and thoughtful memorandum, described by Whyte as 'able',[122] but was also, at the same time, receiving theological advice on whether or not the Mother and Child Scheme was incompatible with Catholic moral teaching.[123] Not only that, but he had already familiarised himself with alternative – and considerably more advanced – versions of Catholic thought, when, as far back as 1949, he had requested Joseph Walshe, Ireland's ambassador to the Holy See, to procure the texts of lectures given by the Franciscan, Fr Agostino Gemelli. Gemelli, who was rector of the Catholic University of Milan, was warm in his praise for the British National Health Service in a lecture which he gave on the vexed topic of 'state medicine', saying that 'in the face of disease all members of the community have equal rights because health is not an individual good, but a common good', and adding, for good measure, that Catholic Italy had 'the duty to do at least as much as Protestant and Labour Britain has already done'. Browne had received the text from Walshe by April 1950, and it surfaced again in the debates which occurred after the fall of the government, when Peadar Cowan, for one, used it as ammunition for his argument that the attitude of the Irish hierarchy to the planned extension of the health services was not adopted by all Catholic authorities on the subject.[124]

The theologian retained by Browne advised him that while the scheme was contrary to Catholic *social* teaching (which a practising Catholic, in all conscience, can disagree with), it was not contrary to Catholic *moral* teaching, defiance of which would lead one into serious sin. Browne described his discussions with this theologian, who continued to request anonymity long after the crisis had ended, a request respected by Browne, who never named him. This episode is of interest for the light it throws on Browne's own cast of mind. Browne's particularly cerebral brand of Catholicism probably owed much to the intellectual rigours of his Jesuit education, for he mentioned in his autobiography that while at Beaumont he 'became quite an authority on the new testament',[125] and while Tim Pat Coogan may have opined that Browne 'can hardly be called an orthodox Catholic',[126] this was valid only in a context which ignores that the practice of the same religion can differ enormously from one culture to another. Irish Catholics with a bent for theological debate (as both Noël Browne and Garret FitzGerald have discovered to their cost) have found it virtually impossible to conduct any sort of intellectual debate in, or with, the Catholic Church in Ireland, on matters of 'faith and morals'. While the intellectual position adopted by the Irish Catholic Church is narrow, defensive, and usually exceptionally reactionary, their immensely powerful position in Irish public life has meant that they have not been obliged to defend stances with any sort of serious intellectual rigour until relatively recently, and then only in a reluctant response to the demands of a changing society. Such distinctions – distinguishing between Catholic social and moral teaching – were altogether too fine to seriously tax the collective minds of the Irish hierarchy, and their response, which simply reiterated all of their previously stated objections to the scheme, coupled with the addition of a few new ones, signalled that the hierarchy would accept nothing less than complete surrender from the unfortunate minister.[127]

The elaborate memorandum prepared by Browne, which contained his considered responses – including his 'magnanimous concessions'[128] – to the letter of the hierarchy of October 1950, registering episcopal unease, was handed by Browne to Costello 'within days of the meeting at the Archbishop's Palace' to be delivered to the hierarchy, in accordance with accepted protocol. For some unexplained reason, which has never been made clear, Costello did not deliver Browne's response to the hierarchy until the end of March 1951, almost six months after it had been written.[129] Yet, as Browne himself pointed out, 'it is clear from statements made by him in the Dáil that Mr Costello was in constant verbal contact with the Archbishop during that time'.[130] This is undoubtedly true. In fact, it appears that Archbishop McQuaid was 'briefed by the Taoiseach about discussions in Cabinet in the course of at least seven secret bilateral meetings',[131] a fact partly confirmed by Costello himself, when he wrote in his covering letter – which contained Browne's memorandum – to the hierarchy that 'His Grace of Dublin has on many occasions seen me in the interval.' Not only that, it appears that Costello was receiving lessons in dictation as well, for, as Cooney has noted, 'McQuaid virtually acted as cabinet secretary by drafting the text of the Government's acceptance of the episcopal condemnation of the scheme.'[132] The suspicion must also exist that McQuaid likewise made suggestions regarding the text of the four letters Costello himself wrote to Browne in March 1951, urging him to make the necessary alterations to the scheme in order to render it compatible with Catholic teaching. Having heard no further response to the memorandum, which, had he but known, had not even been delivered, Browne assumed that he had met the objections of the hierarchy, and that he need concentrate only on the doctors. He realised his error, and was 'genuinely surprised',[133] when, in early March, a 'freezing'[134] letter arrived from the archbishop of Dublin, stating 'bluntly' that McQuaid 'may not approve' of the Mother and Child Scheme, and adding that he 'must reiterate each and every objection' made by him and 'unresolved' by the minister.[135] In fact, as is now realised, 'McQuaid's detailed notes of the crisis confirm that for months he effectively stalked the beleaguered Browne, until he was fully satisfied that he was isolated in Cabinet and was helpless in the face of the medical profession, with whose leaders McQuaid had coalesced behind the scenes.'[136] It is only fair to add that Noël Browne was not the only minister, and the inter-party government was not the only administration, to experience misunderstandings or difficulties in communication with the hierarchy. Fianna Fáil, infinitely more adept as a government, and much more deft in their handling of such issues, also experienced communications difficulties when they came to deal with the Health Act, shortly after their return to power.

By March 1951, therefore, Browne was battling on several fronts, for he faced the medical profession, the hierarchy, most of his Cabinet colleagues, and his own party leader.[137] It was to be unfortunate for Browne, for MacBride, and for Clann na Poblachta that Browne's epic struggle in seeking to implement the Mother and Child Scheme should reach a climax at just about the same time as his relationship with MacBride took a dramatic turn for the worse. As it happened, this relationship, which had functioned reasonably amicably for over two years, began to deteriorate in the latter part of 1950.

 A key feature of this increasingly altered relationship was the enigmatic role played by Noel Hartnett, which has already been alluded to. Busy as he was with the cares and glories of ministerial office, it seems to have taken MacBride some considerable time to acknowledge these altered relationships within Clann na Poblachta. When he finally realised the potential for trouble in these incipient splits, his response was entirely characteristic. On 9 November 1950, he suggested a spot of dinner with Noël Browne in one of his favourite haunts, the Russell Hotel. This was to be the first in a series of utterly extraordinary encounters between the two men from then until the following April, when, with the resignation of Browne from the Cabinet, the various controversies combined to erupt into the public domain. The atmosphere at this weird meal comes through clearly in MacBride's recollection, a closely typed seven-page account which he 'prepared' later that same night.[138] As MacBride subsequently noted, during the dinner, Browne informed MacBride that he 'was sorry to have to say' that he, MacBride, 'had completely failed in [his] leadership of the Clann'. According to Browne, this complete failure had come about because MacBride had spent his time 'looking for praise and admiration' and was 'under the influence of worthless people' whose only interest was to tell MacBride that he was 'a marvellous person and an ideal leader'. However, MacBride's appetite for admiration was not Browne's only cause for complaint. Further criticism centred on the fact that MacBride had 'surrounded' himself with 'the same old [IRA] crowd', and had become 'isolated' from Noel Hartnett.[139] Indeed, the absent Hartnett hovered prominently over proceedings, with Browne, according to MacBride, earnestly saying that 'You have no better friend in the world than Noel Hartnett and his only desire is to help you, if you would let him. As you know I would follow you anywhere if you would only do that',[140] a theme which surfaced again, later, with MacBride attributing to Browne the remark that 'despite his impossible prejudices, ulcers and laziness' Hartnett was the 'most loyal friend' MacBride had 'in the world'.[141]

Browne remembered the dinner – fairly hazily – but remained certain that he did not make any of the threats that MacBride's version attributed to him.[142] Instead of uttering the threats ascribed to him, Browne recalled saying to MacBride that he realised that MacBride and his family had suffered much for their beliefs, and that he also recognised MacBride was 'seriously committed to a united Ireland'.[143] Consequently, he stressed that 'if Clann na Poblachta and the government submitted to the demands of the Roman Catholic Church it would be seriously damaging to that cause'.[144] Furthermore, Browne claimed that he 'warned' MacBride that he 'intended to publicise to the full any such interference by the church, should it occur, in Cabinet'.[145] In fact, it is highly unlikely that Noël Browne expressly informed MacBride of his intention to publicise the interventions of the Catholic Church. Had Browne actually said this, it would undoubtedly have appeared in MacBride's multiple, detailed, and extremely menacing minutes, and not just because it would have been another stick with which to beat Browne, but also because of MacBride's later, stated, reaction to the 'leaking' of the letters to the newspapers, an action MacBride would describe as 'an act of vindictiveness.' The upshot of all of this, according to MacBride, was Noël Browne had decided to 'wreck' the Clann, and, in pursuit of this aim, set himself the task of picking fights with his party leader at every opportunity.[146] MacBride's version has Browne declaring that 'the Clann was static and would break up before or immediately after Christmas whenever he [Browne] resigned . . . That he would have done this before now but that he wanted to get his Mother and Child Scheme through first, or resign on that issue.'[147] Brooding over this, MacBride felt that he knew exactly where to apportion the blame, and let the national executive of the Clann know the direction his thoughts were taking when he told them some time later at their meeting on 10 February 1951, 'Rightly or wrongly, the impression created on my mind was that this line of conduct was carefully planned and was prompted in no small measure by Noel Hartnett.'[148]

Relations deteriorated further in the New Year, with another meeting – subsequently described by MacBride as 'a long session'[149] – taking place in Iveagh House on 4 January, between MacBride, Browne, and Donal O'Donoghue who had been asked – by MacBride – to sit in on the discussion as mediator and minute-taker. Modestly entitled a 'Brief Minute of Discussion between Donal O'Donoghue, Dr N. Browne and Seán MacBride in Iveagh House on Thursday, 4th January 1951', O'Donoghue's account was anything but brief, but still managed to convey the amazing atmosphere and the extraordinary content of this strange meeting. Lasting over three hours, the meeting covered some fairly familiar ground. Once again, this time according to Donal O'Donoghue, Noël Browne found abundant fault with MacBride's leadership. 'He said that S. MacB. should, for sentimental reasons, have proved an ideal leader but that he had failed miserably and absolutely; that he was vain, could not stand criticism and had become completely isolated.'[150] According to O'Donoghue, Browne explained that his notes were not 'in sequence and that these instances were taken at random', and, with that, proceeded with a scattering of grapeshot, peppering MacBride with various accusations, each depicting an example of failed leadership. All told, these accusations totalled eighteen, and ranged from the general – 'That S. MacB. had completely failed in leadership and was unsuitable because he had no "human understanding" . . . S. MacB. is quite inaccessible to the public . . . This is probably due to "his ivory tower complex" and to his "hopelessly inefficient Private Secretary"' – to the specific, where, according to O'Donoghue, Browne complained about some government appointments, as well as some particular government policies and the lack of Clann reaction to them, such as the Prices Tribunal, Connemara Development, Costello's Bog Land Reclamation Proposals, and the Great Northern Railway.

With regard to party matters, he objected to the fact that MacBride had opposed and 'successfully frustrated any attempt to have parliamentary questions asked. That he, N. B., had prepared some questions and had given them to Michael Fitzpatrick to have asked but that S. MacB. had censored them and prevented them from being asked', and that nothing had been done about starting a party paper. Within the Cabinet, his complaints centred on the complete lack of communication between himself and MacBride, and also on the fact 'that S. MacB. has a perfectly ludicrous habit of producing Memos and proposals to the Government on every conceivable topic from Economics to Pearl Fishing . . . That he, S. MacB. might know something about European affairs, and he, N. B. has some doubts about this, but everyone knows that he is not an expert on everything and anything.'[151] Once again, the Mother and Child Scheme featured as a source of private contention between the Clann's two ministers, and possibly others in the Cabinet as well, with Noël Browne, according to O'Donoghue, stating that 'S. MacB. created no help for me, on the contrary, he suggested to Norton a compromise . . . He suggested that I had left out the word "all" from the Scheme and accused him, N. B. of bungling it; he did this at a time when the Att. Genrl. was searching for a flaw in the Scheme. Of course it was a well accepted legal formula and there was no necessity for the word "all".' Above all, according to O'Donoghue's minutes, Noël Browne stated that 'the main reason for his, N. B.'s antipathy to S. MacB. was S. MacB.'s constant habit of telling "skivvies" lies'.[152]

Reading almost like the script of a play, O'Donoghue's detailed minutes continued with MacBride skilfully finessing as he attempted to refute some of the charges. 'S. MacB. reminded N. B . . . that a Cabinet Sub-committee [on Connemara Development] had been appointed on which N. B. had been put at S. MacB.'s suggestion. N. B. said that this was a third lie, that Norton had proposed him. S. MacB. explained that it is not the practice to have formal propositions as to who should compose such sub-Committees but that he and Norton suggested simultaneously that N. B. should be included on it.'[153] James Dillon's role was next discussed, and disputed over. 'N. B. said that he had never been allowed to see Dillon's Memorandum on [Connemara Development] until he obtained a copy of it a few days ago. S.

MacB. said that the Memorandum had been considered at several Cabinet meetings and that N. B. must have had it then; that it was circulated in the ordinary way or given out at a Cabinet meeting by Dillon. N. B. shouted that this was another lie, the "fourth lie". He became very excited and kept on shouting "four lies".'[154] This meeting ended inconclusively, but not, apparently, acrimoniously, with the minute stating that 'S. MacB. pointed out that no progress could be made in the Clann if N. B. continued systematically to create a split . . . D. O'D. appealed to N. B. to realise the position he was creating and to alter his attitude. N. B. promised to think it over and in the meantime to co-operate with S. MacB.'[155]

Of course, matters did not simply rest there, for February brought the multiple resignations of Noel Hartnett from the party, the national executive, and the Clann's innermost sanctum, the standing committee, ostensibly over the Battle of Baltinglass, as referred to earlier. At the same time, Noël Browne himself resigned from the standing committee of the party. These acts gave rise to the meeting of the national executive on 10 February, at which MacBride presented his first report to the executive on the ominous undercurrents rippling beneath the Clann's apparently tranquil surface.[156] As much as the extraordinary account of the dinner in the Russell Hotel, and the subsequent meeting in Iveagh House in early January, the rather baleful minutes of this national executive meeting make for fascinating reading. MacBride's chilling and incredibly detailed report, complete with four extraordinary appendices which were – or purported to be – the minutes of the various private meetings held with Noël Browne on 9 November 1950, 4 January 1951, and 5 February 1951, was intended to set the record straight for the comrades on the national executive, and to reassure the wobbling in the wake of the departure of Noel Hartnett. It is an extraordinary document – detailed, meticulous, and menacing. MacBride's lengthy report set out his version of the unfolding events in some detail. Most of the national executive seem to have taken MacBride's rendition fairly calmly, for they passed a motion affirming their 'confidence in Seán MacBride as Leader of the Party'.[157] However, not all of the national executive were completely reassured; indeed, MacBride's report contained the sort of unnerving detail which prompted McQuillan, appalled and agonised, to ask 'How many more of us have you got files on?'[158]

Further meetings modelled on the earlier ones were to take place. This series of amazing meetings (however disputed their contents) gives a flavour, or a sense, of the extraordinary (and occasionally poisonous) atmosphere in the rarefied circles at the top of the party, and of the relationship between some of the leading players of the Clann during the last year of the inter-party government. Equally, it throws an interesting light on the way those at the top of the Clann – especially MacBride and some of his closest colleagues – chose to do business, and raises questions about how much their forensic approach was influenced by their respective personalities, or whether their backgrounds in the deepest underground of the republican movement had some influence on the way they tried to run their political party. Above all, it appears to corroborate Noël Browne, to a certain extent, with regard to the manner in which elements in Clann na Poblachta sought to run the party (and yet again confirms his inaccuracy with respect to some of the details, because the single, long meeting which was depicted in his book, *Against the Tide*, actually took place over several meetings of the national executive, and not just one).[159]

There matters rested – at least publicly, for behind the scenes there was a brisk trade in vituperative insult along with the more usual full, frank, and meaningful exchange of views – until after MacBride's trip to the United States, in March 1951. Before he left Ireland, on 8 March, MacBride had despatched a letter to Browne, which was written in the sort of paternalistic style guaranteed to set the latter's teeth on edge, for it expressed the 'hope that everything will go smoothly while I am away and that nothing will be done to precipitate a crisis'.[160] Returning to Ireland, MacBride must have realised that matters were swiftly coming to a head, not least because Noel Hartnett, as has been already referred to, had preceded him home by a few weeks.

A further meeting of the Clann's national executive was called for 31 March – its deliberations took it into the early hours of April – to discuss these escalating problems. MacBride sought a strong endorsement of his position, which he received in the form of the following resolution which was 'adopted unanimously' by the assembled national executive: 'That the Ard Comhairle views with grave concern and disapproval the attitude and conduct of Dr Browne and is perturbed by his lack of co-operation and by his apparent disloyalty to the leadership of the party, and requires him to show a greater degree of loyalty and co-operation in his dealings with the organisation.'[161] A second resolution – which featured 'three voting against' (incidentally, the minute does not name the dissenting three, but Noël Browne later did; they were Jack McQuillan, Con Lucey, and Dermot Cochran[162]) – 'requested' that Browne furnish a 'full, written report' for the 'consideration' of the leader of the party, the standing committee, and the national executive, setting out his position.[163] MacBride now knew that he had the full backing of his own party *apparat* in choosing whatever course of action he saw fit to undertake with regard to the recalcitrant Minister for Health.

Meanwhile, the Minister for Health himself was still embroiled with the IMA, and with their robust, and, rather reactionary, allies, the Irish hierarchy, concerning the Mother and Child Scheme. The hierarchy had finally received Browne's 'able' memorandum on 27 March, and had discussed it and dismissed it by 4 April, unanimously accepting Archbishop McQuaid's recommendation that the scheme was contrary to Catholic social teaching. Clinical and efficient as always, McQuaid acted as his own draftsman and his own postman, and he was infinitely better at both than Costello was at either. Therefore, on 5 April, Archbishop McQuaid himself 'glided into Government Buildings in the full solemnity of his Episcopal robes'[164] and personally handed over to Costello the letter from the hierarchy which he himself had just drafted 'intimating that the particular scheme for a Mother and Child health service proposed by the Minister for Health is opposed to Catholic social teaching'.[165] McQuaid – who has been viewed by one commentator as 'effectively the ecclesiastical Taoiseach of a clerical state'[166] – professed himself more than satisfied with the outcome of his journey to Government Buildings: 'The Taoiseach at once and fully accepted our decision, as one would expect.'[167]

Matters were finally resolved around the Cabinet table on 6 April 1951.[168] Browne refused to withdraw or amend the scheme, and instead drew attention to his theologian's advice, which was that Catholics could disregard pronouncements from the hierarchy which derived their theological legitimacy from Catholic social teaching. Such subtle distinctions did not really carry much weight with the Cabinet, and they dismissed Browne's arguments. Finessing beautifully, McQuaid had even briefed Costello on how to deal with such esoteric arguments when he explained the reasoning to use: 'Catholic social teaching meant Catholic moral teaching in regard to things social.'[169] As far as Browne's Cabinet colleagues were concerned, the hierarchy had spoken, and their suggestions had to be heeded, and, if necessary, incorporated into the Health Act. Browne next invoked a time-honoured formula, when he asked for time 'to consider his position', which was granted, but, before he left the Cabinet room, he requested each of his colleagues, individually, to state where they stood on this issue.[170] With the exception of Labour's Michael Keyes,[171] who initially sided with Browne, the rest all agreed that the scheme had to be amended in accordance with the wishes of the hierarchy, each of them invoking variations on the theme of submission, ranging from MacBride's legalistic 'Those in the Government who are Catholics are bound to accept the views of their Church' to MacEoin's humorous 'I don't want to get a belt of a crozier.'[172] Undoubtedly, a majority of the Cabinet were utterly sincere, and utterly certain, in their unquestioning fidelity to their Catholic beliefs. Most of them saw nothing wrong, whatsoever, with the intervention of the Church on the issue; indeed, some of them may have welcomed the reassurance compliance with Church teaching would have brought in its wake, and many of them remained mystified that fault could and would be found with their unquestioning submission to a clerical intervention.

Costello himself remained unapologetic about his actions, as he made clear in a television interview in 1969, when he declared emphatically: 'And if we were told, as we were told, by an authoritative body in the Catholic Church, that a measure if brought into action would be contrary to morality and the teaching of the Church, then we were bound in my opinion – I'd do the same again – and I know the Government would have to do it.'[173] Equally, there is the suspicion that pragmatism, rather than piety, governed the response of some members of the Cabinet. MacBride's reasons for going along with the ecclesiastical rejection of the scheme seem to have been based as much on pragmatic considerations – 'You cannot afford to fight the Church'[174] – as on whatever degree of personal piety he possessed. Although he was in the habit of writing deferential letters to the archbishop of Dublin stating that he 'was at the disposal' of the prelate[175] – an offer McQuaid was only too happy to avail of – this may have been motivated by a practical republican desire to be seen to keep the hierarchy on board. Privately, MacBride was much less respectful about McQuaid,[176] and some of his displays of public piety lacked the necessary emotional authenticity. Jack McQuillan recalled attending the installation of the new bishop of Elphin during the term of office of the inter-party government, and, during the ceremony, sitting beside MacBride who had 'a brand-new prayer-book, so brand-new the pages weren't even cut'.[177] In any case, whether the government accepted the ruling of the hierarchy for reasons of pragmatism, or for reasons of piety, is not the key question: the main point is that the hierarchy's adjudications on the proposed Health Act were accepted promptly.

Meanwhile, in Clann na Poblachta, matters had also swiftly come to a head. A further 'long and stormy' meeting of the national executive took place on 8 April. Once again, the recollections of the principals diverged. Noël Browne claimed that he was 'summoned' to this meeting, which was 'called by Seán MacBride',[178] whereas MacBride maintained that the 'special' meeting was 'summoned by wire at Dr Browne's request'.[179] Especially prolonged and unpleasant, this was the meeting where Noël Browne claimed his Kafkaesque-like 'trial' – which took the form of a ritual discrediting – actually occurred.[180]

On 11 April, MacBride delivered a letter to Browne requesting the latter's resignation as Minister for Health, having already secured the support of his national executive for this course of action at the meeting held three days earlier, when the national executive announced that it 'affirms its complete loyalty to Mr Seán MacBride as leader of the Party, and that each member of it acknowledges the leader's right and the right of the Party's executive bodies to take any action in accordance with the powers vested in them which is required to maintain party discipline and loyalty to the leader'.[181] Indeed, MacBride already held the necessary authority, for the national executive meeting held on 31 March had passed an even stronger resolution. Couched in fairly unambiguous terms, this resolution stated, 'That the Ard Comhairle wish to put on record that if the leader of the Party deems it necessary to call for the resignation or removal of Dr Browne from the Government he can rely on the loyal support of the Ard Comhairle.'[182] Browne complied, bitterly upbraiding MacBride as he did so in a letter best described as a masterpiece of invective. All of this was extraordinary enough, but what elevated the subsequent row to one which rocked the political system – and wrecked Clann na Poblachta – was Browne's action in ensuring that he was not muzzled on losing ministerial office.[183]

Actually, he had already made the necessary arrangements with the editor of *The Irish Times*, R. M. Smyllie, to publish the entire correspondence concerning the ecclesiastical interventions on the Mother and Child Scheme, and the subsequent correspondence between himself and MacBride, when the latter requested his resignation. *The Irish Times* not only gleefully published the entire correspondence – thereby ensuring that the other papers could do no less if they wished to keep abreast of matters – but also offered trenchant support to Browne in a gritty, strongly worded leader, which concluded by saying, 'This is a sad day for Ireland. It is not so important that the Mother and Child Scheme has been withdrawn, to be replaced by an alternative project embodying a means test. What matters more is that an honest, far-sighted and energetic man has been driven out of active politics. The most serious revelation, however, is that the Roman Catholic Church would seem to be the effective Government of this country.'[184]

With the publication of this material, matters which had previously been taboo topics were now, for the first time ever, openly discussed. Certainly, some in the Cabinet – including MacBride, who would later, tellingly, describe Browne's action in making this correspondence available to *The Irish Times* as 'a final act of vindictiveness',[185] adding, in a revealing remark, 'That act, if nothing else, condemns Dr Browne irretrievably'[186] – were profoundly shocked at this unexpected turn of events. This was an attitude which Costello, speaking in the Dáil, probably summed up best when he said: 'All these matters could have been, and ought to have been, dealt with calmly, in quiet and in council, without the public becoming aware of the matter. The public ought never to have become aware of the matter.'[187] In fact, these sentiments were, apparently, as much McQuaid's as Costello's, for it seems that McQuaid lent a helping hand by briefing Costello and suggesting points for Costello's address to the Dáil, which was intended as the official government response to the vigorous and capable statement Noël Browne had earlier made in defence of himself and his actions.

Public awareness was to lead to an interesting sequence of results at the subsequent general election – where the fortunes of the coalition parties fluctuated wildly[188] – and a significant widening of the area of political discourse considered fit for public consumption. In recent times, there has been a tendency for some commentators to doubt that the Mother and Child Scheme debacle was a Church–state crisis.[189] Of course, it was a Church–state crisis, but it was not only that; it was also an intra-party crisis, and, in any logically constructed coalition on a right–left axis, it could well have been, and, perhaps, should well have been, an inter-party crisis.

In particular, this meant that the thorny topic of relations between the Church and the state could now be subject to public scrutiny. At one side of this debate would be found those who contested the right of an unelected interest group (meaning the Catholic Church, not the doctors, in this instance) to dictate policy behind the scenes to an elected government. Noël Browne himself would eventually become the leading, though by no means the only, voice articulating this point of view. A diametrically opposed perspective was offered, naturally enough, by some members of the hierarchy, which, at its extreme, could be seen as somewhat intemperate: 'In a word, their position was that they were the final arbiters of right and wrong even in political matters.'[190] Of course, the right of the hierarchy to make representations drawing attention to their needs and views, just like any other interest group, was not in dispute. Arguing sometime later with an Ulster Unionist who insisted that the Irish Republic was governed by the hierarchy, Seán MacBride, missing the point somewhat, disingenuously replied, 'Surely the leaders of the Church everywhere were entitled to express views concerning legislation which would affect them, just as trade unionists and other bodies had the right to do the same.'[191] In fact, as Seán O'Faolain, writing in *The Bell*, correctly pointed out, the Church is not just like any other interest group. 'There has been a lot of talk about the rights of institutions to advise, comment and consult and so on . . . In practice, the hierarchy does much more than "comment" or "advise". It commands.' Moreover, they are able to command, because, as O'Faolain put it, 'The Maynooth Parliament [i.e. the hierarchy] holds a weapon which none of the other institutions mentioned holds; the weapon of the sacraments.'[192] Thus, while it could be argued that the power wielded by the Church is a moral one, and that it exercises its power mainly in relation to social and moral matters, it could also be argued that while the Catholic Church won that particular battle, it was at the eventual cost of the war. From the very beginning, even Church apologists privately conceded that they had lost the contest in terms of public relations, for the public neither understood nor sympathised with the hierarchy's case. As one bishop put it, years later, 'we allowed ourselves to be used by the doctors, but it won't happen again'.[193] However, while the intervention of the hierarchy over the Mother and Child Scheme is usually seen as the high-water mark in the exercise of ecclesiastical power in Ireland, (and while the hierarchy's intervention undoubtedly killed off the scheme), in some ways it marked the extent of that power. Never again, no matter what the issue, would an Irish Cabinet display such servile obsequiousness in the face of pressure from the Church.[194] Without clerical intervention, the scheme would probably have become law, albeit in a possibly altered or amended form. Without clerical intervention, Clann na Poblachta would still have found a sword to fall on.

There was an irony in the fact that on the one occasion when MacBride successfully usurped Costello's position – in seeking Browne's resignation – it did not benefit him in the least. The fact that it was MacBride who requested Browne's resignation, rather than Costello, the Taoiseach – whose prerogative this was – could be taken as indicative of MacBride's last fling with his old habit of trespassing. However, MacBride saw matters differently, for he has argued that 'There was an understanding that each party leader would select and be responsible for his own Ministers. That's why I finally had to ask Browne to resign. He was my responsibility.'[195] Nevertheless, the effect of this meant that it was to be MacBride who would be tainted with public odium, rather than the Fine Gael party, which makes Costello's judgement in allowing MacBride to relieve him of the burden of having to fire Browne all the sharper, especially as earlier, on the evening of 6 April, after Costello had briefed McQuaid on what had transpired at the Cabinet meeting that day, 'McQuaid was relieved by Costello's assurance that the Cabinet would demand Browne's resignation.'[196] This brings to mind Lemass's speculation that both Costello and MacBride viewed the Mother and Child Scheme debacle as a heaven-sent opportunity to get rid of Browne. Speaking to Michael Mills, of the *Irish Press*, Lemass had remarked: 'The whole situation was mishandled. I am not so sure that it was not allowed to develop in this way because the coalition leaders were anxious to drop Noël Browne, who must have been a very difficult colleague in government.'[197] No wonder that Costello could later remark approvingly – in a classic case of damning with faint praise – 'For MacBride I must say he was always loyal', when discussing his inter-party governments with Michael McInerney.[198]

Browne took up his position on the backbenches, followed by McQuillan, who also left Clann na Poblachta on this issue, and welcomed by Captain Cowan, who had left the Clann long before. In the ensuing Dáil debate, the government proceeded to tear itself apart, or, rather, the government watched while Clann na Poblachta proceeded to tear itself apart, eagerly eyed by Fianna Fáil, who probably couldn't believe their luck. Fianna Fáil's own contribution to this astonishing debate was minimal and was confined to de Valera's muted and uninspiring contribution: 'We have heard enough.'

By summer, the government had fallen, and the ensuing general election completely destroyed Clann na Poblachta as a serious political force. Ó hEithir has correctly pointed out that the inter-party government was not actually brought down by Noël Browne's resignation, 'although that romantic gloss has crept into history', but fell, rather, when some 'rural deputies turned their backs on it for refusing to increase the price of milk'.[199] This is perfectly true, but the public perception also carries considerable truth, even if it is not exactly historically, or literally, correct, because after Browne's resignation and the subsequent open split in the Clann – which was, after all, in effect, the linchpin of the government – its days as a government were clearly numbered, and it seems to have ranked as little more than a lame-duck administration. Costello himself subscribed to this analysis, for, as he told Michael McInerney, 'A month later the Government fell on a matter, officially, of agricultural subsidies, though the Mother and Child controversies were the real cause.'[200]

Support for Browne and his health scheme came from unusual – and sometimes unlikely – sources. In the Dáil, strong, and possibly predictable, support came from Jack McQuillan and Peadar Cowan. Less predictable was the intervention of Oliver J. Flanagan, whose speech in support of Browne could be described as almost fulsome. Among his supporters outside the Dáil could be found the beginnings of what would, in time, become known as the 'liberal' media – which, at the time, was represented mainly by *The Bell* and, of course, *The Irish Times* – a media which would eventually give voice to the aspirations, goals, and self-image of an emerging, and, over time, an increasingly affluent, educated, materialistic, and – perhaps most surprising because most unexpected – secular Irish middle class. However, that was to be found in the far future. In 1951, those expressing this more liberal outlook – in other words, those who publicly supported the Mother and Child Scheme and were thus defying the explicitly expressed diktat of the Catholic hierarchy – were, in public at least, and irrespective of whatever private doubts regarding organised religion some of them may have harboured (and some of them most certainly harboured doubts), not necessarily less *publicly* Catholic (for that was thought to be the way to political oblivion) but were, perhaps, less *piously* Catholic; or, put another way, were considerably less devotional, and less militantly orthodox, in their expression of fidelity to the strictures of the Church of Rome. Some of them, privately, did not even see themselves as Catholic at all; Whyte wrote of interviewing two ex-ministers who informed him that they were not believing Catholics, a fact neither felt that they could reveal in public at the time.[201]

Other groups to offer support for Noël Browne came from part of the trade union movement and from the Irish Housewives' Association (IHA), each of which had already, during the crisis, passed a resolution calling for the implementation of the scheme.[202] With an almost theatrical sense of timing, on 11 April – the very day of Noël Browne's enforced resignation – the committee of the IHA had unanimously passed one of these resolutions, and sent copies to both Browne and Costello. This enthusiastic support continued during the ensuing election campaign, as Hilda Tweedy recalled in an account which vividly captured the atmosphere of the campaign: 'My own particular memory of this period was, somewhere along the line, being on the back of a lorry in College Green, Dublin, with the two assistant honorary secretaries of the IHA, Ruth Deale and Kathleen Swanton, all eager to show IHA support for the scheme. Dr Noël Browne was there and several other supporters and a considerable crowd of people. Every time the would-be speakers raised the megaphone, their words were drowned by the crowd singing "Faith of Our Fathers"!'[203] Indeed, the IHA went even further with their public support for Noël Browne and his planned health reforms in their report for the year 1950–1, opening by observing the niceties with a nod of obeisance in the direction of neutrality – 'We feel sure that our members will agree that, although as a non-party, non-sectarian organisation, we cannot now take sides, yet we cannot but deplore the manner in which an issue vital to the health of the nation was handled'[204] – while yet continuing with a firm declaration of principles which echoed to the hammering sound of colours being nailed to the mast of a former minister: 'We re-affirm our belief in the equal rights of all Irishwomen to happy motherhood, and deplore the resignation of a Minister for Health who had done so much in his term of office for the health of the community.'[205]

MacBride and John Tully from Cavan were returned for Clann na Poblachta, the rest of his political supporters losing their Dáil seats. On the other hand, Browne, and his supporters, such as Jack McQuillan, Peadar Cowan, and a new member, Michael ffrench-O'Carroll, were all easily returned to the Dáil, where – with the exception of McQuillan who voted against both Costello and de Valera during the debate on the nomination of the Taoiseach – they proceeded to prop up a new minority Fianna Fáil government. 'You could hardly call the new Government a new broom; it's the old broom with a few new bristles',[206] scoffed the humorous monthly *Dublin Opinion* in a dryly succinct description of de Valera's second-last, and worst by far, administration. MacBride, for one, showed that he was perfectly aware of the public perception which gave rise to these results, when, in response to a question, he snapped, 'In the public eye Browne appeared as a martyr who was ill-treated by a bunch of politicians.'[207]

Clann na Poblachta's subsequent history is easily told. They were to receive three seats at the 1954 general election, an election which would result in the creation of Costello's second inter-party government. Clann na Poblachta were offered ministerial representation – one post – on the basis of their Dáil numbers, but this offer was turned down, and, instead, they supported the government from the backbenches without holding ministerial rank.[208] They also brought down the government from the backbenches, when they put down a no-confidence motion in early 1957. Somewhat miffed, Costello later informed Michael McInerney that 'MacBride never even hinted to me that he was contemplating the tabling of a motion of no-confidence against the Inter-Party government.'[209] MacBride's stated reasons were to do with the government's poor economic performance, but few doubted that the real reason was the government's crack-down on the recent resurgence of the IRA, which called for an immediate reaction from an ostensibly republican party.[210] Rather than risk defeat from his former colleagues, Costello dissolved the Dáil instead, and called a general election. This resulted in his removal from office, and in MacBride's removal from the Dáil, for Clann na Poblachta were now reduced to one seat, a disability they would not succeed in overcoming. In fact, MacBride sought to regain his Dáil seat on three separate occasions, in the first two instances attempting to replicate his success from the halcyon days of the late forties, for he contested two by-elections in Dublin South-West, one in 1958 and the other in 1959. As it happened, he was unsuccessful on both occasions, and he also failed to take a seat in the general election of 1961. It is only fair to add that MacBride's views on the role of a TD were rather unorthodox by the standards of the political culture within which he operated. An excellent and informed contributor to Dáil debates, MacBride was somewhat deficient in the more traditional forms of constituency work, for he did not believe that a TD's role should include 'getting grants for people'. If necessary, he directed constituents to the relevant authorities, but declined to make representations on their behalf.[211] This, effectively, ended his involvement in parliamentary activity in Ireland, although John Tully continued to sit for the Clann as their sole Dáil representative until 1965, when the party formally dissolved itself.[212]

The reasons offered for the failure of Clann na Poblachta are many. They include the practical, such as their failure to build up their party organisation, and, arising from that, the even more pragmatic, such as the party's failure to establish a secure local base and to build on the successes of the 1947 and 1948 elections. Few of their unsuccessful candidates in these elections – some of whom had come within the proverbial whisker of a Dáil seat, often being deprived by only a handful of votes for the last seat in a constituency – thought to consolidate their electoral base. Of their successful Dáil candidates, as mentioned earlier, only one, Jack McQuillan, thought to safeguard his political future by contesting the local elections in 1950. Much more revealing is the fact that, after the election of 1948, only three new TDs ever sat in the Dáil for Clann na Poblachta.[213] Equally, one can argue that the electoral experience of the Irish electorate was, as yet, confined to the creation of single-party administrations. People had not yet acquired the habit of voting for coalitions, rather than a single party. Coalition governments, and the resultant coalition, or inter-party, voting patterns, would only become a feature of the political landscape from 1951 onwards, by which time Clann na Poblachta would be in no fit condition to take advantage of the altered voting patterns. Tactically, of course, de Valera's action in dissolving the Dáil after the three by-elections in October 1947 worked. Clann na Poblachta were not allowed to develop at a natural pace, but their complete destruction cannot be laid at de Valera's door, much though he may have desired this outcome. He merely prevented them from achieving their full flowering: they themselves managed to commit spectacular suicide.

Personalities count, above all in politics. And here, in that context, MacBride's myriad flaws as leader must also be offered as reasons. He displayed a manifest inability to work closely with people who disagreed with him, except by resort to expulsion or exclusion, as instanced by his treatment of Peadar Cowan and Noel Hartnett in the Clann, and, later, his treatment of Noël Browne (who, admittedly, was not perhaps always the easiest person in the world to work with) in both party and government; perhaps most telling was the poor relationship which developed between Frederick Boland, secretary of the Department of External Affairs, and his minister. This was a flaw which would prove fatal. At the end of the day, attempting to construct a replica Fianna Fáil, MacBride showed that the differences between himself and de Valera were far more significant, to the detriment of the younger man, than any superficial similarities which might have seemed apparent at the time of the launch of the Clann, and that these political and personality differences were, in effect, what made the difference. Seeking to create a new mass party from pretty similar sources, one of them succeeded in creating an amazingly professional political machine, which successfully dominated the political stage in Ireland, and, to a large extent, has succeeded in setting – or, at the very least, strongly influencing – the economic, political, and social agenda of the state to this very day. Whereas, the other certainly created waves, and set in motion many much needed political changes (some of which, undoubtedly, were unintentional by-products of the time spent in government), but the political movement had fatally foundered within a few years. To a certain extent, some elements of the Clann never succeeded in overcoming their inherited IRA legacy of aloof authoritarianism, as their treatment of internal dissent illustrated all too well.

On a more general level, there are also reasons which can be proffered for the collapse of the party, in addition to further questions which can be posed about the Clann. Critically, and catastrophically, the party failed – spectacularly – to safeguard its ideological territory. Indeed, it almost went so far as to facilitate ideological theft (on the part of Fine Gael) of the most blatant and brazen kind. In attempting to become a catch-all party, a mass party, on the Fianna Fáil model, did it cast its net too wide? Were the tensions between the various wings of the party too much, and could it contain those tensions? Evidently not, as events transpired. In a sense, Clann na Poblachta was torn between two competing visions, two competing visions of what it meant to be republican, and one must ask whether their attempt at political experimentation had run its course by 1951. Was there a realisation that some of their concerns were perhaps more left, more socially concerned, than the existing structures could accommodate? Indeed, for that matter, would Clann na Poblachta have split equally dramatically on something else, if the hierarchy had not, with unselfconscious generosity, given them an issue like Church–state relations on a plate? It can be argued that the internal tensions of the party were close to combustion, and that the Mother and Child Scheme crisis, when it came, simply supplied the catalyst for action. Rather than being a catch-all party, there is a sense in which Clann na Poblachta can be seen as a generational movement, in that it was the means by which an entire generation became politically mobilised. Was such a generational electorate a secure enough base in the long run? Evidently not.

It is tempting to speculate whether the Clann's leadership ever gave any consideration to the notion that Clann na Poblachta's best hope perhaps lay in becoming a niche party after 1948, that the dream of becoming a catch-all party wouldn't happen? Strategies devised by small parties have differed over time. Traditionally, small parties used to attempt to become a catch-all, all-embracing party, heading in a determined manner towards the centre of the political spectrum in the hope that the people would faithfully follow. More recently, small parties have tended to see themselves as niche parties, usually concentrating on an agenda, and seeking thereby to influence the content and direction of the political debate.[214] In turn, this raises questions such as to what extent such small parties define or are defined by their niche. However, even within the Clann's electoral swimming water, huge changes were taking place. Could Clann na Poblachta have survived in a meaningful sense after 1951? Just as earlier, they were the conduit, or connection, or means through which a whole plethora of groups and movements mobilised. They had become the means through which the challenge for change in Irish society was mounted in 1946 and 1947; now, in 1951, they were to be the unwitting, and unwilling, means through which certain features – such as episcopal influence – and contours of Irish society were to be exposed in sharp relief. This unintentional exposure wrecked Clann na Poblachta, but it was by no means the only factor in their demise.

The legacy of Clann na Poblachta was interesting. Most political commentators saw it as the archetypal example of a small party which bursts upon the national stage, peaks at its first outing, and then fades completely. For this sort of deterministic model, the only question left to be answered is whether the decline was precipitous, or imperceptible. In any case, these deterministic models are predicated upon an unchanging political system, the subtext of this argument being that new parties cannot hope to break existing moulds, regardless of whether they posit themselves as catch-all or niche parties. The end of Clann na Poblachta meant a return – for a time – to the two and a half party system; it also served to highlight the infinite capacity of Fianna Fáil (and, indeed, Fine Gael) to reabsorb political flotsam, and assimilate ideas. Clann na Poblachta has done rather better than most other small parties in terms of political analysis, partly because it is seen as the exemplar of this model, partly because, in entering government, it projected a high profile and was viewed as a success in the government, as well as helping to create a new form of government – coalition – in the process, and, no doubt, partly because the Clann's leadership cadre were the sort of interesting eccentrics who attracted a lot of attention. In fact, having been successfully stymied by Fianna Fáil in February 1948, the Clann, as earlier stated, were to be faced with two major political choices, or decisions. The first of these concerned entering government, with its attendant dilemmas and compromises. On this matter MacBride never changed his mind that the choice made in February 1948 was the correct one, stressing that entering government enabled him 'to try to get things done, which we were able to get done. And it hasn't been adequately appreciated . . . Most of the issues on which we campaigned in 1948 were, in fact, achieved by 1951, such as the release of all political prisoners, the repeal of the External Relations Act, higher investment in afforestation, new hospitals and improved social services.'[215] Admittedly, this involved the development of certain skills, skills of consensus, negotiation, and compromise, for the very notion of mutual compromise lies at the heart of coalition arrangements. Pointing out that 'The mandate we got was not a mandate for government',[216] MacBride proved himself quite capable of mastering these skills, which meant prioritising some of the goals of his party in government, while yielding to the conservative consensus in other areas. When asked about this seeming contradiction, his reply was revealing, 'You're ignoring the basics of the situation. When you are in a government – with only two out of eleven seats in the government – you can only concentrate on those situations where you can get agreement – not on the others.'[217]

There were a number of ironies awaiting Clann na Poblachta in government. One was that the party – the Clann – which was the catalyst for coalition, the linchpin of the government, the party which had supplied two of the three best ministers in that government, and had done much to give it that air of dynamic enterprise which was to be its hallmark for most of its three years in office – in other words, the party that had made the government 'ball-hungry', to invoke Ó hEithir's marvellous phrase[218] – was the party to emerge from the experience of government in a state of utter collapse. A further irony of the creation of the inter-party government was that, while it had been created with the specific intention of 'putting Fianna Fáil out', nowhere was it suggested that the main result would be to assist in the revival of a 'moribund' Fine Gael party. Moreover, the Fine Gael revival, such as it was, occurred chiefly at Clann na Poblachta's expense – and not at

Labour's, National Labour's, or even that of Fine Gael's natural enemy prior to that, Clann na Talmhan. There were reasons for this, among them the tendency of MacBride to leave himself wide open – for, as the main Cabinet trespasser, he was the one whose wings most needed clipping.

The other key choice, of course, was the decision made at the time of the Mother and Child Scheme debacle to side with the conservative vested interests, rather than with Noël Browne. Indeed, it is interesting to speculate on what might have happened had MacBride chosen to bring down the government on the issue, but, alas, it can only remain an idle, if interesting, speculation. The future of Clann na Poblachta *could* have been very different had he made that choice. More relevantly, one can ask why MacBride didn't see what *would* happen to Clann na Poblachta after the capitulation to the Catholic Church on the Mother and Child Scheme. It was one thing for Fine Gael to back the vested interests, but such an action made no sense at all for a party such as Clann na Poblachta. In any case, this was the choice which did for Clann na Poblachta, and ensured not only that it would never progress from being a party of protest to becoming a credible party of government, but also that the party's own support base – the protest vote, so to speak – was split in two. By his actions, which split the Clann, rather than splitting the government, MacBride effectively ensured that the Clann's days as a radical party, and even as a political party, were numbered.[219] And this answers the query as to why Fine Gael came out of the government with its support enhanced, and its confidence increased, while the Clann was destroyed – and this despite MacBride's genuine, and utterly credible, conviction that the government had been a very good one – when, after all, both the Clann and Fine Gael had enacted much the same policies, and had taken much the same steps in distancing themselves from Browne and his health scheme. As Lee succinctly put it, 'Costello played an adroit hand. MacBride did not . . . The strength of Costello's position was that while his piety was absolutely genuine, it also happened to coincide with the material advantage of the position he represented.'[220] The opposite was to be the case with MacBride and his party. Notwithstanding MacBride's belief that the debacle happened because Browne 'was spoiling for a fight and he got it',[221] Browne's own analysis on this matter is the better one. Referring to how he had received MacBride's letter 'demanding' his resignation, Browne subsequently wrote: 'He thus ensured the collapse of the Coalition government, his own political death warrant, and the disappearance of Clann na Poblachta.'[222]

Notes and References

1: Genesis of the Clann

1 *The Irish Times* of 8 July 1946 refers to the meeting as having occurred on the previous Saturday, the 6th. However, secret police files – 'prepared in the Office of the Minister for Justice for official use only' – with the intriguing title 'Notes on IRA activities etc. 1941–1947', which can be found in the MacEntee papers (P67/550), put the meeting as having taken place on 4 July. The copies of this document were individually numbered, MacEntee's own copy being number five.

2 *The Irish Times*, 8 July 1946, *Irish Independent*, 5 July 1946.

3 'Notes on IRA activities etc. 1941-1947', p. 95, MacEntee papers (P67/550).

4 ibid.

5 Both published and unpublished sources agree that the signatories who composed the provisional executive were as follows; Breathnach, Fionán; Burke, Thomas; Cowan, Peadar; de Staic, Úna Bean Austin; Donnelly, Simon; Ferguson, Michael; Fitzpatrick, Michael; Fitzpatrick, Seán; Hannigan, James; Hartnett, Noel; Kelly, Michael; Killeen, James J.; Lehane, Con; MacBride, Seán; Mac Giobuin, Seán; Moclair, Patrick J.; Ó Cuinn, Maoilseachlainn; O'Donoghue, Donal; O'Donoghue, Pádraig; O'Kelly, Michael A.; Ó Nualláin, Pádraig; O'Riordan, Diarmuid. *The Irish Times,* 8 July 1946, and MacEntee papers (P67/550). Also regarded as having been active from the outset were May Laverty, Patrick MacCartan, and Roger McHugh. From an early stage, The O'Rahilly was also involved.

6 Tom Garvin, *1922: The Birth of Irish Democracy* (Gill & Macmillan, Dublin, 1996), p. 18. The first chapter of Garvin's book is an interesting, intelligent, and thoughtful treatment of the philosophical roots of Irish republicanism.

7 ibid., pp. 10–11.

8 ibid., p. 16.

9 Eric J. Hobsbawm wrote that in the late nineteenth century a major series of mutations occurred within political nationalism which drastically altered the civic, or liberal, revolutionary-democratic doctrines from which it had sprung. The first of these was the emergence of nationalism and patriotism as an ideology taken over by the right (the extreme expression of which became fascism). Second was the belief (foreign to the 'liberal' phase of national movements) that national self-determination up to and including the formation of independent sovereign states applied not just to nations which could demonstrate economic,

political, and cultural viability but to any and all groups which claimed to be a nation. Third was the assumption that 'national self-determination' could not be satisfied by any form of autonomy less than full state independence. Fourth, and finally, was the novel tendency to define a nation in terms of ethnicity and especially in terms of language. E. J. Hobsbawm, *The Age of Empire, 1875–1914* (Sphere Books Ltd, London, 1989), p. 144.

10 Garvin, *1922*, p. 13.

11 ibid., p. 14.

12 ibid., p. 13.

13 E. J. Hobsbawm, *Nations and Nationalism Since 1780*, p. 22.

14 Garvin, *1922*, p. 14.

15 The fairly extensive police files on Saor Éire predate Fianna Fáil's arrival in office, and, as the IRA actively supported Fianna Fáil in the general election of 1932, one might have expected a degree of disdain from Fianna Fáil regarding official files on their erstwhile helpers, but that did not preclude the Fianna Fáil government from relying heavily on them when the need arose. Fianna Fáil found the hierarchy's ban on, and condemnation of, Saor Éire very useful ammunition against Clann na Poblachta in the 1948 election.

16 MacEntee papers (P67/534).

17 Seán Cronin, *Irish Nationalism* (Academy Press, Dublin, 1980), p. 156. Cronin quotes from *Saor Éire, Constitution and Rules*, which were agreed at the Dublin convention held on 26 and 27 September 1931. See also Anthony Jordan, *Seán MacBride* (Blackwater Press, Dublin, 1993), p. 53, where an edited number of Saor Éire's political objectives are set out. The most interesting account of all can be found in a fascinating little booklet entitled 'Confidential – Office of the Minister for Justice. Departmental Notes On Events From 1st January, 1931, to 31st December, 1940, with several Appendices including an Appendix (D) on events prior to 1st January 1931', MacEntee papers (P67/534).

18 Cronin, *Irish Nationalism*, p. 156.

19 ibid.

20 MacEntee papers, (P67/534).

21 Cronin, *Irish Nationalism*, p. 157. Also worth a look on the significance of organisations such as Saor Éire is Richard English's *Radicals and the Republic: Socialist Republicans in the Irish Free State, 1925-1937* (Clarendon, Oxford, 1994).

22 This argument has been made by Noël Browne in interview with the author.

23 Michael Price left the IRA after the defeat of his position at the Republican Congress. He dabbled for a while with a stillborn attempt to revive the Citizen Army. By August 1936, he had openly aligned himself with the Labour Party, 'advocating the cause of official Labour'. MacEntee papers (P67/534, pp. 26–7).

24 ibid.

25 ibid. Also worth a look is Breandán Ó hEithir's *The Begrudger's Guide to Irish Politics* (Poolbeg, Dublin, 1986), p. 73, where O'Donnell's predilection for conspiratorial methods and de Valera's theft of the land annuities issue – 'snatched' is the verb used – are nicely combined with the following comment: 'Although he could never bring himself to abandon his own peculiar cloak and dagger brand of politics, Peadar O'Donnell was realistic enough to see that some issues called for the backing of the big battalions.' Despite the frivolous title, *The Begrudger's Guide to Irish Politics* is both a great read and an intelligent analytical critique of Irish politics and culture as they have developed since independence.

26 Cronin, *Irish Nationalism*, pp. 157-9.

27   The minute-books of both the Republican Congress and the earlier IRA convention seem to have fallen into the hands of the authorities. These are meticulous records – that of the IRA convention was dated 17 March 1934, and is over a hundred pages long, having been transcribed in beautiful copper-plate handwriting which can be viewed in MacEntee's papers (P67/525).

28   Ó hEithir, *Begrudger's Guide*, p. 109. Tim Pat Coogan, whose own researches on the matter are extensive, refers to it as 'the murky and disturbing Hayes affair', and, later on, 'the infamous Hayes affair', and, while accepting that Hayes's 'confession' was an extremely inventive – and necessary – fabrication designed to save his life, contends that Hayes's own role remains somewhat ambiguous. Coogan, *De Valera: Long Fellow, Long Shadow* (Hutchinson, London, 1993), pp. 531 and 623-4.

29   One of these safe houses was owned by Roger McHugh, 'a gentleman on the staff of University College, Dublin' where he lectured in English, who was to become a founding member of Clann na Poblachta. MacEntee papers (P67/540[6]).

30   MacEntee papers (P67/522[7]). This file is part of a much larger secret police file detailing the activities of 'revolutionary organisations' and predates Fianna Fáil's accession to power in 1932.

31   Sheila Humphries papers (P106/2140[1]).

32   ibid.

33   ibid.

34   ibid. 'M.D.'s' constitution ran to four pages, in addition to a covering page dealing with matters such as the sort of language which would be appropriate to use in this revolutionary context. MacBride's constitution, on the other hand, is an intense, closely typed document running to seven pages, and is an interesting pointer as to the way his mind worked at that time.

35   Sheila Humphries papers (P106/2140[10]).

36   Sheila Humphries papers (P106/2140[7a]).

37   Sheila Humphries papers, (P106/2140[7]).

38   Sheila Humphries papers, (P106/2140[1]).

39   Most sources consulted agree that Cumann Poblachta na hÉireann was essentially a front for the headquarters staff of the IRA: see Cronin, *Irish Nationalism,* p. 159; MacEntee papers (P67/539[1]). Both the IRA's Dublin Brigade and Sinn Féin were reported to be against the formation of this new body, while Peadar O'Donnell greeted it with the remark: 'I welcome the movement in so far as it will bring the IRA away from their policy of isolation from political and social issues.' MacEntee papers (P67/534, pp. 49–50).

40   These election results are detailed with sadistic satisfaction by the secret police. After announcing that a number of 'republican' candidates went forward for election, the police account continued laconically, 'They were decidedly unsuccessful', and proceeded to measure 'the vote given to them, in comparison to the total poll'. Madame Maud Gonne MacBride, whose campaign, in fact, was run by her son, Seán MacBride, received 689 votes out of a total of 29,733. Future Clann na Poblachta apparatchik Michael Fitzpatrick (720 votes out of 32,617), and such republican notables as George Gilmore and Frank Ryan, all failed to gain election. MacEntee papers (P67/552[1]), and (P67/534).

41   Ó hEithir, *Begrudger's Guide*, p. 61.

42   MacEntee papers (P67/550). In addition to the police files, Córas na Poblachta actually published an engaging pamphlet entitled *Córas na Poblachta (The Republican Plan)* which sets out party policies and gives the names of its officers and leading members. MacEntee papers (P67/544[3]). Curiously enough, the typeface is identical to that which would be used by Clann na Poblachta a few years later.

43   MacEntee papers (P67/372[24]). MacCool subsequently stood for Clann na Poblachta in 1948, also in Donegal. He was not elected on either occasion.
44   Manifesto of Córas na Poblachta, entitled *Córas na Poblachta (The Republican Plan)*, p. 7, MacEntee papers (P67/544[3]).
45   On this occasion, not content with giving the information that none of the Córas na Poblachta candidates gained election, the police report helpfully adds that they all lost their deposits. MacEntee papers (P67/550).
46   MacEntee papers (P67/552[1]).
47   Sheila Humphries papers (P106/2140[18]). Sheila Humphries herself led a fascinating life: she had been involved with Saor Éire, was a signatory of the Republican Congress, and had later married Donal O'Donoghue. These particular minutes are handwritten in pencil on a child's exercise copybook, and, as a result, not every word is absolutely clear.
48   Sheila Humphries papers (P106/2140[18]).
49   Sheila Humphries papers, (P106/2140[12–13]).
50   Sheila Humphries papers (P106/2140[13]). The Northern comrade, on whose behalf these questions were put, was the Nationalist MP, Patrick McLogan, who had already put in an appearance at the inaugural meeting of Cumann Poblachta na hÉireann. An earlier, handwritten version of this minute can be found in Sheila Humphries papers (P106/2140[18]).

2: The Children of the Republic

1   See Michael McInerney's interview with Gerry Boland, *The Irish Times*, 19 October 1968.
2   From 1989, Fianna Fáil-led administrations have also found themselves obliged to enter coalitions if they wished to attain, or, for that matter, retain, power.
3   Curiously enough, the lengthiest of the secret police files on MacBride in MacEntee's papers gets his date of birth completely wrong, giving it incorrectly as summer 1898. MacEntee papers (P67/550). This is a strange mistake, as members of the British secret police attended his christening, and left files describing the event. Perhaps they confused his birth with that of his sister, Iseult.
4   Anthony Jordan, *Seán MacBride* (Blackwater Press, Dublin, 1993), p. 41. Jordan, in fact, was quoting C. S. 'Todd' Andrews.
5   It is not clear whether MacBride left the IRA in 1937 or 1938. MacBride preferred to stress 1937, arguing that he supported the state from the enactment of the 1937 constitution. Most other sources (Seán Cronin in *Irish Nationalism* (Academy Press, Dublin, 1980), p. 281, J. Bowyer Bell in *The Secret Army: History of the Irish Republican Army, 1916-79* (Academy Press, Dublin, 1979), and Margaret Ward in *Maud Gonne* (Pandora, Unwin Paperbacks, London, 1990, p. 175) suggest 1938, a year after the Army Council declined to ratify his appointment as chief of staff. MacBride, while regarded as a 'political' person with a theoretical cast of mind, seems to have been comprehensively outmanoeuvred by Seán Russell, who displayed a surer grasp of the political realities of rounding up votes and pitching to an audience. This is of relevance for two reasons: firstly, MacBride attempted retrospectively to place a constitutional justification or gloss on his reasons for leaving the IRA, and secondly, and more importantly, it reveals that the tendency, or propensity, of MacBride to be outflanked or outmanoeuvred by people possessing sharper political skills did not commence with his stint in the inter-party government.
6   The definitive biography of MacBride remains to be written. Jordan's account, *Seán MacBride*, while basically accurate, is quite limited. Neither MacBride

himself nor his mother, Maud Gonne, can be regarded as entirely reliable sources. For example, in at least three far from demanding interviews conducted in the early and mid-1980s – *The Sunday Tribune's* interview carries the nauseating title 'Sweet child with golden hair', a reference to a photograph of MacBride as a cherubic child – MacBride was able to assert with a straight face that the British had imprisoned him at the age of fourteen: 'I was in jail for the first time when I was fourteen. Charge? No charge. My father had been executed, and I was put in jail for good measure.' *The Sunday Tribune*, 4 January 1981; see also *Sunday Independent*, 14 September 1980 (their fatuous headline announced 'I was fighting the Tans at fourteen'), and *Spirit of Ireland*, Autumn 1987. The latter two publications also offered as unqueried fact the idea that MacBride – at fourteen – already held officer rank in the IRA. In fact, MacBride and his mother had only managed to return from France in February 1918, and while he did succeed in joining the IRA's youth wing – the Fianna – almost immediately, he was fairly promptly packed off to boarding school in Mount St Benedict's, Gorey, Co. Wexford, following the arrest of his mother, who *was* imprisoned in May 1918. After her release in late 1918, he joined her in London, neither of them being able to return to Ireland until well into 1919. MacBride's own first brush with the British authorities occurred in September 1920, when the car he was driving was stopped because the rear lamp was faulty. As the car was found to contain Countess Markiewicz, the First Dáil's Minister for Labour, all of the occupants were taken into custody. MacBride was later released because, interestingly enough, he was found to be under age. Jordan, *Seán MacBride*, p. 21, and Ward, *Maud Gonne*, p. 126. For a devastating critique of Maud Gonne's economy with the truth, see Conrad A. Balliet's 'The Lives – and Lies – of Maud Gonne', *Éire-Ireland*, 14, iii (1979), pp. 17–44; much thanks to Alan Hayes for drawing my attention to it.

7   Noël Browne, *Against the Tide* (Gill & Macmillan, Dublin, 1986), p. 90.

8   This point is conceded even by Noël Browne, ibid., pp. 138–9. Even the most cursory glance at the respective election campaigns of 1948 and 1951 serves to confirm it.

9   *Irish Press*, 30 May 1946.

10   'Notes on IRA activities etc. 1941–1947', p. 94, approvingly quoted the minister on this topic. MacEntee papers (P67/550).

11   Browne, *Against the Tide*, p. 90.

12   MacEntee papers (P67/551[14]).

13   MacEntee's papers contain a sense of barely controlled quivering excitement when referring to 'The Vanguard', and it *is* frequently referred to. Granted, names such as The Vanguard, The Spark, and any others borrowed from Lenin's lexicon were something of a hostage to fortune in an Irish context, especially one set in the 1940s and 1950s.

14   MacEntee papers (P67/539[2]), (P67/540[6]), and (P67/534). This undertaking was later to be a source of some embarrassment for Lehane in Clann na Poblachta (Jack McQuillan in conversation with the author). However, MacBride himself, as it happened, had also signed a similar undertaking in the Bridewell on 28 May 1940, an undertaking which in the portentous police language of the time ran as follows: 'I, Seán MacBride, do solemnly and sincerely promise as follows, that is to say, that I shall not engage in or encourage any acts prejudicial to the peace, order or security of the State and in particular that I shall not a) Have any unlawful dealings or unlawful communication with any member of the unlawful organisation referred to as the IRA. b) Assist or encourage the agents or armed forces of any other state to enter

this State, or to operate within it or to obtain information save so far as the same may be done in an open, peaceful and lawful manner.' A copy of this undertaking can be found in MacEntee's papers (P67/542[36]).

15   MacEntee papers (P67/378[35]) and (P67/552[1]).

16   MacEntee papers (P67/548[1]). This lengthy file comes with the lurid title 'Communism in Ireland'. An alternative view is offered by Noël Browne when he comments that, while Fitzpatrick was a 'respected old-timer', he had 'little of serious political content to offer'. *Against the Tide*, p. 104. Advertisements alluding to the attractions of the 'Balalaika' ballroom appeared in the *Review* magazine, a publication viewed by the secret police – with some justification – as a 'Communist organ'. The *Review* was edited by John Nolan – a man 'who regards himself as a writer', as he was witheringly described by the secret police. Nolan further featured, with more relevance, in police files as a 'whole time official of the Communist Party of Ireland' – and, what was clearly much worse, as a 'lapsed Catholic'. MacEntee papers (P67/548[1]) and (P67/551[12]). He ran a left-wing bookshop on Pearse Street called 'New Books' which attracted a wide clientele of left-wing, liberal, iconoclastic types, and even a republican readership. Police cameras recorded Captain Peadar Cowan frequently browsing through the subversive literature available, a fact which was used to embarrass MacBride at the Cabinet table some years later. Browne, *Against the Tide*, p. 249. Or, as the secret police file so engagingly phrased it: '[Cowan] frequented 'New Books' in '45, '46, and '47; seen in company of O'Neill, Nolan, FitzGerald, etc. in Mooney's public house, Eden Quay, July '47.' MacEntee papers (P67/548[1]).

Other more prominent citizens were also captured on camera, future Chief Justice Cearbhall Ó Dálaigh being one such. This was not the only time Ó Dálaigh featured in police files. Many years later, when he was actually Chief Justice, he was observed attending a meeting of the Irish–Soviet Friendship Society, a fact which gave rise to considerable agitation on the part of the secretary of the Department of Justice, Peter Berry, who reported it to his minister. Breandán Ó hEithir, *The Begrudger's Guide to Irish Politics* (Poolbeg, Dublin, 1986), p. 123.

17   MacEntee papers (P67/378[35]) and (P67/552[1]). One of the files refers to Fitzpatrick as the 'director' while the other calls him the 'owner' of the 'Balalaika Ballroom'.

18   MacEntee papers (P67/543[2]). Fitzpatrick supported MacBride's opposition to the Republican Congress, and succeeded Tom Barry (who, in turn, had succeeded MacBride) as chief of staff of the IRA in late 1937. In 1938, having strenuously opposed the planned bombing campaign in England, he was ousted by Seán Russell, who had already comprehensively outflanked MacBride. Throughout the existence of Clann na Poblachta, Fitzpatrick remained a strong supporter of MacBride.

19   Browne, *Against the Tide*, p. 100. Browne concentrates on O'Donoghue's dapper appearance in his description: 'O'Donoghue would stand there incongruously in his expensive-looking brown trilby hat and spotlessly clean yellow chamois gloves, gingerly holding at the ready a folded black silk umbrella.'

20   The Workers' Revolutionary Party in Ireland was formed in March 1930, and O'Donoghue's role was extremely minor, being underlined only years later on account of his later activities, especially his links with Clann na Poblachta. The police report on this meeting betrays a note of frustration when it grumbled that the meeting 'was a short one and was confined to a superficial discussion on the weekly paper. Bell [the editor] announced that *The Workers' Voice* would appear during the first week in April and in the event of its suppression it would

be re-named *The Workers' Challenge*, and in the event of a further suppression would again be re-named *The Workers' Weekly.*' MacEntee papers (P67/522[7]). Not only was the topic under discussion not superficial, in that the putative paper faced banning even before birth, but it also appears that the difficulty in coming up with completely new and original names was not confined to the wilder fringes of the republican movement, but afflicted the far left equally.

21   MacEntee papers (P67/548[1]).

22   Browne, *Against the Tide*, p. 100.

23   ibid.

24   MacEntee papers (P67/522[7]) and (P67/543[2]).

25   University College Galway boasted of a student branch which was certainly quite active in 1948. I am indebted to Jack McQuillan for making some of the branch's papers – including a membership list – available to me.

26   MacEntee papers (P67/539[2]). Both Stephen Hayes and his brother-in-law were held in Roger McHugh's house in Glencree for several days and while there were subjected to threats and beatings.

27   Clann na Poblachta's provisional executive contained six lawyers, five teachers, two accountants, four who owned their own business, one farmer, one electrician, and one public health officer. Their candidates would include quite a few young doctors, and one or two older ones, such as Dr Patrick McCartan, the independent republican candidate in the 1945 presidential election whose astonishing vote rocked the political establishment. This prompts a look at what is not represented; thus landless labourers, the unemployed, small farmers, and the working class played little role in the higher administrative structures of Clann na Poblachta, even though the party set out its stall hoping to attract considerable numbers of these votes, in addition to its already existing republican bedrock.

28   The national executive was a larger body than the provisional executive, and contained Seán MacBride, Noel Hartnett, Con Lehane, M. A. O'Kelly, Fionán Breathnach, Donal O'Donoghue, J. J. Killeen, May Laverty, Peadar Cowan, The O'Rahilly, Roger McHugh, Maura Laverty, Dick Batterberry, Mick Kelly, Tom Roycroft, Paid O'Donoghue, Rory Brugha, Frank Hugh O'Donnell, Mick Ferguson, Michael Fitzpatrick, and Austin Stack. *The Irish Times*, 1 December 1947. Of the new additions to the national executive, both Batterberry and Roycroft were teachers, and Ferguson joined Clann na Poblachta immediately on his return from England, where he had languished in prison since his conviction for his involvement in the IRA bombings of the late 1930s. Each province was also represented by four delegates.

29   The national advisory council, 'having due regard to their responsibility for preserving the National position of the Association, always pledged themselves to the ideals of the men of 1916', as they phrased it in a letter kept by MacEntee. MacEntee papers (P67/372[39]).

30   ibid. MacEntee's glee when he came across this letter was justified.

31   ibid.

32   ibid.

33   All of this appears in Article 12 of Clann na Poblachta's constitution, entitled 'Candidates for Parliamentary Elections'. Curiously enough, they did not use the word 'Dáil' in this context.

34   Article 12 of Clann na Poblachta's constitution.

35   Noël Browne's unease emerges in *Against the Tide*, pp. 105–6. Jack McQuillan expressed his misgivings in several interviews with the author.

36   They say that imitation is the sincerest form of flattery, and in that case, Clann clones litter the political landscape, for Fine Gael's current policy – inaugurated

as recently as 1978 by the then newly appointed leader, Dr Garret FitzGerald – regarding the role of their national executive in candidate selection ('parachuting' is the unkind term sometimes used in these latter days) is clearly an expression of grovelling gratitude, which Clann na Poblachta, if they still existed, would doubtless acknowledge with due decorum. Labour, too, give every appearance of laying it on with a trowel.

37 Articles 9 and 10 of Clann na Poblachta's constitution deal with the composition, functions, and powers of the national executive and the standing committee, respectively. The national executive was to be elected by the ard-fheis, while the standing committee was elected by the national executive, with the exception of the five aforementioned additional members who could be co-opted at will, giving MacBride his in-built majority. Both executive bodies were empowered to make any changes in the rules which they saw fit to make, and the standing committee enjoyed 'all of the administrative powers' of the national executive when that body was not in session.

38 Jack McQuillan in an interview with the author.

39 This phrase is an excellent example of former US President George Bush's legendary inarticulacy.

40 J. H. Whyte, *Church and State in Modern Ireland, 1923–1979* (Gill & Macmillan, Dublin, 1979), p. 230.

41 This character analysis comes from a secret police file on Peadar Cowan. MacEntee papers (P67/551[14]).

42 Brian Inglis, *Downstart* (Chatto & Windus, London, 1990), pp. 163–6. Inglis was at that time a columnist for *The Irish Times*, writing the 'Quidnunc' column, and he covered both the by-elections of 1947 and the general election of 1948 for the paper. He devoted considerable attention and space to the Clann's campaigns because 'the main [political] interest centred on how well, or badly "the Clann" would do'.

43 The story usually told to illustrate this point appears in Breandán Ó hEithir's idiosyncratic and highly readable account of his relationship with the GAA, entitled *Over the Bar* (Poolbeg, Dublin, 1991). It was told to Ó hEithir by the poet Máirtín Ó Cadhain, as an illustration of how Ó Cadhain had come to the conclusion that MacBride 'would never do any good in politics because he did not understand Ireland'. *Over the Bar*, pp. 211-12. Apparently, on the second day of an IRA convention held in 1936, delegates who had been extremely pugnacious the previous day were seen to have become restive. MacBride, who was on the platform, noticed this restlessness and wondered as to the reason for it. Ó Cadhain replied that the All-Ireland semi-final was due to be played that particular day, and that the restive delegates were anxious that the IRA convention be deferred *sine die* as many of them wished to attend the football semi-final instead. Surveying the squirming delegates distastefully, MacBride commented 'I see. So a game of football is more important than the future of the Irish Republic.' MacBride's biographer, who refers to this tale, offers the opinion that 'Such a remark displayed a frightening lack of appreciation of the culture of Gaelic sport in Ireland.' Jordan, *Seán MacBride*, p. 69. In fact, as discussed above, that is more than a little overstated, for, despite his lack of interest in sporting matters, MacBride was not blind to their potential as a vote-gathering exercise.

44 Inglis, *Downstart*, p. 165.

45 Jordan, *Seán MacBride*, p. 41.

46 John A. Murphy, *Ireland in the Twentieth Century* (Gill & Macmillan, Dublin, 1975), pp. 117–18.

47 Tim Pat Coogan, *De Valera: Long Fellow, Long Shadow* (Hutchinson, London, 1993), p. 637.

48 They would fail to attract one of the most successful of all when Jack Lynch, then a young Cork barrister and the proud owner of half a dozen All-Ireland medals spanning both hurling and football, turned them down, and stood for Fianna Fáil instead. It was a decision he never regretted.

49 Both Andy Murphy and his cousin, Tommy Murphy, widely regarded as a 'boy wonder' when he graced the football field, stood as Dáil candidates for Clann na Poblachta. Andy Murphy ran in the Carlow–Kilkenny constituency, and Tommy Murphy stood for election in Laois–Offaly. Clann na Poblachta were not the only organisation to express an interest in the potential political prowess of the 'boy wonder'; Oliver J. Flanagan attempted to woo him but was repulsed. This information came from a number of people whom I interviewed in Carlow, among them Johnny 'Quash' Prendergast, a Fianna Fáil activist from the 1940s, Christopher Moran, who lived in both Carlow and Baltinglass during that era, and John McMenamy, who was then a Labour Party activist.

50 See Inglis, *Downstart*, p. 165, Ó hEithir, *Over the Bar*, pp. 211–12, Jordan, *Seán MacBride*, p. 69.

51 Jordan, *Seán MacBride*, p. 50.

52 It is only fair to point out that MacBride in an interview with the author vehemently contested the idea that the Mother and Child Scheme debacle alienated Clann na Poblachta's radical support. He seemed to see it more as a power struggle within the party, and argued that he was attempting to safeguard the Clann.

53 MacBride himself strongly disputed this analysis in an interview with the author. J. J. Lee, *Ireland 1912-1985: Politics and Society* (Cambridge University Press, Cambridge, 1989), p. 318.

3: The Summer of '46

1 Lee puts the blame for the split squarely on the shoulders of William O'Brien. J. J. Lee, *Ireland 1912-1985: Politics and Society* (Cambridge University Press, Cambridge, 1989), pp. 240–1. This is treated comprehensively in Richard Dunphy, *The Making of Fianna Fáil Power in Ireland 1932–1948* (Clarendon Press, Oxford, 1995), pp. 265–71, and also pp. 289–93.

2 Michael Gallagher, *Political Parties in the Republic of Ireland* (Gill & Macmillan, Dublin, 1985), pp. 109–10. This is also treated in considerable detail in Dunphy, *Making of Fianna Fáil Power in Ireland* (Clarendon Press, Oxford, 1995), pp. 265–9, and 289–93.

3 For an interesting look at the options open to Labour at the time see James A. Gaughan, *Thomas Johnston, 1872–1963: First Leader of the Labour Party in Dáil Éireann* (Kingdom Books, Dublin, 1980).

4 *Review*, July 1947. MacEntee papers (P67/541[14]). MacEntee's reading matter seems to have been extremely wide, for *Review* was a strongly left-wing paper.

5 ibid.

6 An interesting example of this attitude in action concerns two by-elections which were held in May 1940, one in Galway and the other in Kilkenny, when the leader of Fine Gael, W. T. Cosgrave, declined to field any candidates because such a 'contest wouldn't be in the interests of the country'. MacEntee papers (P67/534, p. 86a).

7 Dr McCartan was no stranger to politics, and his own republican pedigree was pretty solid, for he had been elected for the constituency of Offaly in 1918 as part of the Sinn Féin landslide, and was subsequently appointed to the Irish 'Embassy' in Washington on behalf of the First Dáil in 1920, where he acted as a very able polemicist and publicist on behalf of the underground Irish government. A respected member of the Irish Republican Brotherhood, and regarded

by British intelligence as a 'particularly dangerous man', McCartan enjoyed extensive links with influential sections of Irish-American opinion. (Ironically enough, a similar diplomatic posting was given to Seán T. O'Kelly – McCartan's opponent for the presidency almost thirty years later – who was sent, at the same time, as Ireland's representative to Paris.) McCartan escorted de Valera around the USA during the latter's extended sojourn on American soil in 1920, and returned to Ireland, at de Valera's behest, to explain de Valera's perspectives to Collins and Griffith in Dublin. On his return to the USA, he and de Valera appear to have fallen out, and de Valera tried, initially unsuccessfully, to undermine him by sweetly suggesting that the twin roles played by McCartan – namely that of an Irish diplomatic envoy and that of an Irish-American polemicist – were fundamentally incompatible. (This was a bit rich coming from a man who would combine directorships in the *Irish Press* with his onerous position as Taoiseach.) Removed from his journalistic power-base, McCartan was next offered the poisoned chalice of being asked to travel to Soviet Russia as Ireland's envoy, a posting which would be used much later by MacEntee to portray him as being unusually sympathetic to the Soviet Union. This was the background to the notorious affair of the Russian crown jewels, which were accepted by the Irish government as collateral for a loan forwarded to Soviet Russia in 1920. These gems would reappear in the bitter correspondence which preceded the 1948 general election (McCartan bitingly enquired of MacEntee what had become of the jewels), and it would fall to be MacBride's lot as Minister for External Affairs to superintend the redemption by the Soviet government of the jewels. By 1947, McCartan had become a firm, and public, supporter of Clann na Poblachta, and was appointed to the Senate in 1948, as one of MacBride's two nominees. Tim Pat Coogan, *De Valera: Long Fellow, Long Shadow* (Hutchinson, London, 1993), pp. 91–182, passim; letters to the *Irish Press* from both MacEntee and McCartan, 16 January 1948.

8   This, in fact, was the first ever presidential election to be held, as the previous President, Dr Douglas Hyde, who had held the office since 1938, was essentially an agreed candidate.

9   The papers of the Fine Gael leader, General Richard Mulcahy, contain an extraordinarily detailed constituency-by-constituency breakdown of the votes in the presidential election of 1945. Mulcahy papers (7b/115[34]) and (7b/115[35]). O'Kelly obtained a total of 537,965 first preferences, MacEoin received 335,543, and McCartan managed to garner 212,834. Of McCartan's votes, 117,886 found their way to MacEoin, while only 27,200 went to O'Kelly. There were 67,748 non-transferable votes.

10   State intervention would come to be seen in an increasingly positive light by the large numbers of young Irish people who had lived and worked in Britain during, and immediately after, the war. Those who worked in the newly created National Health Service (such as Dr Noël Browne, before his return to Ireland) found the idealism of the experience very uplifting. In addition, among several of the people I interviewed there seemed to be a certain reluctant admiration at the thought of Britain's gumption in even contemplating a large state input in areas such as housing, health, and so on, so soon after a world war which had nearly led to bankruptcy. Inevitably, this led to calls on the lines of 'If war-torn Britain can think along these lines, why can't we?'

11   'The tensions – and the liberations – of war, the shared experience, the comradeship in suffering, the new thinking about the future, all these things had passed her by. It was as if an entire people had been condemned to live in Plato's cave, with their backs to the fire of life and deriving their only knowledge of what went on outside from the flickering shadows thrown on the wall before

their eyes by the men and women who passed to and fro behind them. When after six years they emerged, dazzled, from the cave into the light of day, it was to a new and vastly different world.' F. S. L. Lyons, *Ireland Since the Famine* (Fontana, London, 1973), pp. 557–8.

12   For a very interesting critical analysis of the cultural impact of neutrality see the marvellous section entitled 'Plato's Cave?' in Lee, *Ireland,* pp. 258–70. Lee argues (pp. 259–60) that 'It was not neutrality, but the response of the political culture to neutrality, that mattered', continuing with the perceptive observation that the war and its aftermath 'were perceived in Ireland less as an opportunity for a new beginning than as a threat to an inherited achievement, economically as well as politically'.

13   Dunphy, *Making of Fianna Fáil Power in Ireland,* p. 220. Although Industry and Commerce was more normally considered the bailiwick of Lemass, MacEntee held the portfolio from September 1939 until August 1941. MacEntee was more usually Local Government Minister.

14   This was not one of Lemass's brighter ideas. For a discussion of the threatened flour mill strike, and Fianna Fáil reaction to it, see Lee, *Ireland,* p. 289. This is also discussed in Dunphy, *Making of Fianna Fáil Power in Ireland,* pp. 247–8.

15   This happened in north-east County Galway, near the Roscommon border, according to two informants, one of them an uncle of mine, who both recalled the story.

16   Dunphy, *Making of Fianna Fáil Power in Ireland,* p. 251.

17   ibid., p. 226–7. Undoubtedly, this total would have been considerably greater but for the travel restrictions imposed by the Irish government on certain categories of worker – especially the badly paid tillage workers.

18   ibid., p. 227.

19   ibid.

20   Lee, *Ireland 1912–1985*, p. 335.

21   Privately, of course, there were some – such as Seán Lemass, Fianna Fáil's extremely able wartime Minister for Supplies – who felt that the government's overweening economic and ideological dependence on agriculture needed to be jettisoned, and that it should be replaced by greater attention to forms of industrial modernisation. For an interesting discussion on Lemass's attitudes towards agriculture, especially the sort of smallholding which supplied much of Fianna Fáil's electoral support, see Lee, *Ireland,* pp. 230–3. This topic is also discussed in Tim Pat Coogan's *De Valera,* pp. 632–4.

22   Anyone querying the continuing importance of property in Irish politics need look no further than the unsuccessful outcome of the first divorce referendum in 1986, and the impact of the 'rod licence dispute' in the Galway West constituency in 1989 – which was seen essentially as an attack on the established proprietorial rights of fishermen in the Lough Corrib area.

23   MacEntee papers (P67/548[1]).

24   MacEntee (P67/376[6]), and (P67/372[40]). Neither the Lower Prices Council, nor the 'Women's Parliament' (or, to use its official title, the Women's National Council of Action), which is discussed below, has been given anything like the attention organisations mobilising such numbers merit. Given MacEntee's paranoia, it is probably inevitable that his papers contain copious amounts of material on these potentially subversive organisations, including several newspaper cuttings. The tone of the newspaper coverage is unbelievably patronising, but that was the spirit of the age. MacEntee's own tone is characteristically crabby.

25   Hilda Tweedy, *A Link in the Chain: The Story of the Irish Housewives' Association 1942–1992* (Attic Press, Dublin), 1992, p. 101.

26   ibid.

27   MacEntee papers (P67/548[1], p. 61). Hilda Tweedy managed to mingle amuse-
      ment with a sort of perverse pride at the fact that such files had been kept on
      the Irish Housewives' Association. Tweedy, *A Link in the Chain*, p. 16.
28   Tweedy, *A Link in the Chain*, p. 101.
29   MacEntee papers (P67/550). That particular meeting took place in the Engi-
      neer's Hall in February 1941, and drew the usual attentions of the secret police.
      Berthon Waters, who wrote on economic matters for *The Irish Times*, would
      play an interesting role in the formulation of some of the Clann's economic poli-
      cies. Interestingly, she did not attend the Women's Parliament under the aegis
      of the Clann (whereas May Laverty did), but in her capacity as a representative
      of the Irish People's Co-operative Society. MacEntee papers (P67/376[6]) and
      (P67/372[40]).
30   The producer–consumer market was opened by the lord mayor of Dublin on 5
      January 1949. Tweedy, *A Link in the Chain*, p. 102.
31   In fact, the Labour Court was established in August 1946, right in the middle of
      the INTO strike, and was designed precisely for such eventualities, but this did
      not prevent the Fianna Fáil government from ignoring it completely.
32   Breandán Ó hEithir, *The Begrudger's Guide to Irish Politics* (Poolbeg, Dublin,
      1986), p. 110.
33   Interview with Johnny Prendergast.
34   Information from Colm O'Quigley. The words 'ignorant' (with the stress very
      much on both meanings of the word) and 'boorish' constantly recurred in inter-
      views I had, not just with former teachers, such as Colm O'Quigley, formerly of
      the INTO, but also with people who had been in Fianna Fáil itself, such as
      Johnny Prendergast, an ex-army commandant who had served on the party's
      Comhairle Dáilcheantair in Carlow. Interviews with Colm O'Quigley and
      Johnny Prendergast, Carlow.
35   *The Irish Times*, 12 July 1946.
36   Lee, *Ireland*, p. 289.
37   According to Colm O'Quigley, who had been actively involved with the INTO,
      the teachers themselves had approached Archbishop McQuaid to mediate in
      the dispute, and he duly did so. Colm O'Quigley in an interview with the
      author.
38   This All-Ireland final, which featured Kerry and Roscommon, ended in a draw.
      The match has been preserved on film and the invasion of the pitch by the
      teachers at half-time, and the subsequent police reaction leading to their
      removal, are there for all to see. Dermot Keogh, *Twentieth-Century Ireland*
      (Gill & Macmillan, Dublin, 1994), pp. 166–72, deals quite fully with the strike
      and its aftermath.
39   Wasn't it Pyhrrus who said 'one more such victory and we are lost'? Keogh
      (ibid., p. 172) is quite right to stress the enduring bitterness which was a legacy
      of the strike, a bitterness which he found still evident (as, indeed, did I, during
      the course of several interviews) in conversations with striking activists over
      forty years later.
40   At least three of these offerings from the INTO, Tom Roycroft, Margaret Skin-
      nider, and Richard Batterberry, became members of Clann na Poblachta's
      national executive.
41   By 1946, in fact, most of the hundreds interned had already been released,
      leaving a 'hard-core' of thirty-four still in prison at the government's pleasure.
      MacEntee papers (P67/540[6]).
42   Letter from the RPRA to the *Irish Press*, 20 May 1946. Indeed, Donal
      O'Donoghue also rushed into print with a letter stressing that 'it is absolutely
      untrue to suggest that Mr MacBride was the originator or even a member of this

Association', although O'Donoghue conceded that he did address meetings designed to win support for the situation of Seán McCaughey. *Irish Press*, 1 June 1946.

43 MacBride pointed out in a letter to the daily newspapers (*Irish Press* and *The Irish Times*, 1 June 1946) that he 'did not join' the amnesty association. However, he did make some speeches in support of it. The desire of MacBride and the RPRA to demonstrate a degree of distance in public, while privately supporting each other, is interesting, especially in the light of the fact that preparations for the formation of Clann na Poblachta were evidently under way at the time.

44 MacEntee's papers contain a list of each of these capital cases where MacBride acted as defence counsel. Among the cases listed are those involving Tómas Mac Curtain, Patrick McGrath, Francis Harte, Richard Goss, Joseph O'Callaghan, Maurice O'Neill, George Plant, Joseph O'Connor, Michael Walsh, Patrick Davern, Michael Quille, Charles Kerins, and Henry White. MacEntee papers (P67/372[24]). MacEntee's own views on capital punishment are clearly put forward in a nasty memorandum entitled 'Notes upon the General Principles with which, it is suggested, Advice to the President in relation to the Commutation of Death Sentences should Accord', in which he strongly recommends that the advice to commute death sentences should be invoked sparingly, and preferably should not be invoked at all. MacEntee papers (P67/533[9]).

45 MacEntee papers (P67/540[6]) is a graphic and detailed account of the government's point of view. It contains MacEntee's preparations (and speech) for his Dáil response to Michael Donnellan's parliamentary questions resulting from the uproar generated by the inquest. Coogan, in *De Valera*, p. 625, says that McCaughey would have called off his hunger strike if he had been transferred to the Curragh. At the time of his arrest in September 1941, McCaughey held the rank of adjutant general of the IRA. Ironically, McCaughey found himself in prison on account of his role in the 'infamous' Stephen Hayes affair – on his arrest his jacket pocket was found to contain the keys to the manacles chaining Hayes. Other incriminating material was found as well, leading to a death sentence (which was commuted to penal servitude for life) being passed on McCaughey. He landed in Portlaoise Prison, and immediately joined a 'blanket' protest which, in effect, sought 'political status' by objecting to the wearing of prison uniforms and refusing to associate with other prisoners or engage in any prison work. Ó hEithir in *Begrudger's Guide*, p. 88, refers to McCaughey as 'puritanical not to mention single-minded'.

46 MacEntee papers (P67/540[6]).

47 ibid.

48 MacEntee papers (P67/550, p. 93).

49 The four questions are quoted in a letter Seán MacBride wrote to the *Irish Press*, 20 May 1946; they are also in Ó hEithir *Begrudger's Guide*, pp. 109–10, and Coogan, *De Valera*, p. 625. An interesting footnote in Coogan's book tells of how reporters present at the inquest – with police and prison officers still milling about – subsequently read the transcript out to MacBride who had no corrections and only one suggestion to make: 'Before Dr Duane's reply, put "after a pause".' That particular event was recalled years later when MacBride visited the offices of the *Irish Press* shortly before his death.

50 Recalling the drama of this inquest had quite a number of Clann stalwarts starry-eyed and emotional almost half a century later, when I interviewed them. Most remembered the exchange verbatim. MacEntee's papers, on the other hand, are very sour on the topic. MacEntee papers (P67/540[6]).

51   MacEntee papers (P67/540[6]). MacEntee applauded the coroner's decision to confine evidence on McCaughey's state of health 'to the period after he went on hunger-strike, it being clear that he was at the time in good health and that his treatment in prison before that date, *whatever it was,* had nothing to do with his health' (my italics). However, Coogan, in *De Valera,* pp. 623–5, points out that McCaughey had required medical attention while in prison, and that he appeared to have suffered from nervous strain. Of greater interest, from Coogans's point of view, was the yawning chasm between de Valera's delicately expressed concern over the treatment of IRA men imprisoned in Britain and his treatment of those under lock and key in Ireland.

52   MacBride's lack of wartime involvement – in an army where young Cosgraves and young de Valeras held commissions and marched side by side even if their respective fathers were still not on speaking terms – was first used against him in May 1946, and frequently reappeared right up until the 1948 election. His argument that he was devoting all of his time to his legal practice sounded somewhat hollow, but did not really hurt him electorally.

53   In a letter published by the daily newspapers (*The Irish Times* and *Irish Press*) on 1 June 1946, discussing the fall-out from the McCaughey case, MacBride requested that the papers publish his suppressed letter of 10 July 1943. They duly did so.

54   Seán MacBride, letter to *The Irish Times* and *Irish Press*, 1 June 1946.

55   Richard Mulcahy's papers are extensive, and in dozens of letters, notes, detailed memoranda, and exhaustive lists – references to the Tipperary by-election can be found from early in the summer of 1947 – no mention at all is made of Clann na Poblachta. See Mulcahy papers (P7[b]115[25]) and (P7[c]119).

56   Kinnane enjoyed extensive networks, from his IRA and GAA connections. Furthermore, it was pointed out to me (by a Fianna Fáil source) that his brother was a bishop.

57   MacEntee papers (P67/550, p. 98).

58   ibid. The government's invocation of the charge of petty larceny for the ficti-tious felon is especially ironic in the light of the grand larceny which would be undertaken by Clann na Poblachta itself during the three by-elections.

59   *The Irish Times,* 8 July 1946.

60   Dr Ward was probably the intended nominee to the newly created Department of Health. His precipitate departure delayed the finalisation of the legislation which was to become the Health Act, 1947, and was a personal tragedy, for he as a dedicated, if pugnacious, minister. In fact, the charges levelled against Dr Ward came from a Dublin specialist, whose brother had been sacked as manager of the bacon factory. The charges were broadly dismissed by the Dáil committee set up to investigate them, but Dr Ward was found guilty of making incomplete returns to the income tax authorities on the profits from his bacon factory. J. H. Whyte, *Church and State in Modern Ireland*, pp. 138–9.

61   Coogan, *De Valera,* p. 636.

62   Ó hEithir, *Begrudger's Guide,* p. 113.

63   Oliver J. Flanagan was to achieve notoriety in later life as a staunchly Catholic Fine Gael TD enjoying suspiciously close links with organisations such as the Knights of Columbanus. However, at this time he was an Independent TD, having first been elected in Laois–Offaly as a supporter of the 'Monetary Reform Party', witheringly described by Ó hEithir as 'a small European movement of a quasi-Catholic bent which had a certain popularity in France'. Ó hEithir, *Begrudger's Guide,* p. 112. While Flanagan was an excellent muck-raker, and a superb vote-getter – consistently topping the poll in his Laois bailiwick despite

his extremist political opinions and positions – he was a far sharper politician than many gave him credit for.

64 Lee, *Ireland*, pp. 296–7. Also making the same point are, Coogan, *De Valera*, pp. 635–6, Keogh, *Twentieth-Century Ireland*, pp. 181–2, and Ó hEithir, *Begrudger's Guide*, pp. 116–18.

65 *The Irish Times*, 6 November 1947.

66 ibid.

67 ibid. The emphasis on investigating allegations made against 'members of the Oireachtas' contained one interesting omission, in that it served to exclude examination of the role played by the President, who, innocently or not, appeared to have been involved. One source I interviewed (a former ambassador who had been active in Clann na Poblachta) felt that the main function of the tribunal was to divert unwelcome attentions away from President Seán T. O'Kelly's role, as much as exonerate the government. However, Breandán Ó hEithir pointed the finger as much at Flanagan (for his wild allegations) as at Fianna Fáil's particular brand of corruption, when I spoke with him.

68 Locke's Distillery had been founded in 1757, and when the distillery went up for sale the company secretary sought – unsuccessfully – to buy it. After years of lying derelict, the building, an exceedingly handsome one of cut stone, was tastefully restored. The magnificent water-wheels are still extant, and Locke's now includes a coffee-shop, and, astonishingly – since 1994 – a working distillery. As a curiosity, it is possible to buy bottles bearing the Locke's label, which contain coloured liquid. I did so, when I visited the place in 1987. There is no reference to the scandal, or attempted scam, anywhere.

69 *The Irish Times*, 23 October 1947. Minister for Justice Gerry Boland was somewhat embarrassed by the fact that this consortium, and their friends, were treated to 'tea with the president'.

70 Ó hEithir, *Begrudger's Guide*, p. 115.

71 Ó hEithir points out (ibid.) that the stock of whiskey was worth about £660,000 in the money of that time on the black market; this was a time when a TD's annual salary came to £624. Nowadays, the value of that whiskey would realise more than £60 million.

72 *The Irish Times*, 27 October 1947.

73 Ó hEithir, *Begrudger's Guide*, p. 115.

74 *The Irish Times*, 15 October 1947.

75 Keogh, *Twentieth-Century Ireland*, p. 182.

76 *The Irish Times*, 27 October 1947. This, note, was at a time when most Irish people usually walked, or cycled, or used public transport in order to reach their intended destinations.

4: 'Two lovely black eyes could only mean a general election'

1 *The Irish Times*, 1 November 1947.

2 Letters from both men, fighting two parallel running battles, appeared regularly in both papers throughout October 1947. Each gave as good as he got, but MacEntee must have been surprised at the doughty resilience and rapid reflexes of his Clann opponent.

3 The letters page of the *Irish Press*, 23 and 24 October 1947, reads with the raciness of an attention-grabbing thriller. On 24 October, on the one page, letters are featured from Bill Quirke (the 'prominent Senator' at the eye of the storm over Locke's Distillery), MacBride's own lawyers, Kennedy & McGonagle (who threatened libel actions on MacEntee), Tommy Mullins, Seán MacEntee, Gerry Boland, and Fianna Fáil's director of elections, P. J. Burke. MacBride himself

had produced a massive missive the day before, which had given rise to references by the editor of the *Irish Press* to the parallel correspondence in *The Irish Times*, 'which as it was not published in the *Irish Press* clearly did not concern us'.

4   *Irish Press* and *The Irish Times*, 23 and 24 October 1947.

5   *The Irish Times*, 29 October 1947.

6   'Seán MacBride is fighting your battles for a right to live in reasonable comfort in your own country; for a lower cost of living; for food subsidies and price controls; for increased old age pensions; for free secondary education for your children; for decent housing; for proper social services; for municipally owned transport; for a *Christian state in reality, not merely in name.*' This comes from one of MacBride's manifestos, which, along with much of the correspondence from the campaign, can be found in MacEntee's papers (P67/542).

7   This advertisement was extremely eye-catching, attractively constructed, and very well written. Also worth noting are some similarities with policies espoused by that hoary old ghost, Saor Éire.

8   *The Irish Times,* 13 October 1947.

9   *The Irish Times*, 28 October 1947.

10   ibid.

11   *The Irish Times,* 15 September 1947.

12   *The Irish Times*, 27 October 1947.

13   Dermot Keogh, *Twentieth-Century Ireland* (Gill & Macmillan, Dublin, 1994), p. 182, suggests that Tommy Mullins was considerably more left-wing than his Clann opponent, and, for that matter, seemed to be considerably more left-wing than was the norm for Fianna Fáil TDs.

14   *The Irish Times* gave quite generous coverage to MacBride, without openly supporting him, and it is clear that they were able to read the political situation quite accurately, as anyone perusing their issues for October 1947 can see for themselves.

15   A list put together by Mulcahy (who was devoted to drawing up lists) set out eight matters to be attended to by Fine Gael in Tipperary. Most of these were fairly mundane topics – 'roll call of district centres', 'constituency finance', etc. – but one of them, labelled 'Relations with other Parties' deserves closer attention. Mulcahy to J. J. O'Dwyer, 11 May 1947, Mulcahy papers (P7c/119). Could anyone contemplate de Valera ever giving the slightest consideration to the concept of 'relations with other parties'? One could, of course, read into this that Mulcahy was already well disposed to the notion of reaching accommodations with other parties long before the election of 1948.

16   For all that Clann na Talmhan and Fine Gael were in pursuit of the same support, Mulcahy indicated a preference for a common approach when possible. An interesting example of this was his decision not to move the writ for the Tipperary by-election until he had secured agreement from Clann na Talmhan to do so, 'as it would do damage between the Farmers and ourselves'. Richard Mulcahy to J. J. O'Dwyer, 31 May 1947, Mulcahy papers (P7c/119). It is probably of relevance to note that the Tipperary vacancy had come about due to the death of a Clann na Talmhan TD.

17   Mulcahy papers (P7b/115[25]).

18   Results at the end of the first count gave Mullins 16,261 votes, while MacBride polled a truly astonishing 16,062 votes. Fine Gael's Rooney received a very respectable 14,116 votes, and Labour managed 10,067. As the quota had been set at 28,254, it was necessary to persist with two further counts, even though MacBride pulled away almost immediately from his Fianna Fáil opponent. After the second count, his votes totalled 21,755 to Mullins's 17,399, a transfer rate of

almost five to one; MacBride benefited most from the third count also, Rooney's votes going to him in a three to one ratio. The final vote registered for MacBride was 29,629, to Mullins's 20,197. *The Irish Times*, 31 October 1947. This was a comprehensive trouncing, and not simply a routine beating.

19 ibid.

20 ibid.

21 ibid.

22 Rewarding Mulcahy's hopes for 'relations' between parties, the Fine Gael candidate had even led the Clann man (but not Hayes from Fianna Fáil) at the end of the second count, when, with the elimination of the Clann na Talmhan candidate, for once votes had flowed to Fine Gael. However, with the subsequent elimination of Labour, Kinnane overtook Fine Gael again, and, with the further elimination of Col. Ryan himself, Kinnane was able to take the seat with 23,265 votes to Hayes's 21,647. Fianna Fáil rightly regarded this as a disaster.

23 Nowhere is Waterford given the coverage bestowed on the other two constituencies, and this includes the national dailies of the time, and both Mulcahy's and MacEntee's private papers. MacEntee concentrated his fire on Dublin, and Mulcahy seems to have paid most attention to Tipperary. In Waterford, Fianna Fáil's vote fell from 19,259 in the 1944 election to 11,840 votes in 1947. Ormonde could count himself lucky; on the first count he polled 11,840 votes, while the Fine Gael candidate managed 9,941, Kyne for Labour received 7,683, and Clann na Poblachta's Feeney trailed miserably with 2,758. The poor vote garnered by Feeney was about the only consolation that Fianna Fáil could draw from the whole sorry business, for this really represents a failure for the combined opposition rather than a success for Fianna Fáil. Clann na Poblachta were to rationalise their lack of success by pointing to the extremely short duration of their campaign – they had less than a fortnight in which to canvass votes – and to the fact that their candidate, unlike everybody else in the running, had no local government experience. In Waterford, Clann na Poblachta and Labour seem to have had the sort of 'understanding' that Fine Gael and Clann na Talmhan had reached in Tipperary. This meant that, for once, Labour was in a position to benefit from the Clann, rather than the other way around.

24 *The Irish Times*, 1 November 1947.

25 *The Irish Times*, 3 November 1947.

26 This was a beautifully timed jibe, and appeared in *The Irish Times* on 4 November 1947. It achieved a tone at once both needling and condescending, and signed off with the wonderfully barbed conclusion, 'While there are few matters of policy upon which I find myself in agreement with your Government's policy, I thought it well to indicate that the result of the by-elections could only be construed as strengthening your position in the course of the present negotiations.' Given that Fianna Fáil were still smarting, one might well ask how the by-elections 'strengthened' Fianna Fáil, but that, presumably, was the intention of the note.

27 J. J. Lee, *Ireland 1912–1985: Politics and Society* (Cambridge University Press, Cambridge, 1989), pp. 293–6, is bitingly scathing on the subject of this particular constituency carve-up, acidly describing it as 'one of the most delicious pieces of fiction ever devised by even a harassed electoral cartographer to frustrate the will of the people'.

28 The details of the Electoral (Amendment) Bill are set out in *The Irish Times*, 9 October 1947. The straight-faced quote comes from the same day.

29 *The Irish Times*, 6 November 1947. Brian Inglis penned the 'Quidnunc' column at this time; however, later writings (for example, his books *Downstart* (Chatto & Windus, London, 1990), and *West Briton* (Faber and Faber, London, 1962))

show a marked disenchantment with MacBride. Inglis subsequently went on to work with the Irish News Agency, and, later still, became an outstanding editor of *The Spectator*.

30   His biographer, Tony Jordan, states that between the time MacBride took his seat on 5 November, and the Dáil was dissolved on 15 December, MacBride had contributed more than sixty times to debates on an extremely diverse range of topics, demonstrating an enviable breadth of vision, and a singular capacity for generating publicity for himself and for his party. Anthony Jordan, *Seán MacBride* (Blackwater Press, Dublin, 1993), pp. 89–90.

31   *The Irish Times*, 29 October 1947. *The Irish Times* consistently condemned de Valera for turning the by-elections into a vote of confidence. Terms such as 'sadly arrogant', 'rather petulant', 'an unfair threat to the electorate', 'unnecessary ultimatum', and, of course, 'preposterous' were all used in the editorial of 29 October.

32   *The Irish Times*, 3 November 1947.

33   Browne, *Against the Tide*, p. 118.

34   These accounts come from a number of the Clann stalwarts whom I interviewed, chiefly Colm Ó Laoghaire and Liam Ó Laoghaire, with whom I spent a fascinating evening as their recollections sparked further memories from each other. They told me the story concerning the car. Others from the Clann who recalled memories of the 1948 election included Florence O'Riordan, Fursa Breathnach, Labhrás Ó Nualláin, George Lawlor, and Roger McHugh. Cars as status symbols never seemed to hold any attraction for MacBride; at the time I met him, on several occasions in the late seventies and the early to mid-eighties, he drove a medium-sized Renault. When in government, Clann na Poblachta ministers were expected to use their state cars on official business only. Noël Browne, *Against the Tide* (Gill & Macmillan, Dublin, 1986), p. 118.

35   This of course was to de Valera's advantage, for he was perfectly aware of the benefit accruing to those who had access to the airwaves, and of the impact that radio broadcasts could have on the general public. With a straight face, he could claim that Fianna Fáil – as a political party – didn't take to the airwaves either, but that did not preclude him, and his party, from enjoying access to the radio as the government of the country.

36   I must convey my profound gratitude to the late Liam Ó Laoghaire who, along with Brendan Stafford, actually made the film. Ó Laoghaire not only arranged a private viewing of this film for me in August 1979, in the RTÉ studios, but also discussed the making of it with me. It was a marvellous afternoon, and when we had finished, Ó Laoghaire, then well into his seventies, took off on his motorbike, with *Our Country* safely tucked under his arm. Some time later, a very interesting documentary was made about Liam Ó Laoghaire himself, and in it, he discussed the making of *Our Country*.

37   Hartnett was the ideal person to do the commentary, as he was able to draw on his vast radio experience for the task. The film was produced by Liam Ó Laoghaire, and directed and photographed by Brendan Stafford, while the script was written by Maura Laverty.

38   Browne, *Against the Tide*, p. 99, describes the film as 'an able and enlightened effort . . . without doubt fair comment', adding that 'its merits can be verified'.

39   *Irish Press*, 28 January 1948.

40   ibid.

41   This menace was also directed at the National Film Institute of Ireland, an organisation partially funded by the government, which MacEntee felt had somehow assisted in the procurement of facilities in the making of *Our Country*. The 'Irish Film Society' alluded to in MacEntee's correspondence,

which had placed resources at the disposal of Clann na Poblachta, turned out to be 'Irish Civic Films', and mindful of MacEntee's menace (concerning finance in the future) the hapless National Film Institute found themselves issuing a grovelling apology to the minister. See *Irish Press*, 28, 30 and 31 January 1948. See also MacEntee papers (P67/379[1–10]), (P67/376[69]).

42   *Irish Press*, 28 January 1948.

43   *The Daily Film Reuter*, 26 January 1948. MacEntee papers (P67/379[3]).

44   ibid. *The Daily Film Reuter* went on to point out that the decision of Rank not to distribute the film 'has provoked widespread surprise in Eire'.

45   Liam Ó Laoghaire, letter to the *Evening Mail*, 30 January 1948.

46   Liam Ó Laoghaire in conversation with the author.

47   I have never actually heard this LP, but I have interviewed a number of people who had once possessed it. The shellac records of the time were quite fragile, usually ran at 78 rpm, and broke easily. (For the purpose of making discs, or records, the use of vinyl – which was a much more flexible substance than shellac, and was considerably less susceptible to casual breakages – only became widespread from the mid-1950s.) Again, for its time, this was a startling innovation, and certainly contributed to the Clann's image as an open-minded party which would be amenable to comprehensive change.

48   Michael Gallagher, *Political Parties in the Republic of Ireland* (Gill & Macmillan, Dublin, 1975), p. 28.

49   McQuillan had been commissioned in the wartime Irish Army, not the Local Defence Force. He believed that those who had served in the Irish Army were regarded with reserve and contempt in Clann na Poblachta, because their service had been with the Army, rather than the IRA. Jack McQuillan in interview with the author. Earlier still, McQuillan had studied engineering at University College Galway.

50   Interview with Jack McQuillan. This also appears in Browne, *Against the Tide*, p. 100.

51   Browne, *Against the Tide*, p. 100.

52   Captain Peadar Cowan left a very readable unpublished autobiography, which his son kindly permitted me to read.

53   Jack McQuillan was able to give a few instances in the west of Ireland where patently unsuitable people were considered and occasionally selected as candidates merely because they could afford these deposits. One such candidate was a west of Ireland publican, who was considered 'tired and emotional' in the euphemism of the time. More damning, he was also able to give examples where capable candidates were prevented from running; in one case this was because the individual concerned had served as an Irish Army captain rather than with the 'real Army', the IRA.

54   Lee, *Ireland*, pp. 277–93, Tim Pat Coogan, *De Valera: Long Fellow, Long Shadow* (Hutchinson, London, 1993), pp. 630–5, and Michael O'Sullivan, *Seán Lemass, a Biography* (Blackwater Press, Dublin, 1994), pp. 94, 100, 104–5 all devote attention to the clashes between Lemass and MacEntee.

55   F. S. L. Lyons, *Ireland Since the Famine* (Fontana, London, 1973), p. 560, put this rather nicely when he wrote: 'It is doubtful, however, if a new party would have had much success at that particular point if it had put all its eggs in the republican, anti-partition basket.'

56   Jordan, *Seán MacBride*, p. 52.

57   His criticism of the existing poor law health system was sharply worded when he wrote that it was 'tainted at its root and it reeks now, as it did when introduced, of destitution, pauperism, and degradation'. He also thought that such degradation was fundamentally 'un-Christian'. J. H. Whyte, *Church and State*

in Modern Ireland 1923–1979 (Gill & Macmillan), Dublin, 1979, p. 106. Dignan's plan called for the creation of a nationally based health insurance system, and implied, without explicitly stating such, the need for some sort of comprehensive safety net for those not covered by the proposed scheme. Whyte argued (pp. 96–119) that while Dignan's criticisms of the existing health service were trenchantly observed, his ideas for reform were a bit nebulous, but acknowledged that it was a 'sincere attempt by a public-spirited man'. Ironically, Dignan himself had been the first member of the hierarchy to openly support Fianna Fáil in 1932.

58   Lee (who states that 'Dignan's heart was in the right place') suggests that, ideologically, Dignan and Lemass probably had more in common 'than either had with MacEntee'. After being removed from his post, Dr Dignan had bitingly asked the minister, 'The Scheme is based on Christian principles of social justice and charity. Does the Minister mean that a social and economic system based on these principles is impracticable in Ireland?' Lee, *Ireland*, pp. 286–7. Some years later, Dignan would be the only member of the Irish hierarchy who would support the Mother and Child Scheme.

59   Whyte, *Church and State in Modern Ireland*, p. 112.

60   Not surprisingly, the encyclicals referred to were those in which Catholic social teaching was put forward, namely, *Rerum Novarum* (1891), *Quadragesimo Anno* (1931), and *Divini Redemptoris* (1937).

61   *Report of the Commission of Inquiry into Banking, Currency and Credit* (Minority Report No. 3), pp. 638–9.

62   ibid., p. 651. In fact, the Minority Report No. 3 is a beautifully written document reverberating with a righteous, and well-deserved, anger. O'Loghlen's comments on the use of emigration as a tool of social control still make relevant reading, as when he wrote, with glorious fluency, on p. 653: 'My colleagues appear to believe that unemployment and emigration are inevitable, and that they will continue, and possibly increase. I do not feel able to accept the theory that either emigration or unemployment in this country are inevitable, and I am unaware of any reason why in Ireland, alone among the nations, a national decline must be accepted as part of the essential nature of things. I cannot subscribe to the assumption that Ireland presents an isolated pathological phenomenon different from other countries.'

63   ibid., pp. 655–6.

64   MacBride stressed the importance of the Minority Report, and its influence on the evolution of his outlook and policies, in interview with the author.

65   B. Berthon Waters was an economist who wrote for *The Irish Times*. She has already appeared in this narrative lecturing the assembled membership of Córas na Poblachta and taking part in the Women's Parliament. In early 1948, according to Peadar Cowan's unpublished autobiography, she made a further appearance when she adjudicated the respective economic papers – sight unseen – of MacBride and Cowan (the latter declaring that MacBride's economic knowledge was 'rubbish'). Neither had signed his paper, to keep the affair appropriately anonymous, and she found for Cowan, whose thoughts became Clann economic policy. This tale should be treated with just a little caution, for, while Cowan was to find plenty to denounce in MacBride, MacBride's capacity for questioning established economic orthodoxies was never in doubt. Moreover, as Berthon Waters was already advising MacBride (and he was clearly receptive to her advice), what need would there have been for her to find against a paper already reflecting her economic preferences?

66   Ronan Fanning, *The Irish Department of Finance 1922–1958* (Institute of Public Administration, Dublin, 1980), pp. 359 and 408. For example, in 1949, she wrote

a memorandum entitled 'The Monetary Defence of Ireland' in response to the situation generated by the sterling crises (i.e. devaluation) of that year.

67 Seán MacBride, *Our People – Our Money*, a three-part lecture series delivered by MacBride to the Catholic Commercial Club, under the auspices of Clann na Poblachta, on 13, 18, and 22 October 1949. This was later published as a pamphlet by Browne & Nolan, and is now available in the National Library.

68 *The Irish Times,* 1 November 1947.

69 Colm Ó Laoghaire and Liam Ó Laoghaire in conversation with the author.

70 Seán MacBride, *Our People – Our Money*, p. 10.

71 ibid.

72 'Statement by Mr Seán MacBride, S.C. T.D., at the Fifth Ard-Fheis of Clann na Poblachta held in Dublin on 30th June and 1st July 1951', p. 4.

73 Jack McQuillan in conversation with the author. According to McQuillan, the Clann's Irish language policy came to MacBride 'on the train journey from Calais to Paris, about three hours in those days'. Spending three hours drafting an Irish language policy (which was bound to be very predictable coming, as it did, from a party boasting well-watered republican roots) seemed to show a degree of commitment to the topic unusual in 'official' Ireland at that time.

74 John A. Murphy, *Ireland in the Twentieth Century* (Gill & Macmillan, Dublin, 1975), p. 119.

75 Seán MacBride in a radio interview with RTÉ's John Bowman, 29 December 1980. I thank John Bowman for making a copy of this interview available to me.

5: 'Mr de Valera's abhorrence of coalitions is proverbial'

1 Clann na Poblachta obtained over 175,000 votes, and won ten seats, while Fine Gael, on 262,000 votes, managed thirty-one seats. (Anthony Jordan, *Seán MacBride* (Blackwater Press, Dublin, 1993), p. 94.

2 All of these figures come from Michael Gallagher, *Political Parties in the Republic of Ireland* (Gill & Macmillan, Dublin, 1985), Appendix 1, pp. 156–9. Clann na Poblachta even outpolled Clann na Talmhan in the west of Ireland, by 14 per cent to 11 per cent, yet won only one seat, McQuillan's own in Roscommon.

3 Most sources seem to feel that the Clann were hard done by in terms of a return of seats to votes. Both Gallagher, *Political Parties*, p. 113, and J. J. Lee, *Ireland, 1912–1985: Politics and Society* (Cambridge University Press, Cambridge, 1989), p. 297, refer to this number of nineteen potential TDs with evident sympathy. Tim Pat Coogan, in *De Valera: Long Fellow, Long Shadow* (Hutchinson, London, 1993), p. 637, also does so.

4 At least ten Clann candidates were the immediate runners-up in their constituencies. Gallagher, *Political Parties*, p. 113.

5 This, admittedly, was not the norm, but barely concealed hostilities did exist in Roscommon, for example, and in one or two other western constituencies. The source in this instance was Jack McQuillan in conversation with the author.

6 John Bowman interviewing Seán MacBride, on RTÉ Radio, 29 December 1980.

7 ibid.

8 ibid.

9 Coogan, *De Valera*, p. 637.

10 ibid., pp. 637–8.

11 Two Fine Gael candidates, James Hughes and Eamonn Coogan (who were both TDs), died during the election campaign, which necessitated a double by-election within two weeks of the general election. One of them, James Hughes, had been Fine Gael's agriculture spokesman, and was undoubtedly destined for the Agriculture ministry if and when Fine Gael regained power, as Mulcahy's papers

make abundantly clear. See for example Mulcahy's speech in Nenagh, 7 December 1947, Mulcahy papers [P7[c]121–2]. Hughes's seat was retained by his brother Joseph.

12   Information from Oliver J. Flanagan, secretary of the anti-de Valera Independent group, in a letter to the author, January 1981.

13   *Dublin Opinion*, April 1948.

14   Lee, *Ireland*, p. 299.

15   *The Irish Times*, 3 November 1947.

16   *The Irish Times*, 8 November 1947. Roddy Connolly's illustrious ancestry (he was a son of James Connolly), in addition to the fact that he held, as *The Irish Times* approvingly noted, 'an important position in the ranks of Labour', guaranteed that attention was paid to whatever he said. *The Irish Times* correctly chose to interpret Connolly's views as 'an interesting pointer'.

17   ibid.

18   *Irish People*, 15 November 1947. MacEntee papers (P67/541[4]).

19   Mulcahy papers (P7[c]122).

20   ibid.

21   ibid. This speech was interesting in that it occurred during the Carlow – Kilkenny hiatus, between the election (4 February) and the time when, as Mulcahy himself later put it, the election results 'became clear' (10 February).

22   ibid.

23   ibid.

24   Mulcahy seems to have thought at first that Costello wanted his memory primed on material from the Cosgrave government of the 1920s, and sent him a three-page typed rant on the topic. Mulcahy papers (P7d/116). Thanking Mulcahy for his 'memorandum', Costello delicately indicated by return that 'I did not wish to put you to such trouble. Some time before the interview perhaps I could see you for a few minutes merely to verify facts about which I may not be quite sure. In particular, I would like to have a kind of specific statement about the formation of the Inter-Party government.' Mulcahy papers (P7d/116). As Costello was not brought into the picture until well into the negotiations, his lack of detailed recall is not surprising.

25   'Jack' Costello to 'Dick' Mulcahy, 16 May 1967. Mulcahy papers (P7d/116). William Norton was the leader of the Labour Party, and is probably best known now for the vitriolic pen-portrait painted of him by Noël Browne in the latter's autobiography, *Against the Tide* (Gill & Macmillan, Dublin, 1986).

26   Letter from Mulcahy to Costello, 17 July 1967. Mulcahy papers (P7d/116).

27   This was the first letter from Mulcahy to Costello on this matter. That was written (and posted) on 15 May 1967. Mulcahy papers (P7d/116). By the 1960s, Michael McInerney was a most distinguished, decent, and humane political correspondent for *The Irish Times*; earlier, he had been an active sympathiser of the Irish Communist Party, and Mulcahy would most certainly have known of his political background and sympathies from police and Department of Justice files.

28   Morrissey was an auctioneer who had once been a TD for the Labour Party, but, by the forties, was comfortably ensconced in Fine Gael. In the Dáil, he represented Tipperary (as did Mulcahy), and, despite Noël Browne's withering descriptions of him, appeared to be a sharp political fighter, with a keen nose for the business of politics. Mulcahy showed a high regard for him in his papers.

29   Letter from Mulcahy to Costello, 17 July 1967. Mulcahy papers (P7d/116).

30   ibid.; 'the inviting' appears as a later handwritten addition.

31   ibid.

32   ibid.

33   ibid.

34   ibid.

35   ibid. This is interesting because Costello already held a position on the Fine Gael front bench, that of spokesman on external affairs, and so, presumably, he would have been invited to attend that Saturday night meeting (14 February) in his capacity as a potential minister. Costello had a thriving – and lucrative – practice at the Bar, and some observers felt that he faced the prospect of *any* ministerial office with 'considerable reluctance'. Brian Farrell, *Chairman or Chief: The Role of Taoiseach in Irish Government* (Gill & Macmillan, Dublin, 1971), pp. 42–3.

36   Mulcahy papers (P7d/116). This was obviously how Mulcahy spelt 'The O'Rahilly'. The choice of The O'Rahilly to accompany MacBride was an interesting one; in fact, The O'Rahilly was a Cork academic who had been linked with Clann na Poblachta from the earliest days, and he had also been involved with the cabal of economic advisers who advised MacBride and agreed with the recommendations of O'Loghlen's Minority Report No. 3 into the Banking Commission. Nonetheless, it was a curious choice. Everybody else brought potential ministers and/or seasoned political fighters – MacBride brought someone who was not a TD, not a seasoned in-fighter, and not from the ranks of the old IRA group, which was where MacBride's ultimate power-base within the party was to lie. In fact, most unusually, MacBride brought along someone who was a personal friend of his. Margaret Ward (*Maud Gonne*, Pandora, Unwin paperbacks, London, 1990) pp. 167 and 192 refers to this friendship.

37   Letter from Mulcahy to Costello, 17 July 1967. Mulcahy papers (P7d/116).

38   ibid.

39   'Gerry Boland's Story – 11', *The Irish Times*, 19 October 1968 (the eleventh day of a series of interviews conducted by Michael McInerny with Gerry Boland).

40   Gallagher, *Political Parties,* p. 110.

41   ibid.

42   This later letter came about because Costello had made a Dáil speech stressing the 'harmony' he himself had experienced with Labour in two coalition, or inter-party, governments. (There is a suspicion that this speech was made in order to help create a favourable climate for the contemplation of further coalitions in the future.) Once again, Costello called upon Mulcahy's memory to supply relevant supporting data. Mulcahy's response dates from 29 April 1969. Mulcahy papers (P7d/116). Earlier in this letter, he had quoted James Larkin jun. praising Costello.

43   Michael McInerney, 'Mr John A. Costello Remembers – 4', *The Irish Times*, 7 September 1967. This was the fourth in the aforementioned interview, which took the form of a five-part series of interviews with Costello.

44   Mulcahy to Costello, April 29 1969. Mulcahy papers (P7d/116).

45   ibid.

46   ibid.

47   This adjective appeared literally hundreds of times in the hundreds of congratulatory telegrams dispatched to Mulcahy after the formation of the inter-party government. It is also the adjective used by Costello to describe Mulcahy in his series of interviews with Michael McInerney: see *The Irish Times*, 6 and 7 September, 1967.

48   Dermot Keogh, *Twentieth-Century Ireland* (Gill & Macmillan, Dublin, 1994), pp. 185–6, Lee, *Ireland,* p. 299, Jordan, *Seán MacBride,* p. 95, Breandán Ó Eithir, *The Begrudger's Guide to Irish Politics* (Poolbeg, Dublin, 1986), pp. 119–20, Gallagher, *Political Parties,* p. 48. All point to MacBride as having insisted on this decision; only Gallagher says it was a joint Labour–Clann na Poblachta veto. MacBride in an interview with the author accepted that he had objected to Mulcahy as Taoiseach.

49   This is consistent with the rest of Mulcahy's papers where Clann na Poblachta are conspicuous by their absence. However, given their explosive impact on the political landscape, and given Mulcahy's pedantic attention to detail, it is a surprising omission.

50   Patrick Lynch, 'Pages from a Memoir', in Patrick Lynch and James Meenan (eds), *Essays in Memory of Alexis Fitzgerald* (Incorporated Law Society of Ireland, Dublin, 1987), pp. 37–8. Lynch's own source was interesting. Not only did he serve under Costello, but he also cites a letter describing these events which Costello wrote to his son Declan, who was then on holiday in Switzerland. However, Lynch (p. 38) crisply dismissed Brian Farrell's argument that Law Library *bonhomie* had made MacBride predisposed towards Costello, or vice versa, when he wrote: 'I did not accept the legend that his task was eased by his Law Library association with Seán MacBride. They were professional associates at the Bar; Seán MacBride did not form friendships that way; moreover some members of Fine Gael disliked and distrusted him.' See Farrell, *Chairman or Chief?*, pp. 42–4.

51   Strangely enough, this argument has been made to me by members of both Fianna Fáil and Clann na Poblachta.

52   Mulcahy's papers – which are charitable and complimentary about almost everybody else – indicate a marked detestation for both de Valera and Kevin O'Higgins. He blamed O'Higgins for most of the internal problems of the Cosgrave Cabinet of the 1920s – see, for example, Mulcahy papers (P7d/115). Noël Browne seemed to corroborate this to some extent, for he referred to the fact that there was 'much hostility' between the individual Fine Gael ministers, and he also alluded to the 'mixture of levity and contempt' with which Mulcahy was treated by some of his party colleagues. Browne, *Against the Tide*, p. 125.

53   Costello to Mulcahy, 16 May 1967. Mulcahy papers (P7d/116).

54   Michael McInerney, 'Mr John A. Costello Remembers – 4', *The Irish Times*, 7 September 1967. In an attempt to defuse this pressure, Costello went so far as to suggest Morrissey as Taoiseach. This was politely, but firmly, rejected by MacBride. Patrick Lynch, 'Pages from a memoir', p. 37.

55   Michael McInerney, 'Mr John A. Costello Remembers – 4', *The Irish Times*, 7 September 1967.

56   Arthur Cox was a solicitor and, at that time, a partner in one of Dublin's leading law firms. He had attended University College Dublin with Costello in the period shortly before the First World War, and both had shone academically and as members of the university debating societies. Their close friendship dated from that time. Cox later married the widow of Kevin O'Higgins, and later still, after her death, resigned from his law practice and became a priest, whereupon he travelled to Africa as a member of a missionary order. A biography of Arthur Cox, written by Eugene McCague and entitled *Arthur Cox, 1891–1965,* was published in 1994 by Gill & Macmillan.

57   Michael McInerney, 'Mr John A. Costello Remembers – 4', *The Irish Times*, 7 September 1967. Two other friends of Costello's also advised him to bow to the fates, and become Taoiseach. These were Richard F. Browne, chairman of the ESB, and Donal O'Sullivan who wrote a letter describing these further discussions. *The Irish Times*, 11 September 1967.

58   Privately, of course, this was a totally different matter, and Costello seems to have made many people in Fine Gael aware of just what he was sacrificing for the common good. The McInerney interview contained a reference to how 'Costello, of course, had to make a big financial sacrifice to become Taoiseach, and he was worried about his family, but on that Sunday he gave his consent.' *The Irish Times*, 7 September 1967. This whinging note reappeared in a Fine

Gael document circulated at the time Costello retired from active politics, in 1969. Seeking donations for a fund to honour Costello's retirement, his constituency organisation went on: 'It is widely known that as a result of a decision involving considerable financial hardship Mr Costello undertook the leadership of two Inter-Party governments.' Mulcahy papers (P7d/116). Moreover, Costello actually turned down the post of Fine Gael party leader, when it was offered to him in 1959, on the resignation of General Mulcahy. Again his grounds were financial loss: 'My own circumstances are not such as to permit withdrawal from my professional practice.' In fact, Costello would have preferred to continue his practice at the Bar, while accepting the offer, but, by 1959, there were a number in Fine Gael who felt that the party should have a 'full-time' leader. Thus, Costello resigned as leader of the opposition just after Mulcahy resigned as party leader. Mulcahy papers (P7b/122[2]). Patrick Lynch, Costello's economic adviser and occasional secretary, has also written about this, remarking that 'Costello paid a very high financial price . . . and made very substantial sacrifices in accepting the post.' Lynch, 'Pages from a Memoir', p. 42. By way of contrast, Mulcahy himself never complained about not having been chosen as Taoiseach.

59 Patrick Lynch, 'Pages from a Memoir' p. 37.

60 However, it is worth drawing attention to the contrast between the warm understanding of the Labour Party's trials and tribulations – then and later – which all of the Fine Gael sources displayed, and their mute hostility to Clann na Poblachta, both as an architect of, and participant in, the government. Of course, the fact that Clann na Poblachta are no longer around to fight their corner makes their invisibility in all of the Fine Gael sources all the more revealing, as it is quite possible to peruse these sources and be forgiven for concluding that Clann na Poblachta never even existed.

61 Mulcahy papers (P7d/116). See also McGilligan papers (P35/208), which contains a provisional breakdown of the number of portfolios to be allotted to each party. This simply notes that the allocation of the portfolios was to be: '5-2-2-1-1-1'.

62 Seán MacBride in interview with the author.

63 McGilligan papers (P35/208).

64 *Dáil Debates*, Vol. 9, cols. 561–2, 30 October 1924, quoted in Gallagher, *Political Parties*, p. 43.

65 Lynch, 'Pages from a Memoir', p. 42. If this was true, then no wonder many in the Clann became more than a little confused.

66 Seán MacBride in interview with the author felt that Mulcahy 'wasn't a bad Minister for Education, with his interest in the Irish language, and all that'. Interestingly enough, a surprising amount of Mulcahy's private papers are written in Irish.

67 Browne, *Against the Tide*, p. 125.

68 Nöel Browne (ibid., pp. 201–4) was uncharacteristically fulsome in his praise of Tim Murphy's tenure. It is tempting, but uncharitable, to suspect that Browne's warmth towards Murphy had as much to do with the fact that Murphy predeceased the Mother and Child Scheme debacle (he died suddenly in 1949), and thus was not tainted by betrayal in Browne's mind, as with the fact that Murphy had proved himself to have been an enthusiastic, energetic, and capable Minister for Local Government. F. S. L. Lyons, *Ireland Since the Famine* (Fontana, London, 1973), p. 571, largely agrees with Browne's positive assessment of Murphy, as did Costello himself, who informed Michael McInerney that 'Tim Murphy did a magnificent job on housing'. 'Mr John A. Costello Remembers – 4', *The Irish Times*, 7 September 1967. Furthermore, John Garvin, who held the

position of secretary of the Department of Local Government from 1948 until 1966, thought that Tim Murphy was the best minister he had ever served under.

69   Mulcahy had earlier made it clear that his intended nominee for this position was James Hughes who had died during the election campaign. Hughes seems to have been greatly respected by Mulcahy, for he was mourning his loss well into the 1950s at several Fine Gael ard-fheiseanna. James Dillon had quit Fine Gael in 1942 on the issue of neutrality (a vice-president of the party at the time, he disagreed with the policy agreed on by both government and opposition) and had become an Independent. Twelve Independent TDs were elected in 1948. 'Immediately after [the election] a Group of Independents – 11 – who supported the Government was formed. We met every second month in Room 106 Leinster House. Mr Dillon was Chairman. Oliver J. Flanagan was Secretary and called the meetings and did all correspondence with Mr Costello, Taoiseach, and Mr Dillon.' Letter from Oliver J. Flanagan to the author, January 1981. Flanagan's letter also contained a detailed breakdown of the geographical location, as well as the political preferences, of these Independents.

70   MacBride felt that 'Blowick was a hopeless Minister'. Seán MacBride in interview with the author.

71   Seán MacBride in interview with the author. However, it is worth pointing out that Lee, *Ireland*, p. 299, and Fanning, *Independent Ireland* (Helicon, Dublin, 1983), pp. 165–6, both feel that MacBride exerted considerable influence on the composition of the Cabinet, as did Patrick Lynch, 'Pages from a Memoir', p. 42. It is reasonable to infer that his views would have carried considerable weight at that stage.

72   McGilligan papers (P35/208).

73   Michael McInerney, 'Mr John A. Costello Remembers – 1', *The Irish Times*, 4 September 1967.

74   Lynch, 'Pages from a Memoir', p. 40.

75   ibid., pp. 40–1. Lynch recognised Costello's flaws while warmly acknowledging his virtues.

76   Sir Gilbert Laithwaite to the Commonwealth Relations Office, late 1950, *Irish Press*, 1 and 2 January 1981.

77   ibid.

78   Browne, *Against the Tide*, p. 108.

79   ibid., p. 139.

80   ibid., p. 108.

81   ibid., p. 109.

82   The example Noël Browne cites (ibid., pp. 128–9) in support of this concerns the discussions on capital punishment at Cabinet, during the tenure of the inter-party government. There were a number of these, and clemency was occasionally recommended. For example, two death sentences were commuted at a Cabinet meeting on 22 October 1948. However, according to Browne, in those cases where clemency was not recommended, voting usually broke down into grimly predictable party divisions, with most of Fine Gael (along with Clann na Talmhan's Blowick 'in his high-pitched squeak') clamouring for the application of the supreme penalty, and the Clann ministers desperately attempting to stave this off. Admittedly, the Cabinet formula for greasing the axles of those grinding wheels of justice was rather lugubrious, as in the following case, which occurred on 19 November 1948, materialising at Cabinet as 'item 4'.'William Gambon: Under Sentence of Death; Question of Commutation of Sentence. Following consideration of a memorandum, submitted by the Minister for Justice, relative to the case of William Gambon, under sentence of death for the murder of John Long, it was decided that the Government would not be

justified in advising the President to exercise the perogative of clemency in this case and that the law should take its course.'

However, Cabinet voting on this issue was not always as straightforwardly partisan as Noël Browne appeared to suggest. Patrick Lindsay, who himself was a nauseatingly enthusiastic supporter of capital punishment, and who served as Fine Gael's Minister for the Gaeltacht in Costello's second inter-party government, informed me that Costello himself always pleaded for clemency in these situations, and invariably voted against the death penalty.

83 Ó hEithir, *Begrudger's Guide,* p. 118.

84 Seán MacBride in interview with the author.

85 ibid.

86 ibid.

87 Browne, *Against the Tide*, p. 107.

88 Noël Browne's autobiography *Against the Tide* gives a harrowing account of his childhood. In October 1967, Michael McInerney of *The Irish Times* wrote a very sympathetic six-part profile on Noël Browne.

89 A sympathetic account of life in Newcastle Sanatorium, working under Noël Browne, can be found in *TB Or Not TB?* (Centre for Health Promotion Studies, University College Galway, 1995) by Dr Harry Hitchcock.

90 ibid., p. 79.

91 Brian Inglis, *Downstart* (Chatto & Windus, London, 1990), p. 166.

92 Noël Browne in interview with the author.

93 Seán MacBride in interview with the author.

94 ibid.

95 ibid.

96 ibid.

97 Notes from Peadar Cowan's unpublished memoirs.

98 ibid.

99 ibid.

100 ibid. This is also referred to in Ian McCabe, *A Diplomatic History of Ireland 1948–49* (Irish Academic Press, Dublin, 1991), p. 175, Ch. 3, fn 2.

101 Notes from Peadar Cowan's unpublished memoirs.

102 Cowan's expulsion came as a considerable shock to some in the Clann, such as Jack McQuillan, who recalled opening his Sunday papers over breakfast at his home in Roscommon, only to discover, to his amazement, that 'Cowan had been kicked out of the party'. Jack McQuillan in conversation with the author.

103 MacEntee papers (P67/551[14]).

104 This was vintage MacEntee at his nastiest and most virulent. His papers contain a fascinating letter from General M. J. Costello of the Irish Sugar Company offering to help unearth material from Cowan's Army career which 'might show to Cowan's disadvantage'. MacEntee papers (P67/547[10]).

105 MacEntee to Tommy Mullins, 16 July 1947. MacEntee papers (P67/547[12]).

106 MacEntee papers (P67/376[42]). MacEntee's intelligence on the Clann was obviously very good. With the passage of time, at least two people would recall that letter with acute embarrassment.

107 Notes from Peadar Cowan's unpublished memoirs.

108 Frederick Boland was appointed secretary of the Department of External Affairs in 1946, replacing Joseph Walshe, who had been departmental secretary since 1922. Walshe was appointed Ireland's ambassador to the Holy See, a posting which delighted him. Boland remained secretary of the department until 1950, when he was made ambassador to the Court of St James. Boland accepted the London job because 'he could no longer stand MacBride', according to his wife, who spoke with Dermot Keogh. Commenting on this, Boland himself wrote: 'I

could never really work out whether my going to London was due to Seán MacBride's desire to get rid of me or to Jack Costello's feeling that they should have in London someone they could rely on not to intrigue. I never knew exactly.' Keogh, *Twentieth-Century Ireland*, p. 428, fn. 70.

109   Browne, *Against the Tide*, p. 139.

6: 'Ireland still remains the 'sacra insula'

1   'Ireland still remains the *sacra insula*, whose aspirations must on no account be mixed up with the profane class struggles of the rest of the sinful world. Partially, this is certainly honest madness on the part of these people, but it is equally certain that it is partially also a calculated policy of the leaders in order to maintain their domination over the peasant.' Letter from Engels to Marx, dated 9 December 1869, in Karl Marx and Friedrich Engels, *Ireland and the Irish Question* (New York, 1972), p. 396.

2   Dermot Keogh, *Twentieth-Century Ireland* (Gill & Macmillan, Dublin, 1994), p . 187.

3   ibid. Here, Keogh has quoted a junior diplomat who explained the reasons for the sending of this telegram. Keogh, in his later, superb, scholarly study *Ireland and the Vatican* (Cork University Press, Cork, 1995), p. 232, also discusses this telegram and its aftermath.

4   John Bowman, interview with Seán MacBride, RTÉ Radio, 29 December 1980. I thank John Bowman for helping to make a copy of this interview available to me.

5   ibid.

6   Keogh, *Twentieth-Century Ireland*, p. 187; this is also referred to in Keogh, *Ireland and the Vatican*, p. 232.

7   Patrick Lynch, 'Pages from a Memoir', in Patrick Lynch and James Meenan (eds), *Essays in Memory of Alexis Fitzgerald* (Incorporated Law Society of Ireland, Dublin, 1987), p. 39.

8   Tom Garvin, *1922: The Birth of Irish Democracy* (Gill & Macmillan, Dublin, 1996), p. 2. This idea also surfaces on pp. 6 and 200.

9   ibid., p. 200.

10   ibid., p. 33.

11   ibid., p. 6.

12   ibid., pp. 23 and 33–4.

13   ibid., p. 33.

14   ibid., p. 23.

15   J. H. Whyte, *Church and State in Modern Ireland, 1923–1979* (Gill & Macmillan, Dublin, 1979), p. 16. Apart from Whyte, Tom Inglis, *Moral Monopoly: The Catholic Church in Modern Irish Society* (Gill & Macmillan, Dublin, 1987), pp. 53–8, also deals with this.

16   Breandán Ó hEithir, *The Begrudger's Guide to Irish Politics* (Poolbeg, Dublin, 1986), p. 122.

17   Inglis, *Moral Monopoly*, p. 61.

18   Whyte, *Church and State,* p. 18; Inglis, *Moral Monopoly*, p. 57.

19   Inglis, *Moral Monopoly*, pp. 4–5.

20   J. H. Whyte points out that as recently as the census of 1946, 30 per cent of males aged 55–64 were unmarried – a staggering statistic (the international average was just over 10 per cent). Whyte, *Church and State*, p. 33.

21   Lee, *Ireland 1912–1985*, p. 395.

22   ibid., p. 395.

23   J. H. Whyte, *Church and State in Modern Ireland*, p. 32.

24 Inglis, *Moral Monopoly*, pp. 4–5.

25 Tim Pat Coogan, *De Valera – Long Fellow, Long Shadow*, pp. 628–9, quotes from, and discusses this incredible speech, as does Brian Farrell, *Chairman or Chief?*, p. 28. Actually, Coogan, Lee and Ó hEithir (*Begrudger's Guide to Irish Politics*, p. 106), all make the salient point that the gap between de Valera's rhetoric (what he said he wished for) and his policies (what he actually did) was more than usually wide. Tim Pat Coogan argues that, in fact, while de Valera cultivated an other-worldly 'impractical' persona, he actually 'acted in the most flint-edged, self-interested way' (op. cit., p. 628). Indeed, if anything, it can be argued that de Valera's actual policies tended to achieve the opposite effect of his stated rhetoric, a point stressed by Lee, *Ireland, 1912–1985*, p. 334, when he argued that 'The legitimate criticism of the "dream" was not that it was naïve, but that de Valera not only had no idea how to move the existing reality in the direction of his ideal, but that many of his policies directly subverted it.'

26 ibid.

27 ibid.

28 ibid., p. 223.

29 Council of Mortgage Lenders, cited in *The Observer*, 15 January 1995. In a percentage table of owner-occupation – entitled 'Who in the World owns their own homes?' – of the industrialised nations of the world, Ireland headed the table with a truly staggering figure of 81 per cent, trailed by Norway at 79 per cent, and Greece at 76 per cent; by way of contrast, the UK clocked in at 68 per cent, while most of the mainland continental countries – France gave a figure of 54 per cent, Germany 38 per cent – had far lower percentage figures.

30 J. J. Lee, *Ireland 1912–1985: Politics and Society* (Cambridge University Press, Cambridge, 1989), p. 159.

31 Inglis, *Moral Monopoly*, pp. 193–4.

32 ibid.

33 ibid.

34 Lee, *Ireland*, p. 159.

35 Inglis, *Moral Monopoly*, pp. 4–5.

36 ibid., p. 120, gives details about the nature and the cost of this building programme.

37 Ruth Barrington, *Health, Medicine and Politics in Ireland 1900–1970* (Institute of Public Administration, Dublin, 1987), p. 149.

38 Dermot Keogh, 'Church, State and Society', in Brian Farrell (ed.), *De Valera's Constitution and Ours* (RTÉ and Gill & Macmillan, Dublin, 1988), pp. 103–19; also Keogh, *Ireland and the Vatican*, pp. 132–40, and John Bowman, *What the Papers Say*, RTÉ television documentary about John Charles McQuaid, broadcast April 1998.

39 Keogh, *Ireland and the Vatican*, pp. 132–40, discusses this in detail. In fact, the Vatican conferred a benevolent neutrality – a 'friendly and sympathetic silence', to quote Walshe – on de Valera's wording, coming up with the formula 'ni approvo ni non disapprovo; taceremo' – 'we neither approve nor disapprove; we shall maintain silence'. In the circumstances, it was the best that de Valera could have hoped for, and he was pleased with the outcome.

40 The relevant pieces of legislation were the Censorship of Films Act 1923 and the Censorship of Publications Act 1929; the Censorship Board was founded the following year.

41 Ó hEithir, *Begrudger's Guide*, pp. 39–53; also Lee, *Ireland*, pp. 158–9; Terence Brown, *Ireland: A Social and Cultural History, 1922–1979* (Fontana, London, 1981) also deals extensively with this topic.

42 Ó hEithir, *Begrudger's Guide*, pp. 42–8.
43 Lee, *Ireland,* p. 158.
44 ibid.
45 ibid., p. 159.
46 Ó hEithir, *Begrudger's Guide*, p. 41.
47 Whyte, *Church and State*, p. 94.
48 Keogh, *Ireland and the Vatican*, pp. 127–32, deals with the response of de Valera to the Spanish Civil War, as does Whyte, *Church and State*, pp. 91–3.
49 Whyte, *Church and State*, p. 165.
50 Noël Browne, *Against the Tide* (Gill & Macmillan, Dublin, 1986), pp. 222–3.
51 Patrick Lindsay gave me examples of acts of private charity which illustrated the way Costello took his religion personally and seriously.
52 Keogh, *Ireland and the Vatican*, pp. 232–49, gives a fascinating account of the Irish input into the Christian Democrat victory in the elections of April 1948.
53 ibid., pp. 265-304.
54 The real problem with Felici seemed to be that he was at the end of his career, and had not been a high-flyer, meaning that therefore Ireland was not seen as a prestigious appointment in the eyes of the Vatican officials, a point which seems to have rankled somewhat with the Irish authorities, who would have liked their importance to the Vatican to be demonstrated in a fulsome manner. In fact, Felici proved to be an unintrusive and uncontroversial nuncio, whose hands-off approach would be longed for, in other, later, years.
55 Keogh, *Ireland and the Vatican*, p. 271.
56 ibid., pp. 314–15.
57 Browne, *Against the Tide*, pp. 145–6.
58 Information from Noël Browne in conversation with the author. Browne was perversely proud of the fact that he did not visit Rome to attend celebrations for the Holy Year. See also, ibid. and Keogh, *Ireland and the Vatican*, pp. 312–21.
59 Whyte, *Church and State*, pp. 174–9, discusses this in some detail.
60 ibid., pp. 179–83.
61 Noël Browne, letter to *The Irish Times*, 11 March 1996. Whyte deals with the question of adoption in *Church and State*, pp. 183–93.
62 This is discussed in Whyte, *Church and State*, pp. 191–2. It is also referred to in John Bowman's documentary on John Charles McQuaid, *What the Papers Say*, RTÉ Television, 9 April 1998.
63 Inglis, *Moral Monopoly*, p. 75.
64 Austin Clarke, 'Burial of an Irish President (Dr Douglas Hyde)', in *Selected Poems,* ed. Hugh Maxton (Lilliput Press, Dublin, 1991).

7: 'The Fine Gael Party had a sudden brainwave that they would steal the "Long Man's" clothes'

1 F. S. L. Lyons, *Ireland Since the Famine* (Fontana, London, 1973), p. 564.
2 John A. Costello, Memorandum on the Repeal of the External Relations Act, p. 2.
3 ibid.
4 See Seán MacBride, interview with James Downey, *The Irish Times*, 1 and 2 January 1979.
5 J. J. Lee, *Ireland 1912-1985: Politics and Society* (Cambridge University Press, Cambridge, 1989), p. 306.
6 Clann na Poblachta, ard-fheis 1948, *Clár,* p. 16.
7 Costello, Memorandum, p. 2.
8 ibid. See also Lyons, *Ireland Since the Famine*, pp. 563–4, where Costello

stressed this point in both letters and interviews with Lyons.

9   Hickerson was an American diplomat who held the position of Director of European Affairs at the State Department. Ian McCabe, *A Diplomatic History of Ireland 1948–49* (Irish Academic Press, Dublin, 1991), p. 31.

10   ibid., p. 30.

11   ibid., pp. 31–2.

12   *Dublin Opinion*, May 1948.

13   ibid.

14   Costello, Memorandum, p. 1.

15   Tim Pat Coogan, *De Valera: Long Fellow, Long Shadow* (Hutchinson, London, 1993), p. 640.

16   Lee, *Ireland*, p. 300.

17   The link between language, imperialism and power is superbly analysed in a number of works by Edward W. Said, notably in both *Culture & Imperialism* (Chatto and Windus, London, 1993) and *Orientalism* (Penguin, London, 1991; first published by Routledge and Kegan Paul Ltd, 1978).

18   An interesting recent example concerns the lengthy debate which took place in 1990 in the Czechoslovakian Federal Parliament – as it then was – after the collapse of the Communist regime. Deputies agonised over whether the name of the country should take the form of 'Czechoslovakia', 'Czecho-Slovakia', or, the form it actually took until Slovakia subsequently seceded from the federation, 'The Czech and Slovak Federal Republic'.

19   Coogan, *De Valera*, p. 640.

20   ibid.

21   Lyons, *Ireland Since the Famine*, p. 570.

22   ibid.; Lee, *Ireland*, p. 300, touches on the same point.

23   Robert Fisk draws attention to the fact that after the 'bellicose' Chanak affair of 1922, the Australian and Canadian governments were enraged at Britain's arrogant assumption that the dominions would readily supply military assistance when requested to do so and effectively served notice that such aid was no longer automatic. Hence the fact that some of the dominions allowed themselves more than a week before formally allying themselves with Britain's war effort. Robert Fisk, *Ireland in Time of War* (Paladin, London, 1983), pp. 75–6.

24   ibid., p. 76.

25   Ever since the Treaty of Locarno it had been recognised that 'it was entirely for a Dominion to decide whether it should or should not participate in a war'. ibid., p. 126.

26   ibid., pp. 125–6.

27   ibid., p. 126.

28   ibid.

29   This is partly how Lee views the continuing perception of success surrounding the policy of neutrality. See Lee, *Ireland*, pp. 259–62.

30   See Robert Fisk's account of his interview with Con Cremin. Fisk, *In Time of War*, pp. 371–2.

31   T. Ryle Dwyer, *De Valera: The Man and the Myths* (Poolbeg, Dublin, 1991), pp. 292–3.

32   Coogan, *De Valera*, p. 640.

33   ibid.

34   ibid. Coogan cites Lord Longford and T. P. O'Neill's 'official biography', *Eamon de Valera* (Arrow Books, London, 1970), as his source for this point. Officially, de Valera was 'staying his hand' to allow Maffey time to raise the 'revival' of that old hobby-horse, the Council of Ireland, with the British government.

35   Coogan, *De Valera*, p. 640.

36 Dermot Keogh, *Twentieth-Century Ireland* (Gill & Macmillan, Dublin, 1994), p. 190.
37 ibid. Boland is quoted directly.
38 ibid., pp. 190–1.
39 ibid.
40 The invitation appears to have been received on 18 August. Costello himself received a 'communication' from the 'British Representative' on 12 August concerning the vexed question of precedence to be accorded to high commissioners. All of this material appears in NA, S. 14333
41 See NA, S. 14333. The block capitals exist in MacBride's original version of the answer.
42 Brian Farrell, *Chairman or Chief?: The Role of Taoiseach in Irish Government* (Gill & Macmillan, Dublin, 1971), pp. 42–54.
43 Lee, *Ireland*, pp. 306–7, Keogh, *Twentieth-Century Ireland*, pp. 186 and 195, and Noël Browne, *Against the Tide* (Gill & Macmillan, Dublin, 1986), pp. 127–8, all make this point, stressing more MacBride's declining influence rather than Costello's increasing confidence.
44 Keogh, *Twentieth-Century Ireland*, p. 186, uses the expression 'rival Taoiseach' to describe the initial stature of MacBride at the time of the formation of the government.
45 Patrick Keatinge, *The Formulation of Irish Foreign Policy* (Institute of Public Administration, Dublin, 1973), pp. 62–3.
46 Farrell, *Chairman or Chief?*, pp. 42–3, argues that Costello faced the prospect of ministerial office 'with considerable reluctance' and, initially, did not seek *any* portfolio in the new government.
47 Keatinge, *Formulation of Irish Foreign Policy*, p. 63.
48 Browne, *Against the Tide*, p. 133.
49 ibid., p. 203.
50 Lee, *Ireland*, p. 299.
51 Browne, *Against the Tide*, p. 121.
52 Anthony Jordan, *Seán MacBride* (Blackwater Press, Dublin, 1993), p. 165. Jordan states that MacBride was 'almost paranoid' about security within his office, lest it be 'infiltrated'.
53 Keogh, *Twentieth-Century Ireland*, p. 186.
54 ibid.
55 See NA G/3/14 and CAB 2/10, 19 February 1948 and 24 February 1948. See also Patrick Lynch, 'Pages from a Memoir', in Patrick Lynch and James Meenan (eds), *Essays in Memory of Alexis Fitzgerald* (Incorporated Law Society of Ireland, Dublin, 1987), pp. 39–40.
56 Moynihan became secretary of the Department of the Taoiseach in 1937, relinquishing the post in 1960, when he was appointed governor of the Central Bank.
57 Lynch, 'Pages from a Memoir', p. 39.
58 ibid., pp. 39–40. Lee, *Ireland*, p. 306.
59 Lynch, 'Pages from a Memoir', p. 41.
60 A number of ministers have attested to this over the years, among them Seán Lemass and Noël Browne.
61 Farrell, *Chairman or Chief?*, p. 46.
62 Liam Cosgrave in interview with the author. Cosgrave held that minutes should be a concise record of decisions taken, not lengthy accounts of discussions.
63 Browne, *Against the Tide*, p. 180.
64 An unusual exception was Mulcahy, who did have shorthand, as his private papers amply demonstrate. However, he does not appear to have used this facility at Cabinet meetings.

65   Lee, *Ireland*, p. 306.
66   Farrell, *Chairman or Chief?*, pp. 52–3.
67   Patrick Lynch makes this very point in 'Pages from a Memoir', pp. 39–40.
68   NA, S. 14333.
69   NA, S. 14333, MacBride memorandum.
70   ibid., p. 2.
71   ibid. contains this sentence.
72   ibid.
73   NA, CAB 2/10, 19 August 1948.
74   NA, S. 14333. MacBride's dossier includes transcripts from the BBC, extracts from *The Halifax Chronicle* (Nova Scotia), and several articles from both *The Economist* and *The New Statesman and Nation*. These span dates ranging from February to June 1948.
75   NA, S. 14333. This is a later dossier, containing several articles from *The New Statesman and Nation*, all of which date from July 1948.
76   Costello, Memorandum, pp. 2–3, explicitly states that the government had decided to move legislation to repeal the External Relations Act when the Dáil resumed, in October.
77   NA, CAB 2/10, 27 February 1948; the third Cabinet meeting of the inter-party government saw the establishment of an 'Economic Sub-Committee' of the Cabinet, which seems to have had a very extensive brief.
78   NA, CAB 2/10, 7 May 1948; two subcommittees were established concerning the Marshall Aid programme, one dealing with overall policy on the European Recovery Programme, the other to co-ordinate interdepartmental administration of Marshall Aid. Both of these were to enjoy extensive powers of prowling. Contrast these with the subcommittee which was set up to discuss the establishment of the Central Statistics Office, in NA, CAB 2/10, 6 July 1948, which confined itself to its brief.
79   *Dáil Debates*, Vol. 112, cols 2440–1, 6 August 1948.
80   ibid., col. 2441, 6 August 1948.
81   Costello, Memorandum, pp. 2, 3, 6, 8 and 9.
82   ibid., p. 3.
83   *The Citizen*, Vol. 3, No. 1, May 1967. I came across this in Richard Mulcahy's papers (P7(d)118); interestingly enough, that interview was conducted by a rather youthful Vincent Browne, who was then an ardent supporter of Fine Gael's Just Society programme.
84   Michael McInerney, 'Mr John A. Costello Remembers – 5', *The Irish Times*, 8 September 1967.
85   Farrell in *Chairman or Chief?*, p. 49, quotes directly from Costello's memorandum. See also Lyons, *Ireland Since the Famine*, p. 564, and Michael McInerney, 'Mr John A. Costello Remembers – 5', *The Irish Times*, 8 September 1967. When one adds Costello's own memorandum and *The Citizen* to this list of publicly expressed doubts, that means that there are five sources where Costello confessed his doubts as to whether this decision was minuted. Obviously, he was perfectly aware that it had not been minuted.
86   Lyons, *Ireland Since the Famine*, p. 564. Lyons's book was first published in 1971.
87   Hector Legge, letter to *The Irish Times*, 11 December 1991.
88   Of course, all of this makes Ronan Fanning's subsequently stated surprise at the lack of written records on the decision to repeal the Act all the more astonishing. Noël Browne, in *Against the Tide*, p. 131, refers to Fanning's 'puzzled references' in his book, *Independent Ireland*, to the lack of any Cabinet papers relating to a decision to repeal the External Relations Act. Fanning's own surprise emerges clearly on p. 173 of *Independent Ireland*.

89   These are: Farrell, *Chairman or Chief?*, p. 49; Lyons, *Ireland Since the Famine*, p. 564; McInerney, *The Irish Times*, 8 September, 1967; Costello's own memorandum; and *The Citizen*, May 1967.

90   Browne, *Against the Tide*, pp. 129–33, deals with the repeal of the External Relations Act. The direct quote comes from p. 133.

91   ibid., p. 132. This is still a fairly widely held opinion; see for example Seán O'Brien's letter to *The Irish Times*, 1 September 1994, where he states that Costello, while on a state visit to Canada, was kept waiting for half an hour by the Governor-General, Lord Alexander, 'while showering, shaving and searching for his shirt studs', and that he 'repaid the insult' by declaring it to be the government's intention to leave the Commonwealth 'at the banquet' that evening. This account contains countless errors. Costello's trip was not a state visit; he never called on the Governor-General and so was never kept waiting; no speeches were made at the famous 'dinner'; and the famous announcement about leaving the Commonwealth occurred several days later at a prearranged press conference, in the press gallery of Ottawa's House of Commons.

92   Browne, *Against the Tide*, p. 127.

93   This would later be used against him by MacBride, who kept a detailed dossier of Browne's Cabinet meeting attendance, to be produced when needed. He gave me a copy of this in August 1979.

94   NA, CAB 2/10. Each meeting is dated, and those present and absent are noted.

95   A curious early exception to this was Browne's appointment to serve on two Cabinet subcommittees established to consider the question of Irish language tests, and the degree of preference to be awarded to such in competitions for posts in the civil service. NA, CAB 2/10, 12 November 1948. Interestingly, MacBride also served on both of these, along with Mulcahy, McGilligan, and Norton. From the outset of his ministerial career, Browne displayed an interest in the Irish language. See also *Against the Tide*, pp. 119–21. Dillon, who loathed compulsory Irish and kept raising it at Cabinet, seems to have been deliberately kept off this subcommittee.

96   Costello, Memorandum, p. 1.

97   ibid.

98   Keogh, *Twentieth-Century Ireland*, pp. 189–90, states that Boland rather than Costello himself originally drafted this speech, and 'that he had not put anything in the draft' about the External Relations Act, partly because he had tailored the speech to suit what was then Fine Gael policy, and partly because MacBride 'was not anxious' that the External Relations Act should be included in the speech. According to this account, Costello didn't like the draft, remarking, 'It's fine but there's too much of the smell of the Empire about this.' Presumably, he altered the offending parts. Keatinge, in *Formulation of Irish Foreign Policy*, p. 62, has no doubts that the final delivered version of the speech reflected Costello's input, stressing the emphasis it gave to 'the importance of international law to the foreign policy of the Cosgrave government', which Costello himself had been extensively involved with, both as Attorney-General and while representing Cosgrave's government at several of the Commonwealth conferences which occurred while they held office. However, MacBride in an interview with James Downey of *The Irish Times*, 1 and 2 January 1979, claims that he 'worked with [Costello] on the draft', and that in it 'Costello clearly said that the existing relationship with Britain was unrealistic and had to be changed'. Lyons, in *Ireland Since the Famine*, p. 565, seems to agree, for he refers to the speech as 'an able and objective account', and adds that 'Mr Costello did allow himself to refer to the "inaccuracies and infirmities" of those sections of the External Relations Act which dealt with the position of

the Crown.' Costello's own emphasis differs from that of his memorandum in his interview with Michael McInerney in *The Irish Times,* 8 September 1967, when he insisted that 'no hint [of governmental intentions] was given in his speech to the Bar Association'.

99   Costello, Memorandum, p. 2.

100   Seán MacBride, interview with James Downey, *The Irish Times* 1 and 2 January 1979.

101   Costello, Memorandum, pp. 2, 3, 6, 8, and 9, quite adamantly stresses this point.

102   The minutiae of Costello's visit to Canada can be found in his own detailed account, a closely written ten-page memorandum, and also in NA, S. 14331, which includes amazingly accurate and almost embarrassingly detailed expenses for the trip. A copy of Costello's memorandum was given to me by Hector Legge. It also appears, attributed as such, in Farrell, *Chairman or Chief?,* pp. 47–50, and Lyons, *Ireland Since the Famine,* pp. 563–7, and is unattributed, but quoted from extensively, in Costello's interview with Michael McInerney in *The Irish Times,* 8 September 1967.

103   Concerns of protocol had raised their pretty heads well before the trip; protocol decreed that visiting heads of government should stay with the Governor-General in Ottawa, and in the Citadel in Quebec. Costello had made it clear before the visit that 'subject to [John Hearne's] advice in the matter, I must say that I should prefer if arrangements could be made for our stay elsewhere during our visit'. Lynch, 'Pages from a Memoir', p. 51. Alternative arrangements were made, satisfying both Costello and protocol, but Lynch himself later derived some satisfaction from noting the splendid, spectacular – and timely – coincidence of the Citadel's end, when he observed, 'otherwise the Taoiseach's Canadian visit might have been symbolically more eventful and the legend of Roaring Meg extended. At midnight on the night of the Taoiseach's arrival in Quebec City the Citadel went up in flames.' ibid., p. 57.

104   Interview with Patrick Lynch, Ian McCabe, *A Diplomatic History of Ireland 1948–49,* p. 41 (IAP, Dublin, 1991).

105   ibid.

106   Patrick Lynch, 'Pages from a Memoir', p. 50.

107   Costello, Memorandum, p. 4.

108   Noël Browne, *Against the Tide,* p. 130, and again on p. 133, mistakenly refers to the Canadian Governor-General as Lord Allanbrooke, reinforcing his reputation for inaccurate recall.

109   Lynch, 'Pages from a Memoir', p. 52.

110   ibid., pp. 50–1.

111   Information from Florence O'Riordan, a former member of Clann na Poblachta, and later a diplomat.

112   Costello, Memorandum, p. 5.

113   Lynch, 'Pages from a Memoir', pp. 52–3.

114   Costello, Memorandum, pp. 5–6.

115   ibid., p. 6. Astonishingly, Costello quotes Lord Alexander's responses verbatim from the interview in *The Irish Times,* dated 25 March 1961. His own injured tone persists.

116   Costello, Memorandum, p. 8.

117   ibid., p. 7.

118   ibid. This *later* version of the memorandum rather reluctantly accepts Hector Legge's version of how the story came to appear. It is interesting, yet again, to contrast Costello's memorandum with the interview he gave to Michael McInerney in *The Irish Times,* 8 September 1967. In this interview Costello was quite

certain that a 'leak' had occurred, and emphasised that point to McInerney. Some of the direct quotes in the article seem to come from an *earlier* version of Costello's memorandum. Costello refused to tell McInerney whom he thought was responsible for the leak. Lyons, *Ireland Since the Famine*, p. 566, gently speculates about the possibility of a leak.

119 Hector Legge in interview with the author. Lyons, *Ireland Since the Famine*, p. 566, also makes this point.

120 Hector Legge in interview with the author.

121 ibid.

122 Jordan, *Seán MacBride*, pp. 106–7.

123 ibid., p. 107.

124 ibid.

125 Louie O'Brien was referred to with great respect by many of the Clann stalwarts with whom I spoke.

126 This, remember, is the speech which Costello says he wrote in the full knowledge of the impending repeal of the External Relations Act, the same speech which Keogh ascribes to Boland, saying that the repeal was never mentioned, and 'nor was Seán MacBride anxious that [it] should'. Keogh, *Twentieth-Century Ireland*, pp. 189–90. If some hint of the intended repeal did not exist, it is difficult to see, firstly, how astute observers, such as Hector Legge, could have 'read between the lines', and secondly, what purpose could have been served by an advance leak. Costello's interview with Michael McInerney in *The Irish Times,* 8 September 1967, stresses that there was 'no hint' of intended government action contained in the speech, whereas MacBride, in his *Irish Times* interview with James Downey, 1 and 2 January 1979, says that Costello's speech 'clearly said that the existing relationship with Britain was unrealistic and had to be changed'.

127 McCabe, *A Diplomatic History of Ireland*, p. 45.

128 Again, see Lee, *Ireland*, pp. 306–8, Browne, *Against the Tide*, pp. 127–8, and Keogh, *Twentieth-Century Ireland*, pp. 186–7.

129 Hector Legge in interview with the author. Also see his letters to *The Irish Times* 11 December 1991 and 01 January 1992, on this topic. However, Hector Legge did appear to change his mind on his long-held view that the government had decided to repeal the Act in advance of Costello's Canadian trip. Latterly, he inclined more to the opinion that an official formal decision had not been taken.

130 Louie O'Brien (erroneously referred to as J. O'Brien), letter to *The Irish Times*, 24 December 1991. See also Jordan, *Seán MacBride*, pp. 106–7.

131 Maffey notified London of this on the afternoon of 7 September. The British government paid little heed to this communication until *after* newspaper reports of Costello's press conference had appeared. Both Maffey and the British authorities seem to have regarded this as little more than a statement of intent, until the outcome of Costello's press conference persuaded them otherwise.

132 Costello, Memorandum, p. 7.

133 Keatinge, *Formulation of Irish Foreign Policy*, p. 63.

134 Costello, Memorandum, p. 7.

135 ibid., pp. 7–8.

136 ibid., p. 8.

137 ibid. This direct quote also appears in Costello's interview with Michael McInerney in *The Irish Times*, 8 September 1967.

138 Costello, Memorandum, p. 8.

139 This story appeared in *The Irish Times* of 9 July 1994, in the course of a review of Anthony Jordan's biography of Seán MacBride by Tony O'Riordan. O'Riordan cites C. W. Sowby's memoirs, entitled *With Thy Blessing*, where Sowby tells this

tale as related to him by John Hearne. In a letter to *The Irish Times*, published on 22 July 1994, David Sowby confirmed that his father had told him this story in the 1960s, explaining that Hearne had told it to his father in 1950, and adding that he is 'sure that he did not invent it'.

140   Jordan, *Seán MacBride*, p. 107.

141   Costello, Memorandum, p. 9.

142   Mackenzie King was accompanied by Lester B. Pearson, then Under-Secretary of State for External Affairs, who was to be appointed Minister for External Affairs almost immediately, succeeding M. Louis St Laurent, who went on to become Canada's Prime Minister when Mackenzie King retired. Thus, as early as October, Pearson, who was to become known as a 'celebrated' Foreign Minister, represented Canada at the Commonwealth conference, and was both exceedingly well briefed about and extremely sympathetic to Ireland's position.

143   NA, S. 14333; this is from MacBride's minute of both his phone call and subsequent meeting with Maffey, submitted as a memorandum to the Cabinet, 9 September 1948.

144   ibid.

145   ibid. contains Maffey's own file, including the revised, detailed proposed agenda, and Maffey's own accompanying comments, including his written note that the other Commonwealth prime ministers would be 'telegraphed in similar terms'.

146   Owen Dudley Edwards, 'The Repeal Announcement', *The Irish Times*, 3 January 1979.

147   ibid.

148   Seán MacBride in an interview with James Downey , *The Irish Times*, 1 and 2 January 1979.

149   Lyons, *Ireland Since the Famine*, p. 567, remarks that 'Interviewing Dr Browne . . . I had the clear impression that the announcement had taken him by surprise.' See also Browne, *Against the Tide*, pp. 129–33.

150   Keogh, *Twentieth-Century Ireland*, pp. 186–93, and an interesting footnote on p. 428, discuss Boland's increasingly strained relationship with MacBride.

151   Boland is quoted in *The Irish Times*, 1 and 2 January 1979.

152   Keogh, *Twentieth-Century Ireland*, p. 190.

153   ibid., p. 190.

154   ibid., p. 190.

155   Lyons, *Ireland Since the Famine*, p. 567.

156   James Downey, interview with Seán MacBride, *The Irish Times*, 1 and 2 January 1979.

157   Lyons, *Ireland Since the Famine*, p. 567.

158   Browne, *Against the Tide*, p. 132.

159   C. W. Sowby, *With Thy Blessing*, cited by Tony O'Riordan in his review of Anthony Jordan's biography of Seán MacBride, *The Irish Times*, 9 July 1994.

160   Dermot Keogh, *Ireland and the Vatican* (Cork University Press, Cork, 1995), pp. 265–304.

161   NA, CAB 2/10, 9 September 1948. Costello, Blowick, Dillon, O'Higgins, Morrissey, and Murphy were all absent, leaving only the Fine Gael Generals, Mulcahy and MacEoin, in addition to McGilligan, Norton, Everett, and, of course, MacBride and Browne, to pick up the pieces.

162   This quote from Maffey can be found in Martin Cowley, 'The shadow and the substance of the UK link', *The Irish Times*, 4 January 1979. The British Cabinet papers for 1948 had just been released.

163   NA, S. 14331 contains extremely exhaustive details of the costs of official visits. Accounts for 1947–48 were out by £1 9s 4d, which was 'attributable to errors discovered after the Accounts for 1947–48 had been closed'.

164 The subsequent sessions of the Commonwealth conference occurred in Chequers and then in Paris. Evatt's supportive role is discussed in detail in 'How Evatt Outmanoeuvred Whitehall Hard-liners', *The Irish Times*, 3 January 1979.

165 James Downey's interview with Seán MacBride, *The Irish Times*, 1 and 2 January 1979. Peter Fraser, the New Zealand Prime Minister, was something of an unknown quantity, and MacBride had not met him before this conference. As MacBride recalled, 'Fraser was an elderly man with a marked cast in his eye. He leaned over to me and said "How is your dear mother? I used to attend her anti-recruiting meetings when I was in the docks in Glasgow."' Fraser, along with Evatt and Pearson, supplied invaluable support to the Irish position.

166 NA, S. 14331 contains several files on the cost of Costello's Canadian visit. Tucked away at the bottom of one of the pages is the information that 'Car hire, London to Chequers, Halton Aylesbury, etc., and return, Minister for Finance and Minister for External Affairs, 17.10.1948, re Repeal of External Relations Act cost £8.17s.' Little further information is offered.

167 Keogh, *Twentieth-Century Ireland*, p. 190.

168 'Britain reveals details of Irish Commonwealth break', *The Irish Times*, 1 and 2 January, 1979.

169 Owen Dudley Edwards, 'The Repeal Announcement', *The Irish Times*, 3 January 1979.

170 NA, CAB 2/10, 11 October 1948; the topics of the safeguarding of citizenship rights, most favoured nation (trading) status, and other such Commonwealth advantages considerably engaged the minds of the Cabinet at their meeting of 11 October 1948, which occurred before the conference took place.

171 This is also the view taken by Lyons, *Ireland Since the Famine*, pp. 568–9.

172 NA, S. 14331 gives Costello's itinerary in detail.

173 NA, CAB 2/10, 11 October 1948, see also NA, S. 14331. This meeting went on for five hours – commencing at 11.00 a.m. and adjourning at 1.00 p.m., reconvening at 7.30 p.m. and finishing at 10.30 p.m.

174 Browne, *Against the Tide*, p. 130.

175 See both Browne, *Against the Tide*, pp. 131–2, quoting Boland, and Keogh, *Twentieth-Century Ireland,* pp. 189–91. However, Boland makes no mention of the 'caucus' meeting. Bruce Arnold, in *Irish Independent*, 4 February 1984, also says that Costello offered to resign on his return. However, it is only fair to add that Patrick Lynch, Costello's secretary, who accompanied him on the trip, disputed this version of events. Lynch, 'Pages from a Memoir', pp. 60–1.

176 NA, S. 14331 describes every ministerial trip undertaken by any minister in 1948 and early 1949, containing details of the destination, purpose and cost of the visit.

177 NA, CAB 2/10, 11 October 1948, item 2 and annexed Schedule A.

178 NA, S. 14331 contains both the draft and the final version of this minute. The minute was 'approved' and it was dated 'today', i.e. 11 October.

179 The fact that Browne refers to a 'Sunday' (which could only have been 3 October if it were to satisfy all of the required variables), while the minute asks about 'last Thursday' is not of major importance apart from noting Browne's lack of precision with detail; what is of relevance is that some sort of unrecorded meeting does seem to have occurred between Costello's return to Ireland on 1 October, and the time he appeared at a Cabinet meeting on 11 October, and that this serves to confirm Browne's version to some extent. What actually happened at this meeting is still a matter for conjecture.

180 That makes this the *third* Cabinet meeting on this matter – the others being those of 19 August and 9 September – where questions arise over the minutes.

181 See Keogh, *Twentieth-Century Ireland*, p. 191, Lee, *Ireland*, p. 301, Lyons, *Ireland Since the Famine*, pp. 567–9, and Browne, *Against the Tide*, p. 133.

182 Martin Cowley, in *The Irish Times*, 1 and 2 January 1980.

183 Lee, *Ireland*, p. 301.

184 Keogh, *Twentieth-Century Ireland*, p. 189.

185 Browne, *Against the Tide*, p. 133.

186 Sir John Maffey to Sir Eric Machtig, 21 October 1948, quoted in *The Irish Times*, 1 and 2 January, 1979.

187 Sir Gilbert Laithwaite to the Commonwealth Relations Office, late 1950, quoted in *Irish Press*, 1 and 2 January 1981.

188 This is a very good example of where Noël Browne's excessive invective mars what was initially a very important point about MacBride having been outmanoeuvred by Costello on the whole question of the repeal of the External Relations Act. MacBride did not stay away from the GPO as a 'pitiful protest', he was in the US, attending a 'conference with the State Department', from 2 April until 3 May 1949, and Easter Monday fell on 18 April. Browne did indeed attend the Easter ceremonies, but not as a sulky stand-in for MacBride. At the Cabinet meeting of 29 March 1949 an agency order was enacted, enabling Browne, in MacBride's absence, to discharge the duties of the Minister for External Affairs from 2 April until 30 April 1949. Moreover, at the Cabinet meeting of 5 April 1949, MacBride had arranged to have memoranda submitted on the form and content of the Easter ceremonies in his absence.

189 Keatinge, *Formulation of Irish Foreign Policy*, p. 63.

190 Sir John Maffey to Sir Eric Machtig, 21 October 1948, in *The Irish Times*, 1 and 2 January 1979.

191 Costello, Memorandum pp. 1–2.

8: The gradually diminishing eminence of the 'Grey Subsidence'

1 Dermot Keogh, *Twentieth-Century Ireland* (Gill & Macmillan, Dublin, 1994), p. 186.

2 Brian Inglis, *Downstart* (Chatto & Windus, London, 1990), p. 181.

3 Breandán Ó hEithir, *The Begrudger's Guide to Irish Politics* (Poolbeg, Dublin, 1986), p. 72.

4 Keogh, *Twentieth-Century Ireland*, p. 186. J. J. Lee, *Ireland 1912-1985: Politics and Society* (Cambridge University Press, Cambridge, 1989), p. 306.

5 *The Irish Times*, 3 January 1979.

6 Lee, *Ireland*, p. 308, refers to this CIA quote, as do Anthony Jordan, *Seán MacBride* (Blackwater Press, Dublin, 1993), p.124, and Seán Cronin, *Washington's Irish Policy, 1916–1986* (Anvil Press, Dublin, 1987), p. 255.

7 Noël Browne, *Against the Tide* (Gill & Macmillan, Dublin, 1986), p. 128.

8 Lee, *Ireland*, p. 306.

9 Laithwaite had replaced Sir John Maffey – who later became Lord Rugby – in 1949.

10 Sir Gilbert Laithwaite to the Commonwealth Office, 8 March 1950, cited in *Irish Press*, 1 and 2 January 1981.

11 Patrick Keatinge, *The Formulation of Irish Foreign Policy* (Institute of Public Administration, Dublin, 1973), pp. 80–2, heaps praise on MacBride's efforts in Iveagh House: 'indeed, expenditure in the department in relation to total government expenditure has never been so great as in 1950. The headquarters staff was increased and reorganised, press attachés and information officers were introduced, training courses were established and cultural activities were

encouraged . . . His speeches in the Dáil were generally long, comprehensive and detailed . . . MacBride was a pioneer in the sense that he articulated long-term national objectives in a Dáil which all too frequently succumbed to the temptations of short-term partisan advantages.'

12   ibid., p. 81.

13   Other sources worth a look are Ian McCabe, *A Diplomatic History of Ireland 1948–49* (Irish Academic Press, Dublin, 1991), which is detailed and balanced, and Dermot Keogh, *Ireland and the Vatican* (Cork University Press, Cork, 1995), which is rather less fulsome about MacBride's stint in Iveagh House. The Irish News Agency, which initially included some very talented writers, such as Brian Inglis, Douglas Gageby, and Conor Cruise O'Brien, was viewed with open hostility by the domestic print media, which did their best to strangle it at birth. Inglis, *Downstart*, pp. 174–5, points out that 'Irish newspaper editors had disliked the idea of the INA, and in general boycotted its copy.' Keatinge, *Formulation of Irish Foreign Policy*, p. 179, also refers to the INA as 'a victim of sectional interests'.

14   Lee, *Ireland*, p. 301.

15   ibid. However, Ian McCabe views the 'invitation' to join NATO more as a sort of 'pre-invitation' designed to elicit the Irish government's views on the matter before a formal invitation was extended to them, and argues that Ireland's futile attempt to link partition with membership of NATO ensured that a formal invitation would not be forthcoming. McCabe quotes from a succinct Foreign Office summary in making his case: 'The attitude of the State Department has so far been that Eire can take it or leave it, and that partition has nothing to do with the case.' McCabe, *A Diplomatic History of Ireland*, pp. 107–14.

16   Sir Gilbert Laithwaite to the Commonwealth Relations Office, late 1950, *The Irish Times*, 1 and 2 January 1981.

17   Some of the very attractive literature put out by the Mansion House Conference persists with this sort of simplistic analysis, offering pictures of divided houses and then asking whether such divisions are 'fair'. Little cultural or critical analysis is offered.

18   A lot of the literature put out by the Mansion House Conference lays considerable emphasis on the inequities faced by Northern nationalists on a daily basis in their lives, concentrating especially on political aspects such as the gerrymandering of constituencies, limits placed on the franchise, inadequate representation, and so on. See *Ireland's Right To Unity*, an official publication stating the case made by the All-Party Anti-Partition Mansion House Conference.

19   A very interesting critical analysis of the sort of nationalist reiteration of platitudes which sustain political beliefs rather than subjecting such beliefs to any kind of serious interrogation can be found in Clare O'Halloran's excellent *Partition and the Limits of Irish Nationalism* (Gill & Macmillan, Dublin, 1987), which described the Mansion House Conference as an 'advance only in terms of the organisation and resources expended and the full frontal irredentist approach adopted. In its essence, as propaganda, it revealed the traditional unreality of orthodox nationalism' (pp. 185–6).

20   John Bowman in interview with Seán MacBride, RTÉ radio, 29 December 1980. Much thanks to John Bowman for making a copy of this interview available to me.

21   Costello came to be seen as 'emotional' on this topic by both Maffey and his successor, Laithwaite.

22   Sir Gilbert Laithwaite to the Commonwealth Relations Office, late 1950, *Irish Press*, 1 and 2 January 1981.

23   Sir Gilbert Laithwaite, cited in *Irish Press*, 1 and 2 January 1981.

24 Jack McQuillan was able to cite examples of the genre, a number of which he had composed himself.

25 Notes from Captain Peadar Cowan's unpublished memoirs.

26 ibid.

27 Sir Gilbert Laithwaite, 8 March 1950, cited in *Irish Press*, 1 and 2 January 1981.

28 In fact, as Raymond J. Raymond points out, economic planning of a sort had already begun during the war, as part of a desperate plan to ensure political and economic (in that order) survival. Lemass, undoubtedly the most able member of the Fianna Fáil cabinet, was put in charge of the newly created Department of Supplies, with a brief to undertake (and implement) such state-run policies as were necessary to guarantee the nation's survival. According to Raymond, this is what introduced the notion of state planning, even if on an ad hoc, emergency basis, to some of the country's civil servants and their masters. Raymond J. Raymond, 'De Valera, Lemass and Irish Economic Development, 1933–1948' in J. P. O'Carroll and John A. Murphy (eds), *De Valera and His Times* (Cork University Press, Cork, 1983), pp. 113–33.

29 Brian Farrell, *Chairman or Chief?: The Role of Taoiseach in Irish Government* (Gill & Macmillan, Dublin, 1971), p. 46. Farrell also refers to a further confrontation, again involving MacBride and the mandarins from Finance, at the time of the devaluation of the pound in 1949.

30 Discussions on the European Recovery Programme occurred at the Cabinet meetings of 2 March, 2 April, 29 April, and 7 May 1948. The meeting of 7 May is the important one in this context, for that was when it was decided 'that the co-ordination of the data and requirements of the different Departments concerned with the Programme should devolve on the Department of External Affairs, the staffing requirements of the special section to be set up for the purpose to be settled in the normal way by the Minister for Finance'. Furthermore, it was also decided at this meeting 'that the Minister for External Affairs should consult direct with the Ministers for Finance, Industry and Commerce, and Agriculture in relation to administrative matters connected with the Programme and affecting their respective Departments'.

31 Finance's unimaginative, Victorian, strait-jacketed approach to government is well traced in Ronan Fanning's *The Irish Department of Finance 1922–1958* (Institute of Public Administration, Dublin, 1980). Lee, *Ireland*, also offers a devastating analysis of its intellectual poverty.

32 Browne, *Against the Tide*, p. 128, wrote rather nastily, and certainly unfairly, that 'McGilligan shared Hartnett's moderate opinions about MacBride as an intellectual and scholar, [and] also dismissed his seeming expertise on economic or financial matters.'

33 Letter from Sir Gilbert Laithwaite to the Commonwealth Relations Office, written towards the end of 1950, *Irish Press*, 1 and 2 January 1981.

34 Browne, *Against the Tide*, p. 197.

35 This is the opinion of Lee, *Ireland*, p. 312.

36 Browne, *Against the Tide*, p. 108, dismissed MacBride's assertion that 'with a little work, McGilligan was educable', with the blunt comment: 'Of all the men in the Cabinet, McGilligan was easily the one man who under no circumstances would have gone our way.' In fact, by 1948, McGilligan was to show himself to be unusually flexible on economic matters.

37 McGilligan papers (P35C/189).

38 ibid.

39 ibid.

40 Michael McInerney, 'Mr John A. Costello Remembers – 4', *The Irish Times*, 7 September 1967.

41   Michael McInerney, 'Mr John A. Costello Remembers – 3', *The Irish Times*, 6 September 1967.
42   ibid. Admittedly, this was much later, but the self-satisfied tone of the convert remains, and it can be found in earlier contributions from both Costello and Mulcahy – especially Costello – at a sequence of Fine Gael ard-fheiseanna throughout the 1950s. Mulcahy papers (P7C/124).
43   Lee, *Ireland*, p. 312.
44   Inglis, *Downstart*, p. 178.
45   Patrick Lynch, 'Pages from a Memoir', in Patrick Lynch and James Meenan (eds), *Essays in Memory of Alexis Fitzgerald* (Incorporated Law Society of Ireland, Dublin, 1987), p. 35.
46   ibid., pp. 36–7.
47   A very interesting – and critical – alternative view on the importance of this budget is offered by Brian Girvin, who argued that the innovations in the capital budget were minimal, and that economic management in Ireland had been 'utilised to preserve stability rather than to generate a modern industrial economy'. Brian Girvin, *Between Two Worlds* (Gill & Macmillan, Dublin, 1989), pp. 170–2. He went on to state (p. 172) that 'there was a general tendency in the Inter-party government to respond to issues, rather than devising policies to achieve consistent objectives'.
48   Cabinet meeting of 3 February 1950. NA, S. 14731.
49   The other major government initiative concerning economic planning involved the setting-up of the Industrial Development Authority. MacBride was strongly in favour of the project, and was, in this instance, involved in the various committees established to oversee its foundation.
50   Seán MacBride in interview with the author.
51   Sir Gilbert Laithwaite to the Commonwealth Relations Office, late 1950, *Irish Press*, 1 and 2 January 1981.
52   ibid.
53   Farrell, *Chairman or Chief?*, p. 45.
54   Sir Gilbert Laithwaite, 8 March 1950, cited in *Irish Press*, 1 and 2 January 1981.
55   Sir Gilbert Laithwaite to the Commonwealth Relations Office, late 1950, *Irish Press*, 1 and 2 January 1981.
56   This by-election is referred to in Sir Gilbert Laithwaite's letter of 8 March 1950. In fact, the Clann had not done particularly well in Donegal in the general election of 1948, either.
57   Mulcahy papers (P7b/115, pp. 31–3). In the urban district councils, Fianna Fáil obtained 258 seats, Fine Gael 131, Labour 56, and Clann na Poblachta a mere 20, while that bane of local election counts, the category of 'others', received 138 seats. Seats on the corporations were distributed as follows: Fianna Fáil 66, Fine Gael 35, Labour 25, Clann na Poblachta a mere 9, and 'others' 50. The town commissioners were broken down as follows: Fianna Fáil 38 seats, Fine Gael 16, Labour 18, Clann na Poblachta 11, and 'others' 25. That leaves the county councils, arguably the most important of the lot. They were filled thus: Fianna Fáil 288 seats, Fine Gael 149, Labour 56, Clann na Talmhan 24, Clann na Poblachta 19, and the eponymous 'others' 112. These results were a disaster for the Clann. In the country they lay in fifth place, behind Clann na Talmhan, and many of Mulcahy's lists of 'others' appear to have included Clann na Talmhan, for his nation-wide aggregate totals place Clann na Poblachta behind Clann na Talmhan in terms of overall votes acquired. His figures were Fianna Fáil, 376,035 first preferences; Fine Gael, 209,856; Labour, 104,078; Clann na Talmhan, 71,310; Clann na Poblachta, 60,394; Independents, 120,495; and 'others', 33,449.

58 Kevin Rafter, *The Clann: The Story of Clann na Poblachta* (Mercier Press, Cork, 1996), p. 123.

59 Rafter states (ibid.) that the party only succeeded in having twenty-six candidates elected to the various bodies; Mulcahy, in his characteristically exhaustive account of the same elections, comes up with a total of twenty-nine Clann representatives – twenty elected to the urban district councils, and nine to the various corporations. Either way, this was a disastrous result for the Clann.

60 Jack McQuillan easily retained his Dáil seat, firstly, as an Independent, and later, as a member of the small left-wing National Progressive Democrats, which he co-founded in 1957 along with Noël Browne, until 1965. However, in 1965 a number of factors combined to deprive him of his seat. Chief among these was his costly libel action against the *Roscommon Herald*, a paper which had been counted among McQuillan's mortal political enemies since 1948. Although McQuillan won the libel action (he was awarded damages of a penny), the action proved exorbitant in political terms. Of equal relevance in 1965 was the fact that McQuillan had recently married and had moved to Dublin, thus physically removing himself from his electoral base in his constituency. Also worth noting is the fact that the National Progressive Democrats had just been subsumed into the Labour Party, and thus, in 1965, McQuillan ran in Roscommon under the banner of the Labour Party, a factor which some commentators felt did not really help his electoral chances very much. Information from Jack McQuillan in conversation with the author.

61 Rafter, *The Clann*, p. 124. Both Barron and ffrench-O'Carroll would be elected to Dáil seats; Barron, finally, in 1961, for Clann na Poblachta, having contested Dáil seats at every election for the Clann since 1948, and ffrench-O'Carroll in 1951 as an Independent supporting Noël Browne. It is unlikely that either of them would have succeeded in taking a Dáil seat without already having successfully contested for local authority seats.

62 Sir Gilbert Laithwaite to the Commonwealth Relations Office, late 1950, *Irish Press*, 1 and 2 January 1981.

63 Sir Gilbert Laithwaite, 8 March 1950, cited in *Irish Press*, 1 and 2 January 1981.

64 MacEntee papers (P67/547[12]).

65 Minute from Clann na Poblachta Standing Committee meeting, 9 February 1951. Thanks to Seán MacBride for this and other minutes quoted in this chapter.

66 Minute from Clann na Poblachta National Executive meeting, 10–11 February 1951.

67 Noël Hartnett's letter of resignation, published in *Irish Independent*, 16 April 1951.

68 ibid.

69 Baltinglass is a surprisingly attractive town, and, in addition to the aforementioned post office, it contains a magnificent ruined thirteenth-century Cistercian monastery. In 1989, when I visited it, distant relatives of the Cookes were still in charge of the post office, and the post office itself had been renovated to look much as it had appeared earlier in the century. Much thanks to the Murphys for very kindly going to the trouble of specially opening up Baltinglass post office for me late one April evening, and for their guided tour of the premises.

70 Some of the residents of Baltinglass that I interviewed were quite prepared to offer this term as being descriptive of the town's attitudes and outlook as long as it was 'off the record'. Moreover, with the exception of Ben Hooper, who still agreed with the boycott, most of the people I spoke with, including the distant

relatives of the Cookes, felt that the matter had 'got out of hand', and was something of an embarrassment, now that they looked back on it. Most agreed to
speak with me only on condition of a guarantee of anonymity, and their general
attitude seemed to be 'oh, no, you're not bringing *that* up again'.

71 The government and Cabinet minutes are full of these post office positions,
containing goodly numbers of appointments, and a surprising amount of
dismissals, quite a number for petty larceny. At the time, however, post office
appointments were viewed as being one of the few forms of patronage with
which a minister could reward stalwart political followers. See Liam Kavanagh's
interview with Cathal O'Shannon, in his documentary *The Battle of Baltinglass*,
RTÉ Television, 10 October 1996.

72 Ó hEithir, *Begrudger's Guide*, p. 49.

73 Most of the people I spoke with in Baltinglass felt some sympathy for Farrell,
referring to him as 'well-meaning'. His father had been a Labour Party county
councillor – hence the controversial appointment – and the business his family
owned in Baltinglass was one of the largest in the town, for it included a bar, a
butcher's section, a drapery, and a general grocery. Such ventures as he became
involved in had usually ended unsuccessfully. He had been a second lieutenant
in the FCA, a rank he remained rooted in, and his unfortunate appointment to
the post office seems to have been regarded as a regrettable catalyst for political
action.

74 The Cookes were not necessarily as 'popular' as some of the literature written at
the time would appear to imply. For example, Helen Cooke was described as 'a
tough lady', with the added comment that 'she was a rip who'd eat you without
salt', according to a former employee of hers, interviewed by Cathal O'Shannon. Moreover, some of the sources I interviewed – such as former Army
commandant and Fianna Fáil Dáilcheantar member, Johnny Prendergast – held
the view that the 'Misses Cookes' were 'Castle Catholics', and this was in spite of
the fact that Fianna Fáil actually supported the boycott, for apart from the
manifest injustice of depriving the Cookes of their livelihood, there was also the
little matter of being able to embarrass the government on this sort of issue.

75 Laurence Earl wrote a book about it which was published in 1952, entitled *The
Battle of Baltinglass*. Written in a prose style vaguely reminiscent of *The Irish
RM*, this treats the affair with considerable levity. In October 1996, RTÉ Television broadcast a well-researched, brief – but extremely good – documentary on
the Baltinglass affair, *The Battle of Baltinglass*. Researched, written, and
presented by the excellent Cathal O'Shannon, it was fair, sympathetic to the
respective participants, and extremely interesting.

76 Browne, *Against the Tide*, p. 196. MacBride, in interview with the author,
stressed the nature of the inter-party government, and argued that small parties
in coalition governments cannot expect to be able to impose their will on every
matter that concerns them.

77 Seán MacBride in interview with the author.

78 Ben Hooper was one of the leading members of the Boycott Committee and was
headmaster of the local vocational school. When I interviewed him, in April
1989, not long before his death, he remained completely committed to the idea
of the boycott.

79 Ben Hooper in interview with the author.

80 ibid.

81 Browne, *Against the Tide*, p. 139.

82 Seán MacBride in interview with the author.

83 Denis Ireland may have come from unionist stock, but he himself was anti-
partitionist. Two republican sources, both in Clann na Poblachta, informed me

that they believed Denis Ireland to have been an enthusiastic anti-partitionist who had actively supported the IRA. This puts his selection – in the context of bridge-building between the two traditions – in a rather strange light. An even stranger light is thrown on his role by a different charge, subsequently made by Hartnett, and later still supported by Noël Browne, concerning the role of Denis Ireland in connection with the 'invitation' to join NATO. Representing Clann na Poblachta in the Senate, Denis Ireland had urged that the policy of neutrality should be abandoned and that the Republic should give serious consideration to the idea of joining NATO, as part of the anti-communist alliance. Making the point that such speeches could hardly have been made without MacBride's consent (and approval), Browne goes on to write (*Against the Tide*, p. 135) that 'this sudden explosion of official authorised enthusiasm for membership of NATO, albeit conditional, represented a dramatic change in Ireland's defence strategy', and, indeed, in Clann na Poblachta's own actual policy, for that matter. (See Browne, *Against the Tide*, pp. 134–6.) Jack McQuillan in conversation with the author also laid strong emphasis on this theory, and they both felt that Denis Ireland's real role may have been to help generate an atmosphere which would be conducive to contemplating membership of NATO. While seeking to join NATO – (even, if only on the condition that 'the problem' of partition be solved first) – admittedly, had hardly been part of Clann na Poblachta's platform, or policy, there is a sense in which the later objections of Browne and McQuillan to Denis Ireland's machinations read as a retrospective projection of history. In other words, the suspicion is that they were projecting their subsequent views on NATO backwards in time, and using that as another stick with which to beat MacBride. This is not to defend NATO itself, or to offer justifications for MacBride's well-documented attempts to join NATO, but it is to say that the sort of ideological objections which would be raised against the idea of joining NATO in the 1980s would have received very short shrift indeed in the Ireland of 1949. For, in 1949, nobody, but nobody – publicly, at least – doubted that Ireland was on the side of the angels in the global confrontation against 'godless Communism'. In any case, Denis Ireland was not the only Northern senator representing Clann na Poblachta in the Seanad whose surreptitious activities would be a cause for concern. With the resurgence of IRA activity during the ill-fated 'border campaign' of the mid-fifties, a raid on an RUC barracks, bearing the characteristic IRA finger-prints of 'daring exploits and tragic aftermaths', was led – though this fact was not widely known at the time – by Liam Kelly, 'one of the Northern Senators whom Seán MacBride had appointed to the Seanad' for the duration of the term of office of the second Inter-Party government. (Coogan, *Long Fellow, Long Shadow*, p. 669).

84   Seán MacBride in interview with the author.
85   Browne, *Against the Tide*, pp. 134–6.
86   Seán MacBride in interview with the author.
87   Browne, *Against the Tide*, p. 106.
88   ibid. Coming from Noël Browne, who more frequently tended to lean towards variants of political purity, this almost beggars belief. In fact, Browne went on to qualify that statement somewhat when he continued, 'Even if this were not so, Hartnett was one of the few within Clann na Poblachta at that time who had any experience of representative democracy', suggesting that this, if nothing else, merited his elevation to the Senate.
89   ibid., p. 137.
90   ibid., p. 138.
91   J.H. Whyte, *Church and State in Modern Ireland, 1923–1979* (Gill & Macmillan, Dublin, 1979), pp. 210–12.

92   *The Irish Times*, 21 February 1951.
93   Noël Browne in his autobiography *Against the Tide* played down the closeness
     of his friendship at the time with Hartnett, and suggested a degree of objectivity
     that was not, frankly, completely credible, when he remarked: 'Though I did all
     in my power to remain detached from their quarrel, I was unsuccessful. Each
     believed that I was disloyal to the other because I declined to take sides in a
     quarrel of whose origins and causes at that time I was unsure' (p. 138). In fact,
     most contemporary sources regarded Browne as being squarely on Hartnett's
     side, at least by that time.
94   Whyte, *Church and State*, p. 210.
95   In the formal government lists, and, even in the attendance lists for meetings of
     the Cabinet, the Health portfolio was ranked last. Its status as a new ministry,
     with an unknown young minister from a small party, probably contributed to its
     low ranking. Indeed, it is probably only in the wake of the Mother and Child
     Scheme debacle that Health came to be seen as a ministry meriting that little
     bit more attention from experienced politicians.
96   Browne, *Against the Tide*, p. 127.
97   J. H. Whyte has written, 'For it was no routine member of a ministerial team
     who was falling from office, but an outstandingly successful administrator.'
     Whyte, *Church and State*, p. 199.
98   F. S. L. Lyons, *Ireland Since the Famine* (Fontana, London, 1973), pp. 572–3,
     Lee, *Ireland*, p. 315, Ó hEithir, *Begrudger's Guide*, pp. 128–34, and Whyte,
     Church and State, pp. 197–9, all refer to Browne's tenure in the Department of
     Health – especially with regard to the campaign against TB – in almost glowing
     terms. Ruth Barrington is somewhat less fulsome on Browne's performance, for
     she points to the fact that while his personalised campaign mobilised the
     public very effectively in combating TB, it was to leave him vulnerable later on
     at the time of the Mother and Child Scheme debacle. Ruth Barrington, *Health,
     Medicine and Politics in Ireland 1900–1970* (Institute of Public Administra-
     tion, Dublin, 1987), pp. 195–201. Predictably, an alternative – and hardly
     credible – view exists, and it can be found in James Deeny's *To Cure and To
     Care: Memoirs of a Chief Medical Officer* (Glendale Press, Dublin, 1989). In it,
     Deeny appears to completely ignore the contribution made by his former boss
     in the campaign to eradicate TB. At one stage Deeny served under Noël
     Browne as chief medical officer in the Department of Health, and his relations
     with Browne appear to have been quite cool. Harry Hitchcock, who worked
     with them both, finds for Browne in his book *TB Or Not TB?* (Centre for Health
     Promotion Studies, University College Galway, 1995).
99   Seán MacBride in interview with the author.
100 Michael McInerney, 'Mr John A. Costello Remembers – 4', *The Irish Times*, 7
     September 1967.
101 Seán MacBride in interview with the author.
102 Hitchcock, *TB Or Not TB?*, p. 104.
103 Whyte, *Church and State*, p. 197.
104 Hitchcock, *TB Or Not TB?*, p. 61.
105 Lyons, *Ireland Since the Famine*, p. 572.
106 Whyte, *Church and State*, p. 205; Hitchcock, *TB Or Not TB?*, pp. 115 and
     128.
107 Whyte, *Church and State*, p. 205.
108 ibid.; also interviews with former medical personnel, two of whom made clear to
     the author their strong feelings on this topic.
109 Barrington, *Health, Medicine and Politics*, p. 198.
110 ibid.

111 Browne, *Against the Tide*, p. 122. At all times, Noël Browne showed a great respect for the wisdom and loyalty of his senior staff in the Department of Health, especially Patrick Kennedy, the departmental secretary.

112 Whyte, *Church and State*, p. 199.

113 ibid., pp. 199–200.

114 Cabinet Minutes, 25 June 1948. The redrafting was intended to remove some of the compulsory features of the Act, such as the compulsory inspection of schoolchildren, which had already generated controversy. In fact, before the general election, James Dillon, then in opposition, had threatened to undertake a legal action designed to test the constitutionality of the 1947 Act. Ministerial office put paid to this particular challenge, but others lurked in the wings.

115 Noël Browne never made any secret of where his sympathies lay on this question. His liberating and 'refreshing' experience working in the British National Health Service, coupled with his oft-stated belief that he had always found 'the cash nexus between the patient and the doctor indefensible', points to an understandable preference for a salaried state system. Browne, *Against the Tide*, p. 82.

116 Lee, *Ireland*, pp. 315–6.

117 Ó hEithir, *Begrudger's Guide*, p. 131.

118 Keogh, *Twentieth-Century Ireland*, p. 209. In fact, Garret FitzGerald appears to have been the first Taoiseach to take issue with the concept of members of secretive organisations serving in an Irish government. While Taoiseach, he made it clear that membership of organisations such as the Knights of Columbanus was incompatible with membership of his government. He discusses this briefly in his autobiography *All in a Life* (Gill & Macmillan, Dublin, 1991), p. 431.

119 Browne, *Against the Tide*, pp. 157–9, discusses this meeting and its aftermath; it is also dealt with in Whyte, *Church and State*, pp. 213–16.

120 Whyte, *Church and State*, p. 223.

121 This was suggested by John Bowman, in *What the Papers Say*, broadcast by RTÉ Television on 9 April 1998.

122 Whyte, *Church and State*, p. 222.

123 Browne, *Against the Tide*, pp. 163–4.

124 Keogh, *Ireland and the Vatican*, pp. 324–5; Whyte, *Church and State*, pp. 264–5.

125 Browne, *Against the Tide*, p. 52.

126 Tim Pat Coogan, *Ireland Since the Rising* (Pall Mall Press, London, 1966), p. 101.

127 In fact, it is only fair to mention that the hierarchy themselves were not totally united on this issue, either. Bishop John Dignan, who had earlier been sacked by MacEntee as chairman of the National Health Insurance Society for his outspoken criticisms of the poor law system, wrote warmly to Browne, supporting the Mother and Child Scheme. However, his stance was as singular amongst the hierarchy as Browne's was to be in Cabinet. Browne, *Against the Tide*, p. 171; Whyte, *Church and State*, pp. 219–20.

128 Browne, *Against the Tide*, p. 167.

129 ibid., p. 162–3; Whyte, *Church and State*, p. 425, footnote in Appendix B.

130 Browne, *Against the Tide*, p. 163.

131 John Cooney, in *The Irish Times*, 6 April 1998

132 ibid.

133 Browne, *Against the Tide*, p. 167.

134 Whyte, *Church and State*, p. 217.

135 ibid., p. 426.

136 John Cooney, in *The Irish Times*, 6 April 1998.

137 J. J. Lee has put it rather nicely when he wrote with a note of barbed sympathy that 'Browne was probably his own worst enemy, despite the competition from Costello, MacBride, and McQuaid.' Lee, *Ireland*, p. 318.

138 Much thanks to Seán MacBride for making his strange account of that peculiar dinner available to me. Entitled (in MacBride's hand) 'Minute of conversation between Seán MacBride and Noël Browne held at the Russell Hotel and Leinster House on 9 Nov. 1950. Prepared by Seán MacBride the same night', it makes fascinating reading.

139 ibid., pp. 2 and 4.

140 ibid., p. 2.

141 ibid., p. 6.

142 This surreal document could be treated as the creation of a rather paranoid mind – and certainly poses questions about MacBride's own attitudes towards personal and professional relationships – but, despite its air of icy calculation, it should not be dismissed. MacBride's rendition of both his own and Noël Browne's patterns of speech seems to be quite accurate. Harry Hitchcock, an open admirer of Browne's who acted as his locum in Newcastle Sanatorium while Browne was Minister for Health, offers an interesting story which partially supports Browne's contention that the government – or, more to the point, the Clann – was on a slippery slope towards total collapse well before Browne's actual resignation. According to Hitchcock, Browne dropped in on Newcastle Sanatorium in February 1951 for a flying visit, and informed Hitchcock: 'You probably know that my career as Minister is likely to be terminated shortly. I have no option but to resume my post here.' Hitchcock, *TB Or Not TB?*, p. 136. Browne discusses the dinner in *Against the Tide*, pp. 180–1.

143 Browne, *Against the Tide*, p. 180.

144 ibid., pp. 180–1.

145 ibid., p. 181.

146 MacBride clearly regarded this account as being something of a definitive version of events, for almost everybody who ever spoke with him on the topic seems to have received a copy of it. His biographer relates a story of how Muireann McHugh (who was a daughter of Roger McHugh and worked as an occasional secretary to MacBride) and her husband found themselves 'invited to dinner' following a remark made concerning the Mother and Child Scheme. 'During the course of the meal, Seán MacBride produced his file on the Mother and Child Scheme controversy, and proceeded to read his famous memorandum, written after dinner with Noël Browne. This, he felt sure would put [them] right.' Jordan, *Seán MacBride*, p. 165.

147 MacBride minute of the Russell Hotel dinner, pp. 2 and 5.

148 'Note of Report to the National Executive of Clann by Seán MacBride on the 10th February 1951'. Sheila Humphries papers (P106/2177). This is a truly extraordinary document.

149 ibid., p. 7.

150 'Brief Minute of Discussion between Donal O'Donoghue, Dr N. Browne and Seán MacBride in Iveagh House on Thursday, 4th January 1951. Duration about 3 hours (9 p.m. till shortly after midnight)'. Sheila Humphries papers (P106/2175). A fascinating read.

151 ibid.

152 ibid.

153 ibid.

154 ibid.

155 ibid.

156 Minute of Clann na Poblachta National Executive meeting, 10–11 February 1951.

157 ibid.

158 Jack McQuillan in conversation with the author. See also Browne, *Against the Tide*, pp. 177–84. McQuillan's question is referred to on p. 179.

159 Browne, *Against the Tide*, pp. 177–84. In Noël Browne's memory, several appalling national executive meetings seem to have been jumbled into one uniquely horrendous experience.

160 Letter from Seán MacBride to Noël Browne, 8 March 1951. Much thanks to Seán MacBride for this letter.

161 Minute of Clann na Poblachta National Executive meeting, 31 March–1 April 1951. Much thanks to Seán MacBride for this intriguing minute. The use of language in these resolutions makes for fascinating reading.

162 Browne, *Against the Tide*, p. 184.

163 Minute of Clann na Poblachta National Executive meeting, 31 March–1 April 1951.

164 John Cooney, in *The Irish Times*, 6 April 1998.

165 Cabinet Minute for 6 April 1951. NA, S. 14997B.

166 John Cooney talking to John Bowman, in *What the Papers Say*, RTÉ Television, 9 April 1998.

167 John Cooney, in *The Irish Times*, 6 April 1998.

168 Browne states in *Against the Tide*, p. 176, that the Mother and Child Scheme was the only matter discussed at that particular meeting, whereas the minutes themselves show a number of topics to have been addressed. The Mother and Child Scheme features as 'item 3', and, while Browne says that he walked out after this discussion – and, presumably he did – the minutes show that health matters featured further during the course of the meeting, for 'item 8' turned out to be a discussion on special leave for civil servants interested in putting in time with the World Health Organisation.

169 John Cooney, in *The Irish Times*, 6 April 1998.

170 Browne, *Against the Tide*, pp. 176–77. Browne's own account of this Cabinet meeting has remained consistent over the years.

171 Michael Keyes had been appointed Minister for Local Government, in place of Tim Murphy, who had died suddenly in the summer of 1949. Browne, *Against the Tide*, p. 177.

172 ibid.

173 This interview with John A. Costello featured in John Bowman's documentary, *What the Papers Say*, RTÉ Television, 9 April 1998.

174 Browne, *Against the Tide*, p. 170.

175 John Bowman, *What the Papers Say*, RTÉ Television, 9 April 1998.

176 'It was on this occasion that Boland was most unfavourably impressed with MacBride, who spoke with great deference to the Archbishop on the phone, but once having put the receiver down was dismissive of the prelate to the point of being contemptuous.' Keogh, *Ireland and the Vatican*, p. 261, fn 76.

177 Jack McQuillan in conversation with the author.

178 Browne, *Against the Tide*, p. 177.

179 Minute entitled 'Statement Issued by Clann na Poblachta', dated (in MacBride's hand) 15 April 1951, and containing a number (but not all) of the resolutions passed at the national executive meetings of 31 March–1 April and 8 April. Much thanks to Seán MacBride for making a copy of this minute available to me.

180 Browne, *Against the Tide*, pp. 177–84. As argued earlier, while it is perfectly possible that all of these horrors actually took place at this one meeting, on the basis of available sources or minutes, the suspicion must be that this format had occurred at a number of meetings from the beginning of the year. Certainly,

some of the events depicted – such as reading out accounts of conversations noted surreptitiously – had occurred at the earlier meetings.

181 'Statement Issued by Clann na Poblachta', 15 April 1951.

182 ibid.

183 Browne may have done the concept of open government a huge service by releasing the correspondence on the whole matter to the media, but not all of his actions were so praiseworthy. Before leaving his office, he has written about how two of his civil servants 'took care that all documents in our files likely to be used or misused against us were destroyed'. It is unlikely that this was done without Browne's approval. Browne, *Against the Tide*, p. 186.

184 *The Irish Times*, 12 April 1951.

185 'Statement by Mr Seán MacBride, S.C., T.D., at the Fifth Ard-Fheis of Clann na Poblachta held in Dublin on 30th June and 1st July 1951', p. 11. Much thanks to Seán MacBride for this document. Coming from MacBride, who later in his life became a staunch – even passionate – supporter of the idea of open government, and of an enthusiastic and inquisitive press, this almost beggars belief.

186 ibid.

187 *Dáil Debates*, Vol. 125, col. 784, 12 April 1951.

188 The key results in the 1951 election were the remarkable resurrection of Fine Gael – they gained nine seats, increasing their tally from thirty-one to forty – and the complete collapse of the Clann's vote, which fell to about 4 per cent of the national total, down from over 13 per cent in 1948, leaving them with just two Dáil seats which contrasts sharply with their total of 10 seats in 1948. This was a further reduction on the already poor local government results of 1950. Fianna Fáil gained a single seat which brought their total in 1951 to sixty-nine, an increase of one from the sixty-eight they had won in 1948. In 1950, Labour had merged with the God-fearing comrades in National Labour, and the newly reunited party managed to take sixteen seats in 1951, as against fourteen for Labour, and five for National Labour in 1948. Clann na Talmhan held their own, their seats decreasing by one, from seven to six. Fourteen Independents were returned, including in their number such former Clann na Poblachta luminaries as Noël Browne, Jack McQuillan, Peadar Cowan and Michael ffrench-O'Carroll.

189 For example, Keogh, *Twentieth-Century Ireland*, p. 213.

190 Dr Cornelius Lucey, Bishop of Cork and Ross, quoted in Whyte, *Church and State*, p. 312.

191 Seán MacBride, *The Irish Times*, 24 April 1954, quoted in ibid., p. 366.

192 ibid., p. 248–9.

193 Keogh, *Twentieth-Century Ireland*, p. 213.

194 De Valera may well have conceded to the hierarchy as late as 1953, but it could never be said that the hierarchy left with de Valera's scalp – or the head of any of his ministers – dangling from their belts.

195 Seán MacBride in interview with the author.

196 John Cooney, in *The Irish Times*, 6 April 1998.

197 Whyte, *Church and State*, p. 236, and also Lee, *Ireland*, p. 317.

198 Michael McInerney, 'Mr John A. Costello Remembers – 4', *The Irish Times*, 7 September 1967.

199 Ó hEithir, *Begrudger's Guide*, p. 131.

200 Michael McInerney, 'Mr John A. Costello Remembers – 4', *The Irish Times*, 7 September 1967.

201 Whyte, *Church and State*, p. 386, fn 29. He also quoted (pp. 312–13) a letter written by a TD to *The Irish Times* in April 1955, taking strong issue with the statement of the bishop of Cork, Dr Cornelius Lucey, that 'the Bishops were the

final arbiters of right and wrong *even in political matters*'. The TD went on to write that he, as a member of the Dáil, would not 'accept dictation' from a bishop, or bishops, at any time, on matters 'of a political nature'. However, as Whyte pointed out, the really interesting feature of the TD's letter was the fact that he felt he could not reveal his identity, because 'I do not want to finish my political career before it starts.'

202 The National Executive of the ICTU had passed a resolution on 30 March calling for the early implementation of the scheme and were concerned that it might be watered down (Whyte, *Church and State*, p. 227).

203 Hilda Tweedy, *A Link in the Chain: The Story of the Irish Housewives' Association 1942–1992* (Attic Press, Dublin, 1992), pp. 73–4.

204 ibid., p. 73.

205 ibid.

206 *Dublin Opinion*, July 1951.

207 Seán MacBride in interview with the author.

208 Some sources suggest that it was the ministry offered – said to be Posts and Telegraphs – which generated this refusal to serve in the second inter-party government. Jack McQuillan in conversation with the author. However, an alternative view contends that the Clann na Poblachta TDs 'had wished' to join the government, but had been overruled by the party's national executive. MacBride announced this decison 'with regret'. This latter view is held by Michael Gallagher, *Political Parties in the Republic of Ireland* (Gill & Macmillan, Dublin, 1985), p. 113, and Rafter, *The Clann*, p. 166.

209 Michael McInerney, 'Mr John A. Costello Remembers – 4', *The Irish Times*, 7 September 1967.

210 According to MacBride's biographer, Anthony Jordan, the impetus behind this move actually came from the Clann's national executive, not their parliamentarians, in what would later become a familiar tug-of-war for parties like Labour. Apparently, the Clann's three TDs were completely opposed to bringing down the government, but were 'mandated' to do so by the national executive of the party. Interestingly, Jordan remarks that, 'by then Seán MacBride's influence within the party had declined'. Jordan, *Seán MacBride*, p. 150. This same point is also made by Rafter, *The Clann*, pp. 172–3. What is of interest here is that MacBride's influence would appear to have declined considerably in yet another forum, a forum which, in this instance, he himself had founded, and that this further illustrates his perennial inability to achieve results in 'political' organisations.

211 Seán MacBride in interview with the author.

212 Tully continued to sit as an Independent TD for Cavan until 1969, when he retired from politics.

213 These included Joseph Barron, who finally took a seat in Dublin South-Central in 1961, and John Connor, who managed to take a seat in the North Kerry constituency at the general election of 1954. John Connor died in a car accident in December 1955, and his daughter, Kathleen O'Connor, was nominated to contest the by-election on behalf of Clann na Poblachta. In a startling display of inter-party solidarity (presumably to ensure that the seat didn't fall into Fianna Fáil's lap by mistake), the other parties declined to nominate candidates, and so Kathleen O'Connor won the seat formerly held by her father. She refused to stand for the Clann at the following general election, and they failed to even nominate a candidate to contest the seat. Rafter, *The Clann*, pp. 164 and 170–2.

214 Love them or loathe them, one must concede that the Progressive Democrats have been very successful in setting a political agenda; the price, or cost, of their political emasculation was the virtual adoption of their policies by the larger parties.

215   Seán MacBride in interview with the author.
216   ibid.
217   ibid.
218   Ó hEithir, *Begrudger's Guide*, p. 128.
219   Lee, *Ireland*, pp. 317–18, offers a devastating analytical critique of MacBride's deficiencies as leader of a radical party.
220   ibid., p. 317.
221   Seán MacBride in interview with the author.
222   Browne, *Against the Tide*, p. 185.

Bibliography

Primary Sources

National Archives, Dublin
Cabinet Minutes
Cabinet Secretariat files

University College Dublin Archives Department
Sheila Humphries papers
Seán MacEntee papers
Patrick McGilligan papers
Richard Mulcahy papers

Private Sources
Peadar Cowan's unpublished memoirs
Memoranda and minutes of Clann na Poblachta meetings supplied by Seán MacBride.
John A. Costello's private memorandum on the repeal of the External Relations Act
Our Country: film made by Liam Ó Laoghaire, Brendan Stafford, and May Laverty; commissioned by Clann na Poblachta for the 1948 general election
Our Nation: a magazine/periodical published by Clann na Poblachta between 1948 and 1954; some of the earlier editions can be found in the National Library, and much thanks to Labhrás Ó Nualláin for allowing me to peruse an almost complete collection of editions published between 1951 and 1954
Fursa Breathnach, George Lawlor, Seán MacBride, Jack McQuillan, and Florence O'Riordan also furnished me with private material, such as Clann na Poblachta's constitution, standing orders, minutes from some meetings and related information

Newspapers and Periodicals
The Connacht Tribune
Dublin Opinion
Evening Mail
Hot Press
Irish Independent
Irish Press
The Irish Times

RTÉ

John Bowman, interview with Seán MacBride, RTÉ Radio, 29 December 1980
John Bowman *What the Papers Say*, broadcast RTÉ Television, 9 April 1998
Cathal O'Shannon, *The Battle of Baltinglass*, broadcast RTÉ Television, 10 October 1996

Official Publications

Dáil Debates and Reports
Report of the Commission of Inquiry into Banking, Currency and Credit (Minority Report No. 3), 1938

Papal Encyclicals

Rerum Novarum (1891)
Quadragesimo Anno (1931)
Divini Redemptoris (1937)

Interviews

Fursa Breathnach, Noël Browne, Liam Cosgrave, Oliver J. Flanagan, Ben Hooper, George Lawlor, Hector Legge, Con Lehane, Patrick Lindsay, Seán MacBride, Roger McHugh, John McMenamy, Jack McQuillan, Breandán Ó hEithir, Colm Ó Laoghaire, Liam Ó Laoghaire, Labhrás Ó Nualláin, Colm O'Quigley, Florence O'Riordan, Seamus Pattison, Johnny Prendergast, Dr D. Quill, and several others who wished to remain anonymous

Secondary Sources

Barrington, Ruth, *Health Medicine and Politics in Ireland 1900–1970,* Institute of Public Administration, Dublin, 1987
Bell, J. Bowyer, *The Secret Army: History of the Irish Republican Army, 1916–79,* Academy Press, Dublin, 1979
Bew, Paul, and Henry Patterson, *Seán Lemass and the Making of Modern Ireland,* Gill & Macmillan, 1982
Brown, Terence, *Ireland: A Social and Cultural History, 1922–1979,* Fontana, London, 1981
Browne, Noël, *Against the Tide,* Gill & Macmillan, Dublin, 1986
Carty, R. K., *Electoral Politics in Ireland,* Brandon, Dingle, 1983
Coogan, Tim Pat, *Ireland Since the Rising,* Pall Mall Press, London, 1966
Coogan, Tim Pat, *De Valera: Long Fellow, Long Shadow,* Hutchinson, London, 1993
Cronin, Seán, *Irish Nationalism,* Academy Press, Dublin, 1980
Cronin, Seán, *Washington's Irish Policy, 1916–1986,* Anvil Press, Dublin, 1987
Deeny, James, *To Cure and to Care: Memoirs of a Chief Medical Officer,* Glendale Press, Dublin, 1989
Dunphy, Richard, *The Making of Fianna Fáil Power in Ireland 1932–1948,* Clarendon Press, Oxford, 1995
Earl, Lawrence, *The Battle of Baltinglass,* Harrap, London, 1952
English, Richard, *Radicals and the Republic: Socialist Republicans in the Irish Free State, 1925–1937,* Clarendon, Oxford, 1994
Fanning, Ronan, *The Irish Department of Finance 1922–1958,* Institute of Public Administration, Dublin, 1980
Fanning, Ronan, *Independent Ireland,* Helicon Press, Oxford, 1983

Farrell, Brian, *Chairman or Chief?: The Role of Taoiseach in Irish Government*, Gill & Macmillan, Dublin, 1971

Farrell, Brian (ed.), *De Valera's Constitution and Ours*, RTÉ and Gill & Macmillan, Dublin, 1988

Fisk, Robert, *Ireland in Time of War*, Paladin, London, 1983

FitzGerald, Garret, *All in a Life*, Macmillan, London, 1991

Gallagher, Michael, *The Irish Labour Party in Transition, 1957–82*, Manchester University Press, Manchester, 1982

Gallagher, Michael, *Political Parties in the Republic of Ireland*, Gill & Macmillan, Dublin, 1985

Garvin, Tom, *The Evolution of Irish Nationalist Politics*, Holmes & Meier, New York, 1981

Garvin, Tom, *1922: The Birth of Irish Democracy*, Gill & Macmillan, Dublin, 1996

Gaughan, J. A., *Thomas Johnson, 1872–1963: First Leader of the Labour Party in Ireland*, Kingdom Books, Dublin, 1980

Girvin, Brian, *Between Two Worlds*, Gill & Macmillan, Dublin, 1989

Hitchcock, Harry, *TB Or Not TB?* Centre for Health Promotion Studies, University College Galway, 1995

Horgan, John, *Labour: The Price of Power*, Gill & Macmillan, Dublin, 1986

Inglis, Brian, *Downstart*, Chatto & Windus, London, 1990

Inglis, Brian, *West Briton*, Faber and Faber, London, 1962

Inglis, Tom, *Moral Monopoly: The Catholic Church in Modern Irish Society*, Gill & Macmillan, Dublin, 1987

Jordan, Anthony, *Seán MacBride*, Blackwater Press, Dublin, 1993

Kennedy, Kieran, *The Economic Development of Ireland in the Twentieth Century*, Routledge, London, 1988

Keatinge, Patrick, *The Formulation of Irish Foreign Policy*, Institute of Public Administration, Dublin, 1973

Keogh, Dermot, *Twentieth-Century Ireland*, Gill & Macmillan, Dublin, 1994

Keogh, Dermot, *Ireland and the Vatican*, Cork University Press, Cork, 1995

Lee, J. J., *Ireland 1912–1985: Politics and Society*, Cambridge University Press, Cambridge, 1989

Lindsay, Patrick, *Memories*, Blackwater Press, Dublin, 1992

Lynch, Patrick, and James Meenan (eds), *Essays in Memory of Alexis Fitzgerald*, Incorporated Law Society of Ireland, Dublin, 1987

Lyons, F .S. L., *Ireland Since the Famine*, Fontana, London, 1973

MacCabe, Ian, *A Diplomatic History of Ireland, 1948–49*, Irish Academic Press, Dublin, 1991

McCague, Eugene, *Arthur Cox, 1891–1965*, Gill & Macmillan, Dublin, 1994

Mair, Peter, *The Changing Irish Party System*, Pinter, London, 1987

Murphy, John A., *Ireland in the Twentieth Century*, Gill & Macmillan, Dublin, 1975

Nowlan, K. B., and T. Desmond Williams (eds), *Ireland in the War Years and After, 1939–1951*, Gill and Macmillan, Dublin, 1969

O'Carroll, J. P., and John A. Murphy (eds), *De Valera and His Times*, Cork University Press, Cork, 1983

O'Halloran, Clare, *Partition and the Limits of Nationalism*, Gill & Macmillan, Dublin, 1987

Ó hEithir, Breandán, *The Begrudger's Guide to Irish Politics*, Poolbeg, Dublin, 1986

Ó hEithir, Breandán, *Lead Us Into Temptation*, Routledge, London, 1978 and Poolbeg, Dublin, 1991 (originally published in Irish as *Lig Sinn i gCathú* by Sáirséal agus Dill, 1976)

Ó hEithir, Breandán, *Over the Bar,* Poolbeg, Dublin, 1991

O'Keeffe, Patrick D., 'The origins and development of Clann na Poblachta', MA thesis, University College Cork, 1981

O'Sullivan, Michael, *Seán Lemass: A Biography,* Blackwater Press, Dublin, 1994

Rafter, Kevin, *The Clann: The Story of Clann na Poblachta,* Mercier Press, Cork, 1996

Ryle Dwyer, T., *De Valera: The Man and the Myths,* Poolbeg, Dublin, 1991

Tweedy, Hilda, *A Link in the Chain: The Story of the Irish Housewives' Association 1942–1992,* Attic Press, Dublin, 1992

Ward, Margaret, *Maud Gonne: A Biography*, Pandora Press, Unwin Paperbacks, London, 1990

Walsh, Dick, *The Party,* Gill & Macmillan, Dublin, 1986

Whyte, J. H., *Church and State in Modern Ireland: 1923–1979*, Gill & Macmillan, Dublin, 1979

Index